Para Bhairava Hrdaya
Non-Dual Shaivism

In Theory and Practice

Dr. Shreeram Iyer

BLACK MOON PUBLISHING
CINCINNATI, OHIO
USA

Black Moon Manifesto

It is the Will and mission of Bate Cabal/Black Moon to effectively manifest unique and insightful occult Works for the esoteric community in a manner that is unfettered by commercial considerations.

Design © 2024 Black Moon Publishing,LLC

BlackMoonPublishing.com

blackmoonpublishing@gmail.com

Design and layout by
Jo Bounds of Black Moon

ISBN: 979-8-9865228-9-0

Contents

The Crest Jewel of Supreme Bhairava

Book II: Practice. 327

The Heart of Supreme Bhairava

Book 1 :: Theory

Kala Bhairava

Acknowledgement

With deep gratitude and reverence, I extend my heartfelt thanks to those who have profoundly influenced and inspired this spiritual journey.

First and foremost, I am deeply indebted to my parents. Your unwavering support, boundless love, and the values you have instilled in me have been the foundation upon which this work stands. Your encouragement and guidance have been a source of strength and wisdom throughout this endeavor.

I am profoundly grateful to the great Indian Shaivite saints, whose luminous teachings and timeless wisdom have illuminated my path. Abhinavagupta, with his profound insights into the nature of consciousness, and Kṣhemarāja, whose commentaries have unraveled the depths of our sacred traditions, have been guiding lights. Jayaratha's elucidations have further enriched my understanding, providing clarity and depth to the mystical dimensions of Shaivism.

To the great Para Bhairava, the ultimate embodiment of divine consciousness and transcendent reality, I offer my deepest reverence. Your presence and grace are the essence of this work, and it is through your boundless wisdom that the mysteries of existence are revealed.

May the teachings of these revered sages continue to inspire and uplift, and may their divine grace guide all who seek the light of truth.

With sincere thanks and devotion,
Dr. Shreeram Iyer

Foreword

As I grew in my magical path, I came face to face with the works of Kenneth Grant. I had by then some notions of the kalas through other means, which I had learned to be the feminine counterpart of the masculine chakras, used in both vampiric and mediumistic traditions. I had been taught by a mentor in my country (Portugal) that the kalas could only be accessed by sexual magick, and after being by such means unblocked, they could be worked independently. What was more, only rare women could give access to the kalas, the so-called Scarlet Women. The Kalas then could awaken phenomena and reality tunnels. In other words, they were to be taken, literally, as centers of materialization.

With Kenneth Grant and the Typhonian Current's system I obtained a wider view. The kalas were connected to time and rhythm, and with Kali. It would be derived from this that Kali derives from time or produces it. It is time in turn that would produce space and, as a consequence, materializations and phenomena. According to Grant, disregarding debate among tantric lineages, Kali produces sixteen Kalas that function as magical powers and roots of divinity. They are the days when the moon is waxing, and the womb is menstruating. Grant had gotten the idea from David Curwen that the kalas are sexual fluids (or sexual/lunar perfumes). He knew as well that this womb is connected with the Ajna (commonly known as the third eye in the forehead) and depicts consciousness or at least perception. In other words, the kalas were psycho-sexual fluids

secreted by the female tantric adept.

These sixteen Kalas are complemented by their reflex, adding up to 32 kalas, and consequently forming the whole Judaic Tree of Life (ten sephiroth or spheres plus 22 paths or tunnels between them, corresponding these to the 22 Hebrew letters in the Hebrew alphabet), and to different parts of the body as a microcosm.

This was more or less the rudimentary understanding of the West when it came to the Kalas or to what the West erroneously called Tantrism, along with a few valuable additions. In sum, when Kenneth Grant's "Nu Isis Lodge" was built, Grant had obtained a commentary on the Anandalahari (Heart Chakra) by a Kaula adept, and with this interpretation of the text he countered the phallic cult of Crowley with the vulvic menstrual cycle. The volume *Aleister Crowley and the Hidden God* intends to enlighten through Aleister Crowley's sexual magick system by exposing Kali as a goddess of blood and dissolution: the Scarlet Woman. We were not in as bad hands as it might appear from the raw notions listed. Our understanding of the East, in this specific context, was exoteric at best and strangely materialistic but we had an interesting mystic with an esoteric and creative mind explaining the exoteric concepts.

Some misconceptions appear around the Left Hand Path and the Right Hand Path as connected originally to Hinduism and specifically to a supposed tantrism, but I doubt Kenneth Grant, who once told me that to change the future we should change the past, fell into these misconceptions by mistake. He reformulated in this way the Left Hand Path and, again, made it esoteric when it was but exoteric, spiritual when it was but materialistic, and goes on to claim the Left Hand Path is, in truth, an Indian manifestation of a pre-

dynastic Egyptian cult devoted to what he calls the Great Goddess. The end result of Grant's Typhonian Current is an odd but boiling mixture of Thelema, Western Sexual Magick, ufology, Lovecraft imagery, Neo-Vedanta and general Tantra.

Kenneth Grant's embrace of non-duality and Hindu Advaita was genuine and even Grant's fiction proves it. After learning the teachings of Bhagavan Sri Ramana Maharshi he went as far as to write Advaita Vedanta articles for Indian journals. Grant did attempt to learn directly from the masters in India, volunteering for the army and serving in India, to no avail. Instead, he was initiated by Curwen, a student of Swami Pareswara Bikshu from the Holy Order of Krishna, connected to the so-called New Thought, that imports from Vedanta with distortions of Eastern spiritual philosophy.

In pair with this, there is still today a series of initiates in the East-West Kaula Mystery School called AMOOKOS. I have worked and still work with a number of them, a more or less speculative system that dresses Western concepts in Eastern clothes as much as Wicca had dressed the Golden Dawn in the clothes of traditional witchcraft. That is not to say AMOOKOS has no validity and no power, or Wicca, for that matter. It is to say a purely genuine link to Indian esoteric mysteries as they are in their origins (and not just as an influence, no matter how strong) is still missing to this day but will no longer after this book has met its hour of publishing.

I have worked extensively with Kenneth Grant's methods (or my methods derived from his theories) to great effect. My perception of the swollen kalas in a Scarlet Woman led me to cause long-lasting states of trance and orgasms without touch, which led women to meet their Holy Guardian Angel and find their way out of suicide.

Also to speak in tongues and try to cut me in two with a sword, then biting the cook in a restaurant. No wonder Crowley had such a disastrous effect on women! All in all, it seemed to be quite a powerful but obscure science that randomly destroys or enlightens. I decided it was certainly still a chauvinist approach in which women, no matter how much of a decision they thought they had made, had no awareness or control of what was taking place, as much as a non-adept has no control over magic at all.

A system of conscious initiation was deeply lacking, and all we were given was a chasm in which to jump in the hope of finding wings midway, or in which to jump if we had built our wings elsewhere far from the Typhonian Current. To make the case harder, our access to the ancient esoteric science in Hinduism and any promise of an understanding and full initiation had been quite obscured by Theosophy, New Thought and even, ultimately, Kenneth Grant.

To truly understand Grant, I had to dive into his inspirational roots, and maybe be so lucky as to understand these roots better than Grant himself has managed to in his time. Along the way, as it should be, I found Shreeram Iyer. Just like Grant had found his Curwen I had found Shreeram. With the age of the internet, this Eastern wisdom in its origin had not been diluted. To add to it, instead of publishing about "his" teachings, I could easily have him publish them himself directly in the West.

Shreeram addressed me in appreciation, having followed some of my published articles. He was by then working with the magician Nenad Djordjevic-Talerman, compiling a list for him of his own hermetic work with 72 negative intelligences from Mercury. In a matter of seconds, the conversation developed to Kenneth Grant and

I learned that when Shreeram was 17 he had started with a modality of tantra where Bhairava and Kali are worshipped, in addition to starting the South Indian version of sri chakra practices to realize his true divine nature.

In 2011 he found his mentor, in a tradition that was passed from mentor to disciple, the mentor only teaching one or two students in a lifetime. Shreeram's mentor, who knew not English, wished him to write a series starting with tantra from scratch, expanding the concepts of the different modalities and what they represent.

By this time Shreeram had been denied vehemently by teachers and founders of tantric schools not acquainted with genuine training or not learned in any classical tantric treatises.

Shreeram is learned in Sanskrit, and, in addition, he has access to rare works in the museums. Not only is he proficient in his craft, but he has also pursued Western methods such as the works of Franz Bardon, the Golden Dawn system, and so on until landing upon Aleister Crowley and Kenneth Grant, who had, in the words of Shreeram, "revealed a way for everyone to learn genuine magic by creating a system with the thirty-two manifestations of the supreme godhead and making it public."

Quickly I received him in my Horus Maat Lodge Nexus where we started working with N'Aton and the Maatian Current, and he began to teach me Kashmir Shaivism and Advaita-Vedanta. Learning by Shreeram how to operate the 24 tatwas, I was able to devise the system I presented at "The Inner Gateways of LAM – Esoteric Pillars" (Sirius Limited Esoterica) and solve the mystery of the 24 hearts in the crown of the original LAM drawn by Aleister Crowley.

By practicing the teachings at The Heart of Bhairava and other

teachings by Shreeram yet to be published, I could navigate easily, with certainty, and without unnecessary peril, not only the works of Kenneth Grant but also the Voudon Gnostic Workbook by Michael Bertiaux, another of Kenneth Grant's references.

Love & Will,
André Consciência

Influence of Shaiva Tantra in Typhonian Tradition

The Typhonian Tradition, developed by Kenneth Grant, is a distinctive and complex modern occult system that incorporates a diverse range of mystical and esoteric influences. This tradition, deeply rooted in Western esotericism, draws from elements such as Thelema, Tantric practices, and Lovecraftian themes. Grant's work in this tradition seeks to explore hidden and often darker aspects of spiritual and magical knowledge, aiming to reveal truths that lie beyond conventional practices.

Grant's approach is heavily influenced by Thelema, the spiritual philosophy established by Aleister Crowley, which emphasizes the pursuit of personal will and enlightenment. Additionally, Grant incorporates aspects of Tantric practices, focusing on the channeling of spiritual energies for achieving enlightenment. His exploration also includes Lovecraftian themes, such as the existence of ancient cosmic entities and the pursuit of knowledge that transcends ordinary human understanding. At the core of the Typhonian Tradition is the pursuit of mystical and magical practices that engage hidden knowledge and esoteric truths, challenging traditional boundaries of spiritual understanding.

Kenneth Grant's key works, such as *The Magical Revival*, *Nightside of Eden*, and *Aleister Crowley and the Hidden God*, delve into these themes, offering novel interpretations of occult symbols and rituals. His writings are aimed at uncovering the deeper layers

of spiritual and mystical knowledge, often involving complex and unconventional practices. In the context of Shaivism, a major tradition within Hinduism, the concept of the 32 Kalas plays a crucial role. These Kalas are seen as distinct aspects or phases of divine consciousness and creative power, each representing a specific quality or function within the divine and cosmic order. They reflect the multifaceted nature of Shiva, who encompasses all aspects of existence.

My work explores the 32 Kalas in depth, offering a comprehensive examination of their significance and interconnections within the Shaivite framework. This detailed analysis illuminates the profound spiritual and philosophical dimensions of each Kala and how they contribute to the realization of the divine essence. By delving into the 32 Kalas, my research provides a cohesive understanding of Shiva's divine attributes and their impact on spiritual practices and rituals within Shaivism.

Integrating Kenneth Grant's insights into occultism with the study of the 32 Kalas allows for a broader understanding of both Western esoteric traditions and Indian spirituality. Grant's approach to uncovering hidden and esoteric dimensions of knowledge resonates with the exploration of the Kalas, offering a framework for understanding the deeper aspects of Shaivism. My research not only builds on Grant's exploration of hidden spiritual realms but also provides new insights into how ancient Indian spiritual concepts can be understood within a contemporary esoteric context.

By applying Grant's methodology to the study of Shaivism, my work contributes to a richer and more nuanced understanding of Indian spirituality. This synthesis of perspectives enhances the

comprehension of the 32 Kalas and demonstrates how their teachings resonate with modern mystical and occult practices. Through this integration, my research sheds new light on the complexities of Shaivism and offers a fresh perspective on the profound depths of Indian spiritual traditions.

Preface

This work is dedicated to the Monistic school of Shaivism, which has its origins in the Kashmir Valley of Northern India. Some modern Shaivite philosophers refer to this school as Kashmir Shaivism, but that name would be inappropriate since there are other Shaivism schools originating in Kashmir. The peculiarity of this school lies in its absolute non-dual thoughts in both theory and practice. The doctrines of Shaivism are based on canonical texts called Agamas. Another fascinating aspect of these schools is their esoteric nature, sharing their secret knowledge only with students initiated into a spiritual family by a competent teacher. All canonical texts are written in a coded form to ensure that an uninitiated person can never decode the practices and knowledge contained in these classical texts on Shaivism. The Monistic Shaivism, which is the subject of this work, is an amalgamation of different Shaivite schools such as Krama, Spanda, and Pratyabhijnana. This school is also known as Trika or the triadic school of Shaivism, or Rahasya Sampradaya, which literally translates to clandestine sect or school. This system is called triadic because it considers the divine trinity as ultimate. According to this school of thought, the entire cosmos is a triad, namely subject, cognition, and object, where the subject is the ultimate, and cognition and object are always one with the subject.

The entire Monistic doctrines of Shaivism evolved from three major literary sources: the canonical Agamas, and the non-canonical Spanda and Pratyabhijnana doctrines. For every Shaivite follower, the Agamas are considered absolute, and they are said to

be revelatory texts given to humanity by the supreme Para-Shiva. Thus, the Agamas are regarded as the best source for achieving the ultimate goal of self-realization or God-realization. Most Agamic texts are no longer available today. Some important ones include Mrgendra Agama, Kamika Agama, Chandra Jnana Agama, Malini Vijaya Uttara Tantra, Matanga Parameswara Agama, Vijnana Bhairava Tantra, Karana Agama, and Vatula Agama. These Agamas serve as the philosophical and practical spiritual texts for Monistic Shaivism. Although these Agamas have a staunch non-dual outlook and describe numerous spiritual practices, they are not necessarily written in a systematic way. Additionally, for a long time, these Agamas were scattered across various locations. One of the earliest attempts to integrate the collective thoughts of these Agamas was made by Saint Vasu Gupta of Kashmir, who wrote the Shiva Sutra. Many mythical stories surround this text. Some scholars believe it was directly revealed to Vasu Gupta by Para-Shiva, while others think it was revealed to him in dreams by the supreme lord. Another story suggests that the Shiva Sutra was etched on a magical rock that revealed itself to Vasu Gupta. Regardless, historical evidence confirms that Vasu Gupta wrote a work integrating the core concepts of the Agamas through the Shiva Sutra. This text is held in high esteem by followers of Monistic Shaivism. Since its origin, numerous commentaries and expositions have been written on the Shiva Sutra. They include:

1. Shiva Sutra Varttika by Bhaskara
2. Shiva Sutra Vimarshini by Kshema Raja
3. Shiva Sutra Vrtti by an unknown author
4. Shiva Sutra Vrittikam by Varada Raja

Another prolific saint, Bhatta Kallata, wrote an incredible work based on the Spanda doctrine, integrating the philosophical and spiritual aspects of Shaivism. Bhatta Kallata was a direct disciple of Vasu Gupta, and his work, Spanda Karika, is considered revelatory words spoken by Vasu Gupta and written down by Kallata. Spanda refers to the dynamic activity of consciousness, the simultaneous movement of awareness from subjectivity to objectivity and vice versa. Many later saints wrote expositions on this work as well. They include:

1. Spanda Sandoha and Spanda Nirnaya by Kshema Raja
2. Spanda Pradeepika by Utpala
3. Spanda Vivrti by Rajanaka Rama

The third major work influencing Monistic Shaivism is the Pratyabhijnana or the doctrine of recognition. This work philosophically reflects on the nature of self and God. This school logically uses philosophical reflections to show that the limited subject, or man, is inherently one with Para-Shiva, the supreme God. A great saint named Utpala Deva wrote a work called Iswara Pratyabhijnana, which is considered one of the key works of this school of Shaivism. This Utpala Deva is different from Utpala, the author of Spanda Pradeepika mentioned above. Some major expositions on this doctrine, apart from Iswara Pratyabhijnana, are:

1. Pratyabhijnana Vrtti by Utpala Deva himself
2. Pratyabhijnana Vivrtti Vimarshini and Pratyabhijnana Vimarshini by Abhinava Gupta

Another major philosophical work in this school is Shiva Drshti by Somananda. Apart from this, there are other significant works on Monistic Shaivism written by Abhinava Gupta. Abhinava Gupta is the most important figure in Monistic Shaivism. He was a scholar in aesthetics, poetry, music, philosophy, and grammar. He wrote numerous works on philosophy and theology. Some of his works on Shaivism are lost, while two major works on Monistic Shaivism by Abhinava Gupta are Tantra Aloka and Tantra Sara, which cover all major philosophical and practical aspects of Monistic Shaivism.

With that said, let us move forward.

Shaiva Tantra - An Introduction

The word "Tantra" has taken on many meanings over the centuries. In the West, Tantra is often associated with certain ritualized sexual practices, while in the East, it is sometimes considered to be black magic. Both of these descriptions are incorrect. Tantra encompasses practices that lead to the expansion of the practitioner's awareness. In certain religious principles related to the Vedas, Tantra refers to the quintessence of a particular science, philosophy, or doctrine. Tantra is defined as "Tanyate vistaryate jnanam anene," meaning that Tantra is that which elaborates on any field of knowledge and expands it. In this sense, any scientific principle or doctrine that helps us gain knowledge is Tantra.

In this specific work, we will address certain doctrines, principles, mystic phonemes, syllables, and symbols that convey meanings related to non-dual Shaivism, also known as Advaita Shaiva or Shaiva Tantra. According to Shaiva doctrines, the entire cosmos follows a pattern, which applies to every being, including humans. Each of us is a living fragment of this vast cosmos, which is essentially a divine life. The basic concepts of this work are simple. We exist on two planes: one that is corporeal and mundane, and another that is the inner world of thoughts, awareness, and consciousness, which is based on what we call the mind. Both of these dimensions are real and exist relative to us, and the energies and principles governing these two dimensions are tangible and transmutable.

Every spiritual system aims to find a suitable pattern of the

cosmos and use it for the evolution of individuals. An initiate who applies these principles in practice will experience an expansion in awareness and, eventually, reach liberation. This is the purpose of every spiritual initiation.

The subtle nature of these concepts makes them difficult to identify in the initial stages. It is like trying to explain the cosmos in a single word. In fact, the entire cosmos can be expressed in a single sound: AUM. Similarly, the grand unified theory of physics seeks to explain all the fundamental forces of the universe in a single equation, so that all forces and phenomena can be explained within that framework. This represents the ultimate cause of every causation.

If we examine the spiritual systems that exist around the world, we can see a general pattern in symbols, practices, and doctrines that have proven effective for personal evolution. For example, the swastika is used by Hindus and many other religious and spiritual systems in various ways. The hexagram used by Jewish people is also used by Hindus as a symbol representing the union of male and female principles, or the union of higher and lower nature.

Shaivism identifies 36 principles that make up the cosmos. These thirty-six are not final or static; rather, they represent an ever-expanding doctrine. It is simply a convenient way of explaining the succession of principles that constitute the cosmos. However, the ultimate or supreme god, Parama-Shiva, is independent of any pattern or sequence of successions. He is beyond these epithets. When we contemplate the process of manifestation of any object in our thoughts, our awareness does not undergo any sequence or succession. Parama-Shiva is like that. Utpaladeva, a great Shaivite

scholar, in one of his works, states that Shiva is both the cosmos and beyond the cosmos. This implies that he is the pattern of manifestation and beyond the pattern. He is both the sequence and beyond the sequence. He is the object and the subject, entirely free and unlimited, existing in every possible manner.

These thirty-six principles cannot be considered ultimate or absolute. They are merely a pattern grasped by saints and seers to explain the nature of the cosmos in a sensible way using their logic. The oldest schools of philosophy, Sankhya Darshana and Vedanta, consider twenty-five Tatwas, while Nyaya and Vaisheshika have entirely different views on the Tatwas, referring to them as Padarthas and considering sixteen and nine Tatwas, respectively. The Varaha Upanishad mentions ninety-six Tatwas.

Thus, each school of philosophy had its own ideas about the cosmos. Even though these principles, in some way, explain the nature of the cosmos, the reality depicted by these principles is not the nature of absolute reality. These thirty-six principles represent the known nature of the cosmos, or objects of thought, and as such, an object that can be known is not the nature of Parama-Shiva, who is the ultimate subject or knower holding everything in his subjective awareness. Therefore, scholars have suggested that the thirty-seventh Tatwa is Parama-Shiva, who is supreme and beyond the thirty-six Tatwas. If the nature of the cosmos were represented by a thousand principles, Parama-Shiva would be the thousand-and-first principle, transcending all other known principles of the cosmos. The supreme reality, Parama-Shiva, will always elude our understanding, which operates through the limited nature of our mind. The number of principles is not absolute but a convenient

way to explain the nature of the cosmos.

The path called Shaiva Tantra is the result of gnosis, experiences, and beliefs of empirical individuals who have walked this path using the knowledge gained through these Tatwas. It is not a steadfast rule or an absolute system of mysticism but rather a way of life and living in a system that constantly evolves and perfects itself according to the development of individual empirical souls.

As humanity evolves, the meaning held by the Tatwas evolves accordingly. The Tatwas in modern times may differ from their meanings when Abhinava Gupta wrote the Tantra Aloka, but they still fulfill their purpose of satisfying the hunger for knowledge and quenching the thirst for truth. The knowledge gained from these principles is literally inexhaustible; it renews itself with new insights—the more we gain, the more plentiful it becomes.

After initial exploration of these principles, it is natural to question whether to continue this path or to stop considering it a medieval relic from some old library. This is a question that can only be answered by the empirical individual who puts these theories into practice and experiments with them. All one can do is read the doctrines, theories, and teachings of saints and seers, which may or may not be helpful. Each individual practitioner should be able to formulate the Tatwas according to their life within its sequence and patterns. A person who fails to do so is not a Shaiva yogi or Shaivite.

The Tatwas themselves provide a means to connect with inner worlds and states of awareness inaccessible through normal means. It is from these transcended states of consciousness that these theories and doctrines arise; it is not an automatic process. Shaiva Yoga is not for the lazy, ineffectual, or close-minded religious person. It

offers a pattern that is alive, dynamic, and throbbing with light and awareness, which should be experienced, not merely observed.

Such an experience is possible only when we work through these Tatwas and phonemes corresponding to them in the four dimensions: Para (the most transcendent, pure state brimming with consciousness of creation), Pashyanti (where the initial impulses of creation in the form of ideas occur), Madhyama (where creation exists in the state of thoughts), and Vaikhari (the corporeal, physical universe), and the four corresponding states of consciousness: Jagrat, Swapna, Sushupti, and Turiya.

Since the essence of Shaivism exists in the Tatwas, we must focus our minds on the Tatwas to gain information. For a Shaivite, the Tatwas are as fundamental as the cross is to a Christian, the hexagram to a Jew, or the Tree of Life to a Kabbalist. Without a good understanding of the Tatwas and how they work, there is no point in attempting to understand Shaivism, much like watching a Chinese movie without understanding Chinese.

So much has been written about Tantra and Indian mysticism over the last few decades that it is strange how little has been explained. The entire topic appears as a confusing conundrum. Original works are written in Sanskrit with meanings veiled within meanings. People with a linear way of thinking failed to understand these concepts and misinterpreted them. Subsequent writers merely rehashed these misinterpretations for small purposes, eventually turning Tantra into ritualized sex or black magic involving blood sacrifices, orgiastic rituals, and other barbaric practices to appease a dark god who grants material pleasures in return. Only a handful have attempted to present Tantra in a sensible light.

The entire doctrine of Shaiva Tantra is presented like a jigsaw puzzle with breadcrumbs scattered across various scriptural works. The value of the path lies in the spiritual exercises undertaken in the journey of self-realization. In trying to solve these jigsaw puzzles, the individual uses their mental faculties extensively, resulting in the evolution of the empirical self. Approaching this path as a grand jigsaw puzzle offers an opportunity for genuine progress of the mind and soul to those who have the endurance, patience, and perseverance to attempt its solution. Consequently, oriental scriptures on the topic should be considered as hints in solving this puzzle rather than absolute answers. The solution lies in the consciousness of the seeker.

First, we must understand the Tatwas. What are the Tatwas? They are the link connecting the corporeal, immanent physical world and humanity to the most transcendent principle known as god—a sort of chain linking every being with god. Since the Tatwas are expressed in the form of phonetics (sounds), and these sounds are represented as letters, we must gain knowledge about these sounds. Without understanding these phonemes, the entire Tatwas would be nothing more than simple doodled symbols on a white paper.

A phoneme embodies a Tatwa or principle, allowing an individual to realize the idea represented by the Tatwa using these sounds. These sounds effectively connect and commune with the cosmos. Therefore, phonemes can be considered the language of the cosmos or the language of god. They facilitate the exchange of information and ideas within the cosmos.

To commune with the Tatwas, we must establish feasible means within their framework through certain meditations and other spiritual

exercises. Each Tatwa and phoneme should be contemplated with an idea that leads to dynamic spiritual experiences. These experiences should be intelligible to empirical individuals. Once we integrate these ideas into our thoughts, words, and actions, we are effectively learning this cosmic language.

The primary task of this work is to provide a basic understanding of the fundamental concepts of Non-Dual Shaivism and help individuals handle these concepts through specific practices. Anyone can learn these theories, but to make these concepts an integral part of life, they should be practiced in contemplation, meditation, prayers, and other forms.

To commune with the Tatwas, we need to be able to pronounce the phonemes represented by Sanskrit letters, known as Matrikas, and then express ourselves with their words, called mantras. Eventually, we will understand the mechanics and grammar of the Tatwas and learn to systematically arrange these concepts according to the transcendent states of consciousness, which are usually not accessible through normal means.

The goal is to reach infinity through finite means, and the unlimited through limited means. Our concepts of the Tatwas are constrained by numbers and names, but the connection that pervades within these principles to the unlimited Parama-Shiva is infinite and knows no bounds. Though these Tatwas, grasped by individuals with limited understanding and depicted in a linear manner, may seem finite, they are imbued with the awareness of Parama-Shiva, and the force pervading them flows infinitely and incessantly. The Tatwas function like a computer: we can store information in them and access it anytime, but they are the collective consciousness of

everything in the cosmos, dynamic, living, and throbbing with the light of consciousness. To be a Shaiva Yogi is to explore each Tatwa one by one and realize them in our daily lives.

This work is intended to guide readers step by step through the Tatwas, from the gross physical world represented by Prthwi to the most transcendent Shiva. It involves an ascending journey from earth to heaven. In the theoretical part, the Tatwas will be explained in a descending manner, from Shiva to the physical world (in the order of the universe's manifestation from Shiva Tatwa). In the practical part, we will work our way up, from earth to heaven, from the corporeal to the absolute, in an ascending order. We have fallen from heaven; now let us pick ourselves up and climb Jacob's ladder to heaven.

Shaivite Cosmogony - The Tatwas

According to the doctrines of Shaivism, the cosmos manifests in an orderly manner, which is represented by the Tatwas. Tatwas are principles that explain the manifestation of the entire microcosm and macrocosm in an orderly manner, from the absolute transcendent consciousness known as Shiva to the physical world. These principles also reflect within the microcosm as our psycho-spiritual elements. Without understanding this cosmological hierarchy of Shaiva doctrines, it is impossible to grasp the attributes of phonemes or mantras. I will provide a short description of the thirty-six principles that make up the cosmos in a lucid manner. The reality of consciousness is the immanent manifestation of the cosmos through these thirty-six principles.

The thirty-six cosmological principles are divided into three categories:

1. Shuddha (pure)
2. Shuddha-ashuddha (pure-impure)
3. Ashuddha (gross or impure)

The first Tatwa, called Shiva Tatwa, comes under Shantyatita-Kala or the principles beyond peace. The next four Tatwas fall under Shanta-Kala, characterized by a non-distinct state between subject and object. These five Tatwas constitute the Shuddha or pure Tatwas. These five principles make up the Shakti Anda of the cosmos, or the cosmic egg of Shakti, also known as Shuddha Adhva or pure

manifestation. The pure order is transcended and characterized by the absence of object. Here, the subject and object are one and the same. Shiva is the ultimate "I" consciousness, the ultimate subject from which everything emanates. At this stage, Shakti has not yet evolved into matter; the possibility of an objective manifestation is experienced within the subject. Thus, the object is one with the subject at this stage. The entire set of principles emanates from Parama-Shiva, also known as Anashrita-Shiva. Anashrita means "not dependent on anything or anyone." He is beyond all principles and creates the thirty-six principles independently through his own power, called Svatantrya. Since he is beyond all principles, he is called Tatwatita or beyond Tatwas or transcendent above the Tatwas.

The first two principles are Shiva and Shakti. Figuratively speaking, they are two principles, but they are one and the same. At this stage, there is no subject-object diversity. It is the transcendent consciousness. The manifestation of the outer cosmos has not yet begun. Subjectivity in its unadulterated pure state exists here. Shakti is the self-awareness of Shiva, his dynamic nature, his power to create or to act. In Monistic Shaivism, Shiva is always described as Prakasha Vimarshatmaka (one who is with light and reflection or illumination).

The first impulse to emanate the universe is the necessary self-imposed limitation of Para-Shiva, a negation of the sense of fullness in order to create a sense of need. This limitation is caused by the Shakti Tatwa, which is the power of negation. In turn, Para-Shiva effectively limits himself in Shiva Tatwa. At this point, Para-Shiva exists the same as he was prior to the effect of the Shakti Tatwa, except there is a loss of the feeling of unlimited Purna Aham. Shiva

Tatwa is Chaitanya or Prakasha (consciousness), and his nature is self-illumination or self-revealing. This sportive play, which seems limited due to the self-imposed limitation of Purna Aham of Para-Shiva, is his ability to recognize his unlimited nature by manifesting himself as the finite objective world. Thus, what seems to be the limiting factor is more of a limitation of perception. Para-Shiva, who is the self-illuminating light or self-aware consciousness, has manifested himself as consciousness and awareness in Shiva and Shakti Tatwa, respectively.

At this stage, the sense of pure 'I' has no objectivity to superimpose his experience with. In this way, Shiva Tatwa is filled with a sense of rest. To emanate the cosmos with his awareness or Shakti, he has to limit himself in terms of will, knowledge, and action. Because of this limitation he imposes upon himself, the sense of Purna Aham or complete 'I' is lost, leading to a will towards manifestation, a movement towards emanation, and further evolution of the Tatwas so that whatever is forgotten may be realized again. We should remember that consciousness is eternally one with awareness; the nature of Shiva, the light, is self-revealing in the form of Shakti or illumination. Therefore, it follows that this self-imposed limitation of the Para-Samvid is as dependent upon the Shiva Tatwa as it is on the Shakti Tatwa. With Shakti, he imposes the limitation on himself as Shiva.

In fact, the activities of these two Tatwas are not distinct but are an expression of Para-Shiva in two stages, even before Shakti imposes a limitation on Shiva's fullness. In this manner, these two Tatwas are merely the two sides of the same coin called Para-Samvid or supreme consciousness. So, it should be understood that manifestation has

not really begun at the Shiva or Shakti Tatwa. All that has happened is a realization of the possibilities by limiting the Purna Aham, due to the will, knowledge, and action of Para-Shiva as the supreme lord. Both Shiva and Shakti Tatwa are eternal; they have no point of dissolution, for they are the inherently united nature of Para-Shiva depicted as two separate, independent Tatwas. Because of the nature of these two Tatwas, they never dissolve; they remain in Para-Shiva as the tools or seeds to bring the cosmos into light.

In the next stage, called Sadashiva Tatwa or the principle of Sadashiva, the feeling of 'THIS' occurs, i.e., 'I AM THIS' or 'I am the universe.' Here, the universe has yet to manifest, but the duality of subject and object begins to form. The subject and object are merged together, and a feeling of 'I AM THIS' or 'Idamasya Aham' occurs. Shiva feels as if he is the entire cosmos. The formation of duality and the breaking of the united Shiva-Shakti principle start from this principle.

Prior to the evolution of Sadashiva Tatwa, there was only the experience of an 'I' or Aham. Now, there is the experience of Aham becoming or evolving into something, which refers to the successive Tatwas that constitute the cosmos. Becoming in this sense implies a relation to something else. The subject now has an object to realize. The object at this stage still remains elusive; however, the sense of objectivity separate from Aham has already begun. This phenomenon is realized as "I am this" or "Ahameva idam." At this point, Shakti has begun its function, which is to bring the cosmos into light through the power of will or Icha-Shakti. Icha-Shakti is more expressed at this stage due to the will of the subject to experience himself as the object. The main function of Icha-Shakti is to bring

the cosmos into light through the unlimited will aspect of Shiva, so that the supreme subject may experience himself as the object.

The presence of a subject is essential to acquire knowledge of any kind, and subjective consciousness is impossible without the presence of self-awareness or the 'I' consciousness. Objects in the universe can manifest and disappear, but the ultimate universal consciousness that makes everything possible is always present, eternal, transcendent, and the ultimate subject.

The next principle is Ishwara-Tatwa or the principle of Ishwara. At this stage, the universe as an object exists within the subjective consciousness of Shiva. The entire universe is an expansion of Shiva, or "I AM THIS," with greater emphasis on the object being pronounced. This stage marks the beginning of creation. It is akin to a seed that contains all the information required to become a tree but has yet to sprout. This principle characterizes this stage.

In simpler terms, the Idam aspect has become predominant at this stage. Shiva experiences himself as "Idameva Aham" or "this am I." Para-Shiva is now in the process of materializing his glory, exalting his will by manifesting himself as the objective world. The Idam aspect, which was elusive in the previous stage, is now more prominent and apparent. Para-Shiva now experiences himself as both the knower and the known. At this stage, Jnana-Shakti, or the omniscient aspect of Para-Shiva, is predominant.

Para-Shiva, as the ultimate experiencer, has realized that he can manifest as both matter and spirit, as phenomena and noumena. Para-Shiva understands that he can manifest himself as duality and experience objectivity from a perspective, and vice versa. The next principle is characterized by a perfect balance between 'I' and 'This.'

The following principle is Shuddha-Vidya Tatwa. Here, the universe has manifested externally, and a clear distinction between the subject and object occurs. In this stage, the subject and object seem separate and independent from one another, but they are, in fact, one and the same. The notion of duality is more pronounced and evident at this stage. Starting from here, the awareness of unity or oneness fades, and the notion of duality becomes increasingly evident in the succeeding principles. This Tatwa is characterized by the experience "I am this thing and this am I."

Kriya-Shakti is dominant in this stage, marking the initial distinction between the subject and object. This stage is characterized by unity in diversity. From this point onward, the actualization of the idea of creation takes place, thereby creating a distinction between the subject and object.

The five principles can be explained with a simple analogy. If we consider a seed with the potential to grow into a tree, this represents Shiva-Tatwa. When we sow the seed, it germinates and becomes the Shakti-Tatwa. As the seed's shell cracks open and the sapling begins to sprout, this stage can be considered the Sadashiva-Tatwa. When the sapling emerges from the shell, it represents Ishwara-Tatwa. Finally, when the sapling grows and emerges from the ground, this stage can be considered Shuddha-Vidya.

Vidya-Kala, Maya, and the Five Veils

The next five principles can be referred to as principles of obscuration, limitation, or veiling. They are known as the Pancha-Kanchukas or five limiting factors (Raga, Niyati, Vidya, Kala, Kaala). At this stage, Shakti veils herself from her true nature and creates a sense of duality or separation from Shiva. With this sense of separation, the domain of objectivity begins.

In Shaivism, the term Maya refers to the creative potential of the supreme consciousness. Maya is related to Maana, which means to measure. To measure the immeasurable represents a self-limiting action of the supreme lord during the manifestation of the cosmos or the evolution of the Tatwas.

The Maya Tatwa and the five obscurations constitute the Maya Anda or the cosmic egg of Maya. This represents the first step towards the distinction between subject and object. Up until now, we have seen the pure order of the Tatwas; from here onward, Maya and the five veils represent the pure-impure order of Tatwas. This phase is also called Vidya-Kala, and the limited empirical individuals, known as Purusha, are manifested here.

Para-Shiva, through his sportive play, uses his Shakti to create plurality and manifests the five obscurations of Maya. Consequently, he becomes limited in terms of will, knowledge, and action, becoming the limited empirical soul, Purusha.

Shiva brings the cosmos into light through his Maya-Shakti. Maya-Shakti is a fundamental aspect of Shakti-Tatwa; it is an essential principle for bringing the finite cosmos into light. At

this stage, the subject completely forgets his real nature as Purna-Aham and becomes Alpa-Aham, or limited 'I'. Para-Shiva becomes numerous limited subjects to experience his manifestation as finite objects.

The limited Purusha is simply the 'I' mistakenly identifying itself with the objective world. As a result, the limited subject starts to identify with the characteristics and attributes of finite objects.

The Tatwa, or principle, known as Maya represents the creative potential of the supreme lord through his arising Shakti. The self-limiting factor of the principle of Maya creates a state of ignorance regarding the transcended state of consciousness and a denial of the true nature of self. Here, Maya manifests as multitudes of finite objects or an infinite number of finite objects. It organizes every object in existence into patterns and categories. The unlimited becomes limited, the unfathomable becomes fathomable, and the infinite becomes finite under the power of Maya.

Kala, Vidya, Raga, Kaala, Niyati, and Purusha

Kala

The first obscuration caused by Maya is the Kala Tatwa. Kala represents the limited capability to perform tasks, denoting a restriction in the Kriya-Shakti of Shiva. This principle creates the sensation of specific abilities in individuals, such as an artist, musician, or sculptor, each limited to certain skills and ideas. The phenomena of karma and causal efficacy arise from this principle, indicating a limitation in action.

Vidya

The next principle under the domain of Maya-Shakti is Vidya, or knowledge. This knowledge is limited and impure, as it arises from Maya. Vidya creates a sensation of duality, where individuals perceive themselves as separate from each other and from Shiva. It allows one to gain knowledge of finite objects, such as a car or an apple, but does not provide a complete understanding of the infinite or the absolute.

Raga

Raga, or attachment, is the principle that manifests as a lack of self-sufficiency in individuals. It creates a sense of incompleteness, leading individuals to attach themselves to certain objects in an attempt to fulfill this perceived deficiency. This attachment fosters

feelings of anger, disappointment, aversion, and imperfection. Understanding the true nature of the self is necessary to overcome these desires and the resulting emotional states.

Kaala

Kaala, or time, represents the sensation of an orderly progression of events in a linear fashion. This principle restricts an individual's perception to specific events or time frames, limiting the perception of the infinite to a finite experience. Time is constituted by a sequence of events with past, present, and future dimensions. For a Shaivite practitioner, time is not an independent entity but exists within individual consciousness, obscuring the true nature of pure transcended awareness.

Niyati

Niyati, or bondage, refers to spatial limitations and creates the sensation of finite positions within a limited space. This principle results in experiences characterized by duality rather than unity. The illusion of duality leads to bondage and suffering. For example, the perception of colors as distinct entities under Niyati represents diversity rather than unity. True unity is symbolized by light.

Purusha

Purusha is the principle of transcended consciousness veiled by the five impure Tatwas (Kanchukas). The individual soul, immersed in Maya and having lost the non-dual perception, is referred to as Purusha. At this stage, consciousness is inundated with duality, leading to a bifurcation between subject and object. The phenomenal

world is perceived as separate and independent from the self. Unlike in the Shuddha-Vidya stage, where the object is known to be a projection of one's consciousness, in Purusha, the object is perceived as an independent entity.

Pratishta Kala and Prakriti

The next set of principles constitutes the Pratishta Kala or the immanent cosmos, and they form the Prakriti Anda, or cosmic egg of Prakriti. The principle of Prakriti is foundational to all objectivity in the cosmos and is the matrix for all empirical individuals (souls). Prakriti comprises three attributes:

1. Satva: Harmony and balance.
2. Rajas: Movement, passion, and activity.
3. Tamas: Inertia and lack of activity.

These attributes reflect every phenomenon, with Satva representing balance, Rajas representing dynamic activity, and Tamas representing stability. From Prakriti arises the triad of internal organs (Antahkarana Traya): Ahamkara (ego), Manas (mind), and Buddhi (intellect). These internal organs facilitate cognition, conation, and feeling.

Antahkarana or Internal Organs of Senses

The internal organs, or Antahkarana Traya, are responsible for cognitive functions:

- Buddhi: Responsible for cognition.
- Ahamkara: Responsible for conation (action).
- Manas: Responsible for feeling.

In Indian philosophy, these organs are subtle and evolve from Prakriti, aiding consciousness in performing specific functions.

Sense Organs

The five sense organs and their functions are:

1. Granendriya: Organ of olfaction.
2. Rasenendriya: Organ of taste.
3. Rupendriya: Organ of vision.
4. Sparshenendriya: Organ of touch.
5. Srotrendriya: Auditory apparatus.

These organs are subtle elements that facilitate sensory processes, beyond the physical organs like eyes or hands.

Five Tanmatras or Sensory Processes

The five Tanmatras are the subtle elements that correspond to the senses:

1. Shabdha: Sound.
2. Sparsha: Touch.
3. Rasa: Taste.
4. Rupa: Vision.
5. Gandha: Olfaction.

Tanmatras serve as intermediaries between the subtle senses and the gross elements (Pancha Mahabhutas), facilitating cognition.

Five Gross Elements or Maha Bhutas

The five gross elements evolve from the Tanmatras:

1. Akasha (Ether): Related to sound.
2. Vayu (Air): Related to touch.
3. Agni(Fire): Related to vision.
4. Ap/Jala (Water): Related to taste.
5. Prithvi (Earth): Related to smell.

These elements represent the manifestation of the physical universe, derived from the Tanmatras and influenced by the subtle internal organs.

Nivrti Kala and Prithvi Anda

The final Tanmatra is **Gandha**, or odor, which represents the stability of the supreme subject in the physical world as the **Prithvi Tatwa**. This Tatwa constitutes the **Prithvi Anda**, or the cosmic egg of the gross material world. Prithvi signifies the culmination of stability in the action of **Para-Samvid**, representing the full materialization of the physical universe.

The perceptions of various sensory qualities—such as sound, touch, form, flavor, and odor—manifest as:

Vacuity (Akasha/Ether)
Aeriality (Vayu/Air)
Formativity (Agni/Fire)
Fluidity (Ap/Jala/Water)
Solidity (Prithvi/Earth)

This indicates that the objective Mahabhutas (gross elements) arise from the subjective subtle principles present in the sense organs. The process of perceiving these elements involves an intermediary, the Tanmatras, which bridge the subjective awareness and the material objects.

In summary, the cognitive process through the five senses is mediated by the Tanmatras, which serve as intermediaries between subtle sensory principles and gross material elements. The causal relationship between the gross elements and the subtle sensory principles is thus well-understood through this framework.

These concepts should be viewed from the perspective of absolute idealism rather than subjective idealism. This is because, in absolute idealism, the entire cosmos is seen as a reflection of the consciousness of Shiva or the ultimate subject. The material world is perceived as a projection of this consciousness, and the objective reality of the cosmos is thus considered a manifestation of the ultimate, non-dual consciousness.

Shad Adhwas-The six fold existence of the cosmos

In summary, the gross elements emerge from the subtle principles present in the sense organs, passing through the Tanmatras. This causal relation emphasizes that the objective world is a projection of consciousness, where perception through the senses is mediated by subtle principles and manifests in the physical world.

It is necessary to briefly explain this concept here because this chapter is about cosmogenesis according to Shaivite theology. According to Shaivite doctrines, not only monistic Shaivism but also Siddhanta Shaiva doctrines, the universe exists in six forms. Of

these six, three pertain to the objective path, while the other three pertain to subjectivity. Adhwa means path and Shad means six. The objective paths are called Vachya-Adhwa, meaning that which is spoken, observed, cognized, or known. The subjective paths are called Vachaka-Adhwa, where Vachaka refers to the speaker, observer, knower, or the subject.

The three objective aspects of the cosmos are Bhuvana-Adhwa, Tatwa-Adhwa, and Kala-Adhwa. Bhuvana-Adhwa is the most grossly densified path of the universe, while Kala-Adhwa is subtle. Bhuvana means world; here, the world does not refer to the physical universe or a planet but to subtle worlds existing within the Tatwas. The physical universe we live in falls under the Prthwi-Tatwa. There are a total of 118 worlds scattered across 36 Tatwas.

Within the Prthwi-Tatwa, there are sixteen worlds. From Jala-Tatwa to Prakrti-Tatwa, there are a total of 56 worlds or Bhuvanas. From Purusha-Tatwa to Maya-Tatwa, there are 28 Bhuvanas. From Shuddha-Vidya to Shakti, there are 18 Bhuvanas. The total number of these Bhuvanas scattered over the Thirty-Six Tatwas is 118. These worlds are named after the deities presiding over them. The goddess Bhuvaneswari is interpreted as the goddess of the physical world, but her rulership extends over all 118 Bhuvanas, not just the physical world, which is only one among these 118 worlds.

The next path is Tatwa-Adhwa, the path of the Tatwas, which has been explained in detail above. The third path is called Kala-Adhwa. Here, the 36 Tatwas are categorized into five sheaths or Kalas. The first and densest Tatwa, Prthwi, falls under Nivrti-Kala. The Tatwas from Jala to Prakrti, constituting twenty-two Tatwas, fall under Pratishta-Kala. The Tatwas from Purusha to Maya, constituting

eight Tatwas, fall under Vidya-Kala. The Tatwas from Shuddha-Vidya to Shakti constitute Shanti-Kala and are four in number. The final Tatwa of Shiva falls under Shantyatita-Kala and is the subtlest among all the Kalas.

Now, let us briefly look at the subjective paths of the cosmos. They are three in number, like the objective ones: Pada-Adhwa, Mantra-Adhwa, and Varna-Adhwa. Pada refers to the 51 phonemes in Shaivite theology, which we will address later in this work. Next is Mantra-Adhwa; Mantra here refers to the words formed by the combination of phonemes. The last is Varna-Adhwa; Varna refers to sentences made up of words. This Vachaka or subjective path refers to the gradual unfolding of the universe as the divine speech of the supreme subject from the Para state to Pashyanti, which will be discussed in detail later in this book. The yogi or mystic uses these six paths of the cosmos to realize his divine self. Initially, all the Tatwas that make up the macrocosm are meditated upon within the body. Later, the Adhwas are meditated upon as fragments of awareness in the mental processes of the yogi, thus realizing the absolute oneness with Para-Shiva.

Abhasa and The Theory of Manifestation

In Monistic Shaivism, the world we live in is considered a tool for self-realization. Shaivism views every object, both animate and inanimate, as a manifestation of Shiva, making every object equally divine. Accordingly, Shaivism has introduced Abhasa Vada to explain the manifestation of the cosmos. Before delving into the theory of Abhasa or the theory of reflection, we must examine the various cosmological theories in Indian epistemologies and understand how Shaivism differs from them.

Indian Cosmological Theories

Four major cosmological theories are prevalent in Indian epistemologies. These theories are shaped by the understanding of the absolute or ultimate reality, i.e., God. They derive from the ontological view of the universe.

The first theory is known as Paramanu Vada. This theory posits that the entire cosmos is composed of tiny, subtle particles called Anu or atoms. When two such Paramanus combine, they form a Dwyanu. When two Dwayanus combine, they form a Trayanu; Trayanu combine to form Chaturanu, and then Panchanu. When two Panchanus combine, they form a Mahanu, which then combines to form physical materials and gross elements. In this theory, God acts merely as a designer who arranges the Anu to create the material universe. This theory, also called Arambhavada or the theory of

origination, was proposed by Kanada of the Vaiseshika school.

The next theory is Parinama Vada, propounded by Kapila of the Sankhya school of philosophy. This theory asserts that the effect is merely a transformation of the cause. For example, butter exists in milk as an effect, and milk is the cause of butter; milk undergoes transformation to produce butter. Just as milk transforms into butter, this school believes that the effect resides in the cause from the beginning, and the cause transforms to produce the effect. This theory states that the cosmos exists in the Prakriti or root element, similar to how a plant exists in a seed. Due to the disharmony in the three Gunas—Satva, Rajas, and Tamas—the universe forms. Thus, the cosmos is a result of the transformation of Mula-Prakriti. During dissolution, the universe reverts to Prakriti in reverse order. Everything occurs according to absolute universal laws without divine intervention.

Several flaws exist in this theory. Parinama Vada does not explain how Purusha interacts with Prakriti. Additionally, since Prakriti is insentient, it cannot independently give rise to the sentient universe. The theory lacks a causal agent or doer to bring about the transformation of Prakriti.

The next theory, propounded by the Vedanta school of Sankaracharya, is Vivarta Vada or the theory of appearance. This theory is strictly non-dual according to the Vedanta school. Some followers of Vedanta believe that only Brahman is real and the universe is unreal, if it exists at all. They view the universe as unreal. If it exists, it is not the nature of Brahman, contradicting non-dualistic Vedanta doctrines. Therefore, some Vedantic scholars consider the universe to be an illusion. However, even an illusory world should

have an apparent cause. For example, if someone mistakes a rope for a snake in dim light, the rope is real and the snake is an illusion caused by the lack of light. For a Vedanta follower, the absence of light is a real phenomenon. Non-dual Vedantic philosophers attribute this to the phenomenon of Maya.

According to these Vedantic followers, it is an illusion that leads us to believe that a god created the universe. When the illusion is removed, we realize that the universe and the god who created it are illusions. Thus, Vedanta considers the entire cosmos a dream, an illusion, and a false notion, pointing to the belief that both the universe and its creator are illusions caused by ignorance. The notion of a physical universe arises from beginningless ignorance or Avidya. Therefore, ignorance and illusion, or Avidya and Maya, are used interchangeably by some Vedanta followers to depict the same concept.

The Vedanta school attributes Sat, Chit, and Ananda as the three attributes of the supreme Brahman. The term Sat refers to existence; the Indian theory of Sat Karya Vada stems from Sat, which means existence or being. When Sankara used the analogy of a rope in dim light, he suggested that the way we perceive the cosmos (as dual or separate from the supreme) is an illusion. This message conveyed by Sankaracharya through Vivarta Vada was eventually misinterpreted, leading to the view that the universe itself is an illusion.

The concept of Guna Rahita (devoid of properties) was used to describe the supreme lord as lacking the three Gunas of Satva, Rajas, and Tamas, which are subject to limitations, finiteness, and determinate ideas and thoughts. This was misinterpreted as meaning that Brahman is devoid of any properties. Consequently,

later Vedantic philosophers assumed that Brahman lacks creative impulses and thus creation was seen as an illusion.

In contrast, the supreme lord Shiva is attributed with five powers: Chit, Ananda, Icha, Jnana, and Kriya. The triadic powers of Icha, Jnana, and Kriya bring about the cosmos. The Vedantic school includes these triadic powers of the supreme lord under the attribute of Sat, while Chit and Ananda are separately attributed in Shaivism. Sat precedes in Vedantic doctrines, indicating that the nature of Brahman involves creating or manifesting the cosmos. The only illusion that exists is in the mind of the limited empirical individual.

Some Shaivite sects, such as Pashupata-Shaivism, Siddhanta-Shaivism, and Veera-Shaivism, propose that the god created the world out of compassion by modifying the primal matter, similar to how a potter shapes clay using a wheel. However, these theories suggest that divine providence is limited by certain laws and cannot manifest the universe independently but relies on preset laws. In all these theories, the role of God in manifesting the universe is secondary. God is seen as a force that arranges primal matter to create the cosmos, like a weaver using threads or a potter using a wheel. The concept of God in these theories remains incomplete.

Monistic Shaivism, on the other hand, views God as free from all limitations and manifesting the universe out of sheer desire through His independent energy or sovereign power, known as Svatantrya Shakti. Creating the universe is not a necessity but a choice for God, who has the freedom both to create and to refrain from creating. This view asserts that the manifested universe is an expression of God's will. Parama-Shiva does not depend on anything or anyone to manifest the universe; He relies solely on His own free will and

independent power.

Like the Sankhya school of philosophy, Monistic Shaivism holds that Tatwas pre-exist in Parama-Shiva in potential form, akin to how a plant resides in a seed. However, Monistic Shaivism distinguishes between two kinds of movements: Unmesha and Nimesha, or manifestation and dissolution, which can also be described as emanation and withdrawal. Both these acts occur at the will of Para-Shiva.

In contrast, the Sankhya school asserts that there is no god even during withdrawal. The Tatwas are directly reabsorbed into Prakriti, the root element, without any causal agent.

In Monistic Shaivism, the universe emanates from Para-Shiva when the impulse to create arises in His consciousness. This emanation, termed Vama or "vomiting out," is understood as projecting cosmic Tatwas from His consciousness. Scholars of Monistic Shaivism liken this projection to a reflection in a mirror. Parama-Shiva projects the universe from His consciousness like a reflection and does not change His nature during this process. Such projection is only feasible if divine providence is seen as pure awareness and consciousness. The manifested universe thus reflects the consciousness of the absolute, representing an expansion of the supreme lord and an exaltation of His will, resulting in cosmic diversity. The acts of emanation and withdrawal can be termed Spanda or "throb." In other words, all cosmic principles exist in the consciousness of Para-Shiva as pure 'I', in complete unity, without any sense of duality or diversity. Spanda, or the throb, exists in the 'I' consciousness of Shiva, leading to the emanation and withdrawal of the universe, and the conception of the Tatwas of Shiva and Shakti.

When Monistic Shaivism identifies the cosmos as a projection of Parama-Shiva, it is seen as an ideal projection of consciousness, unlike the non-dual Vedanta view, which considers the universe an illusory projection due to beginningless ignorance. Sankhya theory, which holds that the effect is a transformation of the cause, would imply that Para-Shiva transforms into the cosmos, thereby losing His transcendent nature and effectively being destroyed, resulting in the creation of the universe. To illustrate, consider the transformation of milk into butter or curd: the attribute of milk is destroyed, and curd, a different substance, is born from it.

When Parama-Shiva projects the universe from His consciousness, He does not transform into matter; rather, the world, as an ideal projection, is nothing but His own consciousness. Thus, the phenomenal universe is an ideal projection of Parama-Shiva as consciousness. When Parama-Shiva projects the universe from the mirror of His consciousness, it does not create a substance different from His own nature. It is a perfect reflection of His own nature. Whatever is projected is of His nature, and anything not in His nature cannot exist or be known. Therefore, something non-existent in Him will not be projected.

The Shaiva theory of knowledge is thus the theory of cosmogenesis. This projection theory is known as Abhasa Vada or the Theory of Projection. The underlying principle of the Tatwas and the phenomenal world is consciousness. Everything that exists, every object perceived by our senses and mind, and every form that appears and disappears—the ever-changing universe—is nothing but the projection of divine consciousness. This external manifestation of what is within is termed Abhasa.

Knowledge is essentially the 'I' consciousness, the subjective awareness. The subject brings the object into manifestation; that is, the object does not have any independent existence of its own but is dependent on the subject. Objects such as a jar or a pot are identical with self-awareness and are unified within the 'I' consciousness of the subject. When a person says they see colors like blue or pink or objects like a cloth or a pot, it is essentially the 'I' shining as the object. Various objects shine within the subject as knowledge, much like an object of knowledge shining in a mirror. This awareness manifests in two ways: identifying the existence of an object and also its non-existence.

For example, a person identifies a jar on a table. When the jar is removed, the subject then identifies the non-existence of the object that was previously there. Thus, both existence and non-existence are within the subject, a point that will be clarified further in this chapter. Initially, the jar is one with consciousness, which is infinite and unlimited, identical with the nature of consciousness. Then the subject deliberately separates the object from awareness since the object in its indeterminate state is not useful to the subject. Monistic Shaivism denies the exclusive separation of subject and object. Initially, subject and object are regarded as identical in consciousness. The integral unity then splits and manifests as finite subject and object at the time of manifestation. Cognition of the object is possible only through the separation of subject and object from the integral unity. Knowledge is not possible if the object is completely different from or entirely cut off from the subject.

The mutual relationship of objects can be justified only if they exist within subjective awareness. Concepts like a jar, blue, or happiness

exist within subjective awareness. Objects themselves do not have the property to shine independently. The determinate experiences of consciousness manifest the object. This unity is maintained by the ultimate subjective awareness called Shiva.

Both subject and objects are manifestations of universal consciousness. We can compare knowledge phenomena to the rise of two sea waves: subjective and objective waves. The rise of the subjective sea wave represents the shining of the limited subject capable of receiving Abhasa (reflection), while the rise of the objective wave constitutes the manifestation of the object.

In essence, the objective wave is merely a collection of Abhasas, but only a few Abhasas are reflected on the wave of the limited subject. Each Abhasa is a collection of numerous minor Abhasas and requires minor subjective waves for its reflections. The causal efficiency of each Abhasa depends on the determinate cognition by the subject. Cognition is entirely dependent on the subject.

From the above, it is clear that each empirical individual is confined to their own objective world. These worlds are neither illusory nor mere figments of imagination. They are real objective worlds made up of Abhasas that are independent of us (the reasons will be detailed later in the chapter). Each Abhasa is separate, eternal, and the manifestation of these Abhasas depends entirely on their separation and union.

The manifestation of these Abhasas is controlled by universal consciousness through Niyati Tatwa. An object or event is identified by its dissimilarity to other objects. An Abhasa can only be recognized or cognized by its dissimilarity to other Abhasas. An object can be recognized only through its relative dissimilarity to other objects.

This diversity and notion of duality or dissimilarity are caused by Maya Tatwa. The Abhasa of self-luminous consciousness, which is beyond Maya Tatwa, is called Shiva Tatwa. It is Parama-Shiva, who transcends all Tatwas, that alone can unite and separate these Abhasas and control their manifestations.

An objection might arise based on Abhasa Vada: if all objects are illumined together since they are one with self-luminous light, everything should be illuminated at all times. However, the finite subject, which is identical with universal consciousness, does not shine distinctly or separately from the object. In response, Shaivites argue that every object, including the limited subject, is merely a manifestation of light itself. Since nothing is separate from light, the light manifests as limited due to the five obscurations and Maya. When light manifests as a limited subject under the influence of Kanchukas, it is called shunya pramata (a subject who has not realized their true identity with unlimited Shiva).

In this manner, the limited subject perceives only one minor Abhasa among many manifested Abhasas. For example, a person perceiving an object first sees the Abhasa named height, then length, and so on. This ability to perceive a specific Abhasa at a particular time is due to the Svatantrya or independent nature of the limited subject. The perception of Abhasas is restricted to one at a time because light manifests as a limited subject due to the influence of Maya and the five veils on the unlimited subjective light.

According to the universal absolutism of Shaivism, an object has no independent participation in universal being; an object cannot exist independently of the subject. Therefore, the object lacks causal efficiency. The manifested world appears as a reflection in

the mirror of the ultimate subject's consciousness. The supreme subject manifests as many objects, and while the objects may appear to change, the eternal subject remains unchanged and is beyond any notion of duality or diversity. Every object exists within His consciousness in a perfectly unified state.

Our perception is limited to the diversities in objective forms. These forms appear and disappear, but the underlying universal consciousness is everlasting, eternal, self-existent, and unchanging. All Abhasas rise at our will and merge into universal consciousness, much like how rising waves ultimately merge with the ocean. The existence of Abhasas is real in that they are projections of the ultimate Parama-Shiva. However, they are non-existent in the form that we, the limited subjects, experience them. For Parama-Shiva, the entire phenomenal world is an Abhasa. All perceptions and cognitions are Abhasa for the conventional, limited empirical individual.

Puryashtaka or Eight Sense Organs
And The Jiva

Now let us examine the functions of the Puryashtakas. The Puryashtakas consist of the five Tanmatras and the three internal sense organs, or Antahkarana, namely Manas, Buddhi, and Ahamkara. As we have already seen, Ahamkara splits into three entities: Satva, Rajas, and Tamas. Tamas gives rise to the five Tanmatras and to the five Mahabhutas, while Satva gives rise to the ten Indriyas (Jnanendriyas and Karmendriyas), and Rajas acts as the mediating force between the two.

As we know, the supreme subject has two aspects: immanent and transcendent. The supreme subject assumes the form of empirical individuals during its descent into the gross Tattwas. The empirical individual is none other than the almighty veiled in the obscurations of Maya, having assumed a limited and encapsulated form.

Purusha/Soul and the Tatwas in the Dimension of Objectivity

In our exploration thus far, we've established that the soul, referred to as Purusha in the context of the empirical individual, plays a pivotal role in understanding the dimension of objectivity. In Advaita Vedanta, Purusha is often equated with Atma, the core self or essence. With this foundation, let us delve deeper into how the individual soul perceives and interacts with the objective world.

Perception and the Sensory Experience

When we engage with the objective world, our perception is

primarily mediated through the five senses: touch, sight, odour, flavour, and sound. Initially, when we perceive these sensory inputs, they are experienced as distinct objects of our senses. However, as we engage more deeply, this distinction between the sensory inputs and their corresponding objects begins to dissolve. Instead, we start to perceive the sense organs as being intrinsically linked with the objects they engage with.

For instance, consider how we experience sound. When a person listens to music, the variation in volume is initially very apparent. Similarly, changes in the brightness of a television or computer screen are easily noticeable at first. However, over time, our senses become accustomed to these variations, and the initial perceptual clarity fades. This phenomenon illustrates how our sensory perception adjusts and integrates the variations in stimuli.

The Dynamic Nature of Perception

When a person is exposed to a sound that initially lacks variation, and then suddenly experiences multiple variations, the perception of Shabda Tanmatras (sound elements) becomes more nuanced. The variations in sound reveal the diversity inherent within the Shabda Tanmatras. As Purusha, transcending the physical body, engages with these sounds, the experience of sound is perceived as pervading all directions of space.

This perception reflects a deeper understanding: the self or Purusha, devoid of a physical locus, experiences sound as omnipresent. This aligns with the Indian philosophical concept of Kadamba Mukula Nyaya, which suggests that sound propagates in all directions simultaneously. According to this theory, sound

particles (or waves) radiate everywhere without a single medium of travel, making sound and the medium of Akasha (space) inherently intertwined.

Shaivite Doctrine and the Nature of Sound

In the Shaivite doctrine, this concept is further explored through the figure of Para-Bhairava. Para-Bhairava, often depicted as Vyoma Kesha, embodies the essence of space (Akasha) and the radiating waves of sound. "Vyoma" signifies space or the Akasha Mahabhuta (the great element of space), and "Kesha" refers to the dreadlocked hair of Bhairava, symbolizing the lines of radiating waves. This imagery represents the omnipresence and dynamic nature of sound, emphasizing its unity with the medium of space.

Integration of Sensory Experiences and Tatwas

To fully comprehend the interaction between the Purusha and the Tatwas, we must consider how these elements function within the dimension of objectivity. The sensory experiences of touch, sight, sound, and so forth are not merely passive observations but are deeply integrated with the fundamental principles of Tatwas. As these experiences are processed, they contribute to the manifestation of the limited self and its perception of the external world.

The interplay between Purusha and the Tatwas within the realm of objectivity provides a profound understanding of sensory perception and its integration with the cosmic elements. The dynamic interaction between the senses, the self, and the elemental principles reveals a comprehensive view of how we engage with and interpret the world around us. This intricate process underscores the depth of

our connection with the fundamental aspects of existence and their manifestation in our sensory experiences.

In our continued exploration of the Tatwas and their interplay with sensory perception, we turn our attention to two crucial elements: **Sparsha Tanmatra** and **Rupa Tanmatra**. These elements correspond to tactile sensations and visual forms, respectively, and their interaction with the Mahabhutas (great elements) provides a deeper understanding of how we perceive and interpret the world around us.

Sparsha Tanmatra: Tactile Perceptions and the Air Element

The **Sparsha Tanmatra** pertains to the sense of touch and the tactile perceptions associated with it. This Tanmatra is closely linked with the **Vayu Mahabhuta** or the air element. Tactile sensations are primarily concerned with variations in temperature and texture, which are perceived through our sense of touch.

Consider an environment where the temperature is stable with no noticeable fluctuations. In such a scenario, our tactile perception cannot directly discern the temperature's stability but can only detect changes or variations. For instance, we feel temperature changes as hot or cold rather than as an absolute state of temperature.

In practical terms, tactile perception involves detecting variations in the **aeriality** of the surroundings. The variations in the movement of air particles, or the tactile particulates in the environment, create the sense of temperature and texture. This dynamic interaction with the air element allows us to perceive the sensation of warmth or coldness.

Additionally, within the somato-sensory system, various

receptors like **mechanoreceptors** and **proprioceptors** contribute to our tactile experience. These receptors detect changes in pressure, texture, and temperature, helping us interpret the tactile quality of our environment. The fundamental tactile perceptions we experience, such as sensations of hot and cold, arise from variations in the movement and distribution of air particles or the **Vayu Mahabhuta**.

Rupa Tanmatra: Visual Forms and the Fire Element

The **Rupa Tanmatra** relates to visual perception and the ability to discern shapes, colors, and forms. This Tanmatra is associated with the **Agni Mahabhuta** or the fire element, which plays a crucial role in creating and perceiving forms and shapes within the cosmos.

Imagine a scenario where there is an all-pervading, homogeneous color of light. Without any variation in color, it is challenging to form distinct images or perceive objects. It is only when there is a shift or variation in the colors of light that forms and shapes become perceptible. These variations in color create the images and shapes we see, thanks to the activity of the **Rupa Tanmatras**.

The fire element (Agni) is essential in this context because it is the source of the variations in light and color that allow for the formation of visible shapes and images. Just as fire can transform and generate different hues, the Rupa Tanmatra enables the creation, sustenance, and dissolution of forms. The ability to perceive shapes and forms relies on the variations in colors and light, which are manifestations of the fire element within the self.

In essence, the **Rupa Tanmatra** is responsible for the creation of the formative plane of perception, allowing for the infinite variety of objects and images we experience. It provides the dynamic

quality necessary for the perception of shapes and colors, which are essentially variations in the light spectrum.

Integrating Sensory Experiences with the Elements

Both Sparsha and Rupa Tanmatras highlight the dynamic interaction between our sensory perceptions and the fundamental elements of the universe. **Sparsha Tanmatra** deals with the tactile experience and its association with the air element, emphasizing how we perceive changes in temperature and texture through the movement of air particles. On the other hand, **Rupa Tanmatra** focuses on the visual experience of forms and colors, linked with the fire element, which enables the perception of shapes and images through variations in light.

Understanding these elements provides a comprehensive view of how we experience and interpret our environment. The interplay between tactile and visual perceptions, mediated by their respective Tanmatras and elements, reveals the profound connection between sensory experiences and the fundamental principles of existence. This integration not only enhances our understanding of perception but also illustrates the intricate relationship between the individual self and the cosmos.

In our continued exploration of the elemental principles that underpin our perception of the world, we now turn our focus to the sense of taste and its association with the **water element**, or **Jala Mahabhuta**. This element, also known as **Ap Mahabhuta**, plays a crucial role in our sensory experiences, albeit less prominently compared to the other senses.

Sensation of Taste and the Water Element

The **Sparsha Tanmatra**, associated with the sense of touch,

allows us to experience variations in texture and temperature. In a similar vein, the **Rasa Tanmatra** governs the perception of taste. This Tanmatra is intrinsically linked to the water element, which is essential for tasting different flavors.

Taste is experienced through moisture, which facilitates the interaction between taste buds and flavor molecules. This element's ability to dissolve and transport various flavors underscores its importance in our sensory perception. However, unlike the other senses, taste plays a relatively minor role in our daily sensory experiences. Nonetheless, the water element's influence is pervasive and fundamental.

It's important to note that at this stage of perception, the elements are not yet fully localized to specific sensory organs. The manifestation of localized physical structures, such as taste buds, occurs with the development of the **earth element** or **Prthwi Mahabhuta**. Up to this point, the elements have an all-pervading nature, not confined to particular physical points but rather existing in a more diffuse state.

In this context, the soul, referred to as **'Anu'**, interacts with the elements, including the water element, in a more abstract and widespread manner. The variation in taste reflects changes in liquidity and moisture, associated with the water element's qualities.

The Earth Element and Odoriferous Perception

As we move to the next element, **Prthwi Mahabhuta**, or the earth element, we encounter the principle of **Gandha Tanmatra**, which corresponds to the sense of smell. The odoriferous particulates and their variations relate to the stability and cessation of movement, a characteristic inherent to the earth element.

Odor perception reflects the stability and solidity of the earth element. Unlike the other sensory experiences, which are continuous and dynamic, the experience of smell can be intermittent and less constant. This reflects the solid and stable nature of the earth element, marking the completion of the physical realm's manifestation.

The earth element signifies a point of culmination where the sensory experiences of the previous elements coalesce into a stable and solidified physical presence. This culmination results in a sensory experience that is continuous, stable, and indicative of the solid, tangible nature of the physical world.

Integration of the Five Elements in Sensory Experience

The five elements of perception—space (Akasha), air (Vayu), fire (Agni), water (Jala), and earth (Prthwi)—form the foundational principles of the physical cosmos. These elements result from the cosmic experiences of the Purusha and are intrinsically connected to the internal sense organs of the soul.

1. **Space (Akasha)**: Governs the sense of sound and the omnipresence of vibrations.
2. **Air (Vayu)**: Relates to tactile sensations, temperature variations, and the movement of particles.
3. **Fire (Agni)**: Is associated with visual perception, shapes, and the transformative aspect of light and color.
4. **Water (Jala)**: Influences the sense of taste and the role of moisture in flavor perception.
5. **Earth (Prthwi)**: Pertains to the sense of smell and the stability and solidity of the physical realm.

These elements collectively create the diverse and multifaceted experience of the physical world, reflecting the interplay between the external reality and the internal perceptions of the Purusha.

Agni Mahabhuta:
The Principle of Expression and Divine Speech

The **Agni Mahabhuta** (fire element) is particularly significant in the context of divine speech and expression. In Vedic and Vedantic philosophies, **Agni** symbolizes the principle of **expression** and the **exaltation of will** of the supreme subject. Fire is seen as the source of transformative light and speech, manifesting as images and forms.

The principle of fire is not only associated with the creation and perception of forms but also with divine speech, as it represents the dynamic expression of consciousness. Agni is considered the light of consciousness, embodying the supreme speech and the principle of creative manifestation.

Shaivite Perspective on the Tatwas

In the Shaivite tradition, the arrangement of Tatwas emerges from a logical standpoint and reflects the fundamental principles that constitute reality. **Para-Shiva**, the ultimate consciousness, transcends and pervades these principles. Para-Shiva is the supreme subject who experiences all Tatwas as inherently one with him.

The Tatwas are seen as manifestations of Para-Shiva, with each element contributing to the overall fabric of existence. The physical world, composed of these elements, is a product of the experiences of the Purusha, seamlessly integrated with the internal sense organs.

In summary, the interplay of the five Mahabhutas and their

corresponding Tanmatras highlights the profound connection between sensory perception and the fundamental principles of existence. The physical world and its diverse forms are a reflection of these elemental experiences, revealing the unity and complexity of the cosmos as perceived through the lens of the soul and consciousness.

Antahkarana Traya:
The Triad of Internal Sense Organs

To understand the Shaivite aspect of the three internal apparatuses, we must analyze the internal psychic processes from an epistemological point of view. When we recall an object from our memory, speak about something, or cognize an object, numerous operations occur within us. Although we may not pay conscious attention to these processes, they take place in the mental dimension. Due to the swiftness of the Manas-Tattwa, they are often unappreciated.

The first process involves the cognition of a particular object, which includes the association of sensory inputs with the internal organs: Manas, Buddhi, and Ahamkara. Attention must then be focused on sustaining and assimilating the objective knowledge that is cognized. These processes occur simultaneously during cognition; thus, the perception of knowledge is not possible without all of these processes working together.

The entire process is driven by the will to perceive a specific object, which manifests as a desire to acquire knowledge. This involves focusing on the object to be perceived while negating other irrelevant stimuli. For instance, if a person is looking at a

particular car on the road—a blue Lamborghini—the mind focuses on that Lamborghini by disregarding all other objective Abhasas, such as people crossing the road, traffic signals, buildings, and other vehicles. Only the blue Lamborghini is highlighted, and the unnecessary stimuli are filtered out by the psychic apparatuses.

The process of will to cognize an object, followed by the negation of unnecessary Abhasas and the creation of the perceived image, constitutes the second stage of cognition. The first process is the mere sensation or perception through the sense organs, while the second process involves the creation of the mental image. This image-making process is essential for recognizing and identifying the blue Lamborghini.

However, creating an image alone is not sufficient to assimilate the object and recall it when needed or to communicate about it to others. The images we see are variations in the hues of colors, which help us differentiate and create the desired image. The process of image-making involves distinguishing hues and selectively including or excluding elements based on past experiences. The attributes of the recalled object are drawn from past encounters and are integrated into the self. In essence, we are able to recognize an object because the elements of the object and our subjective experiences align.

Philosophically, the image must be experienced, assimilated, and recalled in relation to the self. This process of integrating objective knowledge within the self and endowing it with aspects of the self constitutes the third step in cognition. Yet even this third step does not fully complete the integration of objective knowledge into subjective experience.

Before conveying the knowledge of the blue Lamborghini that

I have assimilated, I must be able to distinguish this car from all others I have seen before. This involves identifying the specific Lamborghini out of all the Lamborghinis and distinguishing it from other brands like Volkswagen. This process of negating previous impressions and focusing on the specific one constitutes the fourth step in cognition.

The internal mental operations involved in this process are carried out by the triad of internal sense organs: Manas, Buddhi, and Ahamkara.

Manas is the entity that triggers the desire to cognize an object. It directs our awareness to a particular object and excludes irrelevant stimuli at that moment. Manas formulates discrete Abhasas (objective impressions) and constructs the image of the object within the mind.

Ahamkara, or the personal ego, stores and assimilates objective experiences in memory. It recalls these experiences as needed, contributing to the sense of personal 'I'. This personal ego, which is essentially a collection of memories, differentiates our personality from others and distinguishes between the object and the subject. While this lower ego represents our individual identity, the higher ego or supreme 'I' is Para-Bhairava, which pervades all empirical beings in the cosmos. The lower ego arises from the identification of the self with objects.

Buddhi is the principle that exists beyond Ahamkara. It represents the deeper, subconscious aspects of the mind. While Ahamkara makes decisions and judgments based on experiences and creates frames of reference, Buddhi transcends this lower ego, representing a more profound, subconscious self. In Western terms, Buddhi can be equated to the subconscious or subliminal self.

Shaivite epistemology incorporates both experiential and logical aspects. It is true that, from a logical standpoint, the three psychic apparatuses exist within the mental dimension of human beings. Experiencing these aspects vividly contributes to the gnosis in Shaivism. Some yogis, mystics, occultists, and magi claim to have experienced states of oneness, where their individual identity dissolved, allowing them to experience unity with all existence—a state of transcendent awareness.

Buddhi is not an incomprehensible or unfathomable principle. It is an experience that transcends the lower ego and influences Ahamkara. For example, when a person wakes from deep sleep, they are initially aware only of the immediate impressions and are unaware of their personal 'I'. At this moment, Buddhi is comprehensible. The state experienced upon waking is related to Buddhi Tatwa. Since Buddhi lacks the sense of lower 'I', it represents a purer, more fundamental aspect of consciousness.

The state of being awake versus asleep is influenced by bodily conditions. Sleep is associated with the dominance of Tamas on Ahamkara, while waking is driven by the predominance of Satwa and Rajas. The supreme subjective state, however, remains ever-active and dynamic, transcending the cycles of sleep and wakefulness tied to the body.

The changes in equilibrium and agitation within the three Gunas (Sattva, Rajas, and Tamas) are fundamental to the states of sleep and wakefulness. The question arises: what causes these fluctuations in the Gunas, leading to different states of awareness? Is it Prakriti, which is inherently inert, disturbing its own equilibrium, or is it Purusha, who, having identified with Prakriti, uses Ahamkara to

create these agitations?

Buddhi represents the universal experience of wholeness but becomes limited due to the influence of the Kanchukas (sheaths) on individual awareness. It embodies a calm state of consciousness, predominantly characterized by Sattva Guna. Buddhi is thus the internal, limited light of consciousness that is untainted by external objective impressions. It represents a state of Purusha that has not yet generated limited objectivity but remains limited as a subject. In other words, Buddhi is the introverted awareness of the limited self.

In the evolution of empirical individuals, Buddhi precedes the sensation of 'I' and concrete objective impressions. It consists of abstract ideas and operates in the background of the concrete ideas formed by Ahamkara. Ahamkara, or the ego, emerges from Buddhi as the next step in the descent of the Tatwas.

Ahamkara comes into play once a person develops a firm sense of self. Unlike Buddhi, which is more abstract, Ahamkara is a concrete affirmation of the self. It is composed of thoughts, emotions, and experiences gained through the cognition of external and internal objects. At any given moment, Ahamkara reflects the sense of 'I' and is connected to both external and internal objective impressions.

Thus, Ahamkara is formed from the accumulation of experiences and memories throughout one's life, significantly shaping personality. It involves the process of focusing on and selecting particular attributes while negating others, thereby shaping the individual's identity. Ahamkara is the process of self-identification and self-affirmation, defining the self in relation to these selected attributes and ideas as 'Me', 'Mine', etc. It is deeply involved in self-arrogation, self-identification, and self-affirmation.

Another perspective on Ahankara is to view it as the power of Shiva to manifest as limited objects. Ahankara embodies the Icha Shakti, or the will aspect of Shiva, in a limited and encapsulated form. In this capacity, Ahankara enables an individual to form judgments, make resolves, and acknowledge the self through actions that are inherently limited. It represents a state of constrained will, coupled with the dynamic Rajas Guna of Prakriti. Since Ahankara is actively involved in the development of character and personality, its predominance of Rajas is understandable, as Rajas represents the dynamic and active aspects of Prakriti.

Now, let us examine the third principle, Manas. Manas originates from Ahankara and is engaged in the process of image-making, constructing objective impressions from the manifold Abhasas perceived through the sense organs. The faculty of attention and concentration is a key attribute of Manas. It is inherently dynamic, continuously shifting from one objective impression to another. Even if the sense organs perceive objects in the external universe, if Manas is not properly synchronized with them, the individual will be unable to perceive these external objects effectively. Therefore, synchronization between Manas and the sense organs is crucial for receiving accurate information from the external world and responding appropriately.

Manas acts as a consolidating factor, gathering and organizing the multitude of sensory inputs into a coherent form that is comprehensible to the self. Once Manas has synthesized this information into a comprehensible form, it transfers this knowledge to Ahankara. Here, the knowledge undergoes further processing, acquiring a concrete and meaningful form after being judged and

contemplated by Buddhi.

It is important to note that as Buddhi gives rise to Ahankara, and Ahankara to Manas, none of the preceding Tatwas cease to exist. Instead, each Tatwa retains its presence alongside those that follow. Manas itself does not possess the capacity to illuminate or make sense of the knowledge it gathers. This illumination and understanding are provided by Buddhi and Ahankara. Thus, Tamas, which is associated with the seat of desires, also plays a role in this process.

This brief exploration of Puryashtaka (the eight principles) highlights how these psychic apparatuses come into play in the process of cognition and the interplay between them within the mental dimension of a limited subject.

The Seven Subjects

Every philosophy around the world has sought to answer a fundamental question: What is life? What is the nature and purpose of life? Different philosophies address this question in various ways. Some view reproduction and growth as signs of life, while others consider attributes such as hunger, thirst, emotions, feelings, and pleasure. These attributes are indeed signs of life, but life encompasses more than just hunger, pain, or reproduction. It also involves consciousness and awareness.Even when functions like pleasure, pain, and hunger cease seamlessly during deep, dreamless sleep, we continue to be alive. An interesting point to note is that some level of awareness persists even in this deep, dreamless state. Although objective reality vanishes, we are able to retain an awareness of the void we experience during deep sleep. In other words, we retain the experience by understanding the complete disappearance of objective impressions.So, what exactly happens when we are in deep sleep? According to Monistic Shaivism, during deep sleep, we experience our own self—the 'I' or inner awareness. However, we are not able to retain this experience because we have not trained ourselves to be aware of our inner self.Monistic Shaivism posits that there are seven states of subjective perception. The nature of consciousness is self-luminous; it illuminates all sensory perceptions received through our sense organs and can manifest itself without relying on external or internal impressions. All our experiences are due to this self-luminous 'I,' which is the ultimate consciousness that gives rise to the objective world.

Non-dual Shaivism holds that matter evolves from consciousness. This consciousness, manifesting in seven stages, is omnipotent, omniscient, eternal, and all-pervading, and is the causative principle of existence. In non-dual Shaivite doctrines, life itself is considered to be consciousness. This consciousness is identical with the cosmic consciousness of Para Shiva. Thus, Shiva is described as "Prakasha Vimarshatmaka" (light and illumination). In essence, the purpose of this light is to bring objects into existence. This ultimate, all-powerful divine providence brings everything into light. The light of consciousness is imbued with self-awareness, which is compared to Vimarsha or reflection. Since the nature of light is illumination, the nature of this consciousness is self-awareness

Due to its creative nature, this consciousness manifests as a multitude of objects. The diversity arises from the veils it creates to obscure its true nature while engaging in creating an infinite variety of objects from its own awareness. Thus, when this all-pervasive light manifests as an empirical soul, it becomes limited in power, constrained in terms of action, knowledge, and will.

Before delving into the seven dimensions of perception or awareness, it is crucial to understand that all these phenomena operate within a triad of consciousness: the subject who gains knowledge of the object, the process of knowing the object, and the object to be known. These are referred to as Pramatr (the knower), Prameya (the known), and Pramana (the means of knowledge) in traditional Sanskrit.

The subjective element in Monistic Shaivism is divided into seven stages, representing the gradual manifestation of divine consciousness as the cosmos. These stages are referred to as the

Sapta Pramatrs or seven subjects. Here is a detailed overview of each state:

1. Sakala State of Subjectivity

The Sakala state represents the first level of subjectivity. It is closely associated with the Prithvi Tatwa (earth element) and is characterized by a clear distinction between the subject and object. In this state, beings are under the illusion of duality, perceiving the objective reality as separate from the subject. They are subjected to all three Malas or impurities: Maya (illusion), Anava (individual ego), and Karma (past actions).

In the Sakala state, when a person focuses on an object, they might temporarily become one with it, mistakenly believing themselves to be the object rather than recognizing that the object exists within the subject. This results in a false identification with the object and an erroneous sense of unity with it.

2. Pralaya Kala

The second state is known as Pralaya Kala, where the subjects are referred to as Pralaya Kala Pramatr. The term Pralaya means the dissolution of objective impressions or thoughts back into consciousness. This state corresponds to the experience of deep, dreamless sleep.

During Pralaya Kala, the impurities of Maya and Anava persist. This state involves a form of negation where awareness rejects or withdraws from external objects, creating a sense of void or non-awareness. Despite the seeming void, this state still involves a distinction between subject and object. The subject rejects the

object, but this negation is not a transcended awareness; rather, it is a form of ignorance or a lack of awareness of the real self.

Saint Abhinava Gupta further divides Pralaya Kala into two stages:

- Apavedhya: Characterized by the complete cessation of all mental activities, both inner and outer. During this state, there is no awareness of this cessation process by the adept.
- Savedhya: In this stage, the adept is aware that both internal and external mental processes have ceased.

3. Vijnana Kala

The third state is called Vijnana Kala, and those residing in this state are known as Vijnana Kala Pramatr. This state is often experienced by yogis and mystics. In Vijnana Kala, there is an incomplete awareness of the real self. Yogis in this state occasionally perceive their true self and experience bliss, but they might not sustain this state continuously. At other times, they may feel limited or separate from the objects around them.

In Vijnana Kala, Karmiya Mala (impurities from past actions) and Anava Mala (ego impurity) are overcome, leaving only Mayiya Mala (illusion impurity). This state provides a glimpse of the bliss associated with higher subjectivity but is not yet fully realized. Yogi's progress from Vijnana Kala may involve shedding the physical body or returning to impart spiritual teachings (Shaktipath) to those in lower states of subjectivity. This process often involves the grace of Shri Kantha Natha, a manifestation of Shiva, who facilitates the evolution of the Purusha Tatwa into the physical cosmos.

Beyond Vijnana Kala, the states of subjectivity correspond directly to the pure Tatwas of subjective experience. While Vijnana Kala is a blend of pure and impure elements, representing a transition phase, the subsequent states pertain to entirely pure subjective experiences. These higher states reveal the profound and untainted aspects of consciousness, reflecting a deeper understanding and realization of the self.

The seven stages of subjectivity in Monistic Shaivism represent a progression from the dualistic perception of Sakala to the increasingly refined and pure experiences of higher states, culminating in the ultimate realization of divine consciousness

In Monistic Shaivism, the journey through the stages of subjectivity reveals a profound evolution of consciousness, culminating in the realization of the ultimate nature of reality. Here is a detailed exploration of the remaining states of subjectivity:

4. Mantra

The fourth state of subjectivity is known as **Mantra**. Beings in this state are called **Mantra Pramatr**, and it resides within the **Tatwa** of **Shuddha Vidya** or **Shadakhya**. In this stage, the yogi achieves a significant realization of their true self, often experienced as **Svachanda**, meaning self-liberated or free.

In the Mantra state, all impurities are eradicated. The adept is free from the three **Malas** (impurities) and restrictions, experiencing a profound sense of bliss and heightened awareness. The yogi gains insight into the infinite will, knowledge, and action of the universal subject. Despite this, the yogi may still not feel completely fulfilled.

The yogi may experience a duality in awareness:

- **"Aham Aham"**: A realization of "I and I alone," where the ego sense is strong.
- **"Na Iti"** or **"Idam Na Iti"**: The perception that everything external is false or an illusion, affirming the inner awareness as the only true reality.

The external world is perceived as an illusion, with the inner awareness being recognized as the sole reality.

5. Mantreswara

The fifth state of subjectivity is called **Mantreswara**, with subjects in this state referred to as **Mantreswara Pramatr**. This state operates within the **Tatwa** of **Ishwara**. In Mantreswara, the yogi experiences the external world as an extension of their own self. The distinction between the internal and external worlds dissolves, leading to a profound sense of oneness with the cosmos.

In this state, the yogi perceives no separation between themselves and the universe, recognizing that all external phenomena are integral parts of their own consciousness.

6. Mantra Maheswara

The sixth stage is known as **Mantra Maheswara**, with subjects residing in this state called **Mantra Maheswara Pramatr**. This stage is associated with the **Sada-Shiva** Tatwa. In this state, the yogi realizes that the entire universe is an emanation of their own consciousness and that it is not separate from their own nature.

Those who reach this stage are fully realized beings, free from the influence of ignorance and the veils of **Maya**. They no longer experience themselves as a **Pashu** (bound being) but as **Pati** (the

universal subject), the ultimate reality underlying all beings in the cosmos.

7. Shiva

The final stage of subjectivity is called **Shiva**, residing in the **Shiva-Shakti** Tatwa. The subject in this state is referred to as **Shiva Pramatr** and represents the absolute realization of being. In this state, there is no distinction between the inner and outer worlds; only pure awareness exists, untainted by notions of duality or form.

This is the highest state of consciousness, characterized by **god consciousness**, where awareness transcends all conceptual limitations and dualities. It is the ultimate, unconditioned state of absolute awareness, beyond words and descriptions.

Additional Considerations: Akala

Certain schools of Monistic Shaivism introduce an additional refinement to the final stage, dividing it into two sub-stages known as **Akala**:

- **Shakta**: The penultimate stage, associated with **Shakti**, the dynamic aspect of divine energy.
- **Shiva**: The ultimate stage, associated with **Shiva**, the static, absolute consciousness.

Each of these states of subjectivity can be further subdivided into more specific categories and sub-Tatwas, which delve deeper into the intricacies of spiritual realization. However, exploring these sub-categories is beyond the scope of this overview.

The progression through these stages of subjectivity illustrates a journey from the illusion of duality to the ultimate realization of non-dual consciousness. Each state represents a deeper level of awareness and understanding, culminating in the pure, unconditioned awareness of the Shiva state. This path reflects the transformative journey of spiritual evolution in Monistic Shaivism, leading to the realization of the divine essence that pervades all existence.

The Five Stages of Subject-Object Experience in the Shuddha Tatwas

In the philosophical system of Monistic Shaivism, the **Shuddha Tatwas** (pure categories of existence) represent different stages of subjective experience. These stages reveal various depths of self-awareness and understanding of the universe. The journey through these stages progresses from the most fundamental to the most refined levels of consciousness. Here, we examine the nature of subjective experiences from **Shiva** to **Shuddha Vidya**.

1. Shuddha Vidya (Mantra Pramatr)

Shuddha Vidya represents a significant stage in the hierarchy of subjective experiences, known as the **Mantra Pramatr** or the subjective state of **Mantra**.

At this stage, the experience can be described as a balance between '**I**' (the subject) and '**This**' (the object). The veil of **Vidya Tatwa**, which represents limited knowledge, is completely purified here, resulting in a state of **complete knowledge** or **omniscience**. This stage signifies the dissolution of limited experiences and the emergence of a more profound understanding. The distinction between subject

and object is obliterated, making them indistinguishable from each other.

Shuddha Vidya facilitates the unity of the knower and the known. Without this Tatwa, the subject and object would remain separate, and the subject would be incapable of affecting or illuminating the object. This stage transcends the limitations of sensory perception, expressing a state of pure, indeterminate knowledge. It shows that the subject's awareness is not influenced by external or internal sense organs but rather by a direct, omniscient understanding.

2. Ishwara-Tatwa

The next stage is **Ishwara-Tatwa**, where the subjective experience reaches a new level of integration between the subject and object.

At the **Ishwara-Tatwa** stage, the object **'This'** merges completely with the subject **'I'**. The distinction between knower and known is effectively dissolved, with the awareness of objectivity being fused with subjectivity. Here, the subject identifies itself with the object, placing more emphasis on the **'Thisness'** of the object.

This stage reflects a more profound realization of unity between the self and the external world. Although the subject's experience of itself as the object becomes dominant, the overall awareness remains fused and integrated. This represents a higher level of consciousness where the subject's identity becomes deeply connected with the object of perception.

3. Sadakhya-Tatwa

Sadakhya-Tatwa is named after the term **Sat**, meaning existence or being. This stage signifies the experience of **'I Am'**.

In the **Sadakhya-Tatwa**, the experience is characterized by '**I Am**', where '**Am**' is experienced through '**I**' as the individual self or the principle of pure experience. This stage reveals the ontological or metaphysical '**I**' in its supreme expression as the pure '**I**'. The **Sadakhya-Tatwa** represents a crucial stage in subjective awareness. Here, the '**I**' perceives the universe as an emanation of itself. This realization reflects the ultimate expression of the self, where the individual self recognizes its role as the source of all experiences. This stage signifies a deep awareness that the universe is a projection of one's own consciousness.

Shakti-Tatwa involves pure mystical experiences and represents the blissful aspect of divine consciousness.

4. The Shakti-Tatwa

The **Shakti-Tatwa**, or the principle of **Vimarsha**, is the aspect of **Para Shiva** that differentiates and actualizes divine consciousness. At this stage, the subjective experience is marked by profound bliss (Ananda). The experience is characterized by a deep sense of inner bliss and divine joy, which cannot be fully articulated in words.

Shakti is the dynamic force behind the emanation and withdrawal of the cosmos. It represents the bliss aspect of divine consciousness and the essential power that underlies all creation and dissolution. This stage reflects the profound, untainted bliss and awareness of the divine essence.

5. Shiva-Tatwa

The final stage in the series is **Shiva-Tatwa**, representing the pure state of subjectivity.

Shiva-Tatwa represents the pure 'I' stage of subjectivity, where the awareness is devoid of any object or duality. This stage is characterized by a complete absence of external and internal distinctions, reflecting the ultimate state of pure consciousness. The experience here is purely subjective, with no object to shine upon, representing the ultimate realization of divine consciousness. **Shiva-Tatwa** is the culmination of subjective experience, embodying the pure, unconditioned awareness. It is the final realization of the **Chit** aspect of **Para Shiva**, where the subject experiences itself in its most refined state. This stage demonstrates the absolute, transcendent nature of consciousness, free from all forms of duality and conceptual limitations.

The five stages of subjective experience from **Shiva** to **Shuddha Vidya** reveal a profound progression in consciousness. Each stage represents a deeper realization of the self and its relationship with the cosmos. **Shuddha Vidya** provides a state of complete knowledge and unity, **Ishwara-Tatwa** integrates the subject and object, **Sadakhya-Tatwa** embodies the ultimate self-realization, **Shakti-Tatwa** signifies divine bliss, and **Shiva-Tatwa** represents the purest state of consciousness.

These stages illustrate the evolution of self-awareness and its expression through different levels of understanding and experience, culminating in the realization of the absolute, unconditioned 'I'

The **Shakti** and **Shiva Tatwas** represent the pinnacle of subjective experience in the framework of Monistic Shaivism. These stages are characterized by profound mystical experiences and deep realizations about the nature of consciousness and reality.

Shakti-Tatwa and Shiva-Tatwa: Mystical Experiences and Their Significance

Shakti-Tatwa is the principle of divine power and bliss, known as **Vimarsha** or the **Ananda** (bliss) aspect of **Para Shiva**. It plays a crucial role in the differentiation and actualization of divine consciousness.

The subjective experience of **Shakti-Tatwa** is characterized by profound bliss and divine joy. This bliss is the pure inner awareness of **Para Shiva**, which transcends verbal expression. In this state, the awareness of bliss is so profound and pure that it cannot be fully captured in words.

Shakti is the dynamic force that enables both the creation and dissolution of the cosmos. She is responsible for the emanation of the universe (Adha-Maya) and its withdrawal (Urdhwa-Maya). Thus, **Shakti** represents the energy and potential that bring the cosmos into existence and also the power that can withdraw it, facilitating the transition between manifestation and pure awareness.In the context of the cosmos, Shakti serves a dual purpose:

1. **Adha-Maya**: The power that causes emanation and manifestation of the cosmos.
2. **Urdhwa-Maya**: The power that facilitates withdrawal and negation of the cosmic form, allowing the pure self-awareness to be experienced.

Shiva-Tatwa represents the ultimate stage of subjectivity, characterized by the pure **'I'** experience without the **'Am'** aspect. This is the highest realization of the self and is the manifestation of

the **Chit** (pure consciousness) aspect of **Para Shiva**.

In **Shiva-Tatwa**, the experience is pure, unconditioned awareness. The subjective state is experienced as 'I' without any object or duality. This stage reflects a state where objectivity ceases to exist, and only the pure 'I' or consciousness is present. It is the stage of pure self-illuminating light of consciousness, free from all forms of duality and conceptual distinctions.

Shiva-Tatwa represents the ultimate realization of the self where the divine essence is fully experienced. It is both the first impulse of cosmic manifestation and the final stage of subjectivity. In this stage:

Shiva embodies the untainted, pure 'I'—the essence of consciousness without any object or form.

Here, all other aspects and distinctions are subdued, and the pure self-illuminating consciousness prevails. The **Shiva-Tatwa** is the absolute, transcendent consciousness that remains as the foundation of all experiences.

Shakti supports the realization of **Shiva-Tatwa** by facilitating the processes of creation and withdrawal. **Shiva** and **Shakti** are inherently one, representing the unified principle of consciousness and energy. While **Shiva** signifies the static, unconditioned awareness, **Shakti** represents the dynamic, active force that brings forth and dissolves the cosmos.

To illustrate this with an analogy, **Shiva** represents the essence and life inherent in the seed. **Shakti** represents the potential and dynamic energy that causes the seed to grow and manifest into a complete tree.

The **Shakti** and **Shiva Tatwas** encapsulate the most profound

levels of subjective experience in Monistic Shaivism. **Shakti-Tatwa** reflects the bliss and dynamic power of consciousness, while **Shiva-Tatwa** represents the pure, unconditioned self-awareness. Together, these Tatwas highlight the dual yet unified nature of divine consciousness and energy, showing how both principles are essential in the manifestation and dissolution of the cosmos.

The experience of these Tatwas demonstrates the ultimate realization of the self as pure awareness and the dynamic interplay between consciousness and its creative potential. Understanding these stages provides insight into the nature of reality and the divine essence that permeates all existence.

Shiva-The Absolute Supreme Consciousness

The concept of supreme consciousness is a complex topic within Indian esoteric traditions, and many saints have attempted to explain it from various perspectives. Theories about supreme consciousness, or the ultimate deity, differ across different philosophical streams. Although some similarities exist, spiritual aspirants often find it challenging to grasp the true nature of supreme consciousness through these varying theories.

When examining the theories from different schools of thought on supreme consciousness, it becomes apparent that, at their core, they are similar. Each school approaches the concept from a distinct angle, which can make them appear different on the surface. However, fundamentally, they convey the same essence. Most major Indian esoteric traditions agree that the essential nature of the supreme deity is consciousness.

Despite the efforts of these esoteric traditions to address the supreme, many of their explanations remain incomplete or inadequately developed. This lack of a thorough explanation can be seen as a form of intellectual dishonesty or negligence, which is contrary to the pursuit of truth. The diversity in approaches to understanding the absolute in different spiritual traditions adds a unique character to each tradition.

In a way, these theories serve as pieces of a large puzzle that needs to be assembled. Each theory offers a specific perspective on

the nature of the supreme deity. A seeker is expected to assimilate these perspectives, reflect on them, and realize the nature of supreme consciousness in a way that is uniquely suited to them. Every theory about the absolute has some element of non-duality. Since the supreme deity is infinite, it cannot be comprehended directly but can only be understood through its infinite manifestations in the realm of finite objects. Therefore, supreme consciousness can be approached from countless angles without ever being fully exhausted.

The absolute, which is beyond all symbols, is expressed through symbols. The divine, which transcends all sounds, is expressed through mantras. The supreme, which surpasses every idea, is expressed through concepts, and the supreme consciousness, which goes beyond all forms, is contemplated through forms and images. For an adept from a purely non-dual school of spiritualism, the divine transcends all these concepts, symbols, and ideas. Nevertheless, they recognize that the manifestation of the divine includes these symbols, sounds, and ideas as well.

This can be illustrated with an analogy: The center of a circle can be reached by drawing countless radii from its perimeter. In this analogy, the center represents the absolute, and each radius represents a different path followed by the adept to reach the supreme deity. An adept follows their chosen path (radius) to reach the center, and while they may not be aware of other paths, each approach to the absolute can lead to the supreme deity

It is reasonable to conclude that every philosophical system has evolved from gnostic experiences, suggesting that the supreme principle is grounded in the value of these experiences. Consequently, the absolute being experienced is often addressed using similar terms

across different systems. To illustrate this further, let's examine the doctrines of Vedanta and Madhyamika Buddhism, which both utilize cognitive experiences to realize the divine principle. Conversely, Shaivites, Shaktas, and Yogacharas rely on the aspect of will to attain a realization of the divine. The Vaishnavism tradition, particularly that of Chaitanya Mahaprabhu, emphasizes Bhakti (devotion) or feeling as a means to realize the absolute.

In Shaivism, the absolute is described as *Swatantra*, or freedom. According to Shaivite doctrines, the absolute is perceived as the knower, the known, and the process of knowing, encompassing the states of emanation, sustenance, withdrawal, and dissolution. Shaivism posits that even in a pure, unadulterated transcendent state, the objective world is not rendered non-existent; instead, it is perceived as one with the supreme consciousness. Parama-Shiva is regarded as the all-pervading supreme consciousness, with no separation between the knower (subject) and the known (object). The known is manifested by the knower independently, without reliance on any external source. This ability to manifest any object from one's awareness is termed *Swatantra* or absolute freedom. If we assume there is no distinction between phenomena and noumena, then both must be seen as aspects of the transcended absolute consciousness. Other theories of absolutism tend to falter because they are typically inclined towards one of these dualities. For example, from the Sankhya perspective, a Purusha (divinity) that requires Prakriti (nature) to initiate cosmic activity is not truly free and lacks the sovereign will to create.

In Shaiva absolutism, freedom is intrinsic to the supreme consciousness, which is referred to as *Prakasha* or the light of

consciousness. This self-luminosity, or *Vimarsha*, corresponds to the absolute freedom to manifest objects or bring the objective world to light. The notion of lack of freedom is associated with the impure *Tatwas* (elements) starting from Purusha, due to the five veils of Maya (illusion). Shaivite saints assert that this perception of limited freedom is, in itself, part of the supreme *Swatantra*, since the supreme subject possesses the freedom both to create and to refrain from creation.

The term "consciousness" in this context conveys the idea of a divine being that transcends all forms, ideas, and objects, going beyond every manifestation. The term "absolute consciousness" is used throughout Shaiva epistemology to express the notion of non-duality.

The concept of *Swatantra*—or absolute freedom—illustrates the omnipotent nature of Shiva's Kriya Shakti, the dynamic power that enables him to perform the profound act of manifesting the cosmos purely through his will. Various terms are used to describe the absolute, including *Swatantra*, *Para-Samvid*, *Para-Shiva*, *Para-Pramatr*, *Chitta*, *Svachanda*, *Ahamta*, *Purna*, *Prakasha*, and *Vimarsha*. Each of these terms reflects different facets of the dynamic supreme consciousness.

The term *Ahamta* refers to the supreme sense of 'I', representing the unity of all manifested objects and a sense of integral wholeness. In contrast, the self-luminous nature of the absolute indicates the way in which the objective world is manifested. *Vimarsha* denotes the process of discerning and determining the elements (*Tatwas*) from the indeterminate, while *Swatantra* signifies the absolute freedom or omnipotence through which Para-Shiva brings the cosmos into

existence.

This concept of total freedom helps bridge the gap between noumenal consciousness and phenomenal matter. It further clarifies that objects are mere manifestations of the subject, reflecting or expressing the will of the universal subject. Through this perspective, Shaivism robustly affirms its doctrine of non-duality. This is perhaps where Shaivism achieves a notable distinction compared to other non-dual schools of Indian philosophy. Other schools, such as Vedanta, have struggled to convey their concept of non-duality without falling into contradictions or producing insufficient justifications for their theories of non-dual absolutism.

Shaivism avoids duality by asserting that Shiva and Shakti are, in essence, the light and its luminosity, respectively. Luminosity is the inherent nature of light, just as Shakti represents the nature of Shiva; in other words, Shakti is the awareness of Shiva, the supreme consciousness. Therefore, Parama-Shiva is seen as embodying the freedom to act. A free act of consciousness is intrinsic to the nature of the supreme subject, and this unique interpretation of freedom in Shaivism sets it apart from other absolutist theories.

Since the supreme subject is conceptualized as consciousness, it cannot be described as a pure, formless being or as mere nothingness, as these interpretations would denote negation. Rather, the supreme subject is the active agent through which all finite objects emerge. Consequently, freedom is attributed to the supreme, resulting from the self-awareness inherent in consciousness. This infinite self-awareness brings forth the myriad finite objects of the cosmos. Thus, the supreme Parama-Shiva can be understood as the unified aspect of consciousness and the freedom of awareness, or the *Samyoga*

(union) of *Chit* (consciousness) and *Swatantra* (freedom). Shiva is regarded as the supreme subject, serving as the foundation for the eternal play or sport known as *Lila* of Shakti. Consequently, Shakti can be defined as the dynamic awareness that manifests in countless forms and objects. Thus, Shiva and Shakti are not two separate realities but are instead two integral aspects of the absolute, through which its presence is made evident to us.

According to Shaiva doctrines, the absolute is described as *Prakasha-Vimarsha*. Here, *Prakasha* refers to the pure, transcendent, and unchanging subjective consciousness, while *Vimarsha* signifies the self-awareness that gives rise to the successive Shaktis of *Icha* (will), *Jnana* (knowledge), and *Kriya* (action). Abhinava Gupta, in his exposition of the *Bimbha-Pratibimbha Vada* or theory of reflection, likens the light to a mirror that reflects objects. In this analogy, *Vimarsha* is the actual act or the potential of the mirror to reflect the light. This concept is referred to as *Aham-Vimarsha*, meaning "I reflect myself." It represents self-awareness or the potential of the subject to know itself, illustrating the power of the subject to be aware of itself, which is *Vimarsha*.

Vimarsha is the self-luminous nature of consciousness, while *Prakasha* represents the supreme subject in the form of pure consciousness. This *Vimarsha* manifests as the self-awareness of Para-Shiva. It is limitless and does not take on the form of a finite object. If it were limited, Shiva would have to rely on an external source for creation, leading to an infinite regress. Similarly, without *Vimarsha* in *Prakasha*, the universal subject would lack self-awareness, rendering it a lifeless substance devoid of self-luminous awareness. Thus, *Vimarsha*, which is worshipped as the divine

feminine and given names such as *Para-Vak*, *Para-Shakti*, *Spanda*, *Aishwarya*, *Anugraha*, and *Ananda*, is essential to the understanding of consciousness.

Returning to the concept of Para-Shiva as the Absolute 'I' or the supreme subject, it becomes clear that supreme consciousness encompasses all reality. This understanding avoids the concept of nothingness as an absolute, which would amount to negation, or the idea that the physical world is merely an illusion caused by ignorance. In Shaiva doctrines, duality is entirely dissolved. The nature of the subject is to emanate the object, meaning the knower's nature is to bring objects into the light of knowledge. Thus, the apparent duality between subject and object is revealed as an illusion.

The Absolute 'I' is dynamic and imbued with awareness. The primary attribute of this 'I' is self-awareness—the ability to be aware of itself, and to reveal itself along with the objects illuminated by its own light. This self-awareness is not a mere accidental phenomenon of the Absolute 'I' but is intrinsic to its nature. This self-awareness forms the basis or principle of unity in the finite experiences of the subject as *Purusha* (limited subject). In the supreme 'I', there is no bifurcation or duality; the distinction between subject and object does not exist. Although a false sense of duality may appear in the gross planes of existence, this dichotomy is grounded in the non-dual supreme Absolute 'I'. Without *Para-Samvid* (supreme knowledge), the existence of both the known and the knower would be impossible. Therefore, the very existence of objects and subjects serves as proof of the existence of this supreme 'I' consciousness.

The supreme 'I' is self-luminous and inherently possesses a constant luminosity that it never negates. It is important to understand

that this self-luminosity of consciousness is not an object of its own awareness. Theoretically, the supreme self could be aware of itself in two distinct ways: one is partial awareness, where the supreme is aware of certain attributes or objects within itself; the other is complete awareness, where the entire supreme light is fully aware of itself and all objects of thought are simultaneously illuminated.

If the former case were true, it would imply distinctions and differentiations within the supreme consciousness, which contradicts the principle of non-duality. On the other hand, if the latter case were accurate, the subject and the object would overlap, leading to a situation where they are indistinguishable. Both scenarios fail to account for the fact that the subject is never an object of awareness or thought. The supreme subject serves as the fundamental substratum through which all things are manifested; it is the agent of knowing, not an object to be known.

Self-luminous consciousness cannot be described as the consciousness of consciousness. Awareness cannot be recognized by a subsequent layer of awareness. For example, when a person says, "I see a tree," and later reflects, "I know I saw a tree," the initial awareness of seeing the tree has dissipated, and the subsequent awareness is a result of a new, distinct awareness. This illustrates that the initial awareness cannot be cognized by the subsequent one. Thus, the subject, being self-revealing, is never an object of awareness.

In the Chandogya Upanishad, there is a concept known as *Akshini Vidya* or the "knowledge of the eye," which suggests that the sight of the seer is immortal. This indicates that supreme consciousness is eternal and continually self-cognizing, rather than

describing a relationship between seer and seen. Self-awareness is inherently possible due to consciousness itself; consciousness is the agent of self-awareness. In simpler terms, we can be aware of our consciousness, but we cannot be conscious of our consciousness in the same way. God, as the ultimate knower or subject, can never be the object of contemplation or knowing; He is the ultimate contemplator and agent of knowing.

Para-Shiva is not a determinate knowledge or a specific form of consciousness, as determination implies duality. Since the supreme 'I' is devoid of any determination, it remains as pure consciousness, characterized by spontaneous self-awareness. The supreme 'I' is pure and free from dualities, owing to the absence of any inherent determination.

When Shaivite saints assert that the supreme god is consciousness endowed with self-awareness, questions might arise about how this consciousness can be aware of itself and what the nature of this awareness is. Is it the same as the self-awareness experienced by every individual? To answer this, we must recognize that humans are *Purushas*, or limited individuals, constrained in knowledge, will, action, and awareness. Our awareness and understanding are bound by time and space, and we remember and recall events in a sequential manner due to our linear perception.

Omniscience, affected by *Maya* (illusion), creates the sensation of limited knowledge within the constraints of time. The manifestations of activities in limited spaces and contexts reflect the limited aspect of omnipresent consciousness. Therefore, in an empirical individual or Purusha, awareness is limited and does not equate to the nature of absolute consciousness. This self-imposed limitation and the

recognition of the true self represent the eternal sport of Shiva and Shakti, the interplay of the dynamic and static aspects of the supreme reality.

Consciousness: A Further Hermeneutical Investigation

The concept of consciousness, characterized by its self-luminescence, is understood in Shaiva philosophy as self-aware and dynamic. The light, which is self-luminous by nature, symbolizes consciousness in its most profound form. Shaivite saints, particularly Saint Utpaladeva, delve into this concept, offering two distinct theories to elaborate on the nature of self-reflective light.

Saint Utpaladeva posits that the self is indeed consciousness, a view supported by the Shiva-Sutras, which affirm this with the verse "Chaitanyam Atma" (Consciousness is the Self). According to Shaiva philosophy, consciousness is dynamic and self-reflective. This complex concept of consciousness, a cornerstone of Shaivite thought, can be seen as an active principle. It is characterized by self-luminous consciousness, which represents the supreme speech or Vak—the sovereign power of the supreme subject to create. This concept encompasses both the freedom to create and the freedom from creating. In all these aspects, the supreme is affirmed as self-aware consciousness.

Thus, the self-aware consciousness, which is the supreme subject, is articulated as one with the supreme speech or Vak. This sovereign freedom enables the supreme to actualize itself as the cosmos. It manifests as a self-affirming or self-verbalizing aspect of the supreme, independent of external means. The supreme consciousness revels in its own manifestations, appearing as a multitude of objects within

the cosmos, and reflecting itself in various forms such as thoughts, words, images, odors, and sounds.

The supreme self-reflective or self-aware consciousness manifests in two primary ways:

1. **Supreme Self-Reflective Infinite Light**: This aspect is characterized by being all-pervading, indeterminate, infinite, and all-knowing. It represents a boundless and unconditioned form of consciousness.
2. **Limited Subjective Awareness**: In the process of actualizing the cosmos, the supreme consciousness manifests as finite, determinate, encapsulated, and confined. This is an inevitable phenomenon when the supreme reality is expressed as the cosmos or the objective world.

The supreme is equated with speech due to its nature of self-expression or self-reflection, which will be explored in greater detail in subsequent chapters. This form of consciousness is self-expressive, revealing its essence through speech and other manifestations.

In Shaiva doctrines, consciousness is explained in two key ways:

1. **Self-Awareness**: The ability of consciousness to be aware of its own existence or to affirm its own presence.
2. **Cause of Manifestation**: The ability of consciousness to create or express itself as the objective world.

From these perspectives, supreme consciousness can be understood as the infinite, all-pervading 'I' consciousness. If

consciousness is indeed omnipotent, omniscient, and omnipresent, it must be complete and whole, able to express itself fully, self-sufficient, and independent of any external dependency. It should be self-sustaining in nature.

Returning to the triad of subject, cognition, and object, consciousness is identified with the subject. In Shaiva philosophy, consciousness is the all-inclusive principle, encompassing both the knowledge of objects and the act of cognition within itself. This understanding highlights the inherent oneness of the object and cognition within the subject, rather than a subsequent amalgamation of two distinct principles. Simply put, the subject, which is consciousness, emanates objects from within itself and actualizes them.

In understanding the dynamics of consciousness, it is crucial to recognize the integral relationship between the subject, the act of emanation, and the object. According to Shaiva philosophy, the principle of consciousness operates through three interrelated components:

1. **The Subject**: This is the consciousness itself, the ultimate reality, or the self that emanates.
2. **The Act of Emanation**: This refers to the cognitive activity or process by which the subject brings objects into manifestation.
3. **The Object**: This is the result of the emanation or the actualized principle—the manifestation that appears as a discrete entity in the world.

This triadic relationship—subject, cognition, and object—is not merely a theoretical construct but is evident in everyday actions and experiences. The realization of this relationship underscores that the synchronization and coordination of discrete cognitions (objects of awareness) are essential for coherent action in the world.

Unification of Object and Cognition with the Subject

In the empirical realm, the seemingly separate forms or objects of awareness, originating from Shakti (or luminosity), are actually unified with the consciousness aspect, identified as Shiva. This unity implies that what appears as manifold manifestations ultimately emanates from a singular source. This reinforces the concept of the supreme consciousness being the ultimate reality, with the universe as a manifestation within this supreme consciousness.

Monistic View of Manifestation

To grasp the nature of consciousness and its manifestations, it is essential to adopt an absolute monistic perspective. According to Shaivite scholars, the universe is not external to the supreme consciousness but manifests within it. This monistic view provides a framework to address and resolve the apparent duality in understanding consciousness and its manifestations.

Prakasha-Vimarsha and Pratibhana

Shaivite scholars propose two primary interpretations to describe the supreme:

1. **Prakasha-Vimarsha**: This concept refers to consciousness as self-affirming and self-aware. Here, *Prakasha* denotes

the supreme light or self-luminous consciousness, while *Vimarsha* signifies the self-awareness or the reflective aspect of consciousness that manifests various forms and objects.

2. **Pratibhana**: This term describes the inner manifesting awareness, which encompasses both the supreme consciousness and empirical souls. *Pratibhana* is the sum total of the inner awareness that gives rise to determinate knowledge. It reflects how consciousness manifests as both the essence of objective knowledge and the experience of the world.

Consider the act of perceiving an object, such as a pot. The inner light, which manifests as the knowledge of the pot, does not reside in the pot itself but within the subject as the light that externalizes the concept of the pot. Similarly, when recognizing a cow, the subject recalls past experiences and features of the cow, such as its shape and color. This process involves the succession of inner light or awareness, which enables the subject to recognize and distinguish the object.

The inner light, which shines on the field of objectivity, represents the very nature of consciousness—the 'I'. The 'I' brings objects into existence by shining light upon them. This dynamic activity is referred to as **Spanda**, the vibratory or pulsating nature of consciousness. The 'I' recalls objects from an indeterminate state and manifests them as determinate knowledge.

The Nature of the Subject and Consciousness

The subject, or 'I', functions as the substratum for both the object

and the act of cognition. The consciousness, or *'I'*, integrates the objective reality within itself and actualizes the cosmos as its own extension. Thus, the self-affirming awareness is a reflection of the subject's ability to illuminate and manifest the objective world.

The subject (Shiva) and the awareness (Pratibhana) are one in Shaiva philosophy. The consciousness manifests as self-affirming awareness, shedding light on objective reality and extending itself into the cosmos. In this framework, consciousness is synonymous with the knowing nature of the subject and its absolute sovereignty in manifesting the objective world.

The concept of consciousness as a unitary principle is indeed present across various Indian philosophical traditions, not exclusively within Shaivism. However, the way Shaivism approaches and interprets this unitary principle presents distinctive aspects that contribute uniquely to its doctrine. To address why Shaivism's approach is notable, especially in the context of similar philosophies like Vedanta, it is helpful to explore both the general philosophical background and the specific contributions of Shaivism.

In philosophies that hold consciousness as a unitary principle, such as Vedanta and Shaivism, the central question is how a singular, undivided consciousness can manifest a diverse and multiplicity-filled objective world without compromising its non-dual nature. Vedanta, for example, posits that the phenomenal world is an illusion (Maya) that obscures the true nature of Brahman (pure consciousness). However, it often leaves the origin of this ignorance unexplained and maintains a stark division between the ultimate reality and its illusory manifestations.

In contrast, non-dual Shaivism offers a more nuanced explanation.

According to Shaiva doctrine, consciousness (Para-Shiva) is not merely a passive, static principle but an active, dynamic force. The supreme consciousness is described as having the inherent power (Shakti) to create and manifest the objective world while retaining its non-dual nature. This view addresses the need for a monistic doctrine by providing an internal mechanism for how unity and multiplicity coexist.

Unlike Vedanta, which tends to emphasize the illusion of the material world, Shaivism sees the world as an expression of the supreme consciousness. Here, consciousness is dynamic and self-affirming, embodying both the power to manifest multiplicity (through Shakti) and the maintenance of its unitary essence. The manifestation is viewed as an extension or expression of the supreme consciousness rather than a mere illusion.

Attributes of Self-Affirming Consciousness:

- **Will (Icha)**: Consciousness has the inherent will to act and know. This will manifests as the drive to create and interact with the world.
- **Reflective Awareness (Vimarsha)**: Consciousness reflects its own self, creating the notion of objects and their perceived reality.
- **Manifestation (Kriya)**: The ability to manifest the objective world in its own nature or image, showing the dynamic aspect of consciousness.

These attributes are fundamental in Shaivism, representing

the powers of Para-Shiva: Icha (will), Jnana (knowledge), and Kriya (action). The dynamic interplay of these powers allows consciousness to manifest the cosmos while remaining unchanged and omnipresent.

Spanda a unique concept in Shaivism refers to the vibratory or pulsating nature of consciousness. It is through Spanda that the supreme consciousness reflects and actualizes the world. This process includes the dynamic act of emanation, where the subjective consciousness manifests the objective reality while maintaining its non-dual essence.In Shaivism, the objective reality is not seen as separate from the subjective consciousness but as an expression or exaltation of the same. During dissolution or withdrawal, the objective reality reverts to its primal state of reflection and is absorbed back into the will, illustrating the cyclical nature of manifestation and withdrawal without disrupting the unitary essence of consciousness.

Shaivism integrates the limited manifestations into the ultimate principle of consciousness. The material world, although seemingly limited, is seen as a reflection of the supreme consciousness. Thus, the world is both an expression of Para-Shiva and a means through which the divine nature is exalted and celebrated.

While the unitary principle of consciousness is not unique to Shaivism, its treatment in Shaiva philosophy offers a distinctive perspective by emphasizing the dynamic, self-affirming nature of consciousness. Unlike Vedantic views that often describe the material world as illusory, Shaivism presents a more integrated approach where the objective world is a legitimate expression of the divine consciousness. This allows Shaivism to maintain a non-dual view while explaining how consciousness can manifest and

interact with the diverse multiplicities of the cosmos without losing its essential unity. The monistic doctrine of Shaivism, therefore, provides a comprehensive framework that reconciles the existence of a pluralistic universe with the underlying unity of consciousness.

Shakti The Dynamic Awareness

The Role of Shakti in Shaivism: The Power of Limitation and Manifestation

It is evident that in Shaivism, the concept of limitation is intrinsically tied to the nature of the supreme subject, known as Para-Shiva. Unlike other philosophical systems where limitations might be viewed as constraints or deficiencies, in Shaivism, these limitations are understood as expressions of the supreme subject's inherent power of Swatantra (freedom). This power enables the supreme subject to impose limitations upon itself and simultaneously transcend these limitations, leading to the creation and evolution of the cosmos.

The Role of Shakti: Power and Manifestation

In Shaivism, Shakti represents the dynamic power of the supreme subject to manifest and limit itself, resulting in the creation of the cosmos. The presence of Shakti is self-evident in the dynamic awareness we experience of the multitude of objects around us. Shakti, in essence, is the active force behind the manifestation and interaction of these objects.

The analogy often used to clarify this concept is that of fire. In this analogy, if Shiva is compared to an eternal fire, then Shakti is akin to the heat and light produced by that fire. Just as heat and light are inseparable aspects of fire, awareness is an inherent aspect of consciousness. The heat and light are not separate from the fire; similarly, awareness is not separate from consciousness but is its fundamental nature.

Shakti as Cause and Effect

Shakti operates as both the cause and the effect in the cosmos. She is responsible for the creation of duality, which allows for the recognition of the self's true nature. By manifesting dualities such as good and evil, large and small, or long and short, Shakti enables the perception and understanding of these contrasts. This duality is not merely a creation of external differences but is essential for the cognitive process itself. Shakti embodies both the process of cognition and the object of cognition, demonstrating her role as both the means and the end of knowledge.

Cause and Effect Theory: Karya-Karana Siddhanta

In Indian philosophy, the theory of cause and effect (Karya-Karana Siddhanta) addresses how causes bring about effects and how effects are inherent in their causes. This theory is discussed in various schools of thought with different interpretations:

1. **Inherent Potency**: Some schools argue that the effect is inherent in the cause, meaning that the cause possesses the potential to bring about the effect. For example, just as milk has the potential to become curd under the right conditions, this inherent power is a reflection of Shakti's role in manifesting effects from causes.

2. **Complete Transformation**: Other schools suggest that the cause entirely transforms into a new object, the effect. In this view, milk changes completely into curd, symbolizing how Shakti can lead to a transformation where the cause becomes a different form entirely.

In both perspectives, the concept of inherent power to produce an effect is crucial. This potency is an aspect of Shakti, illustrating how she operates through processes and phenomena to bring about manifestations.

Understanding Shakti is complex because she is not directly perceivable in isolation from the manifestations through which she operates. Instead, Shakti is realized through inference (Anumana) from observing the processes and phenomena of the cosmos. For instance, the nature of fire is inferred through its attributes like light and heat. Similarly, Shakti's presence and activity are inferred from the observable effects and processes in the universe.

Shaivism presents a nuanced understanding of limitation and manifestation through the concept of Shakti. Shakti, as the dynamic power inherent in the supreme consciousness, enables the manifestation of the cosmos while allowing the supreme subject to both limit and transcend itself. Through Shakti, the supreme consciousness creates the objective world, and the interplay of cause and effect highlights the essential role of Shakti in the continuous evolution and manifestation of the universe. The realization of Shakti, though indirect, provides insight into the dynamic nature of consciousness and its ability to both create and transcend duality.

In Shaivism, the concept of Shakti is crucial for understanding the manifestation and evolution of the cosmos. Shakti, often associated with the term Maya, plays a pivotal role in the creation and dissolution of the universe. Here's a deeper dive into how Shakti functions within the Shaivite framework, its distinction from illusion, and the critique of non-dualistic interpretations of manifestation.

In Shaivism, Maya is derived from the Sanskrit term Maana,

meaning to measure or to manifest. This term reflects Shakti's role as the agent through which every object in existence is brought into reality. Abhinava Gupta, a prominent Shaivite scholar, explains in his work Tantra Aloka that Shakti enables Para-Shiva to accomplish the complex task of creating the cosmos. This complexity involves the manifestation of the thirty-six Tatwas (principles) that constitute the material and subtle aspects of the universe.

It's important to recognize that Shakti is neither a mere illusion nor distinct from the supreme consciousness. Instead, Shakti is the dynamic principle through which Para-Shiva (the supreme consciousness) manifests the cosmos. Thus, Shakti is a real, essential power within the supreme subject and cannot act independently of it. This integration underscores that Shakti is not separate from Para-Shiva but is an intrinsic aspect of his nature.

The concept of Para-Samvid or supreme consciousness is central to understanding Shakti's role. Para-Samvid, characterized by light and illumination, manifests the cosmos through its awareness. This awareness reveals the multitudes of objects and is embodied in Shakti. Consequently, Shakti is the mechanism through which Para-Shiva actualizes the universe. All actions and manifestations of Shakti are rooted in the supreme consciousness, emphasizing that Shakti cannot exist independently of Para-Shiva.

In the process of cosmic manifestation, the eternal light of Para-Shiva undergoes a transformation into thirty-six Tatwas. During creation, these Tatwas evolve and manifest the material world, while in the process of withdrawal or involution, they return to a unified state. Importantly, the first two Tatwas, representing Shakti and Shiva, remain unchanged through evolution and involution. The

changes occur only among the remaining thirty-four Tatwas, from the highest to the lowest.

Shakti's role encompasses both the emanation (creation) and withdrawal (dissolution) of the cosmos. Her power governs the process through which the universe evolves and eventually returns to its original state. This cyclical process highlights Shakti as the ultimate cause behind all phenomena, driving both the emergence and reabsorption of the material world.

Non-dualistic philosophies, particularly those influenced by Vedanta, often describe the material world as an illusion (Maya) to reconcile with the idea of a singular, absolute reality. These schools argue that the apparent duality of the world is illusory and does not reflect the true, undivided nature of the absolute.

However, this view faces several challenges:

- **Origin of Ignorance**: If the material world is an illusion due to ignorance (Avidya), one must explain the origin of this ignorance. If the absolute is truly without attributes (Nirguna), how can it account for the creation of illusion?
- **Omnipotence of the Absolute**: If the absolute is devoid of all attributes, including the ability to create, then how can it be considered omnipotent?

These questions highlight the limitations of strictly non-dualistic theories, which often fail to address the practical and metaphysical implications of manifestation. The critique points out that such views may create an artificial distinction between the material and the absolute, leading to a paradox where non-duality inadvertently

reintroduces duality.

Shakti is not merely an illusion but a fundamental principle of reality. She embodies the power of manifestation and withdrawal, and her relationship with Para-Shiva is integral to the creation and dissolution of the cosmos. Unlike other philosophical schools that struggle with the notion of duality and illusion, Shaivism offers a more cohesive framework by integrating Shakti as a dynamic aspect of the supreme consciousness. This perspective acknowledges the real, dynamic interplay between consciousness and manifestation, providing a more comprehensive understanding of the universe's nature

In many non-dualistic philosophical schools, particularly those influenced by Vedanta, manifestation is often dismissed as an illusion (Maya) to maintain the purity of the absolute reality. These doctrines argue that the material world is an illusion because it introduces duality, which seems to contradict the notion of an undivided, absolute reality. However, this approach has its own limitations and paradoxes.

One significant problem with this view is the question of the origin of manifestation. If the absolute reality is not the cause of manifestation, how did the world come into being? Non-dualistic schools that argue for the illusory nature of the world often claim that this illusion is produced by ignorance (Avidya). Yet, this raises further issues: if the world is an illusion, what is the origin of this illusion?

Additionally, if ignorance is the cause of the cosmos and its dualities, one must consider where this ignorance itself comes from. Is ignorance a product of the absolute, or does it exist independently?

Non-dual schools often assert that ignorance is inherent in the individual mind but do not adequately address its origin or how it arises from the absolute.

Another challenge is related to the attributes of the absolute. If the absolute is defined as Nirguna (without attributes), then how can it be considered omnipotent or capable of creating the universe? The notion of the absolute being devoid of attributes often leads to the conclusion that it is inert and passive, incapable of action or creation.

Furthermore, non-dualistic philosophies, by defining the material world as an illusion, inadvertently create a duality between the absolute and the illusory world. This duality contradicts their aim of establishing a purely non-dual reality.

Moreover, non-dualistic schools often view suffering as a result of ignorance, which exists only in the mind of the individual. This view fails to address why suffering occurs if the absolute reality is fundamentally non-dual and perfect.

Shaivism offers a different perspective by integrating the concepts of Prakasha (light or consciousness) and Vimarsha (awareness or reflection) into the nature of the absolute. In Shaivism, the absolute is understood as encompassing both Prakasha and Vimarsha. Prakasha represents the inherent light or consciousness, while Vimarsha is the reflective awareness that brings the cosmos into manifestation. This duality is not seen as a contradiction but as complementary aspects of the same reality.

The supreme consciousness, which is both self-luminous and self-aware, naturally manifests the cosmos. The process of creation and dissolution is seen as an inherent quality of this absolute consciousness, rather than an external or illusory phenomenon.

By recognizing that awareness is inseparable from consciousness, Shaivism provides a framework that resolves the paradoxes faced by non-dualistic schools. The absolute is both the source of the cosmos and the dynamic principle through which it is manifested and reabsorbed.

In Shaivism, awareness and consciousness are considered as aspects of the same reality. The eternal light of the absolute is never devoid of luminosity; it is always in a state of dynamic expression through Shakti, the power of manifestation. This approach embraces both the unity and the diversity of the universe, providing a more cohesive explanation of the cosmos and its relation to the divine. By recognizing Shakti as the dynamic principle within the supreme consciousness, Shaivism offers a framework that resolves the apparent duality of manifestation with the non-dual nature of the absolute.

In essence, when Shiva manifests, he becomes Shakti, and when Shakti withdraws, she becomes Shiva. The first two Tatwas, Shiva and Shakti, are not distinct entities but represent different aspects of the same principle. The primary difference between them is the degree of manifestation. In states of gross manifestation where duality is prevalent, Shakti is active. Conversely, in non-dual, subjective states of consciousness, Shiva predominates. In transcended states, there is no distinction between Prakasha (light) and Vimarsha (reflection); both exist in a balanced state, which is known as the Parama-Shiva or Para-Shiva state.

Certain Shakta schools regard Shakti as an independently existing, supreme entity. Meanwhile, some Shaivite followers perceive Shiva as a transcended state devoid of attributes, including awareness,

thus considering it inert or Nirguna. Both perspectives fail to fully grasp the interplay between consciousness and awareness, leading to an intellectual void.

Shiva is imbued with the powers of will, knowledge, and action and is never devoid of these attributes. When Vedanta describes the supreme Brahman as Sat, Chit, and Ananda—existence, consciousness, and bliss respectively—it attempts to convey that Brahman expresses itself through existence. Para-Shiva, or the supreme Shiva, is characterized by five powers: Chit (consciousness), Ananda (bliss/awareness), Icha (will), Jnana (knowledge), and Kriya (action).

According to Vedantic teachings, the supreme Brahman is described as Sat (existence), Chit (consciousness), and Ananda (bliss). Sat denotes existence, which leads to the theory of existence or being (Sat Karya Vada). Even the non-dual Vedantic schools acknowledge that Brahman embodies existence. This existence is made possible through the powers of will to create, knowledge of objects to be created, and the act of creation itself. Vedanta broadly encompasses these three powers under the term Sat, as they occur simultaneously.

However, later interpretations by Vedantic followers misinterpreted this understanding, categorizing creation as an illusion. This misinterpretation was reinforced by the term Maya, which is commonly translated as illusion. Consequently, people accepted the notion that the cosmos is an illusion resulting from a lack of knowledge.

Even the ancient Indian epistemology of Sankhya Darshana suggests that Prakriti (nature) operates only with the assistance

of Purusha (consciousness), and Purusha manifests the universe through Prakriti. This aligns with the non-dual principle in Sankhya thought.

Shaivism, on the other hand, adheres strictly to a monistic or non-dual principle. It views the world as an exalted expression of the divine will and asserts that the world is not separate from the supreme subject. Shaivism does not support the idea of Shakti and Shiva, or Purusha and Prakriti, as having independent existence. Instead, it considers Prakriti as the nature of Purusha and Shakti as the nature of Shiva. Through these arguments, Shaivism establishes and justifies its monistic view of the cosmos.

For a Shaivite, the entire cosmos, composed of thirty-six Tatwas, resides within the pure splendor of Para-Shiva. This supreme consciousness is characterized by being complete, infinite, eternal, omnipotent, all-pervading, and eternally radiant. The universe manifests through his inherent awareness, known as Shakti, which is an intrinsic aspect of Shiva.

In this view, Shiva, as the knower, and Shakti, as the process of knowing, together give rise to the object of knowledge, which is the cosmos itself. Therefore, from a Shaivite perspective, the subject (Shiva) only manifests the object (the cosmos) which is identical to him. In essence, Shiva reflects his own nature as the objective world. The process and mirror of this reflection is Shakti.

Shaivite doctrine describes Maya as the principle that creates the apparent distinction between subject and object, whereas certain Vedantic traditions consider it to be an illusion. However, the true illusion is the notion of being separate from the universal subject. Even Vedantic schools attribute Chit and Ananda (consciousness and

awareness) to the supreme Brahman, which indicates that Brahman is not devoid of qualities. The view that Brahman is entirely without attributes (Nirguna) is a fallacy and contradicts the descriptions of Sat, Chit, and Ananda.

It becomes clear that the universal subject is fundamentally consciousness, with awareness as its inherent nature. The awareness of the multitude of objects inherent within this consciousness brings the cosmos into existence. Thus, Shiva and Shakti are two aspects of the same reality; one cannot exist without the other. Their eternal play involves manifesting the cosmos through self-imposed limitations while simultaneously realizing their unlimited nature—a divine sport that encompasses all existence.

Triadic Manifestation of Shakti

The Relationship Between Shakti and Shiva

The relationship between Shakti and Shiva in Shaivism is foundational to understanding the manifestation of the cosmos. Para-Shiva, the ultimate subject, orchestrates different actions through the interplay of Shiva and Shakti. This interplay reveals how Shakti evolves during cosmic manifestation.

Para-Shiva possesses five fundamental powers: consciousness, bliss, will, knowledge, and action. Among these, the powers of will, knowledge, and action are directly involved in the evolution of the Tatwas, the principles that constitute the cosmos. When Shiva brings the cosmos into light, these three powers are actively engaged in the process.

In Monistic Shaivism, Shakti manifests in three primary forms: Para (Aghora), Para-Apara (Ghora), and Apara (Ghora-Tara). Although these forms appear distinct, they all exist in perfect unity within Para-Shiva, reflecting his multifarious nature.

Para (Aghora) – The Supreme State

The state of Para signifies the will aspect of Shiva. In this state, everything exists in perfect unity without diversity or objectivity. This form represents the eternal union with the supreme, known as Samavaya or Samarasya. In the Para state, the distinctions between subject, object, and the process of cognition dissolve into a unified experience. The known and the process of knowing reside solely within the subject. This state corresponds to the will aspect of Para-

Shiva and is also referred to as Shiva Bhava.

Para-Apara (Ghora) – Unity in Diversity

The Para-Apara state represents a unity in diversity. While there is a distinction between subject and object, a partial non-dual aspect persists. In the triad of consciousness, this state signifies the process of knowing or cognition, highlighting the knowledge aspect of Para-Shiva. Here, knowledge is understood as the awareness of the objective world manifested as thoughts. This state reflects the omniscient aspect of the supreme consciousness and is known as Shakti Bhava.

Apara (Ghora-Tara) – The Inferior State

The Apara state is characterized by a clear distinction between subject and object, creating a pronounced duality. Apara manifests the objective universe with a complete division between subject and object. This state introduces the nescience of true self and represents the gross form of Shakti as the entire physical universe. In the triadic manifestations of Shakti, Apara embodies the action or Kriya-Shakti of Shiva—the actual act of creation. This state is also referred to as Nara Bhava.

These three forms of Shakti—Para, Para-Apara, and Apara—illustrate the dynamic evolution of the cosmos from the supreme consciousness of Para-Shiva. While each form reflects different aspects of manifestation and cognition, they all remain unified in the ultimate reality of Para-Shiva. Through this understanding, the process of cosmic creation and dissolution is revealed as an expression of the inherent nature of Shiva and Shakti.

All three powers—consciousness (Chit), bliss (Ananda), and action (Kriya)—exist simultaneously in the Chit-Ananda Shakti of Para-Shiva. For the sake of clarity, a linear explanation is used to describe their manifestation and interaction. The triad of powers that manifests the cosmos remains embedded within the Chit-Ananda Shakti of Para-Shiva.

In the Ghora-Tara or Apara aspect of Shakti, the power of Jnana or knowledge fully blooms and manifests as the objective world through the complete expression of Kriya-Shakti, or action. In the Para-Apara or Ghora stage, the Icha-Shakti, or will, opens up the faculty of Pramana, which is cognition. At this stage, knowledge exists only in an abstract form; it becomes more concrete and vivid as the process progresses.

As Maya Tatwa, combined with the five obscurations, generates a multitude of objects with knowledge of the objective reality, Kriya-Shakti blooms fully to bring about the manifestation of objects in the form of knowledge. The supreme 'I' exists as 'I Am' in the Para aspect, as 'I Am This' in the Para-Apara aspect, with a focus on the 'I' aspect, and as 'I Am THIS' in the Ghora-Tara or Apara aspect, emphasizing the 'THIS' aspect.

The triune structure described is not exclusive to Monistic Shaivism but is also recognized across various Indian spiritual traditions, including priestly doctrines. In the Yoga school of Patanjali and Hatha Yoga, this triad is acknowledged. Vaidika or priestly doctrines, Vedas, and Puranas also recognize a trinity comprising Brahma, Vishnu, and Rudra. The Suta Samhita describes Brahma as the Pingala-Nadi and the energy of the sun, Vishnu as the Ida-Nadi and the energy of the moon, and Rudra as the Sushumna,

associated with fire. Devi Bhagavata relates Brahma, Vishnu, and Rudra to the Kriya, Jnana, and Icha Shaktis of Devi, representing action, knowledge, and will of the Para-Shakti respectively.

In Monistic Shaivism, particularly the Trika tradition, the energies of Aghora, Ghora, and Ghora-Tara correspond to Sushumna, Pingala, and Ida, respectively, and represent subject cognition and object, or will, knowledge, and action. This understanding aligns the trinity with the triad of consciousness. When the Yoga Sutras mention the Nadis, they refer to this triad of consciousness rather than literal nerve plexuses in the body.

The esoteric principle of trinity in Indian tradition is based on the understanding that a transcendent principle underpins the immanent world. This transcendent consciousness, often referred to as Para-Samvid, Para-Shiva, or Parama-Shiva, serves as the foundational matrix for the manifestation of the empirical world. Essentially, this transcendent consciousness can be viewed as a divine principle or god, from which the immanent world emanates.

Empirical individuals, in contrast, are bound by limitations in terms of action, awareness, knowledge, and will. This state of limited freedom, known as Alpa-Aham or Nara Bhava, reflects a restricted condition compared to the boundless nature of the transcendent. The trishika, or triune, in Monistic Shaivism creates a polarity between Shiva Bhava, representing the godly state of unlimited freedom, and Nara Bhava, the limited individual state. The Shakti Bhava, positioned between these extremes, reflects a state with elements of both.

This arrangement should not be misconstrued as a mere transition from a divine state to a human one, or from an unlimited to a limited

form. Instead, it represents how the omnipotent supreme Shiva manifests himself within the limitations of the Nara Bhava. This manifestation is not a transformation akin to physical changes, such as curd turning into milk, as described in Parinama Vada. If Shiva were to undergo such a transformation, the unified unlimited nature would be disrupted. Rather, the descent from Shiva Bhava to Nara Bhava occurs through Shiva's own free will, a process described as Lila or Kreeda—the divine play.

According to Shaivite interpretations of texts like the Bhagavad Gita, the universe is viewed as the Deva Kreedanaga, or the playground of the supreme. The acts of ascent and descent are part of the eternal Lila or divine play of Para-Shiva through his Para-Shakti. When Para-Shiva descends into the Nara Bhava and manifests the diverse objects of the cosmos, his divine nature is veiled by the five attributes of Maya. This veiling results in Shiva appearing as both the objective universe and the multitude of limited individuals inhabiting it.

Epistemologically, the manifestation of Shiva as the limited universe and individual is likened to the reflection of light in a mirror, creating numerous images. From a religious perspective, Shiva and Shakti are revered as the highest divine couple, embodying the principles of divine feminine and masculine. Regardless of their specific worship or interpretation, they represent the light and luminosity, or consciousness and awareness, that gives rise to the phenomenal universe in which we all participate.

The limited manifestation of Shiva is facilitated through his Shakti, which simultaneously obscures his true nature. The universe emerges through this self-obscuration by Shiva's Shakti. If Shiva

did not obscure himself, the cosmos would not manifest. This process of obscuration is part of his inherent nature, demonstrating that even within limitations, Shiva remains omnipotent. His ability to manifest both limited and unlimited forms is a testament to his freedom. The two additional actions of Para-Samvid—Anugraha (revealing) and Nigraha/Tirodhana (obscuring)—are fundamental in the manifestation of the cosmos.

The dynamic act of Parama-Shiva encompasses a dual nature: the descent into the Nara Bhava from the Shiva Bhava, and the ascent back to the Shiva Bhava from the Nara Bhava. This movement involves the concealment and revelation of his true nature. During the process of seeking, the adept realizes the Anugraha Bhava, which allows the limited individual to perceive his true self through the power of divine grace. This dual activity can be metaphorically described as Unmesha and Nimesha, the opening and closing of eyes. When Shiva opens his eyes, he brings the cosmos into manifestation; when he closes them, he withdraws it into himself. It is crucial to understand that this entire process of emanation and withdrawal occurs entirely within Shiva himself and not outside of him. Shiva embodies the creator, the created, and the act of creation. There is nothing existing outside of him. For the sake of clarity, a linear method of explanation is employed, although the actual process is inherently non-linear and cyclical.

The act of creation, or emanation, is perceived as the concealing aspect of the divine. In this phase, Shiva limits and contracts himself to bring the cosmos into being. Conversely, the Samhara, or dissolution phase, is not merely the destruction of the universe but an act of revealing. This revealing process signifies the recognition

of the true nature of the self: that the universe exists within Shiva, highlighting the dissolution of the artificial distinction between subject and object. This dual activity is facilitated by Shiva's Shakti. The downward movement, or descent, is governed by Adha-Maya, while the upward movement, or ascent, is managed by Yoga-Maya. These are represented as Adha Kundalini and Urdhwa Kundalini in the human body, respectively.

It is important to recognize that the awakening of Kundalini is not simply a literal flow of energy within the spinal canal. Rather, it symbolizes the realization of the true self—the understanding that the knower, the known, and the act of knowing are inherently unified. Through Shakti, Shiva assumes the role of a limited Purusha, and it is through her that a limited individual can rediscover his true nature. For instance, through Aghora, an individual realizes his true nature, whereas through Ghora-Tara or Apara, the individual remains obscured from this realization. The entire cosmic play of Para-Shiva, from the Shiva Tatwa to the Prthwi Tatwa, is constructed upon this trinity of Shiva, Shakti, and Nara.

In the advanced practices of Monistic Shaivism, two triads are considered—an upper and a lower triad—which emerge from this fundamental triad. Despite the complexities, the entire system is rooted in this triune framework. Initially, one begins from the Nara Bhava, experiencing the manifestation of the divine as a limited individual. As one progresses, there is a realization that the divine is inherently dynamic, and the very essence of the supreme lord is to emanate the universe. This understanding reveals that the universe itself is an exalted expression of the divine will. Advancing further to the principle of Aghora, the adept comes to see that everything is

unified with the supreme and that all existence is a perfect reflection of the lord. Ultimately, the supreme lord manifests as the knower, the process of knowing, and the known—embodying the roles of subject, cognition, and object.

The ultimate principle in Monistic Shaivism is referred to as Maha-Para, which is understood as a state called Parateetha, transcending even the supreme state. In this state, the divine is realized as the ultimate consciousness—pure, unadulterated, blissful, all-pervading, and omnipotent. This state is symbolized by Kala Sankarshini or Kala Akarshini, often associated with Maha Para Kali. She represents the ultimate metaphysical principle pervading all stages of the supreme lord. Kala Sankarshini Kali is the matrix upon which the different aspects of the divine manifest: Aghora, Ghora, and Ghora-Tara. She is omnipresent in all three states of divine manifestation.

In the absolute state of Para-Shiva or Para-Bhairava, known as Kala Sankarshini Kali, there is no distinction between subjectivity and objectivity. This state is characterized by pure, unblemished consciousness, and it is through her that both subject and object come into existence. Her nature is unfathomable, and she serves as the agent through which the three states—Para, Apara, and Para-Apara—manifest. The term "consciousness" is used to describe the annihilation of relative notions in mental perception, representing the essence of this absolute state.

Realization of this absolute state can only be achieved through profound gnostic experiences, termed Pratibha. These experiences are reached by following the contemplative practices prescribed by Shaivite saints. When an adept achieves Pratibha through these methods, they come to understand that everything is Para-Shiva

or Para-Bhairava, and nothing exists independently or differently from him. The distinctions felt by the empirical individual in the phenomenal world dissolve, revealing the underlying unity.

In the framework of Monistic Shaivism, light and luminosity represent the two aspects of Para-Shiva. The immanent and non-immanent aspects should not be seen as polar opposites but as inherently unified. In the phenomenal world, this unity is expressed through the triad of Shiva, Shakti, and Nara Bhava. In the Para-Apara state, it is understood as will, knowledge, and action. In the state of Para, it is the trinity of subject, cognition, and object. Here, the eternal, unified play of Shiva and Shakti is realized as light and illumination. In the stage of Mahapara, the eternal, self-aware light that pervades everything becomes apparent.

The practices of Monistic Shaivism focus intensely on self-realization. The doctrines of Shaivism assert that the limited individual is not separate from the supreme but rather manifests as a limited form of the divine out of his free will. The spiritual practice is thus oriented toward recognizing one's true self or becoming aware of one's real self, which is termed Jivan Mukti. Abhinava Gupta, in his Tantra Aloka, asserts that Moksha, or liberation, is essentially the awareness of the true self, which is Shiva himself. This realization of identity with Shiva is considered the highest goal in Shaivism.

Shakti, who is foundational to Maya, embodies the principle of obscuring and revealing the self. She facilitates the processes of inclusion and exclusion, and is both the creator and destroyer of duality and nescience. In her pure, undivided state, prior to manifestation, she is known as Shakti-Maya. During the evolution of Tatwas, she is referred to as Tatwa-Maya, and at the time of

manifesting the multitude of objects that constitute the cosmos, she is called Granthi-Maya.

In addition to these forms, Shakti also manifests as Prana-Shakti. Commonly associated with breath, Prana is indeed related to this concept but is more fundamentally understood as the vital force sustaining both the cosmos and individual life. This vital force is essential for all bodily functions and the phenomena of the universe. Prana-Shakti is not merely the breath (Prana-Vayu) but represents a reflection of the supreme awareness through which the universe is manifested.

From a triadic perspective, Prana-Shakti combines Jnana-Shakti (knowledge) and Kriya-Shakti (action). In the context of Prakriti Tatwa, Prana-Shakti illuminates the three internal organs: Manas (mind), Buddhi (intellect), and Ahamkara (ego). In the physical world, Prana-Shakti is manifest as spoken words, composed of sounds. This Shakti constitutes the fifty-one alphabets of the Sanskrit language, which are expressions of the supreme awareness of Shiva.

Prana-Shakti, in essence, is the embodiment of the cosmos in the form of sound. The universe evolves from Tatwas, which are themselves composed of phonemes, and Prana-Shakti represents the totality of the cosmos through sound. The set of Sanskrit alphabets is divided into vowels and consonants, beginning with the sound 'A' and ending with 'h'. The combination of these sounds, particularly 'A', 'h', and Anuswara 'm', forms the mantra 'Aham'. This mantra is considered the primal vibration of Para-Shiva, embodying both the beginning and end of creation. The essence of all phonemes resides in this mantra, making it a key to understanding the power of Prana-Shakti.

Thus, the mystery of Prana-Shakti is intrinsically linked to the alphabets, which are reflections of the supreme awareness known as Para-Shakti. Even the words spoken in daily life are expressions of Para-Shiva, as they are composed of these fundamental phonemes. By engaging in theurgical practices related to the Matrikas (letters), one can experience the bliss of Prana-Shakti. Further exploration of these practices will be covered in subsequent chapters.

Para Shiva the Noumena

In our exploration of Shaivism, we have delved into how the consciousness of the supreme subject, Para-Shiva, brings the cosmos into existence through his inherent power, Shakti. We have established that this self-luminous Shakti is inseparable from the light of consciousness that is Shiva. Now, it's crucial to further understand Para-Shiva, who embodies this self-luminous light within himself.

Shaivism is not merely a collection of metaphysical theories; it also encompasses a rich philosophical framework. It serves as an epistemology that addresses fundamental questions about the nature of the absolute and the nature of the phenomenal world.

In discussing the inherent oneness of Shiva and Shakti, Shaivite scholars assert that Para-Shiva represents the supreme subject, whose essence encompasses both Shiva and Shakti. These principles, manifesting as subject and object within the phenomenal world, are often seen as divine masculine and divine feminine. Although consciousness and awareness may appear as distinct principles within the realm of phenomena, they are, in essence, one unified reality.

Para-Shiva embodies this inherent oneness of light and luminosity, existing in a state of equilibrium between Shiva and Shakti. This balanced state is referred to as Para-Samvid or Para-Shiva. In the phenomenal world, Para-Samvid manifests as the interplay between Shiva and Shakti.

It's important to recognize that Para-Shiva is not merely an

aggregation of Shiva and Shakti. Rather, Para-Shiva represents an eternal unity from which these two principles appear distinct only due to the linear perspective of the empirical mind. They constitute the dual manifestations of Para-Shiva. From the perspective of duality and the phenomenal world, which is influenced by the three impurities that cloud the empirical soul, we see the relationship between light and illumination as distinct.

The realization of the absolute is beyond the capacity of Vikalpa (limited thought constructs). These constructs are inadequate to pierce through the veils of Maya and grasp the noumenon. The absolute subject, also referred to as Purna-Aham (the complete self), represents a state of perfection or completeness. The concept of Purnatha, or completion, in Shaivism, particularly within Monistic Shaivism, is an extensive subject that warrants a comprehensive investigation beyond the scope of this discussion.

In the phenomenal world, Purnatha is obscured by Maya and its five attributes, which prevent the Purusha from recognizing his true nature. This obscuration results in the limited state known as Alpa-Aham, or the limited self. When Para-Shiva manifests as Purusha, an apparent schism occurs within the empirical soul, leading to a perceived division between Shiva and Shakti in the mind of the limited individual.

From the perspective of Alpa-Aham, the limited self perceives Shiva and Shakti in various ways. Some individuals may worship Shiva as the divine masculine principle, while others may revere Shakti as the divine feminine, manifesting as deities like Kali, Lalitha, or others. This distinction is a result of the perceived schism created by the limitations imposed by Maya, reflecting the diverse

ways in which the absolute can be experienced and worshipped in the phenomenal world.

Within the context of Shaivism, the dynamic interplay between Shiva and Shakti is pivotal to understanding the nature of reality. The perceived rift within Purusha creates a duality where Shiva is recognized as the pure light of consciousness, or Bodha, and Shakti is seen as the sovereign power or freedom that enables the manifestation of the cosmos. Shiva, as the knower, embodies the essence of consciousness, while Shakti represents the phenomena of becoming—the objective world, the known, and the act of knowing.

In the experience of Purusha, this fundamental unity appears as light and form. Light, in this context, serves to illuminate forms, while forms necessitate light for their visibility. This interplay underscores a profound relationship where light and form are interdependent: light reveals itself through forms, and forms are illuminated by light. This is akin to sunlight, which can be understood as distinct rays and light; however, the rays are inherently part of the sunlight, and the distinction arises from the limited perception of the individual mind. This relationship is referred to as Tadatmya, which signifies a distinction in unity or duality within non-duality.

Initially, Tadatmya appears as two separate principles—light and form. However, as one transcends ordinary awareness and reaches higher states of consciousness, the underlying oneness of these principles becomes evident. Within the Purusha Tatwa, Tadatmya is seen as matter and its attributes. Just as burning is an inherent property of fire, matter in its essence is identified with its attributes. In the phenomenal world, Shiva and Shakti are often perceived as separate principles. Yet, in transcended consciousness, they are

recognized as one unified principle.

Despite this essential oneness, the distinction between Shiva and Shakti in the immanent world remains significant. This distinction plays a crucial role in both the evolution of the cosmos and the path to self-realization. The recognition of Shakti as both distinct and integral to Shiva is vital for understanding the process of creation and the individual's spiritual journey.

Shaivism identifies five primary powers of Shiva that facilitate his eternal cosmic play. These are Chit (consciousness), Ananda (bliss), Icha (will), Jnana (knowledge), and Kriya (action). These powers enable Shiva to create, sustain, and destroy the cosmos. Additionally, Shiva's actions include concealing (Tirodhana) and granting grace (Anugraha). Each of these aspects will be explored in detail in subsequent discussions.

During the creation phase, Shiva introduces a sense of duality and self-imposed limitations, manifesting a multitude of objects in the form of Tatwas (elements) within the phenomenal world. This manifestation is made possible through his Shakti. The distinction between subject and object arises through this process, facilitated by Shiva's Shakti. Shiva's dynamic action, driven by his Shakti, further emphasizes the unity of Shiva and Shakti. Thus, Shakti is not merely a tool but an intrinsic aspect of Shiva's own being.

To reiterate a key point discussed earlier, the cosmos manifests as Abhasa, a reflection or appearance of reality. Shiva and Shakti are not merely reflections (Abhasas) but are the fundamental agents through which Abhasa arises. They embody the essence of creation, sustaining the cosmos, and their unity remains central to understanding both the process of cosmic manifestation and the path

to self-realization.

In the classical doctrines of Monistic Shaivism, Spanda, or the creative impulse, is a central concept that describes the dynamic nature of Para-Shiva. This dynamic nature is metaphorically explained as the opening and closing of Para-Shiva's eyes, which signifies the processes of emanation and withdrawal.

When Para-Shiva "opens his eyes," the evolution of Tatwas occurs, bringing the cosmos into manifestation. This process involves the outward movement of divine energy, where the latent potential of Para-Shiva is expressed as the structured, ordered reality of the universe. Conversely, when Para-Shiva "closes his eyes," the universe undergoes involution, returning to its original, undifferentiated state. This represents the return to the inherent oneness of light and form with Para-Shiva, where the cosmic play is reabsorbed into the divine essence. This cyclic process of emanation and withdrawal illustrates how Shiva and Shakti operate within the fundamental substrate of Para-Shiva.

Shakti's Manifestations

Shakti, the dynamic energy of Para-Shiva, manifests in a variety of forms. As the self-luminous aspect of consciousness, Shakti embodies self-awareness and has the inherent ability to bring forth various manifestations from Shiva's consciousness. Shakti's multifaceted nature can be understood through different roles:

1. **Icha-Rupini Shakti**: As the will of the absolute, this aspect of Shakti represents the omnipresent, creative aspect of Para-Samvid. It is through Icha-Rupini Shakti that the cosmos is

created, reflecting the supreme will.

2. **Jnana-Shakti**: This aspect embodies omniscience, the power of supreme knowledge through which Para-Shiva sustains the cosmos. It is the principle of knowledge that maintains the order and continuity of the universe.
3. **Kriya-Shakti**: As the power of action, Kriya-Shakti is responsible for the actual process of creation, manifesting the evolution of Tatwas. This aspect facilitates the dynamism and functionality of the cosmos.

Shakti is also crucial in creating distinctions and limitations within the Purusha (individual soul), which influences the experience of duality.

Urdhwa-Maya and Adho-Maya

Shakti's actions are described in terms of two principal movements:

1. **Urdhwa-Maya**: This upward movement refers to the ascent from the realm of duality to the non-dual states of consciousness. It represents the spiritual journey of rising beyond the limitations and dualities of the phenomenal world.
2. **Adho-Maya**: This downward movement involves the descent from higher states of consciousness into the realm of duality and limitations. It is responsible for the manifestation and evolution of Tatwas, and it obscures the true nature of the self.

In individuals, these principles are reflected as **Urdhwa Kundalini** and **Adho Kundalini**. The Adho-Maya obscures the

true nature of the self by creating and maintaining duality, while the Urdhwa-Maya is the force through which the divine nature of Shiva is revealed and realized.

Shakti and Shiva: An Integral Relationship

Shakti is intimately related to Shiva in the same way that thoughts and actions are inherent to an individual. She is not a separate entity but an integral aspect of Shiva's divine essence. This relationship highlights the unity and interdependence between consciousness (Shiva) and its dynamic expression (Shakti).

Vira-Shaivism and Shakti Vishishta Advaita Vada

To address certain misinterpretations of Vedantic doctrines and societal issues like casteism, a variant of Shaivism known as Vira-Shaivism emerged in South India. This tradition emphasizes a nuanced understanding of the relationship between Shiva and Shakti through the concept of **Shakti Vishishta Advaita Vada** (Qualified Monistic Theory of Shakti).

According to this school of thought, the supreme lord possesses three defining properties:

1. **Consciousness**: The essence of divine awareness, fundamental to both Shiva and Shakti.
2. **Luminosity**: The aspect of light that reveals the divine presence and illuminates the cosmos.
3. **Absolute Freedom of Sportive Play**: The inherent freedom of Shiva to engage in the divine play of creation, sustenance, and dissolution.

These properties constitute the core of Shakti Vishishta Advaita Vada, emphasizing the supreme unity of Shiva and Shakti while acknowledging their distinct roles and expressions within the cosmic framework.

According to the Vira Shaivites, the divine union with Parama-Shiva is realized through the process known as Linga Anusandhana. This practice involves the yogi focusing on and identifying themselves with the Shiva Linga. This meditative process culminates in the realization that the limited individual soul, or Purusha, is fundamentally one with Parama-Shiva. This profound unity is referred to as Linga Aikya, which means union with the Linga.

Among the thirty-six Tatwas, the concepts of pure and impure Tatwas start with the principle of Maya. The principle of Maha-Maya exists in the space between the Maya Tatwa and the Shuddha-Vidya Tatwa. When a yogi's awareness transcends the Maya Tatwa, the stage preceding the realization of Shuddha-Vidya is characterized by a sense of negation or voidness. This state is referred to as Maha-Maya.

The Maya Tatwa, which causes limitations and obscuration of the true self, is ever-present. It represents the aspect of Shakti that introduces diversity into the immanent world through the five Kanchukas: Raga, Niyati, Vidya, Kala, and Kaala. Thus, it becomes evident that the fundamental relationship between Shiva and Shakti is one of unity. This unity is known as Samarasya, or Shiva-Shakti Samarasya. According to the Vaisheshika school of thought, Samavayi, or unity, is a concrete principle. Consequently, Shiva and Shakti are in an eternal state of Samavaya, or eternal unity.

Samarasya represents the indistinguishable divine freedom

experienced in the highest state of subjectivity. In essence, Para-Shiva manifests as Prakasha (light) and Vimarsha (reflection) only within the mental plane of a finite, limited individual. From this limited perspective, distinctions are made, but these distinctions are merely from our finite viewpoint and emphasize the necessity of integral unity. It is through this distinction that the cosmos is manifested. The interplay of duality and the recognition of inherent unity is seen as the eternal play of Parama-Shiva. Therefore, it is essential to realize that there are no true distinctions, relations, or divisions in the absolute subject. The perfect 'I', composed of consciousness immersed in its own blissful awareness, encompasses Icha, Jnana, and Kriya Shakti (will, knowledge, and action).

When the impure Tatwas, afflicted by Maya, manifest, they lead to the nescience of inherent oneness and give rise to an illusory perception of duality. Despite this, Shakti is always perceived as one with Shiva.

In transcended states, the principles of Shiva and Shakti correspond to Chit (consciousness) and Ananda (bliss) respectively. Indian philosophical schools discuss inference, or Anumana, as three types: spontaneous inference, such as deducing fire from smoke; inference of an effect from a cause, such as predicting rain from observing thick clouds; and inferring a cause from an effect, like concluding a sexual act from seeing pregnancy. Therefore, for every effect to be manifested, a cause must be present. Consequently, every cause and its corresponding effect reside in the ultimate Shakti, which is the source of all causations in the cosmos. Shakti is the principle of becoming, manifesting as a multitude of phenomena in the universe.

In exploring the eternal play of the absolute in manifesting

the limited universe and realizing its true nature, it becomes crucial to understand the interplay between Shiva and Shakti as consciousness and awareness. Even the concept of non-duality gains significance only when contrasted with duality. To fully assert the concept of monism, one must appreciate duality. The absolute, while fundamentally one, manifests as two in the immanent reality. There is no discord or distinction between these two; instead, their relationship is a beautiful sportive play where unity expresses itself as duality and plurality. Thus, in the phenomenal world, consciousness and awareness, or Shiva and Shakti, appear as distinct entities. However, Shiva-Shakti Samarasya or Samvaya should not be seen as a denial of distinction but rather as an acknowledgment of unity within diversity, or non-duality within duality. Initially perceived as two, Shakti and Shaktimaan (the bearer of Shakti) are ultimately recognized as inherently one.

In this context, consciousness differs significantly from the Western notion. Western perspectives often equate consciousness with the functions of the mind or brain processes, focusing on the distinction between subject and object. Consciousness, in the Western sense, is linked to the limited mental processes and cognitive functions, involving the perception of thoughts arising in the mind. Contemporary psychologists are increasingly exploring consciousness beyond these limitations, yet they often mistake subconscious states for the ultimate consciousness. They are still largely unaware of the transcended or trans-empirical consciousness described in Shaivite doctrines.

The transcended, trans-empirical consciousness, known as Chit, is the supreme light that manifests as countless forms. This light

represents the fundamental principle of existence—the all-pervading and all-encompassing causation behind every phenomenon. In the Rig-Veda, this principle is referred to as Rita-Chit. Chit is the underlying essence of all phenomena and objects. Unlike the Western conceptualization of consciousness, which is confined by cognitive and perceptual limitations, Chit transcends these constraints. It is not bound by time, space, or conventional thought constructs, nor can it be reduced to states of deep sleep.

The limited awareness experienced in ordinary life is a result of Chit being obscured by the five obscurations of Maya Tatwa. This consciousness is the ultimate experiencer, the core of every being, and the essence of all existence. It is the ultimate entity that experiences everything and also manifests as the objects of experience—the knower and the known. Since Chit transcends forms, time, and space, it is infinite, eternal, all-knowing, all-pervading, and omnipotent.

Pentadic Powers of Para-Shiva

In the intricate doctrines of Shaivism, Para-Shiva, the ultimate reality, is depicted through various names that emphasize different aspects of his divine nature. These names include Para-Shiva, which represents the supreme essence; Parameswara, denoting the supreme lord; Para-Samvid, signifying the supreme consciousness; and Para-Pramata, referring to the supreme subject. Despite the use of different terms, all these names converge to point towards the singular ultimate truth.

Para-Shiva, in Shaivite philosophy, manifests in two principal forms. The first form is his cosmic manifestation, wherein he appears as the entirety of the universe, comprising a boundless array of both animate and inanimate objects. This vast creation reflects the infinite diversity and multiplicity within the cosmic expanse. Simultaneously, Para-Shiva exists as the pure, transcendental consciousness, untouched and unblemished by the phenomena of the universe. This dual aspect highlights the paradox of the supreme reality: while Para-Shiva can express himself as the vast and varied cosmos, he remains fundamentally an immutable, transcendent essence.

This manifestation of Para-Shiva is attributed to his inherent power, known as Swatantra Shakti, which translates to sovereign or free power. Swatantra Shakti is characterized by its unrestricted and infinite nature, underscoring the divine independence and absolute freedom of the supreme reality. This sovereign power is expressed through five distinct forms or Shaktis, each representing a different

facet of Para-Shiva's divine activity:

1. **Chit (Consciousness)**: Chit is the power that embodies the consciousness of Para-Shiva. It is through Chit that Para-Shiva reveals himself as the ultimate subject. This consciousness is not merely awareness but the very essence of the 'I' or 'Aham', which signifies the core of his self-experience. In this state, Para-Shiva experiences himself in his purest form, untainted by the dualities of the phenomenal world.

2. **Ananda (Bliss)**: Ananda-Shakti is the divine power of bliss that emanates from the supreme completeness and satisfaction inherent in Para-Shiva. This bliss is a manifestation of the ultimate subject's infinite and absolute nature, embodying a profound sense of contentment and fulfillment. It represents the ultimate state of being where the divine essence is fully realized and experienced as an all-encompassing joy.

3. **Icha (Will)**: Icha-Shakti represents the divine power of will. It is through this power that the desire to create and manifest arises within the consciousness of Para-Shiva. This will can be seen as the raw, unformed potential that drives the creative process. It is the fundamental impulse that initiates the act of creation, bringing forth the cosmos from the divine essence.

4. **Jnana (Knowledge)**: Jnana-Shakti is the divine power associated with knowledge. It is through Jnana that Para-Shiva enables the creation and illumination of the multitudes of objects in the universe. This knowledge is not just an intellectual understanding but a profound, all-encompassing awareness that allows the manifestation of reality. Everything

in the universe is a reflection of this supreme knowledge, which integrates all forms within the divine consciousness.

5. **Kriya (Action)**: Kriya-Shakti is the power of action, which facilitates the actualization of the universe. Through Kriya, Para-Shiva manifests the myriad forms and phenomena of the cosmos. This action is the dynamic aspect of creation, bringing the potential of Icha into tangible reality. It is through this power that Para-Shiva executes the cosmic processes and structures the universe according to his divine will.

The interplay of these five Shaktis illustrates the comprehensive nature of Para-Shiva's creative process. Each Shakti represents a different dimension of the divine activity, from the initial will to create, through the manifestation of knowledge, to the actualization of cosmic forms. Together, they demonstrate how Para-Shiva utilizes his inherent powers to shape and sustain the universe.

Ultimately, the entire cosmos, with its infinite diversity of subjects and objects, is a manifestation of Para-Shiva himself. The universe is not an external entity separate from the divine but rather an expansion and reflection of Para-Shiva's own nature. Through the dynamic expression of Shakti, the supreme reality projects and experiences the cosmos, revealing the profound truth that the entire creation is an integral part of Para-Shiva's divine essence. Thus, the cosmos is a manifestation of the supreme lord's Shakti, embodying the infinite and self-sustaining nature of Para-Shiva in every aspect of existence.

In Indian philosophical traditions, particularly within the context of Shaivism, the divine actions attributed to Para-Shiva encompass

five fundamental processes, known as the **Pancha-Kritya**. These five actions outline the comprehensive functions of the supreme deity and reflect the dynamic interplay between creation, preservation, dissolution, concealment, and grace. Here is a detailed exploration of each of these actions:

Srishti (Creation)

Srishti, or creation, refers to the process through which Para-Shiva manifests the universe from his inherent divine power, known as Swatantra Shakti. This act of creation originates from Para-Shiva's own mind, which serves as the canvas upon which the universe is drawn. Utilizing his free will and the power of Maya (illusion), Para-Shiva limits himself into myriad forms of objects and subjects. This process transforms the abstract idea of the cosmos within Para-Shiva into a tangible, gross reality. Thus, Srishti embodies the unfolding of the universe from the divine essence, marking the beginning of the cosmic play.

Stithi (Preservation)

Once creation has occurred, the supreme lord engages in Stithi, or preservation, which involves the sustenance and maintenance of the universe. This action ensures that the created cosmos continues to exist in a stable and ordered state. Stithi represents Para-Shiva's role in upholding the integrity and functionality of the universe, allowing it to operate harmoniously according to the divine plan. This phase is crucial for the ongoing balance and persistence of the cosmic order, demonstrating Para-Shiva's commitment to sustaining creation.

Samhara (Reabsorption)

Samhara, often translated as reabsorption, is the action wherein Para-Shiva withdraws the manifested universe back into his own being. Unlike destruction, which implies annihilation, Samhara represents a return to the unmanifested state. The cosmos is absorbed into Para-Shiva, reverting to its original, primordial form. This process allows for the potential re-emergence of the universe in a new cycle of creation. Through Samhara, Para-Shiva demonstrates his ability to dissolve the cosmos back into himself, preparing it for future re-manifestation through his Kriya-Shakti.

Vilayana (Concealing)

During the cosmic manifestation, Para-Shiva undergoes Vilayana, or concealing, which involves the veiling of his true nature. By limiting himself into finite forms and subjects, Para-Shiva obscures his infinite essence behind the veil of the empirical world. This action results in the empirical individual souls becoming ignorant of their divine nature. The true self of Para-Shiva is hidden by the limitations imposed through his five powers, creating a sense of duality and separation in the world. Vilayana thus represents the divine act of concealment, where the supreme reality is veiled by the phenomena of the manifested universe.

Anugraha (Grace or Revealing)

Anugraha, or grace, is the divine action through which Para-Shiva reveals the true nature of the self to the limited souls. This grace allows empirical beings to recognize their inherent identity with the supreme lord. It is a unique and profound act that transcends

the ordinary processes of creation, preservation, and dissolution. Through Anugraha, Para-Shiva dispels the obscurations and limitations imposed during Vilayana, allowing the individual souls to return to their original state of unity with the divine. The flow of grace is a restorative force that culminates the cosmic play (Lila), enabling the transition from the limited experience of duality back to the infinite, blissful nature of Para-Shiva.

In addition to these cosmic actions, the Pancha-Kritya also reflects on the mental and spiritual processes of individual beings. Within the limited sphere of human experience, these actions manifest as follows:

1. **Creation (Srishti)**: The creation of mental perceptions and thoughts.
2. **Preservation (Stithi)**: The retention and maintenance of these perceptions in the mind.
3. **Dissolution (Samhara)**: The merging of these perceptions into the broader consciousness.
4. **Concealing (Vilayana)**: The obscuration of these perceptions or thoughts, which are then deposited into the consciousness.
5. **Grace (Anugraha)**: The complete integration and unification of these mental impressions, where they are absorbed into the consciousness without the intention of separate recall.

Thus, the Pancha-Kritya encompasses both the grand cosmic functions and the subtle mental processes, illustrating the interconnectedness of the divine actions and human experience in the realm of Shaivism.

Metaphysically speaking, there is a sixth power in Shaivism that integrates and represents the actions of the five primary powers of Para-Shiva. This sixth power is symbolically represented by the downward-facing head of Para-Shiva, which is embodied by Devi. In South Indian cults, particularly within the worship of Murugan, Kartikeya is revered in his six principal forms, each representing different aspects of divine power. Kartikeya's six faces symbolize the embodiment of these powers, with the sixth face, known as Sarvato Vaktra, representing the encompassing presence of all other powers. This face signifies the integration of the five primary powers into a unified expression.

A yogi who meditates on the attribute embodied by the sixth face of Kartikeya comes to realize that everything manifested in the immanent world is an expression of these five powers. The phenomenal world, brought into existence by Para-Shakti, is thus composed of these six powers. According to the Panch Brahma Upanishad, everything in existence is made of the five powers of Shiva, while the sixth power acts as the vehicle through which these five powers manifest in the world. By meditating on these five powers within oneself, a yogi can achieve self-realization. This concept follows the principle of "As Above, So Below," asserting that the microcosm reflects the macrocosm. Thus, the mental processes of an individual are representations of these powers, and by contemplating them, a yogi can attain liberation.

Consciousness serves as the fundamental substrate for the manifestation of the immanent world. Our reality is shaped by our consciousness, with awareness shifting rapidly from one object to another. Thoughts flow continuously, often without our full

awareness. While our mind is always engaged with some object of awareness, it is rare that we are fully conscious of every thought. Our awareness often narrows to a limited objective reality, constraining our experience. However, when awareness is withdrawn from the external world and directed inward, a profound inner awareness can develop. This inner awareness reveals the true, unlimited nature of the self.

In the philosophy of Pratyabhijnana, a school of Monistic Shaivism, self-awareness arises spontaneously, though this may be challenging for novices to grasp. Inner awareness is inherent and needs to be recognized, usually through intense spiritual practice. These practices often involve withdrawing from external reality, which facilitates the realization of the self as Para-Bhairava. The doctrine of recognition emphasizes that one need only recognize their true nature, which arises spontaneously when identification with the limited, objective world ceases.

Abhinava Gupta, a significant figure in Shaivism, suggests that to eliminate limited notions of objectivity, one must practice Sat-Tarka, or right reasoning and discernment. Sat-Tarka, according to Gupta, is a manifestation of Shuddha-Vidya, representing Para-Shiva as the principle of knowledge or consciousness exercising its power of knowing.

Bliss, or Ananda, is another crucial aspect of this philosophy. In the context of Para-Shiva, bliss represents the ultimate state of fulfillment when residing in Purna-Aham, or complete self. While we experience moments of happiness and satisfaction in daily life—such as meeting a loved one, achieving a goal, or obtaining something we desire—these are merely limited reflections of bliss

within the objective world. The Ananda Shakti of Para-Shiva arises spontaneously from inner awareness and recognition of the Purna-Aham.

To experience this bliss, a yogi must expand their awareness and recognize that external objects are mere reflections of the internal world. Understanding that the subject consciously creates reality helps in recognizing this bliss. As the yogi's awareness grows, they become less tethered to external objects and more attuned to the bliss within. This state of bliss, untethered from external objects, results from heightened self-awareness. Many spiritual practices in Shaivism focus on developing this inner awareness and abiding in the subjective state, ultimately leading to the realization of eternal bliss.

The next Shakti, known as Icha or will, represents the boundless creative potential of the supreme lord and signifies the omnipresent aspect of the Supreme Subject. In everyday life, our experience of Icha-Shakti manifests as a limited form of will. This limited will is what drives our desire to act, to accomplish tasks, or to express ourselves. It is the initial impulse or stir that precedes any action, giving rise to the remarkable creations of humanity. This limited Icha-Shakti stems from the foundational powers of Chit (consciousness) and Ananda (bliss). Without self-aware consciousness, the concept of will is inconceivable. To access the unlimited aspect of will, one must turn inward and shift their awareness away from the external, finite world.

The ordinary will is often directed towards performing specific, limited tasks or actions, constrained by external circumstances. However, the unlimited will, or Icha-Shakti, can be realized by

dwelling in the blissful state of inner awareness. When one's awareness is centered in this pure, unadulterated state of self-expression, the unlimited Icha-Shakti becomes apparent. By concentrating on the initial internal stir that precedes all thoughts and actions, a yogi can connect with this boundless will. Recognizing and resting in this primal impulse reveals the unlimited will aspect of Para-Samvid, the supreme consciousness.

When a yogi attains this awareness, every act or will becomes a manifestation of the supreme self, reflecting the divine essence of Para-Shiva. Actions then take on a divine significance, infused with a profound awareness filled with bliss. The yogi's actions are seen as expressions of the supreme lord himself, and the individual's life becomes a reflection of this divine essence.

The next power is Jnana-Shakti, or the power of knowledge. Jnana-Shakti represents the omniscient aspect of the supreme lord, encompassing all knowledge. In our finite experience, Jnana-Shakti manifests as the understanding of specific objects and concepts within the limited world of objective reality. For the will to be enacted, there must be knowledge of the action to be performed. This means that the will is driven by knowledge, and effective action requires a clear understanding or idea.

Jnana-Shakti in empirical individuals appears as patterns of thoughts, ideas, and images necessary for carrying out actions. For instance, a musician's knowledge of music or a physician's understanding of medicine are expressions of Jnana-Shakti. It embodies the comprehensive body of information and skills in any given field.

The fifth power, Kriya-Shakti, represents the actual act of creation

and the manifestation of the cosmos. Kriya-Shakti is the omnipotent aspect of the supreme lord, actualizing the cosmos from the abstract ideas of the previous powers. Without Kriya-Shakti, the concepts of creation would remain merely as potentialities within the supreme awareness and would never be realized. It is through Kriya-Shakti that consciousness actualizes the objective world, bringing it into form. All finite objects in the cosmos are results of Kriya-Shakti, which brings these objects into existence from the awareness of the supreme subject.

Kriya-Shakti is characterized by its spontaneity and unlimited nature, unrestrained by finite limitations or the veils of Maya (illusion) or Mala (impurities). It is an act of self-expression of the Purna-Aham, the complete self. For the individual, Kriya-Shakti manifests as Karma (action), which will be explored in further detail in subsequent discussions. The Kriya-Shakti of the supreme lord is not constrained by external conditions, reflecting a state of ultimate freedom and self-expression.

By contemplating these five actions—Srishti (creation), Stithi (preservation), Samhara (reabsorption), Vilayana (concealing), and Anugraha (grace or revealing)—a yogi gains insight into the true nature of consciousness and experience. Understanding how these actions operate within the individual reveals that one's own consciousness and experience are fundamentally identical with the supreme subject. Through this realization, the yogi attains Shivahood or Jivan Mukti (liberation), achieving a state of liberation while still in the physical body.

Three Impurities —The Cause of Bondage

Almost every Indian spiritual and philosophical school opines that the state of bondage is the result of Avidya, or ignorance, while the knowledge of the true self is the means for liberation. Each school has propounded its own views on the nature of ignorance and liberation. The doctrines of Shaivism advocate that bondage is the result of the perception of duality, and it can be dispelled through various methods. Bondage arises due to the limitations in the three powers of Para-Shiva, namely Icha (Will), Jnana (Knowledge), and Kriya (Action).

However, a significant challenge that a non-dual Shaivite encounters is the assumption that this limitation is self-imposed. When Shiva manifests the cosmos, He imposes limitations on His powers to create finite, limited objects from His infinitely potent consciousness. Firstly, if bondage is a self-imposed limitation, then discussing liberation becomes moot. The pursuit of spiritual practices would appear absurd. Secondly, achieving liberation would be pointless if there is no real distinction between liberation and bondage, since both states could be viewed as two different aspects of divinity.

To further elucidate this point, the great saint Abhinavagupta, an extraordinary yogi from Kashmir, raises a profound question: what exactly is bondage if every empirical individual is, in essence, the supreme lord? If the highest lord alone is the self, from what

constraints does an individual need to free themselves? From an absolute perspective, there is no bondage. Abhinavagupta, in his work *Gitartasangraha*, asserts that there is neither Bandha (bondage) nor Moksha (liberation); rather, the concepts of bondage and freedom are rooted in duality and do not exist in the absolute sense.

Even in the state of empirical individuality, which is identical with Shiva, one may forget their true nature of freedom and thus be considered bound. Nonetheless, even in this state, the individual is absolutely pure and free, referred to as Purusha. The state of Purusha is essentially a result of ignorance or a lack of awareness of one's true identity. In this context, liberation in Monistic Shaivism can be understood as nothing more than the recognition of the true self. This recognition involves identifying the absolute self with the universal subject, Shiva. This process is termed Shambhava Samavesha.

Through Shambhava Samavesha, an individual realizes that everything that exists is a reflection of the consciousness of Para-Shiva. Ontologically speaking, in Monistic Shaivism, there is no differentiation between consciousness and object; the latter is merely a manifestation of the former.

Since the empirical individual is identified as being identical with Shiva, one might ask what the relationship is between Shiva and bondage. From the perspective of the universal subject, bondage appears as part of Shiva's divine play, known as Lila. In this play, the Lord, out of His own free will, assumes a state of bondage. Shiva possesses the freedom to be both infinite and finite, and His very desire to experience Himself as bound is referred to as impurity or Malas.

Shaivism recognizes three primary Malas: Anava-Mala, Mayiya-

Mala, and Karmiya-Mala. All of these impurities are considered to arise from Maya. Unlike the Vedic conception of Maya as mere illusion, Shaivism views Maya as the divine capability of the Lord to create limited states of existence and finite objects. Anava-Mala is regarded as the fundamental cause of all limitations experienced by an individual, or Purusha. It is the root impurity that gives rise to various forms of existential constraints.

Mayiya-Mala, on the other hand, leads to a sense of separation and duality. This impurity causes an individual to experience a perceived division between oneself and others, fostering a feeling of separateness. The experience of duality and the consequent sense of being separate from the divine unity are attributed to Mayiya-Mala.

Anava-Mala

The term "Anava," derived from the root term "Anu," which means "atom" or "minute particle," refers to an impurity that engenders a sensation of limited nature within us. Despite the fact that Purusha is fundamentally identical with the limitless and omnipotent universal subject, Anava-Mala creates a sense of a limited 'I' or ego within the Purusha. In other words, Anava-Mala instills a perception of limited identity, which manifests as a restricted self-concept.

This impurity results in the experience of spatial and temporal limitations. The omnipresence of the divine Lord is perceived as being confined to specific spatial locations, while the omniscience of the Lord appears restricted by the sequential flow of time. These limitations create a false sense of impermanence and finitude, which is perceived by the empirical individual.

It is important to clarify that this does not imply that the great

Lord Himself becomes limited; rather, it is the Purusha who temporarily experiences a sense of limitation and finitude. The empirical individual, under the influence of ignorance, perceives itself as imperfect and finite, identifying with this limited 'I' or ego. Anava-Mala is considered the root impurity because it encompasses and gives rise to the subsequent two impurities. It serves as the foundational cause of the perception of limitation and the sense of a constrained self.

Mayiya-Mala

The second impurity, known as Mayiya-Mala, pertains to the impurity of Maya. This impurity is responsible for creating a profound sense of division and separation. It can be conceptualized as a form of Vibhaga, or disunion, which arises through processes of comparison, such as distinguishing between a cow and a horse. This sense of division is brought about through contrast, exclusion, and differentiation.

As a result, Mayiya-Mala fosters a sense of separation within the individual or Purusha. Consequently, the empirical soul becomes unaware of its intrinsic unity with the universal subject and instead experiences a feeling of being separate. From the perspective of Para-Samvid, or universal consciousness, which is Shiva, the individual perceives himself as entirely distinct from the universal subject and remains ignorant of his essential nature.

In the state of ignorance, the Purusha identifies with an empirical, limited ego, taking on various forms, shapes, and names, and exists as though it were a separate entity in its own right. It is only through the process of Shambhava Samavesha that the Purusha can recognize

its true self and transcend the sense of duality, differentiation, or diversity.

The nature of knowledge derived from Maya is inherently dualistic, giving rise to the experience of duality and the perception of a limited self. As one transcends the sense of separation and limitation, Mayiya-Mala dissipates. It is evident that Mayiya-Mala exists within the context of Anava-Mala, and by eliminating Anava-Mala, one also eradicates the duality caused by Mayiya-Mala. Thus, the dissolution of Anava-Mala leads to the removal of the divisive effects of Mayiya-Mala as well.

Karma-Mala

The third impurity, known as Karma-Mala, refers to the impurity of action. This impurity arises from the actions of an individual who is unaware of their true self or who perceives themselves as limited in nature. Actions performed by such a limited individual are not spontaneous but are driven by the pursuit of specific goals and outcomes. These goals are pursued due to a lack of self-awareness and a sense of dependency, coupled with a feeling of incompleteness influenced by Raga-Tatwa.

In an attempt to overcome this sense of insufficiency, the individual engages in actions to achieve certain goals and to enjoy the results, hoping to alleviate the feeling of inadequacy. However, since this sense of insufficiency is rooted in a self-imposed illusion of limitation, the fruits of these actions are not permanent. The actions and their results are thus bound by illusion, constrained by the very limitations that give rise to them.

Under the influence of Karma-Mala, actions are performed in

a state of ignorance. The individual who acts under this influence inevitably experiences the consequences or fruits of their actions, whether they are positive or negative, wholesome or unwholesome. The empirical individual, limited by Karma-Mala, cannot escape the outcomes of their actions. These actions represent a restricted form of Kriya-Shakti, the omnipotence of the supreme Lord. When Kriya-Shakti is influenced by Maya and Karma-Mala, it becomes limited and manifests as finite actions or karma.

For a realized person, however, their actions reflect the pure, unbounded Kriya-Shakti of the universal subject. In this state, actions are manifestations of pure consciousness, free from limitations and the three Malas. Such actions are untainted by the five veils and the impurities of Anava-Mala, Mayiya-Mala, and Karma-Mala. They embody the essence of the supreme consciousness and are not subject to the constraints and illusions that define ordinary actions.

It is now evident that the Purusha, or individual soul, experiences bondage due to the influence of these impurities. These impurities act as a veil, obscuring us from our true, real self. It is important to understand that the presence of these impurities is not objective in nature. Instead, they represent a tendency or movement of awareness toward a limited nature, which is termed as impurity. As long as the Purusha or individual awareness remains under the influence of these impurities, it will never realize its true nature. It remains continuously shrouded by these Malas.

The eradication of impurities leads to the realization of the true self. Transcending or overcoming these impurities means that the individual is no longer constrained by Maya and has achieved absolute freedom and autonomy. The realization of the true self

signifies that the individual has transcended the dualistic notions of bondage and liberation, and it also encompasses the process of Shambhava Samavesha.

If we thoroughly understand the concept of liberation, we can define it in two ways: liberation is the dissolution of impurities, or it is the realization of the self, specifically through Shambhava Samavesha. In nearly every Indian spiritual tradition, liberation is explained both positively and negatively, and Shaivism follows this pattern as well. Liberation is considered negative in that it represents freedom from impurities and bondage. However, it is also positive as it involves the recognition of the true self as Para-Bhairava (supreme Bhairava) or the process of Shambhava Samavesha.

Therefore, liberation encompasses both the removal of the obscuring impurities and the profound recognition of the divine essence within us, aligning with the highest state of realization and unity with the supreme consciousness.

Nescience, Karma, and Evil

The concept of evil presents a complex challenge in every religious and philosophical tradition. If a deity created everything, including evil, it raises troubling questions about the nature of that deity. Could such a deity be considered sadistic or malevolent? Conversely, if the all-pervading deity is not evil, does this imply that evil exists independently of the divine or is necessitated by some other force? Alternatively, could evil be a product of ignorance?

If evil is indeed a product of ignorance, then the deity who underpins this ignorance might also be considered evil. When we consider the immanent world as a manifestation of the bliss of the

Supreme Subject, it becomes challenging to reconcile this view with the existence of evil, which manifests as jealousy, greed, murder, rape, bloodshed, and abuse. How could such negative phenomena arise from a source that is entirely blissful and full of light?

If the absolute deity manifested the cosmos in His own image and nature, it is difficult to understand the presence of suffering and violence within such a creation. The prevalence of suffering and hardships might lead one to question the nature of the Supreme Subject, potentially even perceiving Him as malevolent. Some Western left-hand path philosophies, for instance, view the creative principle as evil, suggesting that a deity who invents torture and temptation to judge His creations is, at best, a psychopath. An omnipotent being who seems to derive amusement from tricking, tempting, and causing suffering among His creations—through diseases, poverty, and other forms of hardship—appears to fall below the moral standards of His own creatures. In this scenario, the deity's moral sensibility is questioned, undermining the concept of supreme divinity.

Many religious adherents attempt to address the problem of evil by invoking the concept of Karma, which suggests that suffering is the result of sinful deeds committed in past lives. However, this perspective raises further issues. If the deity is omnipotent and omniscient, aware of all forthcoming moral evils, why did He not prevent them from occurring in the first place by altering the behavior of His creatures? Some argue that preventing such evils would violate the principle of free will. Yet, if free will is upheld, the effectiveness of prayers and the assertion that "God has a plan for everyone" seem contradictory to the notion of free will, creating

a paradox.

Ultimately, explaining evil from an absolute perspective remains a profound challenge, both logically and ontologically. The tension between free will, divine omniscience, and the presence of evil continues to provoke deep questions and debates across religious and philosophical traditions.

We will revisit the topic of evil after examining karma and its manifestation within the realm of nescience. It is established that when the Supreme Subject manifests as the objective world, He imposes limitations on His powers of will, action, and knowledge. This limitation is referred to as Khyati, specifically Swarupa Khyati in this context.

According to Shaivite doctrine, the Supreme God is attributed five functions, which include the traditionally accepted three—creation, preservation, and destruction—as well as consciousness and bliss. These functions undergo a transformation that imposes limitations on the spheres of activity, manifesting as restricted will, knowledge, and action. These three limited powers ultimately culminate in the actions of empirical individuals, who engage in activities aimed at achieving specific goals. These goals, however, are inherently limited because they are affected by the three impurities.

The goals pursued by individuals are influenced by their Alpa-Aham, or limited self, which arises from the sensation of the nonexistence of their omnipresent nature. In their quest to attain certain objectives in order to feel complete, individuals become attached to objects. Because these limited activities are driven by the restricted will of the empirical self, they produce limited effects. Consequently, individuals experience the fruits of their actions in

terms of limitations, categorized as good and evil, wholesome and unwholesome, which leads to the experience of both suffering and pleasure.

Karma must be understood in two stages: Karma-Mala and Karma-Samskara. Karma-Mala, as previously explained, refers to the impurity that affects the actions of the limited individual. At this stage, the actions performed by the limited self act as seeds. Repeated actions towards the same end nurture these seeds, bringing them to fruition. This process is termed Karma-Samskara.

To illustrate this concept with a simple analogy, consider the process of physical training. Hitting the gym once will not result in significant strength or health improvements. Continuous training, combined with proper diet and adequate sleep, will eventually yield stronger muscles. In this analogy, going to the gym represents the seed. The proper diet, sufficient sleep, and consistent training serve as the Karma-Samskaras, akin to soil, fertilizer, and water that nourish the seed and facilitate its growth.

The actions of the limited individual, influenced by Karma-Mala, act as seeds that, through the repeated efforts and conditions provided by Karma-Samskara, eventually come to fruition. This process illustrates how limited actions lead to specific outcomes, reflecting the interplay between impurities and the manifestation of karma.

The next stage in the process of karma is its fruition, known as **Phalonmukatha**. After sustained and directed efforts over a proper amount of time, the fruition of karma becomes inevitable. At this stage, the realization of the particular karmic fruit is unavoidable. Experiencing Phalonmukatha—the outcomes of one's karma—is

essential for understanding the true self. Once the fruits of karma are reaped and experienced, the individual is finally able to recognize the light of Shaktipath (Grace), leading to the realization of their inherent oneness with Para-Samvid (Supreme Consciousness).

To fully understand how actions manifest, it is crucial to consider karma from both subjective and objective perspectives. Objectively, karma manifests through concrete results in the physical world. Subjectively, it involves analyzing how actions come into existence.

The empirical subject, or individual, is limited in terms of will, knowledge, and action. These three aspects are always interrelated. In every action performed, there is an initial stage of impulse—a formless will—followed by the knowledge of the action to be undertaken and an understanding of the goal to be achieved. This is then followed by the actual execution of the action. Thus, the external action is merely an expression of the will aspect of the self, and achieving the goal represents the fulfillment of that will.

It is essential to understand that the empirical will, knowledge, and action, despite their limitations, are ultimately expressions of the supreme subject. The individual who performs the action is, in essence, the supreme subject, and it is the supreme subject who experiences the fruits of these actions, whether they manifest as pleasure, pain, suffering, or happiness.

Now, turning back to the concept of evil, let us connect these ideas. From the absolute state of consciousness, the notions of good and evil are merely vague constructs of a limited mind. They do not exist in the pure state of Shiva. The supreme subject manifests Himself in various states of consciousness, and the concept of evil becomes relevant only within specific stages of existence. Therefore, the idea

of evil assumes a separation between the creator and the created. However, from a non-dual perspective, suffering and the sufferer are expressions of the supreme subject alone. Every experience, regardless of its nature, arises from and rests within Para-Samvid, the supreme consciousness.

In this view, both suffering and the concept of evil are understood as integral aspects of the supreme subject's manifold expressions, rather than independent or opposing forces.

He is the one who experiences everything. A pressing question arises: how can an all-powerful, omnipotent deity subject Himself to suffering? How can He become limited, especially given that bliss is one of His inherent aspects and suffering seems contrary to His nature? Evil, as a concept, is inherently relative and dependent on the notion of "good"; it cannot exist in isolation. The appearance of suffering and the tendency to induce suffering arise from the nescience regarding the omnifarious nature of the individual. Thus, good and evil manifest only during the process of cosmic manifestation.

Within the limited subjective mind, suffering appears as evil. However, when the limited self realizes its true nature, this so-called evil merges into the infinite bliss of the self. The root of evil, along with the suffering associated with it, disappears. Yet, this does not imply that evil can be entirely ignored or considered insignificant. The suffering experienced in the material world cannot be dismissed as mere illusion. The atrocities committed by individuals are not figments of imagination but undeniable realities.

Shaivism posits that the cosmos is an exalted expression of the absolute will of the Supreme Subject. Consequently, the existence

of evil as a material reality is also part of Him. The individual who suffers and the evil causing the suffering are ultimately expressions of the Supreme Subject. There is nothing beyond Him. Within the gross plane of existence, distinctions are made on various grounds, which means that evil results from ignorance—a sensation of incompleteness and dissatisfaction caused by the loss of Purnatha, or omnifariousness.

However, ignorance alone cannot account for heinous acts like sexual crimes or murder. Such acts involve a misuse of free will and an abuse of the freedom granted to the empirical individual. While everyone experiences anger and hatred, not everyone engages in violent acts. Most individuals choose to avoid committing heinous acts. Similarly, although sexual arousal is a universal experience, not everyone chooses to commit sexual abuses. Choices are made even in states of profound ignorance. Thus, evil arises from a disassociation with transcendent awareness and an abuse of free will, compounded by the influence of the three impurities and absolute nescience of the self.

The evolution and involution of the cosmos are intrinsic to Shiva's nature. He is both the creator of heaven and hell and the one who sows the seeds and reaps the fruits of happiness and suffering, good and evil. Duality and perception of such contrasts become evident only within the physical world and do not exist in higher planes of subjectivity. In absolute objectivity, or Sakala Pramatr, the subject mistakes itself for the object and identifies with the attributes of the object. This identification leads the subject to become both the object of suffering and the sufferer.

When the subject realizes his true nature, the identification with

the object of suffering is eradicated, thereby eliminating suffering and evil. In simpler terms, a person who recognizes his true nature—one with all and everyone—will never commit atrocities. Such a person will neither inflict mental nor physical pain on himself or others, nor will he be subjected to evil and suffering. He embodies wholeness and holiness, with a perception filled with bliss. Once the disassociated self acknowledges its true nature and becomes whole, it ceases to identify with or attach to external objects. This realization leads to a state of completeness and infinite bliss, where evil dissolves in the pure awareness of the self.

Karma And Causal Efficacy

Now that we have established that Karma refers to the limited actions performed by a limited individual, let us delve deeper into the intricate nature of karma and its effability. In the framework of Monistic Shaivism, the supreme reality is conceived as light and luminosity. This supreme reality, known as Para-Samvid, is characterized by its all-pervading and all-inclusive nature. It encompasses everything and is simultaneously the source of the cosmos and its diverse manifestations.

A fundamental concept in this philosophy is Vimarsha, or Shakti, which acts as both an all-limiting and controlling factor. This means that the supreme reality has the capacity to manifest itself in both limited and unlimited forms. Despite having the power to both manifest and limit itself, Para-Samvid creates the cosmos without altering or diminishing its own inherent nature. This ability to manifest different forms within itself is attributed to the Shakti aspect or Vimarsha aspect of the supreme reality. The actual process

of manifestation occurs through the various Shaktis inherent in Para Shiva, the supreme deity.

Everything in our perception—every object, event, and experience—is an exalted manifestation of Para-Samvid, governed by his three principal Shaktis: will, knowledge, and action. The will aspect of Para Shiva is crucial because it serves as both the instrumental and material cause for the creation and ongoing evolution of the cosmos. The question then arises: If everything is in perfect harmony and each action performed by an individual is a manifestation of divine providence, how can individuals experience pain, sorrow, or pleasure? After all, bliss is the essential nature of Para-Samvid.

To address this query, Abhinava Gupta provides a comprehensive explanation in his monumental work, Tantra-āloka, particularly in the ninth and tenth chapters. According to Gupta, the theory of Karma extends beyond the limited actions of individual beings and encompasses the entirety of the universe. The universe itself is the cumulative result of all the Karmas—actions and their consequences—experienced by every individual being across the cosmos.

It is essential to understand that the cosmos is not a random or capricious manifestation but rather the result of the supreme reality's desire to experience a myriad of limited forms and sensations. This grand design of the universe is fundamentally centered around the supreme lord's wish to manifest and experience diverse aspects of existence.

The limited self, within this cosmic framework, is constrained by limitations in will, knowledge, and action. These limitations result

in the self's actions and experiences being restricted and diminished. Unlike the supreme reality's unlimited and spontaneous impulse to create, the limited will of the individual manifests as a focused drive to utilize the limited knowledge at their disposal to perform actions within their empirical existence. As a result, individuals assume various physical forms that are suited for experiencing the limited outcomes of their actions.

These limited associations, which give rise to Karma, are attributes of the self rather than mere connections to the physical body. Thus, Karma is intrinsically tied to the self and its limitations. The limitations in will, knowledge, and action are considered to be beginningless, reflecting the inherent nature of the supreme reality to manifest these limitations.

It is crucial to note, however, that the experience of limited results and their associated fruits do not persist in the self-realized or transcended state. The true nature of the eternal self is the unlimited nature of Para-Shiva, and as such, the limitations imposed by Karma do not affect the self. Once an individual realizes their true nature, which is one with the infinite and unbounded reality of Para-Shiva, these self-imposed limitations dissolve. The phenomena of Karma, which are only applicable within the limited physical world, are transcended.

The realization of the true self breaks through the self-imposed limitations that manifest as Karma in the physical world. When one achieves this self-realization, the apparent dualities and limitations associated with Karma are dissolved, revealing the boundless, blissful nature of the supreme reality that underlies all existence.

In addition to the traditionally recognized three functions of the

divine—creation, preservation, and destruction—Shaivite doctrines introduce two additional functions: obscuration and revealing. These five functions collectively offer a more nuanced understanding of the divine activities.

The function of obscuration, also known as Avarana Shakti, introduces a limitation to the divine nature. It acts to veil or obscure the true nature of the supreme reality, creating the illusion of separation and limitation. This obscuration allows for the experience of duality and the sense of individuality within the cosmic play. The functions of creation, preservation, and destruction are influenced by Maya Tatwa, the principle of illusion or cosmic ignorance, which affects the processes of will, knowledge, and action respectively. In contrast, the functions of obscuration and revealing remain unaffected by Maya; they operate independently of the cosmic illusion.

The entire manifestation of the cosmos serves to execute the limited will of the individual beings and to allow them to experience the fruits of their actions. This limited cosmos, with all its associated experiences and phenomena, is essentially designed for the enjoyment of these actions and their results. This enjoyment and the process of experiencing the fruits of one's actions constitute the primary purpose of this limited cosmic framework.

It becomes clear that the self, influenced by limitations in will, knowledge, and action, tends to identify with external objects and the body. This identification is facilitated through the five Tanmatras (subtle elements) and the three internal organs (manas, buddhi, and ahamkara), which serve as the basis for executing limited actions and enjoying their results. These limitations create the perception

of moral distinctions such as good and evil deeds, and sinful versus pious activities.

From an absolute perspective, concepts like sin, piety, good, and evil are meaningless. In this ultimate state of reality, such distinctions do not exist. However, at the empirical level, individuals remain ignorant of the divine will that orchestrates all actions. They perceive themselves as the ultimate doers and experience the fruits of their actions as good and evil, pain and pleasure. This erroneous self-identification with the limited doer leads to attachment to the results of actions, whether they are pleasurable or painful.

When an individual recognizes their true nature as one with the supreme subject, the actions performed become expressions of the divine sportive play, or Lila. The fruits of these actions are then understood as part of this divine play, transcending the limitations and attachments previously experienced.

The term *Karma* is used to describe the limited results obtained from executing the will, knowledge, and actions of empirical individuals, all of which are afflicted by the Malas (impurities). For every association and dissociation an individual makes, a cause is set into motion, leading to corresponding effects.

In contrast, the unlimited power of action, known as Kriya-Shakti, refers to the divine actions performed by the supreme subject. Unlike the limited actions of individuals, Kriya-Shakti is not constrained by any limitations. Thus, the actions of Para Shiva, which are not bound by the Malas or Maya Kanchukas (veils), are not considered Karma. Instead, they represent the unlimited, divine activity that transcends the Karmic framework and the illusions of the material world.

Fruition of Karma

In our previous discussion on Malas, we examined the essential factors required to bring Karma into fruition. To revisit this concept, let's delve deeper into Karma Mala and Karma Samskara. Karma Mala, as previously discussed, represents the limited will and desires of the empirical individual. Karma Samskara refers to the effects produced on an individual that lead to the fruition of Karma. Together, these two aspects constitute the phenomena we refer to as Karma.

To clarify, Karma, from this perspective, is the factor that remains unrecognized, acting as the foundation for the differing results of the same actions performed by different individuals. For instance, consider a group of students studying under the same teacher and learning from the same syllabus. Despite the uniformity in their education, not all students secure the same grades. This disparity is primarily influenced by Karma Samskara. Karma Mala can be likened to a seed, while Karma Samskara functions as the necessary fertilizers, water, and other conditions required to bring this seed to fruition. The fruition of Karma occurs due to the process of self-arrogation, which is the root cause behind the perception of the fruits of actions—whether they are pleasurable, painful, meritorious, or unwholesome.

In simpler terms, self-arrogation is the primary reason for Karma. It is the individual's perception and identification with their limited self that determines how they experience the results of their actions. This self-arrogation influences how the fruits of Karma are perceived, whether as pleasure or pain, and whether they are seen as wholesome or unwholesome.

Moreover, the effect or fruit of Karma is not solely based on the self-arrogation of the isolated individual; it can also impact other empirical individuals, provided they are receptive to it. For example, when a doctor treats and cures patients, the action of the doctor is inherently linked with the well-being of the patients. Thus, the Karma performed by the doctor affects not just the doctor but also the patients. In this case, the Karma involves not just the actions of one individual but the interplay between individuals. The doctor is karmically inclined to provide treatment, and the patient is karmically inclined to receive it.

Karma is fundamentally connected to the limited self rather than the physical body. Consequently, the effects of Karma persist beyond the lifetime of the physical body. Even if the body is destroyed or dies, the fruits of Karma can manifest in future incarnations or after death. The seeds of Karma await suitable conditions to come to fruition and will express themselves at the appropriate time. The effects of these fruits are inevitable and must be experienced. Even if an individual achieves self-realization and identifies with the supreme subject during their lifetime, they still must reap what they have sown. At this stage, the individual gains complete understanding of the nature and reasons behind their Karma and embraces the responsibility for their actions with a sense of blissful acceptance, completing their karmic cycle with clarity and equanimity.

Destruction of Karma and Jivan Mukti

In the landscape of Indian spiritual philosophies, the destruction of Karma is often considered a crucial element for attaining liberation. However, within the framework of Shaivism, the obliteration

of Karma alone does not lead to liberation. Shaivite doctrine delineates a more nuanced understanding, positing that even after the destruction of Karmiya-Mala (the impurity of Karma), further purification is required. Specifically, the yogi must also eradicate Anava-Mala (the impurity of ego) and Mayiya-Mala (the impurity of illusion) to achieve full liberation.

Shaivite Perspective on Liberation

Unlike other spiritual systems that might view physical birth and the cycle of reincarnation as bondage, with death marking the ultimate liberation, Shaivism presents a distinct perspective. For a Shaivite, liberation is not merely the cessation of physical existence or the end of reincarnation. Instead, it is the realization of the true self and the recognition of one's inherent oneness with Para-Shiva. This realization signifies that the limited actions performed by the empirical self are merely reflections of the infinite will, knowledge, and action of the supreme subject.

In the state of nescience, the individual (Purusha) is constrained by limitations of freedom, volition, and action. This restricted self identifies with its limited actions and physical form, thereby experiencing awareness as confined within these constraints. When the grace or Shakti Path of Para-Shiva illuminates the Purusha, nescience is dispelled, revealing the true self's unity with Para-Shiva. This realization obliterates the self-arrogation tied to limited actions and bodies, leading to the burning away of Karma in the transformative fires of Kalagni Rudra. Ultimately, the only remaining reality is the pure, untainted bliss of Para-Bhairava.

Bhogya-Karma and Residual Karma

Shaivite doctrine asserts that each action is linked to its results by a residual trace known as Bhogya-Karma. This term refers to the fruits of actions that are yet to be experienced by the limited subject. These residual Karmic effects contribute to the sense of limitation or bondage. Karma encompasses both the actions that generate these residual effects and the residues themselves. Whether actions are deemed wholesome or unwholesome, constructive or destructive, they function as shackles for the empirical individual until all fruits of these actions have been fully experienced.

Karma is only transformed when the limited subject has thoroughly experienced the outcomes of past actions. As the soul endures the consequences of previous limited actions, Bhogya-Karma is gradually eradicated.

Classifications of Karma

Indian spiritual traditions often classify Karma into three distinct categories based on their origin and the timing of their fruits:

1. **Prarabdha-Karma**: This type of Karma refers to the Karmic debts from past actions that are currently being experienced in the present lifetime. It denotes the actions whose results are already in motion, explaining why the individual is manifested in their current form and circumstances. Prarabdha-Karma is essentially the result of previous actions coming to fruition in the present life.

2. **Sanchita-Karma**: This category consists of accumulated Karma that is not yet active but will be experienced in the

future. Sanchita-Karma encompasses the results of actions that are yet to unfold. It is influenced by the present actions, making today's Prarabdha-Karma a result of yesterday's Sanchita-Karma. In essence, Sanchita-Karma represents the reservoir of past actions awaiting their turn for fruition.

3. **Agamya-Karma**: Agamya-Karma includes actions that have not yet been initiated and thus have not yet started to bear fruit. This category of Karma consists of seeds that are yet to be sown, implying potential actions and their future outcomes that remain unrealized until they are enacted.

The Shaivite view of Karma and liberation involves a comprehensive understanding of how Karma influences the self and its journey towards ultimate realization. Destruction of Karma, while essential, is only part of the broader spiritual process that includes transcending the impurities of ego and illusion to fully experience the bliss of unity with the supreme self.

In Shaivism, the concept of Karma is deeply intertwined with the understanding of cosmic manifestation and the nature of the self. Karma, in this context, refers to the actions performed by individuals and the resultant effects of these actions. To fully grasp the role of Karma in spiritual practice and liberation, we need to explore its connection with Maya (illusion) and the three Malas (impurities) as well as its relationship with the divine process of self-realization.

Understanding Karma and Maya

Karma encompasses the actions undertaken by individuals, which bring about specific results or fruits. These results are influenced by

the interplay of individual will, knowledge, and action, all of which are limited by the inherent constraints of the empirical world. Karma, thus, shapes the experiences and circumstances of the empirical individual, contributing to the formation of a finite cosmos.

Maya, on the other hand, is the principle of illusion that obscures the true nature of the self. It manifests the cosmos and creates the illusion of multiplicity and limitation. Through Maya, the infinite appears as finite, and the self perceives itself as separate from the divine. This illusion of separateness and limitation is what creates the experience of Karma. The process of cosmic manifestation and reabsorption involves Maya repeatedly generating and withdrawing the illusion of the objective world.

The Role of the Three Malas

In Shaivism, the **three Malas** are crucial in understanding the nature of Karma and its effects:

1. **Anava-Mala** represents the impurity of ego or self-assertion, which creates a sense of separation from the divine.
2. **Mayiya-Mala** is the impurity of ignorance or illusion, which blinds the individual to their true nature.
3. **Karma-Mala** is related to the limited actions and their results, which further bind the individual to the cycle of actions and consequences.

These Malas are not merely obstacles but are integral to the

process of cosmic manifestation. They create the sense of limitation and separation that allows for the experience of Karma. The interplay between Karma and Maya, along with the influence of the Malas, results in the empirical individual experiencing a finite world with distinct actions and outcomes.

The Destruction of Karma and Liberation

To achieve liberation, or **Jivan Mukti**, one must transcend the limitations imposed by the Malas. This process involves several key elements:

1. **Vanquishing Self-Arrogation**: This means overcoming the mistaken belief that one is the limited doer of actions. When the individual realizes that they are not confined by their actions or physical body, they move beyond the limitations of Karma.
2. **Experiencing the Fruits of Karma**: The individual must undergo the outcomes of their past actions, known as Bhogya-Karma. This experience is necessary for the dissolution of residual Karmic effects. Even after realizing one's true nature, the fruits of past actions must be experienced until they are exhausted.
3. **Realizing the True Self**: The ultimate goal is to recognize the self's unity with Para-Shiva, the supreme divine. This realization involves transcending the limitations imposed by the Malas and experiencing the pure bliss of unity with the divine.

In Shaivism, Para-Shiva is both the creator and the destroyer of the cosmos. He manifests as the limited universe and the individuals within it, obscuring himself with his own power of Maya. This process of self-limitation and the resultant creation of Karma are seen as part of Para-Shiva's divine sportive play.

Para-Shiva's powers include:

- **Concealment**: Using Maya to impose limitations and create the illusion of the finite.
- **Grace**: Using his divine grace to reveal the true nature of the self and liberate himself and others from these limitations.

From the absolute perspective, the entire process of cosmic manifestation, including the creation and dissolution of Karma and the operation of the Malas, is a manifestation of Para-Shiva's infinite freedom. The divine play involves both the imposition of limitations and their transcendence, reflecting the ultimate sovereignty of Para-Shiva, who, through his divine will, manifests and then transcends the apparent dualities of existence.

The concept of Karma in Shaivism is deeply connected to the principles of Maya and the three Malas. Karma shapes the finite experiences of individuals, while Maya creates the illusion of separateness and limitation. The Malas impose constraints on awareness, contributing to the cycle of actions and their results. Liberation, or Jivan Mukti, involves transcending these limitations and realizing the true self's unity with Para-Shiva. This process reflects the divine play of Para-Shiva, who, through his infinite

freedom, creates and transcends the cosmos, embodying both the imposition and the resolution of limitations.

Jivan Mukthi and The Upayas

In Monistic Shaivism, the concept of liberation, or Jivan Mukti, stands distinct from other Indian philosophical traditions. Unlike those traditions that may view liberation as a dissolution of identity or an escape from the cycle of rebirth (Samsara), Monistic Shaivism presents liberation as a profound recognition of one's true self.

Liberation, in the context of Monistic Shaivism, is not about becoming something new or achieving unity with a separate deity. Instead, it is about the recognition of one's inherent oneness with Para-Bhairava or Para-Shiva, the supreme consciousness. The process of liberation involves the realization that one's true nature is already identical with the divine.

In Monistic Shaivism, the experience of liberation is the direct realization of one's unity with the supreme subject. This realization transcends the apparent distinctions between subject and object. The individual perceives everything as a manifestation of the supreme consciousness, and the illusion of separateness dissolves.

This state of realization is facilitated by the descent of divine grace, known as Anugraha Shakti. This divine grace is an aspect of the supreme subject's self-revealing power. When Anugraha Shakti descends upon a practitioner or yogi, it brings about a profound transformation, allowing the individual to recognize their true nature.

The Process of Liberation

1. **Overcoming Self-Imposed Limitations:** Liberation involves freeing oneself from the self-imposed limitations and constraints created by the divine through his own power of Maya. This process is about recognizing and shedding the false sense of limitation imposed by the three Malas (impurities).

2. **Mala-Paka:** The purification process, known as Mala-Paka, is crucial for this realization. Mala-Paka involves the elimination of the three Malas—Anava-Mala (ego), Mayiya-Mala (ignorance), and Karma-Mala (limited actions). These impurities obscure the true nature of Shiva. Through spiritual practices and divine grace, these impurities are removed, leading to the recognition of one's inherent divinity.

3. **Anugraha Shakti:** The divine grace, or Anugraha Shakti, reveals the true nature of the self. This grace transforms the individual's awareness, removing the veils of Maya and the Kanchukas (limiting factors). The result is a profound awareness of the self as the supreme consciousness.

Essence of Jivan Mukti

Jivan Mukti is the realization of the supreme consciousness manifesting through the individual. It involves the complete removal of ignorance and the recognition that the entire cosmos is a reflection of one's own divine nature. This realization is not confined by time or words; it is an absolute state of bliss and unity with the cosmos.

In this state, the individual experiences a profound sense of oneness with the divine, often referred to as the Shambhava Samavesha, where the identity with Para Samvid (the supreme consciousness) is fully realized.

The Vedantic declaration "Aham Brahmasmi" (I am Brahman) expresses a similar realization of unity with the divine. However, in Monistic Shaivism, this realization is emphasized with a focus on the inherent identity between the supreme lord (Para-Shiva) and the individual self. The recognition is that the supreme consciousness and the individual 'I' are fundamentally one and the same, transcending any notion of partial distinction.

In Monistic Shaivism, liberation is not a process of achieving something new but of uncovering the inherent divinity within oneself. The journey to Jivan Mukti is about recognizing and realizing one's true nature as Para-Shiva, facilitated by the divine grace that removes all illusions and impurities.

With our understanding of liberation in Monistic Shaivism established, we now turn to the means of achieving this liberation, known as Upayas. The nature of Para-Shiva encompasses the manifestation of the cosmos itself. As previously discussed, if the supreme deity were unable to manifest the cosmos or assume the form of the objective world, he would not be fully independent or omnipotent. This ability to manifest and interact with the universe underscores his boundless power and freedom.

The process of liberation involves transcending the influence of the Malas, or impurities, which obscure our true nature. The divine

grace or Anugraha from Para-Shiva is the key to overcoming these obstacles. The process of removing these impurities is called Mala-Paka, and it is achieved through various spiritual means, referred to as Upayas. In Monistic Shaivism, there are four primary Upayas: Anupaya, Shambhavopaya, Shaktopaya, and Anavopaya.

Anupaya

Anupaya, which translates to "little effort," represents a highly advanced stage of realization. At this stage, the realization of the true self happens spontaneously when the potent grace from Para-Bhairava descends upon the practitioner. This form of realization requires minimal effort from the individual, as the grace directly elevates the consciousness to its highest state. Once this grace descends, the yogi is immediately absorbed into the supreme consciousness, experiencing a profound awakening known as Anupaya.

Shambhavopaya

Shambhavopaya involves a more structured approach to spiritual practice. According to the doctrines, various spiritual exercises are tailored to different stages of an individual's spiritual evolution. Abhinava Gupta's Tantra Aloka and the Shiva Sutra of Vasugupta provide detailed descriptions of these practices. The first aphorism of the Shiva Sutra, "Chaitanyam Atma," translates to "consciousness is the nature of self," highlighting that the true nature of self is consciousness itself. This self-aware consciousness manifests

through will, knowledge, and action.

In Shambhavopaya, also known as Ichopya or the means of will, the yogi utilizes the will aspect to merge with the divine will, or Icha-Shakti, of Para-Shiva. This method is characterized by the dynamic expression of awareness, which leads to the spontaneous realization of the supreme self. Kshema Raja, in his commentary, describes this as the "flashing forth of dynamic awareness," which is essential for achieving Shambhava Samavesha. This approach is sometimes referred to as Abhedopaya, or the means of non-dual state.

The Malini Vijaya Uttara Tantra, a classical text in Monistic Trika Shaivism, elaborates on Shambhavopaya as the realization that occurs when the yogi eliminates all contrived ideas and experiences a spontaneous awakening. This awakening happens when the mind ceases to accept or reject any particular idea, leading to a state where ideation halts and self-aware consciousness is recognized. This state of awareness, free from the limited constructs of thought, represents the essence of Shambhava Upaya. It emphasizes the recognition of the unified state of consciousness, which precedes the manifestation of thoughts.

The Upayas in Monistic Shaivism are essential pathways to achieving liberation. Each method offers a unique approach to transcending the limitations imposed by the Malas and realizing one's inherent oneness with Para-Shiva. While Anupaya involves minimal effort and immediate grace, Shambhavopaya focuses on the dynamic use of will and awareness to achieve spontaneous realization. Together, these Upayas provide a comprehensive framework for overcoming the obstacles to liberation and attaining the ultimate recognition of the divine self.

In the transformative process of **Shambhava Samavesha**, the limited ego, or the lower 'I', is entirely dissolved into the Supreme 'I', resulting in the disappearance of any perceived objective universe outside the yogi's consciousness. This profound realization occurs when the yogi perceives the cosmos not as something separate from himself but as an extension of his own supreme self. The distinction between subject and object vanishes, and the yogi's awareness merges with the absolute sovereign Shakti of Para-Bhairava.

At this elevated state, the yogi becomes acutely aware of **Mantra Virya**, which represents the full potency of mantras. This potency is not to be confused with semen, as sometimes misinterpreted in certain Tantric interpretations. Instead, **Virya** refers to the essential energy or potential inherent in the mantras, formed from the fifty phonemes, which are aligned with the awareness of Para-Bhairava. This awareness encompasses the complete awakening of **Kundalini**, the self-reflecting awareness in the form of mantras, which plays a central role in manifesting, sustaining, and withdrawing the universe. The dynamics of Kundalini-Shakti, which Shiva uses to reveal and conceal his true nature, will be discussed in detail in a separate chapter.

In the practice of **Shambhavopaya**, a key technique involves focusing on the gap between successive thoughts, which is often likened to the pause between inhalation and exhalation in breathing. This gap, referred to as **Sandhya**, is a crucial aspect of meditation in Monistic Shaivism.

Sandhya Vandhana is a practice where the practitioner concentrates on the transition periods or gaps that occur between thoughts or between breaths. This concept is deeply rooted in the

idea that in these moments of stillness—whether it is between two breaths or two thoughts—there is a state of pure, unconditioned awareness. The aim of this practice is to become intimately aware of these gaps, as they are believed to hold the essence of absolute consciousness.

By focusing on the Sandhya, or the space between inhalation and exhalation, the practitioner can access a state of profound awareness that transcends ordinary mental activity. This practice helps the yogi to experience a direct awareness of the unchanging, absolute self beyond the fluctuations of thoughts and external stimuli. It is through this refined awareness of the Sandhya that one can approach the state of Shambhavopaya, where the distinction between subject and object fades, leading to the realization of the supreme consciousness.

This method highlights the integration of breath control and mental focus, where the practitioner uses the natural rhythm of breathing as a tool to enhance their meditative experience. By becoming more attuned to the pauses and gaps in their own mental and physical processes, the yogi deepens their understanding of the pure, undifferentiated awareness that exists beyond the surface of ordinary consciousness.

In practice, this involves introspective meditation, where attention is given to the pattern of thoughts and their intervals. By consistently focusing on these gaps or moments of silence, the adept gradually recognizes his oneness with the supreme 'I'. Shambhavopaya, therefore, is characterized by its spontaneous nature. It emerges when the mind is sufficiently trained to be free of external distractions and judgments, allowing thoughts to dissipate and revealing a flash of pure awareness. This realization is often reached after mastering the

previous Upayas, **Anavopaya** and **Shaktopaya**.

Upon attaining Shambhavopaya, the yogi naturally progresses to the ultimate stage of **Anupaya**. This process is spontaneous, occurring without expectations. Through deep contemplation of mental processes, the yogi's awareness turns inward, culminating in a heightened state of subjective awareness. The individual, initially focused on external reality, now embraces a state of subjectivity, recognizing the supreme subjective state of Bhairava.

This transformation involves the dissolution of limited thought constructs. The supreme consciousness, initially contracting into a limited subject, manifests as a limited objective reality. When this awareness retracts, it returns to its superior, unlimited nature. The process of dissolving these limited thought forms is crucial for realizing the boundless nature of the supreme 'I' or **Para-Samvid**.

J. Krishnamurti, a renowned philosopher and adept, frequently discussed the importance of observing thoughts as a means to transcend them. By adopting a passive, observational stance towards thoughts—without judgment or attachment—these thoughts eventually cease to obscure our true nature. Similarly, Franz Bardon, a twentieth-century Western occultist, advocated for a practice of passive observation of thoughts as the first step in his training. Over time, this practice helps one master their thoughts and attain a higher level of awareness.

Shaktopaya is a pivotal method in Shaivism for overcoming the bondage of ignorance and achieving liberation. Known also as **Jnanaopya, Bhavanopaya**, and **Mantropaya**, this approach

primarily involves the use of mantras, which are sacred sounds embodying the consciousness of Para-Shiva. By aligning oneself with these mantras, the yogi can realize their inherent self as the supreme reality.

Shaktopaya

Shaktopaya follows **Shambhavopaya** in the sequence of practices for liberation. When a practitioner finds it challenging to recognize the divine light through will alone, they may turn to the luminous nature of consciousness represented by sounds and letters in mantras. The primary tool here is the mantra, which embodies the divine Shakti or consciousness of Para-Shiva.

The state of **Vikalpa-Kshaya**, or the mind's vacant state, can be elusive for many. For those who struggle to achieve this state, **Shaktopaya** offers a solution through the use of **Shuddha Vikalpa**—pure contemplation in the form of mantras.

Pure vs. Impure Thoughts

In Shaivism, **Ashudha-Vikalpa** (impure thoughts) arise from a limited self and are the result of restricted will and knowledge. These thoughts are characterized by identification with finite objects, creating spiritual darkness and ignorance. In contrast, **Shuddha-Vikalpa** (pure thoughts) are free from such limitations. They represent pure, unadulterated attributes of the supreme reality and help dissolve the duality perceived by the limited self.

To achieve realization, one must employ logic and discernment to understand the self. The yogi must recognize that their identity is not defined by actions, thoughts, or emotions. Instead, the self

is consciousness, the backdrop against which thoughts and objects manifest. Pure Vikalpa aims to dissolve the illusion of separation between subject and object, revealing their inherent oneness.

Mantra

The first aphorism of the second chapter of the **Shiva Sutra** states, "Chittam Mantrah"—consciousness is mantra. This suggests that mantras are not merely sounds but are expressions of pure, transcendent consciousness. Mantras are composed of syllables that embody divine awareness and help the practitioner recognize their unity with the supreme reality. Mantras are not effective through mere mechanical repetition but through their intrinsic connection to divine consciousness. True practice involves understanding and internalizing the essence of these sacred sounds. The first aphorism of the second chapter of the Shiva Sutra states, "Chittam Mantrah," which translates to "consciousness is mantra." This declaration emphasizes that the essence of consciousness is not the limited awareness afflicted by Maya (illusion) and the three Malas (impurities or obstacles). Instead, it refers to the pure, transcendent consciousness, known as Para-Samvid. Mantras, in this context, emerge from the pure awareness of Para-Shiva, representing the luminosity and the Vimarsha (reflection or awareness) of divine Shakti.

The term "mantra" is composed of two syllables: "Mana" and "Tra." "Tra" signifies protection or salvation, derived from the Sanskrit word "Tranana," which means "to save." "Mana," or "Manana," refers to awareness. Thus, mantras are not merely sounds; they embody awareness that protects and liberates us from

ignorance. They facilitate the recognition of the fundamental unity between subject and object, transcending the apparent duality.

Divine Para-Shakti manifests in the form of 51 letters, which constitute the structure of mantras. Each mantra, therefore, is a manifestation of this divine Shakti and is intrinsically linked to her. By engaging in these mantras, an individual aligns themselves with the divine awareness and realizes their oneness with the Supreme Subject. However, it is important to note that merely repeating mantras mechanically, as some modern Tantric schools suggest, does not yield true results. The effective use of mantras involves understanding and internalizing their deeper significance, which will be further explored in the practical section of this study.

Mantras help the practitioner reach the state of pure Vikalpa. In this context, Shuddha-Vikalpa refers to the recognition of the supreme 'I' within oneself. Through the practice of Shaktopaya, the constructs of thought that exist within the realm of duality are overcome, leading to a state where the thoughts that arise are direct reflections of fully realized consciousness. This consciousness is aligned with the supreme subject, revealing the non-differentiated state of unity.

Shiva, in his divine aspect, manifests the cosmos through the letters known as Matrikas. Recognizing these Matrikas within oneself is key to understanding and experiencing the supreme self. The ignorance of one's true self is often due to the lack of awareness of these Matrikas. By focusing on the mantra and contemplating it, the practitioner identifies with the supreme 'I'. This process removes ignorance and the three Malas, leading the individual to the state of

Supreme 'I', where everything shines in the Para-Samvid.

The ultimate state achieved through the practice of mantras is referred to as Unnamana Shakti, which culminates in the Khechari state. "Kha" represents the supreme consciousness, while "Chara" denotes movement. Thus, through repetitive contemplation of the mantra, the yogi attains the Khechari state, characterized by the constant awareness of the supreme 'I' within. In this state, the practitioner's awareness remains permanently immersed in the supreme consciousness.

Sat Tarka and Bhavana

Bhavana (Pure Thought): Bhavana involves cultivating pure contemplation, which aligns with the attributes of the supreme reality. This process helps to rise above dualistic thoughts and attain a state of unity with the divine. It is a means to dissolve the dual perception created by impure thoughts.

Sat Tarka (Right Discernment): Discernment is crucial in recognizing the self. Through reasoning and logical analysis, the yogi realizes that their true self is not limited by actions, thoughts, or emotions but is the consciousness that underlies these phenomena. This discernment helps in understanding that the known is merely an emanation of the knower, leading to the recognition of the inherent oneness of subject and object.

Sat-Tarka, or right discernment, is an essential aspect of the Shaktopaya, aimed at achieving proper knowledge and understanding. It involves the application of logic and analytical

reasoning to the teachings received from scriptures and teachers. The core teaching that the nature of the self is consciousness, which is one with the supreme, must be thoroughly examined and verified through discernment. A student must approach this inquiry with an open mind and a willingness to experiment with the teachings to arrive at a profound understanding.

Sat-Tarka involves critically assessing and validating the correctness of these teachings, using logical analysis to reinforce accurate ideas while discarding those that are illusory or misleading. This process of discernment helps the student to distill and solidify their knowledge, leading to a more profound spiritual insight.

Following the process of right discernment, the next phase is Bhavana, which translates to spiritual attention or creative imagination. In this context, Bhavana refers to the practice of continuously reinforcing the recognition of the inherent oneness with the supreme. This is achieved through repeated, focused contemplation and creative visualization, which helps the adept to internalize the knowledge of their true self.

As the practitioner engages in this creative contemplation, the distinction between subject (the knower), cognition (the process of knowing), and object (the known) begins to dissolve. The knowledge, initially perceived as an object of thought, is eventually absorbed into the supreme self. This process eliminates the separation between the knower, the act of knowing, and the known, leading to a unified experience of consciousness.

Additionally, within Shaktopaya, there is another method that involves meditating on the gap between two thoughts. This practice requires the yogi to focus on the space or interval between

successive thoughts. By concentrating on this gap, the practitioner gradually reaches a state where every thought arises within a context of oneness, merging seamlessly into the supreme 'I'. This state of pure awareness, free from the fluctuations of individual thoughts, represents the ultimate goal of absorption into the supreme consciousness.

An analogous practice can be performed by paying attention to the gap between inhalation and exhalation. This gap, similar to the space between thoughts, provides a point of focus for the yogi to experience the stillness and unity of the supreme consciousness. Through sustained attention to this subtle space, the practitioner moves closer to a direct experience of their own inherent oneness with the supreme 'I'.

Shaktopaya uses mantras and pure contemplation to transcend limited thoughts and dualistic perceptions. By integrating mantras, cultivating pure thoughts, and employing right discernment, the practitioner can recognize their inherent unity with the supreme consciousness, advancing towards liberation. This method is essential for those who struggle with willpower alone and provides a profound means of realizing one's divine nature through the sacred power of sound and awareness.

Anavopaya

Anavopaya represents the most foundational and accessible approach among the three Upayas for spiritual realization, being considered the least advanced of the methods. This approach contrasts significantly with the more refined practices of Shambhavopaya and

Shaktopaya. While Shambhavopaya transcends reliance on external objects and focuses solely on the practitioner's inner will and the recognition of the supreme light through Mantras, Anavopaya begins with a more concrete and practical engagement with the world of limited objects and external means.

In Anavopaya, the practitioner uses tangible, external tools and techniques to facilitate spiritual progress. This method becomes necessary when the individual is unable to refine their thought constructs or attain higher states of awareness through the more subtle means of will or Mantras. Hence, Anavopaya is often employed when there is less grace or Anugraha, indicating a need for more structured, external methods to achieve success in spiritual practice.

The term Anavopaya derives from "Anu," meaning limited or small, referring to the approach that starts from the limited self or ego. It is also known as Anava Yoga and Bhedopaya, reflecting its focus on navigating and transcending the realm of duality. Another designation for Anavopaya is Kriya Upaya, highlighting its reliance on various actions and practices such as rituals, rites, and breathing exercises (Pranayama) to achieve spiritual realization. We have seen that Shambhavopaya does not use any object or means where the awareness of the yogi is fixed; rather, it relies on the impeccable will of the yogi. In Shambhavopaya, the awareness is not fixed on any external object or any point of the body, but it uses Mantras as the means to recognize the supreme light. In Anavopaya, the limited subject depends on external, limited objects, thought constructs, objects of concentration, and parts of the body.

When a practitioner is unable to refine their thought constructs through Mantras or will, they have to rely on other limited means to achieve success. This method is advisable when the amount of grace or Anugraha in the individual is less. It is called Anavopaya because it starts with the limited self (Anu/Anava), also known as Anava Yoga, and is also referred to as Bhedopaya because it begins with the dimension of duality. This is also called Kriya Upaya, as it uses various actions such as rituals, rites, and breathing exercises (Pranayama) to recognize the real self. An individual may use gross Prana, subtle Prana, or Buddhi for Anavopaya, and may also use external objects called Sthana Kalpana. Anavopaya consists of Dhyana, Ucchara, Varna, Karana, and Sthana Kalpana.

Dhyana

Dhyana means to be aware or contemplate, and it is used synonymously with meditation. In non-dual Shaivism, the practitioner should meditate by contemplating the known object and knowing or cognition as one with the subject or knower, devoid of any mutual distinction. This will ultimately lead to the realization of the self. The fire of consciousness will be enkindled, and the person will recognize his oneness with Para-Bhairava. The adept should meditate on the processes of the five sense organs and the knowledge gained through them, and then, using his creative imagination, he should contemplate the knowledge of the five senses as abiding in the inner self. The prolonged practice of this meditation completely annihilates the distinction between subject and object, eventually leading the Subject to recognize the outer world as an expression

of the eternal subjective self, which is one with Para-Shiva. Other practical methods will be mentioned in the practical part.

Ucchara specifically refers to Prana, which can be considered both as sound and as the vital force in man. The primary aspect of Prana here is its ability to rise and express itself as sound. Abhinava Gupta discusses seven kinds of bliss in this context, with the seventh being Jagad-Ananda, or universal bliss.

The practice of Ucchara involves repeating a mantra while synchronizing it with one's breath. This should not be confused with the exercise in Shaktopaya where a yogi meditates on a specific mantra as the ultimate awareness of the junction between inhalation and exhalation. In Ucchara, the yogi vocalizes a mantra, generating sound in the physical plane while coordinating it with his breath.

Initially, this practice leads to a state of voidness, where the adept experiences a form of bliss called Nija-Ananda. In this state, the adept perceives the self as the real subject who experiences the objects. The next stage involves the realization that internal experiences are not entirely governed by external objects. This stage is marked by the freedom of the self from external objects perceived through the five senses, resulting in a type of bliss called Nira-Ananda.

In the subsequent stage, the Prana rises and manifests as gross physical sound, with the knowing subject experiencing objectivity through the rising Prana in the form of knowledge. The bliss experienced at this stage is Para-Ananda, characterized by the bliss of objectivity, with the bliss of subjectivity being lost.

Following this, the bliss arising from the incoming breath is characterized by the experience of all objects abiding in a single body of oneness, with all objects having a singular identity. This

bliss is called Brahma-Ananda, where the distinction between objects completely vanishes. The next stage is marked by the complete annihilation of objectivity, with all objective senses in the form of knowledge resting in the deep awareness of the self. The bliss that arises spontaneously at this stage is called Maha-Ananda, or great bliss.

If the yogi manages to reside in the 'I' devoid of any objectivity, he experiences the final state of bliss called Jagad-Ananda. In Jagad-Ananda, the adept realizes that everything abides in his own nature and is identical with him. The outer world is no longer separate from him; instead, he sees the outer world as a reflection of his own nature. This procedure is known as Prana-Yoga and is distinct from the Pranayama of the Patanjali Yoga Sutras.

As a result of these practices, six phenomena occur in an adept. They are:

1. Ananda
2. Udbhava
3. Kampa
4. Nidra
5. Ghurni
6. Maha-Vyapti

Ananda, or bliss, arises as a result of the recognition of the oneness between the objective reality and the subject. The distinction between the subject and the object vanishes, and the adept feels that the external world is a manifestation of his internal self.

Udbhava is the stage characterized by a sudden upsurge in the

body of the adept, which manifests as soon as the adept reaches the blissful state.

Following the state of Udbhava, the yogi, abiding in his real self, stops identifying himself in relation to external objects. As a result, his awareness of the physical body temporarily starts to wane, and the ignorance that had tethered the adept to his body is eliminated. This state manifests as a mild tremor or shaking of the entire body, which is referred to as Kampa.

The next stage is Nidra. The state of Nidra, or sleep, is characterized by a complete withdrawal from the objects of the sense organs, or the disappearance of the knowledge of external senses. However, unlike normal sleep, even though the external senses are shut, the yogi maintains a focused internal awareness during this stage. This internal awareness is the awareness of the self.

The inner alertness in the state of Nidra is strengthened through repeated practice. This strengthening of alertness culminates in a sensation of whirling, known as Ghurnatha or Ghurna. The whirling is felt as a result of coming into contact with the throbbing awareness.

The next stage, called Maha-Vyapti, is characterized by the complete dissolution of the limited subject and the recognition of the oneness of the self with the all-pervading consciousness or Para-Samvid. This stage is marked by the complete disappearance of the lesser subject, leaving only the pure, blissful state of Para-Bhairava.

These seven states of bliss and the six stages of Prana-Yoga are directly related to the awakening of Kundalini, which will be discussed in detail in a separate chapter.

Varna

We have now seen how Prana manifests as gross sound in Ucchara.

Doctrines of Shaivism state that before a word manifests on the gross physical plane, it exists as the unstruck, inarticulate sound. All letters reside in this indeterminate state, known as Varna, which is essentially the primal vibration of sounds. Intense contemplation on this sound is referred to as the Yoga of Varna. Certain other religious sects in India call it Shabda-Yoga.

Human breathing patterns are considered to be the emanation and dissolution of objective reality. The exhalation, which represents emanation, is depicted by the Srshti Bija, or the seed of creation, which is the letter 'sa'. The Samhara Bija, or the letter of dissolution, represents inhalation. This breathing cycle occurs 21,600 times a day in an individual. Fixing the mind on the inhalation and exhalation, and on these two seed sounds, constitutes the Varna Yoga. The Ham-Sah Mantra is called the Ajapa-Gayatri, or the non-recited Gayatri. This Ajapa-Gayatri represents the entire phenomenon of self-aware consciousness within us, which is a manifestation of the sound AUM. The manifestation of AUM takes place in nine stages, which will be covered in the practical part of this work.

Karana

The next aspect in Anavopaya is Karana, which occurs in seven stages:

1. Grahya
2. Grahaka
3. Chit
4. Nivesha
5. Vyapti

6. Tyaga
7. Akshepa

This technique aims to assimilate the objective world into consciousness, ultimately helping us realize that the objective world abides in the subject, and every object arises and rests in the supreme subject alone.

Grahya represents the objective world, while Grahaka represents the sense organs that help us perceive the immanent reality. In the stage of Chit, the adept deposits the objects of external senses into their consciousness, realizing that the knowledge of the external objects rests within the consciousness. Once the external objects are completely assimilated, the adept establishes their awareness in this inner consciousness, reaching the stage of Nivesha. At this stage, the external objects abide solely in the inner self, and the distinction between subject and object disappears. The next stage, Vyapti, is characterized by the realization that the entire universe is merely a mental emanation of the supreme subject. Here, the entire universe appears as abiding in the subject. The following stage, Tyaga, represents the abandonment of effort, and it signifies the transition to Shambhavopaya. Tyaga means abandonment; at this stage, a person can remain in the non-distinct state without further effort. The final stage, Akshepa, represents emanation. In this stage, the adept perceives the entire universe as an emanation of their own self, which is one with the supreme subject, Para-Shiva.

Sthana Kalpana
For those who find it challenging to practice the previously

mentioned methods, they can direct their attention to external objects such as idols, Yantras, images, icons, or symbols. By contemplating the meanings of these objects, the Vikalpas (mental constructs) gradually dissolve, merging with the awareness reflected by these icons and images. This process leads the adept to reach the stage of pure awareness, revealing their true inner nature.

The applications of these methods and their practical aspects will be discussed later. For now, from a scriptural perspective, the information provided serves as a foundational introduction.

Knowledge - The Light of Supreme

The concept of knowledge in Monistic Shaivism has been discussed in the context of the inherent power of the manifestation of the supreme light. Since self-awareness is the nature of this light, and manifesting the multitudes of objects through awareness is done in the form of knowledge, knowledge is essentially the awareness of these multitudes of objects. Therefore, the Shaivite doctrines consider knowledge to be an inherent power of the supreme subject. As we have already seen, the power of Shaktis cannot exist independently of each other, and the supreme light is the substratum through which they manifest; knowledge is also explained from this same perspective.

Since knowledge is nothing but the Jnana-Shakti, which is required to bring the Kriya-Shakti into fruition, the self-luminous light in its aspect of light or Prakasha serves as the substratum through which the Shakti manifests forms as objects. In other words, the Shakti is what enables the light to be aware of itself both as subject and object. This Vimarsha creates unity within duality and plurality. Thus, Vimarsha manifests the objects by being aware of them in the form of knowledge.

In the philosophical school of Pratyabhijnana (doctrine of recognition) within Shaivism, the Shaivites establish that knowledge is a manifestation of the supreme light. The Shaivites refute the Anatma Vada of Buddhist schools through multiple arguments. The Buddhist theory of Anatma Vada posits that there exists no subject or self, and that the self is impermanent like everything else. Due to

this no-self approach, Anatma Vada fails to explain the phenomenon of knowledge from an absolute point of view.

According to the no-self theory, there exists no permanent subject, i.e., there exists no permanent light. In this case, it would be literally impossible to cognize objects. Simply put, there would be no existence in the absence of a self-aware subject. Additionally, if the supreme is taken as Nirguna (without attributes), then the supreme light would be inert and could not manifest the cosmos; it would be devoid of awareness and knowledge. In both cases, the light would be unable to manifest the objective world from its inner awareness.

The Pratyabhijnana philosophy also explains the phenomenon of memory as a limited power of the unlimited Jnana-Shakti in the limited individual. The Anatma Vada fails to explain the phenomenon of memory, which is one of the essential attributes of Purusha, due to its notion of the absence of the supreme subject. Going deeper into the Pratyabhijnana philosophy or the Vijñānavāda school is not the purpose of this chapter, but proper examples will be cited and comparisons will be made throughout this chapter based on the aforementioned philosophies.

To understand the nature of knowledge, it is necessary to determine whether the phenomenon of knowledge is possible without the existence of a self-aware subject. The absence of a subject would only lead us to a nihilistic end, and reality would have to be accepted as something devoid of attributes. Therefore, the existence of a self, from an epistemological perspective, was established to justify the existence of the cosmos. However, if the existence of the supreme subject is established solely for epistemological needs,

then the existence of the subject could be questioned in the absence of empirical evidence. Thus, to address the concept of knowledge, multiple principles must be taken into consideration.

The Shaivite schools logically established the existence of a supreme subject by affirming that the subject exists as a knower in every cognition and as a doer in every action. However, the self is established only as 'a priori' from an epistemological perspective. Even if the supreme subject is considered to be an ontological existence, it must be assumed that the supreme is not material but is the agent through which everything material and immanent manifests. This supreme subject would be completely independent of the objects of thought and would be the ultimate consciousness that experiences everything.

If we consider the 'a priori' assumption of the existence of a subject, we need to address the existence of knowledge—whether knowledge is an inherent nature of consciousness or an extraneous property of consciousness is another problem. If knowledge is considered to be an adventitious factor, then a rift or schism is created between the subject and the knowledge of the object, since knowledge as an extraneous factor can only reside in consciousness when the subject temporarily becomes aware of the objective knowledge. If we consider this rift to be real, then the absolute view completely breaks down here. The Nyaya and Vaiseshika schools of philosophy consider knowledge to be impermanent. They consider the distinction between the knower and the known to be real and justify it by citing that the subject is not aware of its existence during the states of deep sleep, where only a void exists.

In contrast, Monistic Shaivism initially considers knowledge to

be an attribute and later uses logical explanations to establish that knowledge is an inherent nature of the self-aware consciousness. They use the analogy of sunlight obscured by clouds; when the clouds drift apart, the sun shines again. In the same way, the self is obscured by sleep, like a cloud obscuring the sun. To be more accurate, the adept resides in the Pralaya Kala state of subjectivity while drifting into sleep. Even while transcending from the Pralaya Kala to Vijnana Kala subjectivity and into higher states, the adept needs to traverse the Maha Maya Tatwa, which is situated between the Maya and Shuddha-Vidya Tatwa. During these phases, a subject afflicted by the Malas cannot appreciate the existence of the supreme subject in deep sleep. If the subject were not permanent, the empirical individual would forget everything after waking from sleep. The supreme subject, through his power of Smarana or Smriti (memory), is able to recall the events experienced before sleep. Smriti is an attribute of limited Jnana-Shakti in the Purusha or the limited individual.

Hence, through these experiences, the existence of a metaphysical Subject, and the knowledge being one with the known, is established. The Shaivites conclude that knowledge is inherent in the known, and they are analogous to light and illumination; attempting to differentiate between them is considered erroneous. Therefore, the concept of the absence of the subject is termed Mithya Jnana or erroneous knowledge.

For a Shaivite, the power of knowledge is an active power. Since the nature of the supreme is to bring objective reality into the light of consciousness, and the objective world is in the form of knowledge, knowledge is always creative in nature. Thus, it is an active power

of the Para Samvid or the supreme subject. The perception of knowledge is termed Indriya Artha Grahana. Indriyas refer to the sense organs, both internal and external, Artha refers to knowledge, and Grahana refers to grasp. Hence, the cognition of knowledge, or the act of knowing, is always active in nature.

The existence of the supreme light is self-evident. The knowledge of 'I' the limited subject, is like the images in a reflected mirror, limited by the Kaala and Niyati Tatwa, or the temporo-spatial limitations, and thus appears as the successive progression of objects. Memory also operates in succession due to these limitations created by the two Tatwas. This light, which manifests as the multitudes of objects in the form of knowledge, is the supreme subject. Due to the freedom of this subject, the supreme 'I' manifests as determinate and indeterminate knowledge, as unity and plurality, as subject and object, as knower and known. All differentiation, unification, segregation, agglomeration, and relations are made possible by this subject.

From the Shaivite point of view, knowledge, being an activity, is also self-luminous and thus self-revealing in nature. The moment we recognize that all actions and knowledge presuppose a doer and a knower, we understand that knowledge or activity is not possible without a subject who performs the activities in the form of knowledge. This conclusion establishes the ontological existence of a subject. Thus, the existence of the subject is self-evident through every action and thought.

In the absence of a subject, cognition is not possible, and existence would plunge into eternal darkness; it would be impossible to know the cosmos. In other words, the manifestation of the universe is not

possible. The cosmos has no way of knowing itself or revealing itself in the absence of a subject or awareness. Mere existence of knowledge is not revealing if it cannot reflect upon itself. Therefore, it is the subject who holds the knowledge in himself in the form of self-luminous light and reveals himself through every action he performs.

So the self is the foundation of all mental activities within us. We should understand that the self reveals itself through these mental activities, and these activities are the nature of the self. The activities are inherently one with the self; it is not as if the activities reside in the self, or that the self and activities overlap each other at regular intervals. Their inherent oneness is the only reason itself can reveal itself as knowledge.

Two Types of Knowledge

Monistic Shaivism is a doctrine of non-duality; as such, they have maintained their non-dual view throughout their praxis and work. The non-dual Vedantic school considers only the Brahman to be real, and the way we perceive the material world is unreal or an illusion. As such, the only way to realize the Brahman is to negate the illusion that obscures the Brahman. So they came to the conclusion that the negation of illusion caused by ignorance or nescience will finally lead to their salvation by uniting them with the ultimate Brahman.

The knowledge of the illusory world perceived by the individual who is afflicted by nescience or Avidya is illusory, since the material world, which appears as isolated from the Brahman, is illusory. So

the principle of Brahman alone is real. This is how the Monistic Vedanta scholars maintained absolutism in their scriptures and practices.

According to Monistic Vedanta followers, the phenomena of negation of Maya and Maya itself make up the two types of knowledge. The phenomenal knowledge is what an empirical individual perceives, and the transcendent knowledge is what happens when the illusory knowledge is negated. The illusory or unreal knowledge is nothing but the subject-object distinction in the phenomenal world, while the transcendent knowledge is nothing but the non-distinction of subject and object, everything being one with the subject. As per the view of Monistic Vedanta, the illusory world is real for the existence of life and serves that purpose. If the illusory world is for survival and, as per their theory, life itself is illusory, then why do they need to survive, since survival itself is not the nature of Brahman? The Monistic Vedanta school contradicts its own views using useless arguments.

Shaivites have considered two types of knowledge: Paurusha (empirical) and Baudha (supernal). The worldly knowledge uses the sense organs, both external and internal, to acquire knowledge about the limited objective reality. The Paurusha-Jnana is characterized by a schism between subject and object. Since the phenomenal knowledge uses the limited means of sense organs and inference, it is limited in many ways.

The nature of the supernal or transcended knowledge is different from the empirical knowledge in terms of subject-object distinction. In the most transcended states of awareness, the knowledge or the experiences are in terms of unity; a schism between subject and

object does not exist in this perception. The very nature of this type of knowledge is the ultimate realization that the object is one with the subject and cannot independently exist apart from the subject, and the nature of the subject is awareness which manifests the object. So the empirical individual finally recognizes his true nature through supernal knowledge and realizes that he is not a limited empirical individual, but his very nature is that of Para-Bhairava. This recognition is termed as Moksha or liberation or Jivan Mukti in Shaivism.

The dual division of knowledge is not exclusive to Shaivism alone; it has been seen in the Mahayana and Vedanta doctrines as well. The epistemological distinction of knowledge has its ontological origins in Buddhism and Vedanta. Even Sankaracharya, while using the simile of a rope being mistaken for a snake in twilight, has borrowed it from the Madhyamika school of Buddhism. While Buddhism and Monistic Vedanta schools have only given an epistemological importance to the Paurusha-Jnana or limited knowledge since they completely negate the concept of duality, Shaivites consider the subject-object distinction to be unreal but as necessary for the realization of unity. Since unity has no value without the distinction at first, the subject-object schism is dependent on the inherent oneness of the subject with the object because the former cannot be experienced without the latter. So Shaivites have accepted the subject-object schism from both an ontological and an epistemological perspective.

Empirical Knowledge

The empirical knowledge, which is gained as a result of

phenomenal perception, is limited in scope, but this does not mean that this empirical knowledge lacks ontological importance or a divine purpose. The self, even though it seems to be limited in nature, is identical with the supreme subject. The limitation that overlaps the empirical knowledge is limited in terms of limited thinking and limited activities, i.e., the limitation is perceived as a mental phenomenon or a physical phenomenon. At this stage, where Purusha is afflicted by all three Malas, he cannot recognize his true nature; hence, the Purusha acts on his whims and feels bound.

Another property of the limited knowledge worth mentioning here is that it has a nature and form. As per Indian thought, a substance or Padartha should have physical existence, it should be known through a name, and the perception of the substance through its properties should be expressed by the name. All limited knowledge is determinate in nature. So this kind of determination in the name of limited forms and names is always limited in scope.

The other aspect of limited scope is the two attributes of Samanya and Visesha. Samanya is nothing but similarity or identical appearance. Samanya is said to be "Vridhi Karana" or "Aprthak Bhava" or "Tulyartha Hi Samanyam." Samanya refers to "Tulya Artha" or similarity, or Samanya may also refer to the increase of the same substance. Vishesha is "Vipareeta" or "Viparya." Vishesha is also called "Prthak Bhava." Vishesha is the property that causes distinction and division or a negation of similar properties. So the determinate knowledge can only be expressed in terms of similarity and increase or distinction and decrease. Identifying one property as dissimilar from another is basically a negation of determinate knowledge.

These limited cognitions of objects based on their physical identifications like name, forms, etc., are rooted in the root principle or Prakriti Tatwa, which is afflicted by the three Gunas, viz., Satwa, Rajas, and Tamas. This kind of knowledge, as per Shaivism, is not permanent. Still, they consider this momentary interaction of the limited subject and object as an extension of Shiva in the Nara Bhava.

We have already seen that Para-Shiva limits himself as finite objects while manifesting the cosmos. When a limited individual cognizes a determinate finite knowledge, there exists an initial stage of indeterminate knowledge in the form of pure impulse. For example, when we say 'A Jar,' the jar exists as an image in our mind just before we utter that word. Before the jar appears as an image in the mind, there is a stage of pure impulse that is indeterminate in nature; this is called Bhasa or pure illumination. This indeterminate knowledge is in perfect unity with the subject; here, the inherent union of subject and object is evident. The indeterminate state of perception will be explained in detail later while dealing with the concept of goddess Kali as the ultimate metaphysical principle.

Supernal Knowledge

Supernal knowledge or Baudha-Jnana, by its very nature, is gnostic. It is the knowledge of the unity of subject and object; as such, it is not perceived by sense organs or logic. So a genuine question may arise as to how this knowledge, which is beyond logic and reasoning or which cannot be perceived by external senses, can be validated or inferred. In certain schools of Indian philosophy, it is called Yoga Lakshana Pratyashati, literally translated as knowledge

gained through Yoga or union, or self-realization.

As we have already seen, the empirical knowledge depends on limited means to apprehend the limited objects, owing to the fact that it uses the internal (Manas, Buddhi, and Ahamkara) and external sense organs (five sense organs). This phenomenal knowledge manifests as subject-object distinction. So it is not suitable to achieve the ultimate goal of self-realization. Also, intellectual knowledge initially is afflicted by Malas. So the intellectual knowledge will be confined to the logic based on internal and external sense organs; hence, it is limited in nature. Thus, the intellect, upon overcoming the three impurities, finally recognizes the nature of the real self; as a result, the supernal knowledge flashes and the person reaches the state of subject-object unity.

This supernal knowledge can be attributed to the indeterminate state when there is an initial impulse before the thoughts manifest as images in the mind. This state cannot be comprehended or fathomed. This knowledge, since it is free from any limitations and not afflicted by Maya and the five Kanchukas, is unlimited in nature; hence, it cannot be grasped by limited shapes, forms, and names. This knowledge is self-evident in the form of awareness. This knowledge is attained through Vikalpa Kshaya (disappearance of thought constructs). A question can easily arise in our minds as to how knowledge can be realized without the use of words, forms, and images.

Certain knowledge can only be experienced in our mind. The sweet smell of jasmine flowers can never be completely conveyed through words, even though words like pleasant, sweet, etc., may partially convey the idea of the smell of jasmine. But it is far from the

real experience that a person goes through while smelling the flower. This experiential knowledge can never be completely conveyed through words. As such, this state of awareness, which is the knowledge of the self, can only be experienced in the indeterminate state mentioned earlier. When a person passively observes his thoughts and eventually identifies himself as independent of the thought constructs, the awareness withdraws from the external objects of senses in the form of images, sounds, etc. At this stage, the mind reaches a vacant state which is free from Vikalpa, and then a profound state of awareness is experienced, eventually dissolving the barrier between the subject and object. The yogi finally identifies the object as an emanation of the subject.

These concepts are born from the orientation towards certain internal processes. When a Shaivite tries to convey the experience through words, images, or forms, it becomes conceptual and determinate. No amount of words can completely convey the experiences that the individual goes through in the transcended states of awareness. Hence, the Shaivites termed it as Pratyabhijnana, or recognition. Since the experience is some kind of recognition, they were very clear about the fact that this knowledge is completely experiential and not conceptual.

The Paurusha-Jnana or phenomenal knowledge is also experiential in nature, experienced mentally or through the five sense organs. The major difference of experiences exists within the nature of perception. In the case of empirical knowledge, the object of experience exists external to the self. While the supernal knowledge is achieved by being aware of the self, the object is internal; i.e., the subject himself becomes the object of knowledge.

It is the knowledge of self that plays a major role in Baudha-Jnana. Later on, the experiences expand to the outside reality and eventually the person reaches Bhairava Vyapti or recognizes his identity with Bhairava. The entire universe arising and resting in Bhairava alone. He realizes that the object is just a reflection of the subject in the form of awareness, and the reflection takes place within the subject.

In order to make it clearer, let us consider the knowledge that is gained through the sense organs in everyday life. The senses act as a medium to establish a connection between the subject and object. So, when the contact between the sense organs and the objects of senses is established, the three internal sense organs—mind, intellect, and ego—comprehend it and ensure that the self is able to cognize it. Later, when the individual wants to convey the experiences he went through to another person, the subject or self uses the help of the three internal sense organs and the Karma Indriyas (organs of action), especially Vak (speech), to convey the message in the form of words. If the knowledge gained is conveyed through a picture, then the Karma Indriya Pani (hands) are used, and so on. A certain amount of limited experience and inference accompanied with logic is used in these experiences to gain knowledge and to conceptualize the knowledge along with the use of Indriyas.

In the case of supernal knowledge, which is in the form of awareness, it cannot be explained or conceptualized in the manner described above. Since this awareness is the medium through which the conceptualized knowledge manifests, the agent of conceptualized knowledge can never be conveyed as an object of conceptualized knowledge. But it is experienced in states of awareness that transcend the sense organs and the conceptualized thoughts. This knowledge,

which is in the form of transcended awareness, is not an object of conceptualized knowledge; hence, it cannot be conveyed through empirical means.

So now it is safe to say that supernal knowledge is formless and shapeless, and without any images. The supreme knowledge is the knowledge of consciousness itself, and the nature of consciousness cannot be expressed in any verbal language. Consciousness is always with awareness; with this awareness, consciousness gives rise to images, forms, and words. As such, the knowledge of consciousness can never be conveyed through the objects of awareness. While this knowledge becomes self-evident when it is realized.

Theory of Causal Efficacy and Illusion

When it comes to epistemology, every theory should be logical. Now, the validation of supernal knowledge is necessary from an epistemological point of view. Some Indian philosophical schools opine that knowledge should be validated through external and internal senses, while other schools opine that the knowledge is self-validated.

The causal efficacy theory accepted by Indian philosophy can be easily depicted with an example. If a person perceives a jar, it could only be validated as real knowledge if the jar serves the purpose of holding water. So the knowledge of a jar is affirmed by the ability of the jar to hold water in itself. But Shaivites refute this view by citing an example where a person sees a jar filled with water in a dream state. For the time being, the jar is real and also satisfies the causal efficacy theory. The above dream may be felt as real but is

just an illusory knowledge that fades away after the person awakes from sleep.

If we examine the case from another perspective, the illusory knowledge of a dream has some valid influence on the person even after he wakes up. In cases where a person gets mentally traumatized after a nightmare, or in cases where a person mistakes a rope for a serpent in twilight and suffers a mental shock, the illusory knowledge has a direct impact on the mental dimension of the person. Even though in both cases the illusory knowledge is a projection of the mind, it still has concrete effects on the subjective reality of the person. So it is as real as any physical matter until the person is freed from the mental shock, i.e., after realizing that the perception of the snake and events in the nightmare are unreal.

In the same way, a person frees himself from the illusion of subject-object distinction once he understands that duality is a mental projection. Similar to the projection of a serpent on the rope, the empirical individual projects the idea of duality in the non-dual world. Where did this duality come from? In the former case, the person has perceived the serpent through stories and in reality, which created fear in him. How could an empirical individual project duality without experiencing it firsthand? Monistic Vedanta and other Indian philosophical schools failed to answer these questions. For a Shaivite, the all-pervading subject, while manifesting the cosmos, reflects it from his awareness in his own image. However, he contracts himself and limits himself to manifest the infinite as seemingly finite. In the due process, the lord, being shrunken to a finite aspect, manifests duality in the empirical individual.

While Monistic Vedanta failed to answer this question and

attributed it to a primal Maya (illusion in this context) or Avidya (ignorance) with no beginning, they again failed to answer the origin of illusion or ignorance.

From a Shaivite point of view, knowledge is nothing but self-revealing. Knowledge is manifestation. Knowledge is identical with forms and appearance. If that is the case, we may have to suspect the illusory knowledge as being real. As we have seen in the above example, illusory knowledge is real as long as it lasts, like dreams or mistaking a rope for a snake, etc. It is upon the realization of the true nature of self that the illusion ends. Shaivites accepted a hierarchical arrangement of ideal reality. As we have seen in the part discussing Abhasa, how our reality is a reflection of our awareness and how the cosmos along with all the limited subjects in it are a reflection of the supreme subject. It is clear that the illusory knowledge, owing to its limitations, is impermanent. As such, one of the major differences between the limited and supernal knowledge lies in the impermanence of a limited subject. So it has to be understood that illusory knowledge is unreal from an ontological view, and it is real from an axiological perspective.

Erroneous Knowledge as the Cause of Ignorance

As per the doctrines of Shaivism, ignorance is a partial knowledge or incomplete knowledge. Ignorance can never be considered as the absence of knowledge. When a person mistakes a rope for a serpent, or mistakes a statue for a real person in dim light, the person only has incomplete knowledge about the object. A rope shares some attributes with a serpent, and a statue may look like a real man in

dim light. In both cases, the observer projects a certain element onto the real object. For this mental projection to be possible, the person should have cognized the appearance of a man and a serpent beforehand, and the memory has been recalled at the appropriate time and overlapped with the real object, thus creating an illusion. This kind of partial knowledge is called Apurnakhyati. So in order for Apurnakhyati to manifest, the consciousness must project itself as an object. Thus, the erroneous knowledge, which is the cause of ignorance, is incomplete knowledge, but not Abhava or absence of knowledge. This illusory knowledge is similar to the limited empirical knowledge acquired by the internal and external sense organs, owing to the fact that both are partial.

As to the ontological position of the limited individuals, the world that we perceive as outside us and the limited subjects which perceive the objects are in truth a reflection of the supreme universal subject Parama-Shiva. If we consider the world to be independent of the universal subject, then there exist two mutually exclusive, independent autonomous entities with a mutual causal relationship. That is absurd from a logical and ontological perspective. The erroneous knowledge here is the subject-object distinction felt in the immanent world.

While explaining ignorance, it is necessary to explain the concept of liberation in Indian philosophical schools. Certain schools consider liberation to be a freedom from the Samsaric cycle of birth, death, and rebirth, and a fulfillment of the karmic debts that have been accumulated. It is considered that a person continues to take births in different bodies, depending on his actions or Karma. A person who lives his life sticking to the scriptures of Dharma will

eventually be liberated from his karmic fruitions and will halt the cycle of birth, rebirth, and death. Then the person will be finally absorbed in the all-pervading god.

The above view has been accepted by many Indian schools, while Shaivites consider a limited person as already complete and identical with Para Bhairava. However, the individual is not able to recognize his real nature. Since everything that manifests is of the nature of supreme Bhairava and can manifest only in him, being re-absorbed into the supreme god is absurd. The liberated person is someone who has recognized his true nature and has eliminated the distinction of subject and object in the immanent world and has realized the whole world to be the exalted will of Bhairava. Birth, rebirth, and death are nothing but a shift in awareness from one Abhasa to another Abhasa for a Shaivite. The entire birth, rebirth, and death are just shifts in Abhasas done playfully by the self-realized yogi.

So vanquishing the partial knowledge or ignorance is the key to liberation in Shaivism.

Ignorance or partial knowledge is also of two types: Baudha-Ajnana and Paurusha-Ajnana. The Paurusha-Ajnana manifests as the lesser 'I', or the limited subject. It gives the sensation of an identity with regards to name, place, activities, etc., while it negates the real nature of the self. The Baudha-Ajnana manifests in the form of conceptual knowledge and logic, in the form of thought constructs. In both cases, the individual is deprived of self-awareness; instead, the awareness is oriented towards the limited self, and the individual cognizes the world within the bounds of five veils and Maya, resulting in the distinction of the subject and object.

Shaivites opine that all determinate knowledge arises from the

indeterminate state. Before the self becomes aware of external objects, there is always an impulse to become aware of a particular object. For example, a person sees a jar on a table. Initially, the Abhasas in the form of table and jar are reflected in his vision and reach his mind, and the self cognizes the Abhasas in the form of objects, i.e., jar and table. But when the person says he sees a jar, we need to understand that the self became aware of the Abhasa called a jar out of the other Abhasas.

Here, the Manas, being an internal sense organ, is limited in its perception. To illustrate this attribute, Indian philosophers propounded a theory with an example called Utpala Shata Patra Nyaya. It says that if a person stacks a hundred lotus leaves together and stabs them with a needle from one end until it reaches the other end, even though the needle may seem to penetrate all the leaves at once, it can only penetrate one leaf at a time. So the determinate knowledge which the self perceives using the three internal sense organs and the external sense organs is limited in nature due to Maya and the five veils.

The Baudha-Ajnana, which is more mental in nature and creates the sensation of a limited 'I', along with the Paurusha-Ajnana, causes ignorance and a bound state. As a result, only partial knowledge of the objects can be attained through the external and internal sense organs, and eventually, the self resides in the schism created between subject and object.

Triadic Power of the Empirical Individual

As we have understood, knowledge is nothing but the manifestation of the supreme consciousness as the cosmos. In a limited individual,

i.e., Purusha, the limited power of knowledge has three aspects: limited Jnana-Shakti or the power of knowing finite things, Smriti-Shakti or the power to recall previously perceived objects, and Apohana-Shakti or the power of distinction or discernment. Within the constraints of the five veils of Maya, an individual operates in the limited world with these three powers. With the limited power of knowing, we are able to cognize limited Abhasas that arise from the infinite light of consciousness. For example, an Abhasa called a jar, pot, car, tree, etc., is perceived separately due to this limited power of knowing.

The power of Smriti or remembrance is the factor which maintains the continuous functioning of the Jnana-Shakti. The power of remembrance or recalling the Abhasa previously experienced helps the limited Purusha to function properly in daily life. Without the ability to recall previously perceived Abhasas, a person cannot function in the immanent world. The Para-Samvid, which manifests as limited Purusha, is able to retain and recall or revive the finite Abhasas using the power of remembrance.

The Apohana-Shakti is the power of discernment. The subject and object, prior to manifestation, exist in unity; the limited knowledge which manifests as the subject-object distinction became possible thanks to Apohana-Shakti. It is the Apohana-Shakti that made the subject manifest as distinct from itself. Apohana-Shakti makes the cognition of finite things possible by creating distinctions in the objective world. For example, a cow is distinct from a dog. The distinction which manifests in the objective world is in the form of dissimilarities and negations.

Smriti: A Further Investigation

Shaivites refuted the Buddhist view of the impermanence of objective knowledge, using the concept of the power of recalling or memory as their tool to refute it. Shaivites argued that the existence of a self is impossible if the subject is impermanent. This, in turn, would make the cognition and synthesis of different objects impossible in the mundane world. If the subject and the objects of experiences are impermanent, then the recalling power should not exist. The Buddhists cannot account for the existence of memory using their Anatma Vada.

The object of memory may seem to shine from past experiences, but whenever it is recalled, the object is experienced in the present. So, the object from the past reflects in the present moment, owing to the power of Smriti-Shakti. The limited subject unifies the Abhasas experienced in the past into the present moment and brings about the unification of the past Abhasa with the present Abhasa. This object of limited Vimarsha is divided into two: one is a permanent Vimarsha, and another is a momentary Vimarsha. Momentary Vimarshas dissolve back into the 'I' immediately after they are recalled into awareness, while the permanent Vimarshas persist. This explains the mental traumas and post-traumatic stress disorder that people go through after an unwholesome or nightmarish experience.

Memory exists in the form of thoughts and is another determinate knowledge. The memory of an object is possible only if the limited subject has cognized the Abhasa previously. When a subject recalls an object from his memory and relives it, the memory manifests as exclusion or inclusion. For example, if we recall a car that we saw

earlier, our mind distinguishes it from other cars while bringing the features of the particular car to the present, like the color, company, or size of the car, etc. Our mind spontaneously recognizes the similarity and dissimilarity in the recalled Abhasa. Prior to the time of recollection of the objects of memories, an indeterminate state exists; this phase is the impulse exerted by the subject to recall the particular object of memory. The 'I' still exists as the observer and the doer during the recalling phase, and there exists a moment of indeterminacy. The Purusha or the limited consciousness pulls back the objects of memories from the limited Abhasa cognized previously and brings them into the present. It must be understood that the impulse to recollect an object from the previously experienced Abhasa is an act of will, to bring back a particular Abhasa into light from the past.

By contemplating on the awareness of the self while the self recalls each moment of past Abhasa, a person can realize his true nature. To do this, we have to keep in mind that the ability to recall a previously experienced object is possible because it is one with the universal subject and manifests as determinate memories in the limited 'I'. It is through this power that a Yogi uses and manifests the power of Mantras, which is nothing but the reflection of awareness in the immanent world. The adept will realize this truth once he starts to concentrate on the indeterminate knowledge which exists as an impulse prior to recalling an object of the past to the present. In this way, the adept realizes the true nature of the self, how the supreme subject brings the cosmos into light through his awareness, in the same way the limited individual brings the object into light from his memory.

Manifestation of the Word

One of the interesting concepts in Shaivism is the notion of Shakti as the spoken word or Vak, which is the ultimate power of creation. The concept of Vak and Vak-Shakti is not exclusive to Shaivites; even the Sanskrit grammarians considered reality to be a manifestation of the words spoken by the supreme subject. Shaivites consider Vak to be an inherent nature of the supreme consciousness, while the grammarians considered Vak to be independent of the consciousness of the supreme. Somananda, a great Shaivite saint, in his work *Shiva Drishti*, criticizes the view of grammarians and establishes that Vak, or the divine word, is one with the Chit-Shakti of Para-Shiva. The grammarians considered only three stages of speech: Pasyanti, the visionary stage of speech; Madhyama, the intermediate stage; and Vaikhari, the gross stage where the articulations of vocal cords, etc., are involved.

As we have already seen, Shakti is the self-luminosity or the Vimarsha, and the doctrines of non-dual Shaivism, being absolute Monistic, maintain that consciousness is the ultimate principle. All thoughts are in the form of words of a specific language, and every word is made of phonetics, which are called Shabda. Since the phonemes are one with Shiva and are a reflection of awareness, the spoken word or Vak is assumed to be the Shakti.

Para-Vak

The concept of the Four-fold speech is not exclusive to Shaivism; the Vedas also accept the four stages of speech. In the previous

chapters, we saw that the inherent nature of light is Vimarsha or reflection. Furthermore, the true nature of self is consciousness, which is active in the form of self-awareness or Pratyavamarsha. The Para-Vak is nothing but the freedom of the supreme subject to manifest or actualize the cosmos; it represents the sovereign power of the supreme consciousness to create, unaffected by space and time, and is the essence or core of the Para-Samvid. This freedom is the result of the Ananda-Shakti or bliss, which is described as eternal consciousness without beginning or end, with no birth or death, and unaffected by any determinate, limited thought constructs or space and time. The very nature of this consciousness is the spontaneous expression of will in the form of the cosmos.

This aspect also represents the Purna-Aham, which was explained in the previous chapters. In the doctrines of Shaivism, this speech is also known by many names, such as Kali, who performs the five actions; Chandi, who holds the cosmic egg in her womb; Karshini, who devours; Hrdaya, or essence; Vani, or speech; and Tri-Shakti, who is the embodiment of the three powers of Will, Knowledge, and Action. From the perspective of the doctrines, it is clear that the supreme speech or Para-Vak is identical with the supreme self-aware consciousness. So, Chit-Shakti of Para-Shiva is nothing but Para-Vak. The different names used in different contexts reveal the multitude of attributes embodied by this consciousness and the actions executed by the supreme. For example, if the universe is expressed as speech, then the self-reflective or self-aware consciousness is the Para-Vak. The ability to be self-aware is the real Shakti or power or potential of the consciousness to create. This Para-Vak constitutes the inner speech, which is infinite and indeterminate and devoid of

any objectivity, which is full of bliss and abides in self-awareness. This indeterminate word, in the form of reflection or self-luminosity, is the causative factor for the actualization of the determinate words and cosmos in the form of the thirty-six Tatwas and the letters that make up the Tatwas.

Pashyanti

In one of the previous chapters, we saw that creation starts from the Icha-Shakti, or will aspect of Para-Shiva. In the phonematic emanation of the cosmos, this Icha-Shakti manifests in two ways: unagitated (Akshobatmaka) and agitated (Kshobatmaka). When a calm water body gets agitated, there is an imperceptible initial subtle movement in the water body that culminates in bigger waves. Similarly, there is an imperceptible movement in the Icha-Shakti of Para-Shiva before the movement towards creation begins.

Then the multitudes of objects in the form of the universe appear suddenly in the awareness of the supreme subject, which is termed Knowledge or Jnana-Shakti. This then culminates in Kriya-Shakti, where the actualization of the cosmos is complete.

Pashyanti is the state of speech when the Will aspect of Shiva becomes agitated, and it starts to move towards the act of creation. The literal meaning of Pashyanti refers to the act of seeing. Here, the subject sees the objective world in his mental awareness in its completeness. Even though there exists a slight distinction between the seen and the seer in this stage, the distinction is not manifest. In the triadic manifestation of Shakti, this refers to the Ghora state or Parapara state. It abides in the Bhedabheda state, or partly dual and partly unified state. This state is a general state of indeterminate

knowledge. A simple analogy may suffice to clarify the concept here: the white light, which consists of visible and invisible spectra, exists as white light before splitting into its component parts; the white light prior to its splitting is in the stage of Pashyanti.

In Pashyanti, subjectivity is more dominant than objectivity. The Vikalpas are not determinate in this stage. In the stage of Pashyanti, the universe exists as pure knowledge, without distinctions and determinate thought constructs. This stage is marked by an inner awareness of what is to manifest in an indeterminate manner. Here, Shiva feels as 'I AM THIS,' with the objective universe held in the subjective awareness in an undifferentiated manner.

Madhyama-Vak

Madhyama-Vak is literally translated as the intermediate speech. It is the dimension of speech characterized by mild distinction. This stage also abides in the dimension of Ghora or Parapara Shakti. Previously, in Pashyanti, the object resided in the subject; here, in the intermediate state of Vak, the object and subject have a distinction and determinate forms, and knowledge arises. This stage is seen in the Tatwas of Mana, Buddhi, and Ahankara. Buddhi bestows the power of differentiation and distinction within the self. In the stage of Madhyama, the object has not externalized, but the tendency to externalize the objective world reaches an ultimatum here. However, the object still remains in the internal organs in the intermediate stage. The state of Madhyama marks the first stage of distinction between the knower and the known; as such, it is also the initial manifestation of spoken words, sentences, etc. Since the object has not been externalized here, the knower and the known

seem to have overlapped with each other.

Vaikhari-Vak

It is the final stage of manifestation of speech; this is the gross speech. This is the stage of speech characterized by the complete seeming externalization of the objectivity from the subject. The knower and known are seemingly distinct in this dimension. This is the speech where the vocal cords are involved. Every spoken language, word, and sentence comes under this stage. This stage of Vaikhari is actualized in the Prthwi Tatwa, or the gross physical word. This corresponds to the Apara or Ghora Tara form of Shakti. Even though the Vaikhari state of speech may seem to reside in the state of Malas or impurities, it is still one with Para.

Speech: A Further Thought

Now that we have briefly understood the concept of Vak, let us see what other schools of Indian philosophy think of Vak. The concept of Vak, as we have seen, is not exclusive to Shaivism. In the Rig-Veda, Vak is said to be one with the supreme Brahman. The Brhad Aranyaka Upanishad states that Vak is the supreme, and only through Vak is the supreme known. Vak is nothing but the logos, the monad which gives rise to the cosmos. In Shaivism, the entire universe is considered a manifestation of the divine Vak, while the phonemes in the form of letters constitute the fundamental, structural, and functional unit of Vak. It is a fact that thoughts manifest as speech in humans; as such, it is assumed that the cosmos in divine consciousness manifests as speech.

The supreme feminine principle is said to be the embodiment of

all the phonetics and the four stages of Vak, which is nothing but the pure, unadulterated real nature of self. From the indeterminate stage, when the supreme subject wants to express himself in the form of the cosmos, the Para state transforms into the initial thought forms where the universe exists in an undifferentiated, indeterminate state, in an all-comprehensive vision which is yet to be. In this manner, Para assumes the form of Pashyanti. This Pashyanti is the all-comprehensive vision of the universe that is to be actualized; this stage corresponds to the Sada-Shiva Tatwa.

The Pashyanti undergoes further evolution, and the knowledge of the objects becomes distinguishable as 'That' or 'This'. This stage is termed Madhyama or the intermediate stage. This is also called the Hiranya-Garbha Shabda or the sound of Hiranya Garbha. This state is characterized by the existence of thoughts in the mental realm in the form of words, sentences, etc., before they manifest as gross sound in the physical world. The Madhyama form of speech corresponds to the Ishwara Tatwa, and the Madhyama coming out as the gross speech, which uses the articulation of vocal cords, etc., is called Vaikhari and corresponds to the Shuddha-Vidya Tatwa. The four stages of speech correspond to the five powers of Para-Bhairava, which have been explained in detail in a previous chapter.

It is clear at this point that the supreme god Parama-Shiva is not an inert, actionless nothingness or void, but is an ever-dynamic, self-affirming consciousness which expresses itself in the form of creation. It is both transcendent and immanent. It is transcendent in the sense that it is the self-affirming light of consciousness and maintains its infinite potential, and immanent in the sense that it has the ability to express itself by manifesting the cosmos within

itself in all its pristine glory. So the supreme consciousness is an eternal principle that is both self-expanding and self-contracting in nature. Hence, creation is nothing but the self-manifestation and self-contraction of the self-aware consciousness. Nothing apart from it exists, and it depends on no extraneous powers to actualize these effects.

The adepts of Shaivism have confirmed that the supreme speech, or Para-Vak, is nothing but the light of pure consciousness. The indeterminate word or logos, which shines forth as the causation for the manifestation of the immanent world, is termed Shabda-Brahman or the Logos. This indeterminate logos constitutes the cosmos and every object existing in the cosmos. In other words, the majestic, magnanimous sound or logos is nothing but the potency of all creative powers, reflected as the self-affirming awareness of consciousness, emerging as the cosmos. This transcendental sound is the supra-causal principle which is one with the self-luminous consciousness. This supra-causal awareness holds within itself all the determinate and indeterminate sounds of all phonemes, alphabets, etc.

All the 50 letters of the alphabet, all the mantras, all the divine words and sentences, and also all the mundane words, languages, etc., are pervaded by this supra-causal logo. The supreme self-luminous light manifests itself as the logos, which in turn expresses itself through the multitudes of objects in the universe, through space and time, through different stages of life, matter, and all the cyclical events. It is the quintessence of every word ever spoken and every thought that arises in the minds of sentient beings.

Four States of Consciousness

Experience is the fundamental idea upon which non-dual Shaivism is developed. Experience is nothing but self-awareness; experience is being conscious of objects. When we say "I experience," we are essentially affirming that "I am conscious." Self-aware consciousness is what gives rise to experience; every experience is a fragment of awareness that arises in the consciousness of the limited subject. Experience is what constitutes individual reality. It is necessary to reassert that reality is created by consciousness, and reality will turn to cinders when consciousness ceases to exist. Consciousness is a factual truth; it is immanent and real.

For a Shaivite, consciousness is as real as the material world around them, since reality is something that cannot be denied or disproved. Even if we deny the existence of the self, the self is proved through the act of denial itself. Consciousness is the supreme principle, and the existence of the supreme god is self-evident through the consciousness of every empirical subject in the cosmos. Para-Shiva is recognized as the core self of every limited empirical subject. Every empirical individual is conscious. Para-Shiva cannot be denied, as the denier himself is Para-Shiva. As such, the existence of divine providence is self-evident. Experience is not possible in the absence of consciousness. Consciousness is identical with immanent existence. The recognition of the inherent oneness between consciousness and existence is the Ananda-Shakti, or bliss, of Para-Shiva.

According to Shaivites, consciousness exists in four states. Now

let us explore these four states and what constitutes consciousness.

Jagrat - The Wakeful State

Jagrat literally translates to the wakeful state of consciousness. In our everyday life, our awareness operates in the state of duality. We perceive the immanent world, which is filled with a multitude of finite objects. It is through this experience that our wakeful awareness expresses itself.

There are four states of consciousness accepted in Shaivite doctrines, and each state of experience and consciousness is recognized through this framework. We perceive the immanent world, which is shrouded by the five principles of Maya, and we experience a distinction between subject and object in terms of space and time.

When we contemplate these facts, we infer that our percepts have no inherent value or meaning without concepts or ideas attached to them. For example, a beautiful flower may remind us of a loved one, a yellow rose might symbolize friendship, a red rose might represent love, and white flags are associated with peace. Thus, while perceiving an object in the immanent world, our memories serve the function of attaching ideas to it, thereby giving the object meaning.

Consciousness is able to discern, recall ideas, and attach meanings to objects. Consequently, Shaivism accepts four dimensions of consciousness: Jagrat (the waking state), Swapna (the dream state), Sushupti (the dreamless state), and Turiya (the transcended state).

We will examine these states one by one. As previously mentioned, the waking state is concerned with the immanent corporeal world,

where we are conscious of objects that are separate from us, and perception involves a distinction between the knower and the known. Since the state of Jagrat deals with a limited objective world and determinate ideas associated with it, it is limited in its awareness and capacity to perceive.

The four states of consciousness are purely ontological, accepted based on the logical analysis of Shaivite scholars and Shaiva epistemology.

Swapna - The State of Dreams

Swapna literally translates to dreams. Dreams have intrigued many psychologists, and numerous studies have been conducted on this dimension by various psychologists since the early twentieth century. For a Shaivite, the dream state is as important as the wakeful state, as dreams reflect certain deeply buried ideas and objects that subsequently precipitate into the wakeful state. Psychologists and psychiatrists often ignore the ontological and philosophical implications of dreams and this dimension of consciousness.

Humans spend an average of one-third of their life sleeping, and dreams arise spontaneously during this sleep. In these states of dreams, the human mind projects many objective realities. These may seem unreal, but for a sleeping person, and for the duration of sleep, they are as real as the immanent world. As previously noted, a horrible nightmare can have lasting effects on us; it can traumatize us for a considerable amount of time until the nightmare is recognized as unreal. Nightmares can also create enduring fears, such as the fear of death, losing a cherished object, or a loved one. All these are manifestations of the dimension filled with dreams.

Even though dreams may seem unreal, they have genuine effects on the human psyche.

A psychologist might consider dreams to be a manifestation of deeper desires and fears buried within humans or that dreams may be stimulated by external factors present during sleep. For a Shaivite, perception is determinate and finite in the wakeful state, but this is not the case with dreams. Continuous chains of memories, attention, and discernment pre-necessitate the wakeful state of consciousness, whereas dreams are not restricted by criteria of limited space, time, and knowledge. Dreams are free, spontaneous, and entirely driven by playful imagination. What may seem completely opposite and contradictory can manifest in dreams. It is unrestrained imagination. For a Shaivite adept, dreams are nothing but spontaneous perception.

What kind of ontological and epistemological significance do dreams hold in Shaivism? They signify a dimension of pure perception filled with ideas, thoughts, and objects that are unrestrained and not affected by external impressions. Awareness in the dream state is free from external objects, regardless of what those objects might be. Dreams represent the intrinsic attributes of consciousness.

Dreams are not only independent of external objects chronologically but also free and spontaneous, enjoying a certain freedom from the more determinate ideas of the Jagrat state. Dreams appear real to us primarily due to the ideas and meanings associated with them. It is the ideas associated with images and objects that spontaneously bring dreams into reality or animate them. The state of Jagrat, characterized by determinate conscious ideas, seems independent of unconscious percepts. For example, mistaking a rope for a snake illustrates how, once the true nature of the rope

is recognized, the illusion of the snake disappears. This indicates that by carefully examining the impressions, the illusion altogether vanishes. Thus, perceptions work without the complete awareness of the individual. Additionally, perceptions associated with conscious ideas and superimposed by illusory knowledge lose their reality and are mistaken for the illusory idea imposed upon them.

The pure ideas arising from the subconscious mind are rarely recognized except in the case of some artists, poets, and musicians, who tap into the infinite source of inspiration and creativity found in their subconscious mind. The author does not intend to suggest that dreams are more immanent than physical reality. Instead, dreams provide proof of certain possibilities for great inspiration and creativity, manifesting as ideas, ideals, and similar objects. Whatever manifests from an individual has its origin in the subconscious mind.

To understand this dimension of consciousness, an adept needs to develop keen observation of what arises in their awareness in the form of thoughts. Our understanding of this field of consciousness is directly proportional to our ability to free ourselves from the influence of external physical objects. The more we identify ourselves as independent of external objects, the more mental freedom we enjoy. Once we transcend the notion of identifying ourselves in terms of objects outside ourselves, we can better penetrate the messages and ideas conveyed by the subconscious mind through dreams. The state of dreams and experiences in this state of awareness is called Taijas, meaning light or fire; it is characterized by cognition. This state is spontaneous perception, independent of any outside object.

Sushupti - The Dreamless State

This state is a layer deeper than the state of dreams. Even though dreams are determinate, finite, and have forms, they are part of thoughts that arise in our mental dimension. The third state, Sushupti, pertains to the dimension of ideas and concepts. The renowned Sanskrit grammarian Panini discusses how six such concepts can be integrated into a determinate thought. For example, consider a man swimming in a freshwater river at sunset, which is located near a hill. We have the man, the river, the sunset, the hill, and the water. In other words, we have an agent, space, time, and objects all combined to create vivid images in our mind.

To produce a single thought entity, our mind summons various ideas and weaves them together to form a coherent image. Where do these ideas come from? How do they arrange themselves into a specific pattern that gives us a concrete meaning? An agent synchronizes these ideas into a single, meaningful thought form in a harmonious manner. As previously mentioned, thoughts are merely objects of awareness and represent the play of the supreme consciousness. The subjective consciousness, manifesting in the form of imagination, weaves these objects into a single thought form and presents it meaningfully. All these processes are spontaneous. There is always a doer, an actor who creates thought patterns.

Whenever there is an object of awareness, there is a subject who becomes aware of that object. In other words, there is always a knower whenever there is a known object. Whether the objects are known in the fully awakened state or in the state of dreams, there is always a subject who is the knower. The subject and object are essential for the actualization of any experience. The relationship

between subject and object is universal. They are always together. The very nature of the subject is to become aware of or to know the object, and the object cannot exist without the knower. Thus, it is clear that consciousness has two aspects: a subject and an object. The knower and the known are the two attributes that constitute the self-affirming consciousness. Consciousness gives rise to these two phenomena but transcends them as well. Experience always demonstrates that the known exists only in the knower. A fundamental aspect of all conscious experiences is that knowledge presents itself as an absolute unity of all objects within the subject. Thus, light illuminates itself in the form of subject and object. This is the epistemological view of Shaivites.

What does this dreamless state signify for a mystic? What knowledge does it convey for those in search of their inner self? When people experience dreamless sleep, they usually feel a void state of mind. Even though they may recall this state as a void, they cannot fully understand the nature of this void. Consciousness is not suspended even during deep dreamless sleep, which is why the subject considers it a state of voidness.

The dreamless sleep is essentially devoid of any objective thought. If it is devoid of any determinate thoughts, how can we consider the dreamless stage as a state of awareness or knowledge? How could there be any Jnana-Shakti (knowledge power) of Parama-Shiva in this state if there is no objectivity? Can a blind person be aware that they cannot see certain images? They are simply not aware of the existence of these forms and images. After waking from deep sleep, we have a notion of the voidness we experienced. This suggests that there was some awareness during this state that helped us recognize

the nothingness we felt. We can understand that the nothingness of the dreamless state is recalled from memory, but it is not inferred. A person might say they had a sound sleep because they had no dreams. Now, the memory of having no dreams exists in the subject, which implies that there was an inner self aware of this no-dream state. That is to say, the inner self was aware of the negation of all objective thoughts. Nothingness is the negation of objective thoughts, and the knowledge of this negation exists in the individual even in the dreamless sleep.

We cannot infer something that we have not perceived before. For example, a person might imagine an apple with spines. The spines and apples have already been perceived before, and during imagination, the person simply combines these objects of awareness to create an apple with spines in their mind. Another way to understand this is to consider a person sitting in a completely dark room, painted with a perfect black that absorbs all light. In this case, the person cannot perceive any objects with their eyes. This indicates that the negation of objects is a form of awareness. The person is aware that they cannot perceive any objects, hence they still possess knowledge of the negation. They are also aware of their own existence. As long as they are aware of themselves, they are also aware of the existence of the dark room. So when a person wakes from the dreamless state, they recall the voidness characterized by the negation of all objective thoughts. This indicates that the awareness of negation exists, and thus, the knowledge of the negation of objectivity also exists. Therefore, the dreamless sleep is accompanied by knowledge— knowledge abiding in subjectivity rather than objectivity. The dreamless sleep is characterized by the annihilation of objectivity.

As discussed in previous chapters, the person can recall events that happened prior to sleep, indicating a continuity of events in the mental dimension. Therefore, consciousness never ceases to exist. During dreamless sleep, consciousness is always present, along with self-affirming knowledge. This demonstrates that the soul, which is nothing but consciousness, exists at all times and is not dependent on the waking state or pure objectivity. Rather, the knowledge of objects depends on it.

The word *Sushupti* is translated as "to abide in oneself." This state of consciousness is crucial from both an ontological and epistemological perspective, as it helps prove the existence of an awareness that is free from all forms of objectivity, such as ideals, ideas, and images. It demonstrates that there is a self-knowledge or inner awareness that transcends any ideal or determinate objective knowledge.

In the state of dreams (*Swapna*), we can infer that the object abides within the subject and manifests independently of external influences. In the state of dreamless sleep (*Sushupti*), we can infer that there is awareness without objectivity, or an awareness that is free from determinate objects.

In the states of *Swapna* and *Jagrat*, we perceive the objective world, but objects cannot be perceived without the ideas associated with them. For example, whenever we see a pen, we automatically think about its use for writing; the impression of writing spontaneously arises in our mind. However, in the state of dreamless sleep, there is an opportunity to perceive objects without these determinate ideas. Knowledge can exist without objectivity. The knower and the known are the self in this state. Here, there is a possibility for the knower

to recognize their oneness with the known. The knower becomes aware of themselves in the form of the known.

This does not mean that the individual is completely conscious of the self in dreamless states, but it does open up the possibility of realizing the oneness of object and subject. The empirical individual naturally reaches this state during deep sleep, while a mystic or yogi can willfully achieve this state of consciousness through meditation and by withdrawing their awareness from the objects of the sense organs. In this state, the self becomes aware of itself, free from limited thought forms and untainted by *Smriti* (memory), which constructs the picture of limited objective reality within the mental dimension.

Turiya – The Fourth State

Almost every esoteric doctrine opines that each of us is part of a greater reality and united through a supreme principle. In non-dual Shaivism, it is believed that all individuals, or limited subjects, are manifestations of the supreme subject, and the distinctions between them, as well as isolated existence, are illusions caused by the obscuring power of Maya. While theoretical postulations are possible, they must be validated through logic and experience.

To understand this, we first need to grasp the fundamental nature of our existence. We are not isolated beings existing independently of each other. Every living being is connected to others through the oxygen they breathe. We cannot survive without vegetation; plants are the sole producers of food, sustaining all animal life, including humans. We are composed of the same atoms as planets and stars, and these particles also form dirt and complex life forms. Furthermore,

humans and animals interact for various purposes. We are inherently social creatures, and our interactions reflect a form of mental union. On a grand scale, everything on this planet is one with Mother Earth and interconnected through her. These interactions, exchanges of ideas, and emotions suggest a common substratum underlying these connections.

Returning to our exploration of oneness, a Shaivite must realize this transcendent state if it indeed exists. To facilitate these interactions, there must be a higher state of 'I' that gives rise to the lesser 'I'. This higher state is known by various names, and in this context, *Para-Samvid* is particularly apt.

When an individual undergoes experiences in the material world, three elements are present: the individual who experiences, the act of experiencing, and the experience itself. These three elements make up the triad of consciousness. Although the object of experience may vary over time, the subject who experiences remains constant. In every experience, the subject is a constant.

When we think about something or perform an action, who is performing it? Is it the body that performs the action or the mind that generates images based on memories? The 'I' performing these actions is nothing but self-aware consciousness. It becomes aware of itself through the multitude of actions it performs and asserts its existence through these actions and thoughts. Therefore, it can be concluded that the subject cannot be identified solely with limited actions and thought-forms. The self is the agent through which actions and thoughts are actualized. The 'I' is the ultimate through which everything comes into existence. As previously noted, the 'I' is not an object of meditation or contemplation; rather, it is the 'I'

that meditates and contemplates.

The fourth state, Turiya, is realized when the 'I' withdraws from all limited activities related to finite objects. When the 'I' withdraws from outer reality and ceases to identify its existence with limited objects of knowledge and action, it begins to reveal its true nature. The 'I' is essentially veiled by the limited actions it performs and the limited knowledge it possesses, which are the results of karma and its fruits.

Consider a bright light bulb that emits light in all directions. When this light bulb is covered by an opaque clay pot, its light is contained within the pot and cannot shine outside of it. Similarly, the all-pervading consciousness is obscured by karma and its fruits, which act like the clay pot, limiting its luminosity. To free oneself from this obscuration, an individual must cease identifying with the limited actions performed under the influence of limited will and knowledge. Once the clay pot, symbolizing karma, is removed, the limited subject realizes their true nature and the full extent of their luminosity. This state of self-awareness, free from any limitations related to will, knowledge, or action, is known as Turiya.

In the state of Sushupti, all limited thought forms and objectivity disappear, and self-awareness predominates. In the state of Turiya, the limited subject transforms into the supreme subject. Turiya is characterized by the annihilation of the lesser 'I' and the realization of a supreme principle that gives rise to immanent existence. While a mystic in the state of Sushupti is aware of their lesser self, even though it is devoid of objectivity, the awareness still pertains to the lesser self. In contrast, in the state of Turiya, the awareness is oriented towards the supreme subject. The mystic experiences the

entire universe as being within their awareness. This identification with the supreme subject is possible only when the lesser self is transcended.

There are no distinctions or dualities between the states of Sushupti and Turiya. In Sushupti, objectivity disappears, while in Turiya, the entire objective world is recognized as not separate from the supreme subject. In Turiya, objectivity resides within subjectivity. The lesser subject in Sushupti negates the objective world and abides in their own self, whereas a yogi who reaches the Turiya state of consciousness asserts a higher existence by negating the lower self. As a result, they identify themselves with the supreme subject, recognizing the objective world as an expression of the self.

The Sixteen States of Awareness

The four states of consciousness—Jagrat, Swapna, Sushupti, and Turiya—interpenetrate and exist within each other. Here's a detailed look at how these states are experienced and their various stages:

1. Jagrat (Wakeful State):

- **Jagrat-Jagrat (Wakefulness in Wakefulness):** This state is characterized by complete ignorance of the 'I' and a total absence of self-awareness. The subject is fully absorbed in the object, with no awareness of their own self. This is also known as Abuddha, meaning total nescience.
- **Jagrat-Swapna (Daydreaming in Wakefulness):** This state involves daydreaming or mental impressions while awake. A person might be cognizing an object but thinking about something else. Here, there is a partial awareness of the self,

known as Buddha Avastha, or partial awareness.

- **Jagrat-Sushupti (Wakefulness in Dreamless State):** In this state, despite being fully awake, the individual is not aware of any internal or external impressions. This can be achieved through practices like Trataka or Shambhavi Mudra. It is referred to as Prabuddha, or self-aware.
- **Jagrat-Turiya (Wakefulness in Turiya State):** Here, when external and internal objective impressions are lost, a mild awareness of the inner self develops. This state of self-awareness in wakefulness is known as Jagrat-Turiya Avastha, or Suprabuddha, meaning total absolute awareness.

2. Swapna (Dream State):

- **Swapna-Jagrat (Dreaming in Wakefulness):** This state involves experiencing objective impressions from the waking state in dreams. Dream impressions might be illogical, and self-awareness is minimal. The individual may not be aware of the dream's illogical nature. This state is known as Gatagata, meaning that which comes and goes.
- **Swapna-Swapna (Dreaming in the Dream State):** Here, the person experiences dreams that are completely illogical, and there is no awareness of these illogical impressions. This state is characterized by a total lack of self-awareness and is known as Suviksiptha, meaning discreet and dispersed awareness.
- **Swapna-Sushupti (Dreaming in Dreamless State):** In this stage, the individual starts to become aware that they are

dreaming. This is where dreams become lucid, and a partial form of self-awareness develops. It is known as Sanghatta, or the state of occasional awareness.

- **Swapna-Turiya (Dreaming in Turiya State):** In this state, the individual is fully aware of their self and can recognize that they are dreaming. They can cast away the dream's impressions and objects, attaining the state of Para-Bhairava. However, this state is temporary, and the person often returns to the objective impressions of dreams and forgets their true nature upon waking. This state is called Susamahitam, or complete awareness.

Each of these states represents a different level of awareness, ranging from complete ignorance of the self to a high degree of self-realization, illustrating the interplay between consciousness and self-awareness in both waking and dreaming states.

3. States of Sushupti (Dreamless State):

- **Sushupti-Jagrat (Dreamless Wakefulness):** In this state, characterized by complete voidness during deep sleep, the individual loses awareness of time, space, and self. This state is marked by a profound negation of objective impressions and a sensation of pure void. This state is known as **Udita** or the **rise of consciousness.**
- **Sushupti-Swapna (Dreamless Dreaming):** Here, there is a faint awareness of subjectivity. While the person is unaware of the process of negating objective impressions in deep sleep,

a slight awareness emerges. This stage signifies a gradual increase in self-awareness. This is referred to as **Vipula** or **gradual increase of self-awareness**.

- **Sushupti-Sushupti (Dreamless Dreamless State):** In this stage, subjective experience is more pronounced. The individual maintains an awareness of the negation of objectivity and abides more consistently in subjectivity. However, the person may still lack full realization of the supreme state of consciousness. This state is known as **Shanta** or the **peaceful state**.

- **Sushupti-Turiya (Dreamless Turiya):** Here, the residual objective impressions are completely negated, and the individual experiences profound bliss (Ananda) in subjectivity. While inner awareness is highly developed, it is still centered around the lesser 'I' rather than the supreme 'I'. This state is called **Suprasanna** or **blissful awareness**.

4. States of Turiya (The Fourth State):

- **Turiya-Jagrat (Turiya in Wakefulness):** This stage is characterized by the dawning of awareness of the supreme subjective principle. Although the awareness of the supreme subject exists in the background, the awareness of the lesser self remains dominant. This state is also known as **Manonmani** or **thoughtless awareness**, transcending mental constructs.

- **Turiya-Swapna (Turiya in Dreaming):** In this state, there is a more developed awareness of the supreme principle (Para-

Bhairava), though some residual traces of the lower self remain. The awareness exists in both the higher and lower selves. This state is termed **Ananta** or **unlimited/infinite** awareness.

- **Turiya-Sushupti (Turiya in Dreamless State):** Here, the lower self is completely dissolved, and the awareness is fully identified with the supreme subject. This state represents the pinnacle of self-realization, where the individual is fully aware of the supreme 'I'. It is called **Sarvartha** or **all-pervading consciousness**.

5. Turiyateetha (Beyond Turiya):

Turiyateetha (Transcendence Beyond Turiya): This is the most supreme state of consciousness, transcending even the fourth state of Turiya. It represents pure consciousness that pervades all the previous fifteen states of awareness. In this state, there is no duality or relativity; it is the supreme Bhairava in its pure, unadulterated form. It signifies the ultimate reality and unity beyond all conceptual distinctions.

These sixteen states collectively illustrate a journey through various levels of awareness, from complete ignorance of the self to the realization of pure consciousness beyond all states. Each stage represents a different degree of self-awareness and consciousness, culminating in the highest state of transcendental awareness.

Phonematic Cosmogony In
Non-Dual Shaivism

The present chapter will explore the fundamental aspects of phonemes and mantras within the framework of classical non-dual Shaivism. Shaivism encompasses various schools of thought, each offering nuanced perspectives on the nature of the cosmos and the self. Despite their differences, all these traditions aim to address the profound existential questions concerning the nature of the universe and individual identity.

This chapter will briefly examine the concept of phonemes, their role in constituting the cosmos, and the significance of mantras in Shaivite theurgical practices. Shaivite doctrine features a variety of spiritual exercises, categorized based on the practitioner's level of understanding and recognition of divinity. Among these practices, mantras—constructed from the letters of the Sanskrit alphabet—hold a revered place.

In Shaivism, the Sanskrit letters, known as **Matrikas**, are considered essential components in spiritual practice. The belief is that the use of phonemes can produce results more swiftly than traditional methods such as outward rituals, idolatry, fire sacrifices, and ceremonies. The first letter of the Matrika is 'a', and the last phoneme is 'Ksha'. Additionally, practitioners employ a method known as **Malini**, which involves a distinct arrangement of phonemes and is regarded as a reflection of divine presence within the immanent world.

The Role of Phonemes in Shaivite Cosmology

In Shaivite theology, the supreme deity is **Para-Shiva**, who embodies pure consciousness, referred to as Shiva. The awareness associated with this supreme consciousness is termed **Shakti**. Para-Shiva, through the medium of phonemes, brings the cosmos into existence by being consciously aware of it. Therefore, phonemes are viewed as fragments of the divine awareness of Para-Shiva, integral to the creation and structure of the cosmos.

Phonemes in this context are not mere sounds but manifestations of divine consciousness. They are the building blocks through which the supreme consciousness—Shiva—manifests and orders the cosmos. Since the supreme self is consciousness itself, it possesses complete self-awareness and infinite potential. This self-aware consciousness, or **Chit**, is not only aware of its own infinite nature but also possesses the absolute freedom to enact its will, thus creating and sustaining the universe.

The idea that phonemes are fragments of divine awareness highlights their fundamental role in shaping and sustaining the cosmos. Each phoneme or sound is a reflection of the cosmic order and the divine will of Para-Shiva. In Shaivite practice, understanding and utilizing these phonemes can lead to a deeper realization of the divine nature of existence. By engaging with the Matrikas and the Malini arrangement, practitioners align themselves with the divine order and gain insight into the intrinsic nature of reality.

This chapter will delve into the esoteric significance of phonemes and mantras within non-dual Shaivism. By exploring these concepts, we uncover how the divine consciousness of Para-Shiva manifests through the Matrikas and how these sacred sounds facilitate spiritual

practices and the recognition of divinity in both the microcosm and macrocosm.

Within the phonematic ontology, the letters of the Sanskrit alphabet are regarded as fragments of divine awareness or Shakti. This understanding highlights the supreme feminine principle, known as **Shri-Matra**, meaning "one who is composed of the letters." Mantras, which are considered to embody certain absolute and unadulterated divine forces, are crafted from these mystical phonemes. Without a profound comprehension of the attributes and awakening of these phonemes, attempts to use mantras effectively are often in vain. Some practitioners engage in mechanical chanting of mantras thousands of times, a practice that typically stems from a lack of understanding of the underlying principles governing the use of phonemes and mantras.

Phonemes and Their Spiritual Significance

The phonemes, in both their **Matrika** and **Malini** forms, are employed to achieve the highest spiritual goal: recognizing or realizing the inherent oneness of the individual with the divine. Non-dual Shaivite doctrines assert that man and God are fundamentally the same. This truth, or the true nature of the self, can be realized through meditating on phonemes. The supreme principle is represented as self-affirming consciousness, an absolute consciousness that reflects the cosmos within itself. This reflection is systematically organized into a hierarchy known as **Tatwas**, which are also represented by phonemes.

In Shaivite cosmogony, the supreme deity is endowed with five principal powers, which manifest as sixteen vowels. These vowels, in

turn, reflect the phenomenal cosmos through thirty-four consonants. To understand the formation of the cosmos through phonemes, we must explore these five powers and their relationship to the phonetic elements.

As previously discussed, the entire manifestation is viewed as an expression of **Para-Shiva** through his divine speech or **Vak**, which is synonymous with **Para-Shakti**. Each phoneme represents a different aspect of the divine creative potential of the Lord. The letters are arranged in two primary forms: **Matrika** and **Malini**.

- **Matrika** refers to the creative energy of phonemes, or the "Mother" of the sounds. This arrangement follows a regular sequence, with vowels preceding the consonants.
- **Malini**, on the other hand, signifies the goddess who adorns herself with a garland made of phonemes. In some contexts, **Matrika** is also referred to as **Purva Malini**, which means "the one who precedes Malini." The term **Malini** carries an additional meaning, referring to the holding of the cosmos within the sounds.

Theological Aspects of Phonemes

To delve into the theological dimension of phonemes, it is essential to recognize that the phonetic elements are more than mere sounds; they are manifestations of the divine creative energy of Para-Shiva. These phonemes, whether in the Matrika or Malini arrangement, serve as tools for spiritual realization and alignment with the divine essence. The Matrika arrangement reflects a structured approach to phonemes, while Malini represents a more fluid and integrated

form of divine expression. Both forms are crucial for understanding the profound relationship between language, divinity, and cosmic creation in Shaivite thought.

By exploring these aspects, one can gain deeper insights into how phonemes function as divine tools in the spiritual journey toward recognizing the unity between the individual self and the supreme divine consciousness.

The first letter of the **Matrika**, which is **'a'**, is said to embody the **Chit Shakti**, or consciousness, of **Para-Shiva**. Within the classical Agamas, this initial phoneme is given multiple interpretations as representing the supreme consciousness. As the first sound, **'a'** is considered the source of all other sounds in Sanskrit and signifies the most transcendent aspect of the supreme lord, known as **Anuttara**, meaning "the most transcended."

Phonemes and Their Divine Significance - Vowels

- **'a'**: The initial phoneme, **'a'**, is seen as the embodiment of the ultimate consciousness of Para-Shiva. It represents the pure, unconditioned awareness from which all subsequent sounds and forms emerge. This phoneme symbolizes the absolute, undifferentiated state of the supreme consciousness before any manifestation occurs.
- **'ā'**: The second phoneme, **'ā'**, is an elongated version of the first sound and is referred to as **Ananda Kali**, representing the **Ananda Shakti** or bliss aspect of the supreme principle. This bliss arises from the self-awareness of its own infinite nature. **'ā'** signifies a state of unity and completeness, indicating that no external emanation has yet occurred, and the awareness

remains abstract and undifferentiated.

- **'i' and 'ī'**: The third and fourth phonemes, **'i'** and **'ī'**, represent the **Icha Shakti**, or the will aspect of the supreme consciousness. The will is expressed in two ways:

  'i': This represents the unagitated will of the supreme, embodying a calm and steady aspect of divine intention.

  'ī': The elongated version **'ī'** denotes the agitated will, which involves a dynamic aspect of the divine intent to manifest the cosmos within itself. This agitation does not imply a desire to externalize but rather a will to manifest the object in its own image.

- **'u' and 'ū'**: The next two phonemes, **'u'** and **'ū'**, correspond to the **Jnana Shakti**, or the knowledge aspect of the supreme lord. These letters emerge from the combination of the first two letters **'a'** (Chit Shakti) and **'ā'** (Ananda Shakti) with the will aspects **'i'** and **'ī'**. The knowledge aspect manifests in two ways:

  'u': This phoneme represents the tendency to manifest externally. It is called **Unmesha**, meaning "to open up" or "to expand."

  'ū': The phoneme **'ū'** represents the tendency to retract or decrease, known as **Unata**, which involves the internal contraction or withdrawal of the manifested object.

The phonemes **'a'**, **'ā'**, **'i'**, **'ī'**, **'u'**, and **'ū'** each represent distinct aspects of the divine consciousness and powers of Para-Shiva. They illustrate how the supreme consciousness manifests itself

and interacts with the cosmos through various forms of will and knowledge, ultimately reflecting the nature of the divine in the material world.

The next four phonemes, known as the **Amrita Kalas** or **immortal phonemes**, are characterized by their neutral nature and are collectively referred to as **Shikandi** or **hermaphrodite** phonemes. These phonemes include 'ṛ', 'ṝ', 'ḷ', and 'ḹ'. They are defined by their tendency to repose in the undifferentiated state of oneness and unity, reflecting a profound, undisturbed consciousness. These phonemes are not oriented towards external manifestation but are instead focused on pure subjectivity and an intrinsic state of non-agitation. Due to their nature of representing inherent oneness and undifferentiated awareness, these letters are considered immortal and transcendental. They do not actualize or manifest any external cosmos because they embody a state of repose in the supreme, undifferentiated consciousness.

When the letters 'a' and 'ā' combine with 'e', the resultant phoneme is 'o'. Similarly, when 'a' and 'ā' combine with 'o', the phoneme 'au' is formed.

Phonemes Representing Kriya-Shakti

The subsequent four phonemes represent the stages of **Kriya-Shakti,** or the power of action of the supreme lord. These phonemes are:

- 'e'
- 'ai'
- 'o'
- 'au'

Each of these letters reflects a different state of the action or manifestation of the supreme consciousness:

- **'e'**: This phoneme symbolizes the initial, abstract action, known as **Asphuta Kriya-Shakti**. In this state, the action is indeterminate and not yet concretized. It represents the first stirrings of action within the divine will, still in an abstract form.
- **'ai'**: The phoneme **'ai'** represents **Sphuta-Kriya Shakti**, where the action begins to take form. **Sphuta** means clear or with form, indicating that the action is becoming more concrete and defined compared to the abstract nature of the previous stage.
- **'o'**: This phoneme signifies **Sphuta-Tara Kriya-Shakti**, which denotes a further clarification and concreteness of action. It represents a more definitive and structured manifestation of action compared to the earlier stages.
- **'au'**: The phoneme **'au'** is associated with the most concrete and determinate form of action, known as **Sphuta-Tama Kriya-Shakti**. It is also called **Trishula-Bija** or the seed syllable of the trident because it encompasses all three powers: **Icha** (will), **Jnana** (knowledge), and **Kriya** (action). This phoneme represents the culmination of the action process in its fullest form.

The principles outlined by these phonemes illustrate how the supreme, self-aware consciousness manifests the cosmos through various stages of intention and action. The progression from abstract

to concrete forms shows how the divine will and knowledge translate into the physical and phenomenal world. The transformation of indeterminate will into specific, manifest actions reveals the process by which the supreme consciousness actualizes the entire immanent cosmos.

In Shaivite cosmogony, the cosmos is regarded as a reflection of the divine nature of Para-Shiva. Even though Para-Shiva initiates the creation of the cosmos through his own powers, he remains unchanged in his intrinsic nature. The act of creation does not alter his undifferentiated, non-distinct state. This state of undifferentiated consciousness is symbolized by 'ṃ', known as **Anuswara**, which represents the seminal power of the supreme god and is depicted as a dot.

The process of emanation, where the cosmos is reflected or manifested within Para-Shiva's own essence, is denoted by **Visarga**, symbolized by the sound 'ḥ' (:) and represented by two dots. This signifies the reflection of Shiva's seminal power into the cosmos. In this stage, the cosmos emerges from Para-Shiva in his own image, maintaining the essence of his divinity.

The sixteen vowels, which embody the **sixteen Kalas**, are known as **Para-Shiva Tatwas**. These sixteen Kalas are the foundational elements from which the manifested cosmos arises, represented by the consonants. The consonants correspond to different levels of the manifested cosmos, starting from the more abstract and higher Tatwas and descending through the various stages to the more concrete and lower Tatwas.

For the purpose of understanding, it is instructive to begin with the last consonant in the hierarchy and then descend through the

levels, eventually reaching the first consonant **'ka'**. This approach provides a clearer perspective on how the cosmic manifestation unfolds from its highest, most abstract form to its more concrete expressions.

The Consonants and Their Cosmic Representation

The consonants, beginning with **'ka'** and progressing to higher categories, represent various aspects of the manifested cosmos. Each consonant corresponds to a specific Tatwa or principle in the cosmic hierarchy. By starting with the highest consonant and moving downward, one can trace the descending levels of cosmic manifestation. This hierarchical approach helps in understanding how the abstract, divine essence transitions into the more tangible aspects of the cosmos.

Each consonant represents a particular stage or aspect of the cosmic process. The higher consonants reflect the more abstract and subtle aspects of the cosmos, while the lower consonants represent the more concrete and manifest forms.

This systematic exploration of the consonants, from the highest to the lowest, provides insight into how Para-Shiva's essence is expressed through the cosmos, illustrating the interplay between the divine and the manifested world.

In Shaivite cosmogony, the cosmos is perceived as a reflection of the supreme deity, Para-Shiva. Even though Para-Shiva creates the cosmos through his inherent powers, he remains unchanged in his essence. During the process of emanation, the supreme deity maintains his undifferentiated and non-distinct state, represented by the phoneme **'ṃ'**, known as **Anuswara**. This phoneme, depicted as

a dot, signifies the seminal power of the supreme god. As the cosmos is reflected or emanated, it is represented by **Visarga**, denoted by the sound 'ḥ' and symbolized by two dots. This indicates the reflection of the seminal power of Shiva as the cosmos.

The sixteen vowels in Sanskrit, representing the sixteen Kalas, are identified as **Para-Shiva Tatwas**. These Kalas reflect as the manifested cosmos, which is expressed through the consonants. To understand the consonants better, we start from the higher Tatwa and descend to the lower categories, eventually reaching the first consonant **Ka**.

kṣa

The phoneme 'kṣa' is known as **Shiva Tatwa** and signifies the initial movement toward creation. It represents the first pulsation or the primordial vibration that begins the process of manifesting the cosmos contained within Para-Shiva. This phoneme is formed by combining 'ka' (the first consonant) and 'ṣa' (the last consonant), symbolizing a union of the beginning and the end, akin to the Kabbalistic concept of "Atah," which represents the union of **Aleph** and **Tau**. In this stage, **Chit Shakti**, or pure consciousness, is dominant.

ha

The phoneme 'ha' represents the **Shakti Tatwa**. It is referred to as **"nisheda vyapara rupa"**, meaning negation. This phoneme embodies the negation of objectivity, where there is no distinction between subject and object. **Shakti** is the creative potential of Shiva. Here, **Shiva** remains as the supreme subject without any trace of

objectivity. For the cosmos to manifest, a distinction between subject and object is required. **Shakti** creates this distinction, enabling the cosmos to emerge from a unified state of subjectivity. **Shakti** is not separate from Shiva but is inherently one with him, reflecting his self-luminosity. **Shakti** is described as **Aham-Vimarsha**, the reflection of the self, and is responsible for the Will, Knowledge, and Action aspects of Shiva. In the Shakti Tatwa, the **Ananda** (bliss) aspect is dominant, manifesting as self-affirming awareness.

sa

The phoneme **'sa'** corresponds to the **Sada-Shiva Tatwa** (also known as **Sadakhya Tatwa**). It signifies the will to experience objectivity within oneself. Here, the supreme principle manifests as **'I Am'**, where **'Am'** is undifferentiated from **'I'**. Objectivity remains abstract and buried deep within subjectivity, without significant determinate knowledge. In this stage, **Sada-Shiva** starts to differentiate as objectivity, but this objectivity is still abstract and indeterminate. The concept of **'This'** is one with **'I'**, and there is a fusion of knower and known within consciousness.

ṣa

The phoneme **'ṣa'** represents the **Iswara-Tatwa**. This Tatwa is characterized by **'I Am This'**, where **'This'** becomes clearer and more determinate. This phoneme highlights the manifestation of objectivity, with **Jnana-Shakti** (Knowledge aspect) being predominant. Here, there is a clear conception of what is to be manifested, including the multitude of finite objects in the universe.

Śa

The phoneme '**Śa**' is associated with the **Shuddha-Vidya Tatwa**. In this state, the action or **Kriya** aspect is predominant. Both subjectivity and objectivity, or '**I**' and '**This**', exist equally, akin to the balanced pans of a common scale. Although there is equality, a distinct separation between subject and object exists. This stage represents a unity in diversity, where subject and object are balanced but clearly differentiated.

As we progress further, the distinction between subject and object increases, emphasizing objectivity. The subsequent letters introduce the principle of **Maya**, representing the limiting aspect of the infinite, undetermined supreme consciousness. This self-imposed limitation leads to the manifestation of the phenomenal world, which is finite and limited. This limitation enhances the perceived distinction between the knower and the known, creating the illusion of separation between the divine and the mundane.

The phonemes and their corresponding Tatwas illustrate the gradual unfolding of the divine from an abstract, unified state to a more differentiated and manifest cosmos. Each phoneme represents a specific stage in this cosmic evolution, showing how the infinite consciousness of **Para-Shiva** manifests into the finite, differentiated universe.

va

The phoneme '**va**' embodies the **Maya Tatwa**, derived from the root word **Mana**, which means "to measure." Measurement refers to defining and limiting objects, making this Tatwa the creative principle responsible for constraining the infinite, undifferentiated

consciousness into the seemingly limited and finite cosmos. Up to the state of **Shuddha-Vidya**, the awareness encompasses the totality of existence. However, with the influence of **Maya**, a veil is drawn over pure consciousness, causing it to perceive itself as a limited, objective universe. This concept bears similarity to the **Tzimtzum** in Kabbalistic doctrine, where a divine contraction creates a space for the creation of the finite world.

la

The phoneme 'la' represents two Tatwas: **Kala** (space) and **Kaala** (time). These principles introduce limitations regarding action and temporal aspects, respectively.

- **Kala** denotes the constraint on action, contrasting with the omnipotent nature of Para-Shiva. This Tatwa creates the sensation of undertaking specific, determinate tasks and is integral to the phenomena of Karma and causal efficacy.
- **Kaala** signifies time, marking the orderly progression of events as past, present, and future. This principle introduces limitations on cognition and perception, segmenting knowledge into temporal dimensions. The Tatwa associated with 'la' is sometimes linked with the element of earth in certain yoga traditions. However, this should not be confused with the Mahabhuta, as this element pertains to the conceptualization of finite ideas and the solidification of the infinite into the gross aspects of divine consciousness.

ra

The phoneme 'ra' is associated with **Tejas**, commonly interpreted as the fire element. In classical doctrines, it corresponds to **Pramana-Tejas**, or the fire of cognition. This phoneme enables perception of the physical world through sensory organs, hence it is also known as **Vidya Tatwa**.

This principle introduces limitations in knowledge, as it narrows the omniscient nature of the supreme principle to finite knowledge about objects. '**Ra**' illuminates objectivity, facilitating the movement of awareness from the subject to the object and creating a sense of limitation in knowledge. This Tatwa contributes to the manifestation of the multitude of finite objects within the cosmos.

ya

The phoneme 'ya' encompasses two Tatwas: **Raga** and **Niyati**.

- **Raga** represents attachment, signifying limitations within the self. It induces a sense of incompleteness, causing individuals to feel dissatisfied and seek attachment to finite objects. This Tatwa fosters identification with limited entities and obscures one's awareness of the true nature of pure supreme consciousness. In **Sri-Vidya** practices, associated with the worship of **Sri-Chakra**, **Raga** and its counterpart **Dwesha** (aversion) are symbolized by the rope and elephant goad held by the goddess. Divinities named **Aswaruda** and **Sampath-Prada** embody **Raga** and **Dwesha** respectively.
- **Raga** contributes to the multiplicity within the cosmos, creating variations in appearance and attributes. This Tatwa,

by fostering attachment, links the supreme principle to the objective world to actualize the cosmos. In empirical individuals, this results in attachment to limited objects and experiences of happiness and sadness.

Due to its role in generating multiplicity and variations in the objective world, **'ya'** is often equated with the element of air.

Ashuddha Tatwas

The following Tatwas are known as **Ashuddha** or impure Tatwas because they are entirely obscured by **Maya** and its effects. These Tatwas reflect the complete veil that Maya casts over pure consciousness, contributing to the perception of a limited and differentiated cosmos.

ma

The phoneme **'ma'** embodies the **Purusha Tatwa**. In this context, **Purusha** refers to the empirical individual or the limited subject. It does not exclusively denote humans; rather, it encompasses every sentient being within the cosmos, all of which are inherently limited. Therefore, the **Purusha Tatwa** constitutes the totality of all limited subjects in existence. It represents the essence of limitedness within the cosmos, reflecting the constraint and finitude that characterize every individual being. In classical doctrines, Purusha is described as **"Purnatva Abhavena Paramitatwad Anutavam,"** which translates to the absence of the infinite and complete nature of the supreme god, hence being termed as **Anu**. The term **Anu** signifies a tiny fragment, highlighting the notion that Purusha, being unaware

of its infinite nature, perceives itself as fundamentally limited.

bha

The phoneme 'bha' represents the **Prakriti Tatwa**. **Prakriti** is the objective manifestation of the supreme principle. In contrast to Purusha, which embodies the limited knower, **Prakriti** signifies the limited object or the 'This' of the supreme principle. While Purusha is the finite observer, Prakriti is the observed object. Within an empirical individual, Prakriti manifests as the matrix of objectivity, consisting of the three **Gunas** (attributes) — **Satva**, **Rajas**, and **Tamas**. These Gunas represent the limited forms of knowledge, will, and action, respectively. Thus, these three Gunas are the gross manifestations of the **Jnana** (knowledge), **Icha** (will), and **Kriya** (action) aspects of the divine.

bā

The phoneme 'bā' signifies the principle of **Buddhi**, which is the power of discernment and differentiation within the limited subject. On a cosmic scale, this Tatwa facilitates the differentiation and manifestation of a multitude of objects within the cosmos. It underscores the divinity's capability to produce an infinite array of variations in the objective world, reflecting the diverse and multifaceted nature of the cosmic manifestation.

pha

The phoneme 'pha' embodies the **Ahamkara Tatwa**, which is derived from the **Buddhi Tatwa**. **Ahamkara** refers to the sense of ego or self-identification, the aspect of awareness that asserts the

self as a distinct, limited subject. This Tatwa enables the perception of both external and internal objects. Externally, it allows one to perceive objects like "I see a cow" or "I observe a jar." Internally, it facilitates introspection and thoughts such as "I am thinking about a dog" or "I am considering a car." The presence of Ahamkara is crucial for the ability to perceive and interact with both the external world and one's internal thoughts. This principle contributes to the development of the five senses and the related perceptual processes.

pa

The phoneme **'pa'** represents the principle of **Manas**. In Western terminology, **Manas** is often translated as "mind," but this is a misinterpretation in this context. While "mind" in Western philosophy typically refers to consciousness, **Manas** in this system denotes an internal sense organ or psychic apparatus. It is responsible for converting sensory experiences into determinate perceptions and knowledge. **Manas** plays a crucial role in the cognition of ideas, forms, images, and thoughts. Essentially, it aids in the process of recognizing and interpreting objects within the immanent world, facilitating the overall process of cognition and perception.

na

The phoneme **'na'** represents the organ of sound, known as **Shrotra**. This principle is associated with the ability to perceive sound, reflecting our capacity to hear and interpret auditory stimuli. On a deeper level, this Tatwa encompasses the principle of **conation**, which is the drive or intention behind actions. In our daily lives, our

thoughts often precede and guide our actions, and these thoughts are often actualized and expressed through words. Hence, sound, as articulated through words, is intrinsically linked to the process of thinking and action. This Tatwa embodies the foundational aspect of how we perceive and process sound, aligning our sensory experiences with our mental intentions.

dha

The phoneme **'dha'** represents the **Twak Tatwa**, which is the organ of **tactility**, associated with the sense of touch and the skin. **Tactile perceptions** refer to the ability to interact with or come into physical contact with objects. This principle underscores the association of empirical awareness with finite objects through the sense of touch. By facilitating direct interaction with physical entities, this Tatwa allows us to perceive textures, temperatures, and other tactile sensations, providing a tangible connection to the external world.

da

The phoneme **'da'** embodies the sense of **visual perception**, which is associated with the eyes. This principle is crucial for perceiving forms and images, and it plays a significant role in recognizing and interpreting the visual aspects of the physical world. The **visual perception** allows us to see and identify the distinct shapes, colors, and patterns of objects. In a more transcendent sense, this principle also refers to the ability to create and manifest forms, which constitute the diverse array of objects in the physical universe.

tha

The phoneme **'tha'** represents the principle of **taste**, associated with the tongue, buccal cavity, and alimentary canal. **Taste** involves perceiving and experiencing flavors, which entails the union or conjunction with certain substances to understand their characteristics. This sense of taste allows for the assimilation and digestion of sensory experiences, integrating them into the self. It reflects the cognitive process of discerning and internalizing knowledge through sensory engagement with various substances.

ta

The phoneme **'ta'** signifies the **Ghrana Tatwa**, or the principle of **smell**, associated with the nose. The nose, as the organ of smell, is not only crucial for breathing but also for the life force that animates empirical individuals. **Ghrana** encompasses the processes of cognition, association, digestion, and assimilation of olfactory information. It also involves the elimination of unnecessary knowledge or sensory inputs. This principle underlines how the sense of smell contributes to our perception and understanding of the environment.

The following set of principles, known as **Karmendriyas**, pertains to the organs of action. These principles are essential for performing various activities and functions within the empirical world. They complement the sensory organs by facilitating the execution of actions based on sensory perceptions and cognitive processes.

ṇa

The phoneme **'ṇa'** signifies the principle of **speech**, embodied by the vocal cords and related organs. This principle is intrinsically linked to the ability to think and manifest thoughts as spoken words. In the empirical individual, **'ṇa'** represents the locus of thinking and conation, where thoughts are articulated and expressed. Speech facilitates the externalization of internal processes, translating cognitive activities into verbal expressions, thereby serving as a crucial element in communication and action.

ḍha

The phoneme **'ḍha'** embodies the principle of **Pani** or **Hasta**, referring to our hands. Hands are instrumental in performing various actions and manipulating objects, representing our capability to grasp, hold, and interact with the world. This principle underscores the ability to associate and dissociate with different objects through physical engagement. **'ḍha'** symbolizes the hands' role in executing actions and managing interactions with the environment, reflecting a fundamental aspect of practical functionality.

ḍa

The phoneme **'ḍa'** represents the **Pada Tatwa**, which pertains to the **feet** and, by extension, the principle of locomotion. This principle encompasses movement, the dynamic nature of progress, and the capacity to traverse from one location to another. In the context of divine providence, this principle reflects the ongoing, dynamic nature of cosmic activities, as the divine engages in the five primary actions of creation. **'ḍa'** signifies the continuous motion and

dynamism present in both the cosmos and the individual experience.

ṭa

The phoneme 'ṭa' denotes the **Payu Tatwa**, associated with the **organs of excretion**. This principle involves the ability to expel what is no longer needed and to maintain a balance by eliminating unnecessary elements. It reflects the process of absorption and expulsion, where the body discards waste while retaining what is essential. 'ṭa' thus represents the vital function of processing and managing inputs and outputs, ensuring both physical and metaphorical purification and balance.

ṭha

The phoneme 'ṭha' corresponds to the **sexual organs**, which are essential for procreation and experiencing intense pleasure. This principle represents the objectified manifestation of **Ananda** or bliss, as experienced by the supreme consciousness in the act of cosmic emanation. 'ṭha' embodies the creative and generative aspects of existence, reflecting the blissful engagement of the divine in the continuous cycle of creation and manifestation.

Tanmatras and Their Correspondence to Elements

In the Shaivite cosmology, the processes or **Tanmatras** represent the subtle elements that evolve into the five physical elements. These Tanmatras are fundamental sensory qualities that reflect the nature of perception and are integral to the manifestation of the physical world. They are:

1. **Sabdha (Sound)** - Represented by the letter **'ña'**. This Tanmatra embodies the auditory quality and the potential for sound to manifest in the physical realm.
2. **Sparsha (Touch)** - Represented by the letter **'jha'**. This Tanmatra corresponds to the sense of touch and tactile sensations, facilitating physical contact and texture perception.
3. **Rasa (Taste)** - Represented by the letter **'ja'**. This Tanmatra is associated with taste, the quality that enables the perception of flavors and the enjoyment of sensory experiences related to taste.
4. **Rupa (Vision)** - Represented by the letter **'cha'**. This Tanmatra pertains to visual perception, the quality of form and color that allows one to see and interpret visual stimuli.
5. **Gandha (Olfaction)** - Represented by the letter **'ca'**. This Tanmatra relates to the sense of smell, which perceives odors and fragrances.

These Tanmatras manifest in the physical world as the five classical elements, each associated with one of the sensory qualities:

1. **Akasha (Ether)** - Represented by the letter **'ṅa'**. Ether is associated with the auditory process and the quality of sound, providing the space through which sound travels.
2. **Vayu (Air)** - Represented by the letter **'gha'**. Air corresponds to tactility and touch, influencing the experience of texture and the movement of the wind.
3. **Agni (Fire)** - Represented by the letter **'ga'**. Fire is linked to vision and light, governing the perception of color and the

experience of warmth.

4. **Ap/Jala (Water)** - Represented by the letter **'kha'**. Water is connected to taste, facilitating the ability to savor and experience different flavors.

5. **Prithvi (Earth)** - Represented by the letter **'ka'**. Earth relates to olfaction and the sense of smell, as well as providing the solid, stable foundation upon which other elements interact.

The Tanmatras are the subtle qualities that evolve into the tangible physical elements. Each Tanmatra corresponds to a specific element and sensory process, reflecting the intricate relationship between perception and the material world.

Malini

Malini represents a distinct order of phonemes emanating from the divine, and its complexity warrants an extensive exploration that could fill an entire volume. Here, we can only provide a brief overview.

Malini is a consequence of the emanation of **Matrika** in the dimension of objectivity. While Malini embodies the objectified cosmos, it remains rooted in the ultimate subject. Essentially, Malini reflects the fragmented awareness of the supreme subject when it manifests as the objective cosmos. In the third stage of **Madhyama**, the objectivity becomes more pronounced and closer to manifestation. At this stage, the phonemes are reflected as if in a mirror, creating what is known as Malini.

In Malini, the order of phonemes is entirely scrambled and reorganized. The vowels and consonants of **Matrika** are

intermingled, resulting in a new sequence. The first sixteen letters of Malini represent a reflection of Shiva in Shakti, unlike Matrika, which embodies the pure Shiva Tatwa. The remaining thirty-four letters represent the Tatwas from **Sadashiva** to **Prithvi**.

Shaivite doctrines assert that Malini is both a reflection of the supreme consciousness as the immanent cosmos and a reflection of Shiva as Shakti. It is described as the combination of the Shiva and Shakti Tatwas—the seed (vowels) and the womb (consonants) phonemes. Thus, Malini can be understood as the objectivity of Shakti emerging in the **Madhyama** stage of manifestation.

The symbolism of Malini often draws from the concept of the sacred sexual union, reflecting the union of seed and womb phonemes. This union is portrayed in later Shaivite scriptures as a symbolic representation of divine creation. The reflection of Shiva as Shakti, or the emanation of objectivity from the subject, are essentially the same phenomenon in this context. The self-replicating or reflecting power of Shiva is termed Shakti, and the emanation or reflection is consistent with this power.

Although Malini manifests in the Madhyama stage of **Vak** (speech), it remains unified with the Para state. Malini represents the unity in diversity, illustrating the supreme consciousness's power to appear as multiple objects while maintaining its inherent unity.

As the phonemes evolve and reach their final emanation in the stage of **Vaikhari**, which represents the physical world, they manifest as vocalized sounds in the form of alphabets, written and spoken words, and other expressions. Although the Shiva Tatwas appear veiled and constrained by **Maya** in this final stage, they remain intrinsically one with the supreme consciousness. Thus, even

at this ultimate level of manifestation, the phonemes retain their connection with the divine subject and contain the full potential of divine providence within them.

Having previously discussed Malini as the reflection of Shiva as Shakti, it is insightful to explore this concept further from a philosophical perspective. We have already examined **Svatantrya Shakti**, the sovereign power of freedom inherent in Para-Shiva or Para-Bhairava, to manifest the objective world. The entire cosmos and its categories of Tatwas are reflections within the supreme consciousness. Since the supreme consciousness itself cannot be reflected (as it is the agent of reflection), all categories of existence are reflections within this consciousness. Consciousness alone brings the Tatwas into illumination. The myriad objects and the diverse Shakti that expresses itself through the infinite variety of the phenomenal world are merely expansions of the supreme consciousness.

Abhinava Gupta elaborates on the concept of reflection and Tatwas by asserting that each Tatwa embodies the entire universe within itself. Every Tatwa contains the pristine glory of Para-Shiva in its entirety. For the sake of understanding, Tatwas are often explained in a sequential manner, where each Tatwa is considered to give rise to the next. However, each Tatwa also contains elements of the succeeding Tatwa, as well as the preceding ones. Consequently, the final gross objectified state, known as **Prithvi** (Earth), encompasses all 34 previous Tatwas within it in their full glory, rendering it complete in every sense. Thus, the physical world represents the exalted will of the divine, with each category of existence being complete in its own right.

In this manner, the supreme subject expresses itself as the objective reality within itself without losing its limitless state of freedom. Malini, too, embodies the complete glory of the supreme in every category of existence. It signifies that all levels of existence and dimensions of reality are inherently united with the supreme state of **Bhairava**.

To integrate the concept of Malini into practice, one should contemplate the manifestation of the supreme in every immanent object. This involves recognizing the oneness of objective reality with the supreme state of subjectivity. Ultimately, the mystic comes to realize that even a tiny fragment of an object is imbued with the complete glory of **Para-Samvid**.

Here is a comprehensive listing of the Shakti Tatwas in Malini, including their corresponding phonemes:

TATWA	PHONEME
Sadashiva	gha
Iswara	ṅa
Shuddha-Vidya	i
Maya	a
Niyati	va
Kaala	bha
Raga	ya
Vidya	da
Kala	ḍha
Purusha	ṭha

Prakriti	jha
Buddhi	na
Ahankara	ja
anas	ra
Strota	ṭa
Twak	pa
Chakshu	cha
Rasana	la
Ghrana	ā
Vak	sa
Pani	ḥ
Pada	ha
Upastha	ṣa
Payu	kṣa
Shabda	ma
Sparsha	Śa
Rupa	ṃ
Rasa	ta
Gandha	e
Akasha	ai
Vayu	o
Agni	au
Jala	da
Prithvi	pha

Each Tatwa represents a different aspect of the divine manifesting through the phonemes, illustrating the rich interconnection between sound, consciousness, and material reality.

Malini Arrangement of Shiva Tatwas

In the Malini arrangement of the phonemes, each sound reflects deeper aspects of the divine consciousness and its manifestations. The first phoneme in the Malini arrangement is **'Na'**. In the Matrika scheme, 'Na' corresponds to the Shrotra Tatwa, the principle of hearing. However, within the Malini framework, it reflects **Aham-Vimarsha**, the self-reflective 'I' consciousness of Para-Shiva. This phoneme signifies the self-awareness of the supreme consciousness, representing the fundamental realization of the self.

The next four letters in the Malini arrangement are the **four Amrita Bijas**: ṛ, ṝ, ḷ, and ḹ. These Bijas do not undergo differentiation in the Malini arrangement and symbolize the ability of Shiva to repose in his non-dual state of 'I'. They represent **Nada**, the primordial sound or vibration, which is elaborated further in the text.

The phoneme **'Tha'**, which in the Matrika arrangement is associated with Rasana (the organ of taste), signifies the experience of savoring in the context of taste. In the Malini arrangement, 'Tha' symbolizes the savoring of infinite bliss as the supreme 'I' consciousness. This reflects the enjoyment of the divine essence and the recognition of the blissful nature of the supreme self.

The phoneme **'Ca'** represents the Gandha Tanmatra, related to odoriferous particulates, and is associated with the element of earth in the Matrika scheme. It signifies the densification of the objective world. In Malini, 'Ca' reflects the realization of the supreme self

as pure, infinite, and blissful consciousness, emphasizing that all manifested forms are fundamentally one with the supreme consciousness.

The phoneme **'Dha'** in the Matrika arrangement stands for tactile sensation or touch. In the Malini context, 'Dha' represents the touch of the supreme consciousness, which eliminates the distinction between subject and object. It symbolizes the contact of subjective Shiva with the objective Shakti, leading to the realization of their inherent oneness.

The phoneme **'Ṅa'** represents Vak Tatwa, the power of speech, in Matrika. Esoterically, it signifies the supreme lord's capacity to perform actions. In the Malini arrangement, 'Ṅa' reflects Maya-Shakti and the actions performed through Maya. It underscores that the power to act ultimately resides within the supreme consciousness, or Para-Samvid alone.

The phoneme **'Ba'**, which corresponds to Buddhi Tatwa in Matrika, signifies the power of determination. In the Malini arrangement, 'Ba' asserts and determines its own perfect supreme state within the framework of objectivity. It represents the realization that Para-Shiva is not only the subject but also manifests as the object itself.

The phoneme **'Ka'** represents the earth element in Matrika, symbolizing the densification of the subject into the object. In the Malini arrangement, 'Ka' signifies the cementing of the 'I' consciousness in its supreme, transcended state. It denotes an awareness that is focused inwardly, toward the inner self.

The phoneme **'Kha'** is associated with the Jala or water element in Matrika, symbolizing fluidity and the sense of taste. In Malini, 'Kha' represents the taste of bliss that comes from the realization of

the self as Para-Shiva. It reflects the experience of divine pleasure through the perfect recognition of one's true nature.

The phoneme **'Ga'** in Matrika represents fire, the light principle, and the formative plane. In Malini, 'Ga' signifies Shiva shedding light on his own self, culminating in the recognition of his perfect nature, even as he manifests objectivity within himself.

With this brief overview of the theological and ontological aspects of the phonemes in Shaivite cosmogony, the hope is to provide the reader with a clear understanding of how these letters and Mantras function within Shaivite spiritual practices.

Kali - The Supreme Ontologic Principle

In Monistic Shaivism, Kali is a complex and profound figure who transcends her common associations in religious practice. Although Kali's name might evoke fear or awe depending on context, her role in Shaivism is deeply philosophical and ontological, reflecting core aspects of reality and consciousness.

Understanding Kali through the Concept of Kala

The name Kali derives from the root Kala, which means "to throw" or "to emanate." This is distinct from the common interpretation of Kali as "time" or Kaala. In Monistic Shaivism, Kali is understood as a principle deeply entwined with the actions of the supreme subject, Para-Bhairava (or Parama-Shiva), rather than simply being a representation of time.

The term Kalana (which relates to Kala) can be understood in several ways:

1. **Manifestation:** Kalana refers to the process of manifesting what lies within externally. It involves the emergence of potential into actual form.
2. **Assimilation:** It denotes the assimilation or integration of what appears to be identical with itself. This reflects the principle of unity and identity.
3. **Distinction:** Kalana involves the property of distinction—differentiating between subject and object or between two objects through similarities and dissimilarities.

4. **Self-Replication:** It signifies manifesting in its own image or the self-replicating principle of the supreme subject, illustrating the inherent capacity for self-expression and continuity.

5. **Withdrawal and Digestion:** Kalana also refers to the process of eventual withdrawal and digestion of what has been manifested, culminating in the realization of the supreme 'I' or self-affirming consciousness.

The Five Stages of Manifestation through Kali

In Monistic Shaivism, Kali facilitates the process of cosmic manifestation, which occurs through five key stages:

Kshepa

The cosmos, along with everything that exists prior to its manifestation, resides within the pure consciousness of Parama-Shiva. He manifests the cosmos in his own image; thus, the manifested cosmos is an expression of his will. Everything that exists within the consciousness of Parama-Shiva possesses the potential to be actualized. This inherent potential to bring forth the cosmos in his own image constitutes his sovereign power of expression.

His sovereign power of freedom, or Swatantra, manifests the cosmos externally through the force of will, known as Icha-Shakti. This tendency to project the cosmos from within himself—where Parama-Shiva manifests the cosmos within his own being—is referred to as Vamana, which means "to vomit" in this context. The names Vama-Deva and Vamakeswari, as well as the concept of

Vama-Marga, are associated with this phenomenon.

Before the cosmos is manifested, the entire creation exists within the consciousness of the supreme subject as one with him. The process of actualizing the cosmos from the consciousness of Parama-Shiva is known as Kshepa. This is the initial stage where the supreme consciousness (Parama-Shiva) projects or throws out the potentiality of the universe. It is the act of initiating the process of manifestation from the unmanifested state.

Jnana

This represents the second stage of manifestation. It is characterized by an indeterminate knowledge of objects. At this stage, the cosmos begins to actualize within the consciousness of the divine, or Godhead. The objective world takes on a very vague and formless state during this phase. There are no distinct forms or images present; distinctions are absent in this primordial state. The term **Jnana**, which is literally translated as "knowledge," refers to the differentiation or distinction between object and subject at this level.

Sankhyayana

The third stage of manifestation is characterized by definite objective ideas and distinct forms. At this stage, knowledge pertains to recognizing forms through their attributes, such as color, shape, and other defining features. Determinate knowledge arises through contrast and exclusion, involving distinctions between objects. This

means that an object is identified by differentiating it from both similar and dissimilar objects.

Gati

The fourth stage, known as **Gati**, literally translates to "movement" and is characterized by the movement of the subjective consciousness of the supreme Godhead toward the objects. At this stage, a clear distinction between the subject and the object is observed. The manifestation of the universe reaches its completion here. This state emerges when the awareness inherent in the consciousness of Parama-Shiva transforms into definite, determinate objects, thereby giving rise to the immanent universe.

Nada

The fifth stage is called **Nada** and is characterized by the dissolution of the awareness of the objective world into the self of the supreme Godhead. This stage can be seen as the dissolution of all objective reality into the subjective mind. It represents an inward-oriented awareness, where self-awareness of the subjective consciousness prevails. At this point, awareness has ceased to move towards the objective reality and instead remains firmly rooted in pure subjectivity.

In Monistic Shaivism, Kali is not merely a deity of destruction or darkness; she is the embodiment of the ontological principles of manifestation and dissolution. She represents the dynamic interplay of creation, preservation, and dissolution, acting as the supreme

principle that orchestrates the cosmic process. Through Kali, the processes of projection, knowledge, enumeration, movement, and vibration are actualized, reflecting the continuous cycle of creation and reabsorption in the universal consciousness.

Thus, Kali's role is central to understanding the nature of reality and consciousness in Monistic Shaivism. She embodies the principle of Kalana, manifesting the divine cosmic play and guiding the return of all manifestations to their ultimate source.

These five stages are symbolized by the five faces of Parama-Shiva and correspond to the five actions of the supreme Godhead: creation, preservation, destruction, obscuration of his nature, and the revealing of his nature through his grace.

The first action of Parama-Shiva corresponds to the manifestation of the objective world, known as creation, and falls under the activity of Kshepa. This activity represents the Icha-Shakti, or willpower, of Parama-Shiva. The second action is the preservation of what has been emitted or actualized through Vamana, and this is denoted by the stage of Jnana. The third action involves the withdrawal of the objects that have been emanated or manifested from his consciousness, which is represented by the stage of Nada.

When the awareness of Parama-Shiva is manifested as the objective world, there occurs an obscuration of his true divine self. This obscuration arises because Shiva, as a limited individual, is unable to fully realize his true nature. The stage of obscuration is associated with Sankhyana. In the final act of revealing his true nature through his grace, the individual realizes their divine essence, where the illusion of duality dissolves and everything is recognized as an expansion of Parama-Shiva. The limited perception of duality

completely disappears, and the distinction between object and subject vanishes, with the object being felt as existing within the subjective consciousness.

The mystical teachings centered around the twelve Kalis, which is the major topic of this chapter, are referred to as Kali Krama or Krama Kali, literally translated as the "succession of Kali" or the "Way of Kali."

In this Krama system, Kali is considered to be the Para-Samvid, or the supreme subjective principle, which transcends spatial and temporal constraints and is free from patterns or succession. Since succession of time and space applies only to the limited subject and not to the Para-Samvid, Kali is also known as Matrsadbhava, as she performs the five functions relative to the supreme absolute principle.

According to this system, all experiences of the limited and supreme subjects are framed in terms of cognition. An act of knowing the objective world and the awareness associated with this action are manifestations of the sovereign free will of the supreme consciousness. Whether limited or unlimited, everything is attributed to the supreme principle known as Kala Sankarshini Kali in this system. Just as a limited subject experiences sensations, thoughts, objects, and emotions within their mind, the supreme principle experiences the cosmos within its awareness alone. Similarly, just as a dream is experienced by a limited individual during sleep, the supreme consciousness, aware of the cosmos, manifests it spontaneously as part of its freedom to create.

In this system, the succession of the twelve Kalis is meditated upon as mental processes, one after another. The adept identifies

the states of awareness of the supreme subject within the limited subject and recognizes their identity with the supreme ontological principle. In essence, the limited empirical subject attains liberation by identifying the twelve Kalis within themselves.

The supreme form of Kali is also known as **Vyomeswari**, **Vameswari**, or **Vyoma-Vameswari**, as she actualizes the pentads of actions and powers of the supreme, which are the ultimate causation for all causes and phenomena in existence. Vyomeswari pervades everything; nothing exists independently of her, as she is the all-pervading consciousness or Para-Samvid itself. This system also aligns the supreme with **Para-Vak**, the highest state of the spoken word. The supreme state of speech, known as Para-Vak, is unified with the Para-Samvid, as previously discussed, and Para-Vak is also considered to be identical with the Swatantra, or the sovereign freedom of the supreme.

The essence of the Krama system lies in the purification of determinate ideas and in recognizing these thoughts as expressions of pure consciousness, which is identical with Para-Samvid. Every determinate thought and idea arises from the supreme indeterminate infinite Para-Samvid. By dissolving these determinate ideas into the indeterminate state of awareness, one can realize the supreme principle. This state of realization is referred to as **Maha Bhairava Chanda Ugra Ghora Kali**.

It is important to understand that the indeterminate state of awareness presupposes determinate thoughts and ideas. Therefore, the determinate ideas and thoughts, when dissolved into the indeterminate state, are identified as Para-Samvid or Vyomeswari. Vyomeswari holds four powers within herself to actualize

determinate ideas and knowledge into the form of the universe. These four powers are:

1. **Khechari**, the power of subjectivity.
2. **Dikchari**, the power of the internal sense organs.
3. **Gochari**, the power of the external sense organs.
4. **Bhuchari**, which ultimately manifests the objective universe that appears distinct and external from the subject.

Thus, Vyomeswari embodies **Chit Shakti**, or the consciousness that brings forth the cosmos from itself in its own image. Vyomeswari ultimately gives rise to the principles of subject, cognition, and object. These five manifestations of Kali correspond to the embodiment of the five powers of the supreme subject: **Chit**, **Ananda**, **Icha**, **Jnana**, and **Kriya**, respectively.

In terms of the manifestation of speech, these five forms are **Para**, **Sukshma**, **Pashyanti**, **Madhyama**, and **Vaikhari**. The four stages of speech have been detailed in a previous chapter, and we will explore the concept of Sukshma later in this chapter.

From the perspective of creation, these aspects are referred to as **Srishti** (creation), **Stithi** (preservation), **Samhara** (withdrawal), **Nirakhya** (the indeterminate state), and **Bhasa** (supreme consciousness).

In terms of articulated and inarticulated sounds, they correspond to **Vimarsha**, **Bindu**, **Nada**, **Sphota**, and **Shabda** (sounds), respectively. These powers form the triad of subject, cognition, and object, represented by the three eyes of Para-Shiva, and are known as **Murti**, **Prakasha**, and **Ananda** chakras. **Murti** has seventeen

aspects, **Prakasha** has sixteen aspects, and **Ananda** has twelve aspects, corresponding to the Will or **Icha**, Knowledge or **Jnana**, and Action or **Kriya** aspects of the supreme subject, respectively.

It should now be clear that Vyomeswari represents the totality of existence in terms of subject, cognition, and object, encompassing all the powers necessary to actualize this triad and to withdraw it back into the source.

Wheel of Twelve Kalis

The twelve Kalis are essential to the spiritual evolution of a Shaiva Yogi. They are described in various oriental texts such as the *Kali Kula Panchashatika* and the *Chit Gagana Chandrika*. The author has made every effort to present this tradition and system in a manner that is accessible to a general audience, despite the challenges of translating such complex concepts into Western languages. The aim is to make these intricate ideas understandable and applicable in practice.

The **Krama Chakra**, which comprises the twelve Kalis, is one of the Pancha Vahas, or five wheels. Vyomeswari and the four powers represent the five actions and powers of Para-Samvid, with creation, preservation, destruction, and the indeterminate states corresponding to wheels with ten, twenty-two, eleven, and twelve aspects, respectively. The **Nirakhya** or **Anakhya** Chakra, which corresponds to the indeterminate state of existence, includes the twelve Kalis. The other Chakras will be detailed in the practical section of this work.

Shaivite saint Abhinava Gupta suggests that in the state of

Anakhya, Kali appears as twelve forms in succession within the mystic's mind, symbolizing the dissolution of all determinate thoughts into the infinite Para-Samvid. This process facilitates the liberation of the mystic. The following twelve Kalis encompass the four states of creation, sustenance, dissolution, and the indeterminate state, relating to subject, cognition, and object.

1 - Srishti Kali

Srishti literally means creation. When the will to actualize the cosmos arises within the supreme subjective principle, it is manifested as objective reality within the awareness of the supreme. This action is termed **Srishti Kali** or the creative principle of the supreme consciousness. Srishti Kali represents the creative power in relation to the object, and at this stage, there is a sensation of distinction between the subject and the object.

2 - Rakta Kali

Rakta literally translates to blood. In the context of dark occultism, Rakta Kali is often misinterpreted as a destroyer and vampiric goddess, both in Eastern and Western traditions. However, Rakta Kali represents the principle of maintenance in relation to the object. She embodies the gross sense organs within us that allow us to perceive the world through the five senses. Rakta Kali symbolizes the act of cognition or the means of acquiring knowledge of the supreme principle. She is the principle behind the existence of the objective world, which manifests as the sustenance of objective reality through the five senses.

From an absolute monistic perspective, it should be understood

that the act of cognition may appear as the outward manifestation of the subject. This act manifests as cognition or the means of acquiring knowledge about objective reality, which is related to the object. Thus, the subject and object are perceived as distinct, and all relationships are made within these terms of distinction. Cognition is oriented towards the objective world, while subjective awareness remains unaffected. Additionally, the object does not have independent existence; its existence is entirely dependent on the act of cognition and the subject, as the object is a reflection of the subject.

3 - Stithi Nasha Kali

Stithi Nasha refers to the destruction or termination of cognition, or the dissolution of the principle of existence or sustenance. This form of the supreme consciousness arises when she withdraws her awareness from the objective world, or when she terminates the act of cognition, resulting in the withdrawal of the principle of maintenance or existence. At this stage, the subject experiences the feeling of "I have known the object in its complete form" and then withdraws awareness from the objective reality, focusing on abiding in pure inner awareness.

From an absolute monistic point of view, the entire cosmos or every form of existence is considered a momentary object of the supreme consciousness's awareness. Everything, including the subject, the act of knowing, and the object, is merely an object of awareness within the supreme principle, akin to a thought in the mind of an empirical individual. Due to the effects of **Malas** and **Kanchukas**, the object may appear as an external form of the

subject. However, the external existence of the object, which is identical to the subject, is momentary and exists only as long as it is within the awareness of the subject. Objects are recreated anew when awareness shifts from one objective knowledge to another, as discussed in the chapter on **Abhasa**. This means that as soon as an object is completely cognized and known, it is withdrawn and dissolved back into the subject. **Stithi Nasha Kali** embodies this principle of the supreme consciousness.

4 - Yama Kali

Yama is the god of death in many Indian spiritual traditions, particularly in the Vedas and Puranas. The term "Yama" also means 'to restrain.' Yama Kali represents the indeterminate power that emerges during the experience of limited objects by the limited empirical individual. She embodies the limited subjective principle of the supreme consciousness, bestowing the limited subjective awareness with the power of distinction. This creates various forms of dualities and pluralities within the subjective mind.

The distinctions created by Yama Kali are often based on concepts of wholesomeness versus unwholesomeness and similarities versus dissimilarities. For example, notions such as 'This is a cow' and 'This is a horse,' or 'This is a horse because it lacks horns,' arise from this principle. Additionally, distinctions like one being better than another or one being different from another manifest within limited subjective awareness because of Yama Kali. In a broader sense, Yama Kali also manifests as notions of good and evil, divinity and profanity, and moral values and virtues within subjective awareness.

Various schools of Indian philosophy have specific doctrines and

often refute the views of other schools. For instance, the dualistic school of Madhava refutes the non-dual Vedantic thoughts of Sankara, while the qualified non-dualism of Ramanuja challenges Sankaracharya's non-dualism. Similarly, different Shaiva schools may agree with or oppose the non-dual doctrines of Monistic Shaivism described here. Despite the differences in doctrines and practices across various spiritual systems worldwide, they all ultimately aim at recognizing the true nature of the self. In a more refined state of Yama Kali, the limited subject realizes that everything manifest or immanent is an expression of supreme awareness. Thus, in its most transcended form, everything is free from external objectivity. This realization helps one understand divine principles from various perspectives, as explained in earlier chapters. This unity in diversity within the limited subject is a manifestation of Yama Kali.

5 - Samhara Kali

Samhara literally translates to destruction. After reconciling dualities and pluralities within the mind of the limited individual, the object is perceived as one with the subject in terms of the act of cognition. This phase is known as **Samhara Kali**. Samhara Kali represents the creative phase in the act of cognition or knowing. In the stage of **Stithi Nasha Kali**, the object is perceived as external to the subject. Samhara Kali, however, represents the understanding that the object is recognized as one with the subject through the act of knowing.

6 - Mrtyu Kali

Mrtyu means death, and **Mrtyu Kali** encompasses even

Samhara Kali. At the level of Samhara Kali, the external cognition of objects disappears, yet the objectivity becomes immanent and part of the subject. In the phase of Mrtyu Kali, objective reality merges with the subject and is freed from any inherent objectivity. Here, the subject recognizes the object as an emanation of the subject itself and as a manifestation brought forth by the act of knowing. This phase represents the maintenance or sustenance of the act of cognition. All notions of independent objectivity external to the subject vanish, leaving the subject to perceive the manifestation of objects as changes in cognition or awareness.

7 - Rudra Kali / Bhadra Kali

Rudra Kali and **Bhadra Kali** represent the dissolution or destruction aspect of cognition. The term "Bha" means *Bhedana*, or cutting, and "Dra" means *Dravana*, or liquefaction or dissolution. This phase involves the dissolution of the multitude of objects within the subject, effectively making them disappear and reintegrating them into the subject. This dissolution is different from Yama Kali. While Yama Kali deals with dissolving dualities in the external manifestation of the objective world, Rudra Kali addresses the dissolution of multiplicity within the act of knowing or cognition.

In the context of the limited individual, Rudra Kali signifies the disappearance of all dualities within the subject's mind. Unlike Yama Kali, which resolves dualities in the external world, Rudra Kali focuses on the internal cognitive process. Here, the distinctions and dualities that arise in the mind are reconciled, making every form of objective knowledge shine as a unified whole. In this phase, all multiplicities and pluralities vanish. The term "Ru" refers to light or

gross manifestation, while "Dra" again signifies dissolution. Thus, what has been manifested as a gross object is dissolved back into its fundamental essence. This two-way mechanism, where dissolution and manifestation occur, is why Rudra Kali is also known as such.

8 - Martanda Kali

Martanda refers to the sun and the twelve zodiacs associated with it in mystical contexts. The twelve *Indriyas* or sense organs, including the five external senses, five organs of action, and the two internal organs—*Manas* (mind) and *Buddhi* (intellect)—are considered the twelve suns or zodiacs in this context. Although the *Ahankara* (ego principle) is an internal sense organ, it is not included here because it coordinates all twelve organs, aiding in perception and action.

Martanda Kali represents the principle of the union of all twelve sense organs or suns. This phase embodies the indeterminate or *Anakhya* state of cognition. She is the supreme act that brings together all twelve means of knowledge and action within the *Ahamkara* (ego principle). In this sense, Martanda Kali signifies the identification of the twelve Indriyas as one with the Ahamkara or in union with the Ahamkara Tatwa, representing the indeterminate phase of cognition.

9 - Parama Arka Kali

The preceding tetrad of Kalis addresses the four phases related to the act of knowing. The phase starting with **Parama Arka Kali** represents the four phases related to the subject. Parama Arka Kali is said to envelop or devour the twelve suns of Martanda Kali. This

phase marks the emergence of the limited 'I' or self. It illustrates the distinction between the limited and the unlimited subjects: the limited subject is constrained by space, time, and determinacy, while the unlimited subject is free from such constraints.

This phase represents the origin or emanation of the limited subject and signifies the merging of Ahamkara into the limited subjective consciousness. In essence, Parama Arka Kali symbolizes the transition from the unbounded, infinite self to the bounded, finite self, thus marking the formation of the limited 'I'.

10 - Kala Agni Rudra Kali

Kala Agni Rudra Kali signifies the phase where the limited subject merges with the supreme subject. At this stage, the entire cosmos is experienced within the consciousness of the supreme subject. Here, the limited subject is recognized as one with the supreme subject, reflecting the sustenance or maintenance of the limited self. This phase represents the realization of oneself as all-pervading, encompassing the entire cosmos. Although it is determinate in nature—since the limited subject is identified with the supreme subject—it transcends the limitations of the individual self, embracing the cosmos within the supreme consciousness.

The self is inherently conscious and self-luminous, serving as the foundation for all knowledge. This consciousness cannot be an object of perception or contemplation since it illuminates the entire objective reality. Duality arises when the objective world is seen as separate from subjective awareness, an illusion created by Maya. When duality is transcended and the true nature of objectivity is recognized as unified with the self, this realization is termed Kala

Agni Rudra Kali.

11 - Maha Kala Kali

In **Maha Kala Kali**, the objective world subsumed in the greater 'I' ceases to exist. This phase is marked by the pure 'I', untainted by any external thoughts or objects. It represents the dissolution or destruction of all forms and objects within the supreme subject. Here, the 'I' exists solely in its own essence, with all relational and objective elements dissipating completely. The pure 'I' is self-contained, and the phase signifies a profound internal state where every form of objectivity and relation vanishes, leaving only the undisturbed self.

12 - Maha Bhairava Chanda Ugra Ghora Kali

Maha Bhairava Chanda Ugra Ghora Kali is the ultimate state of supreme consciousness, where all notions of subject, object, and cognition dissolve. What remains is the pure 'I' consciousness, free from any dualistic or objective distinctions. This state is beyond verbal description, as it transcends the limited notions of language and relates to the indeterminate state or Nirakhya concerning the subject. It embodies the self-luminous nature of consciousness, devoid of any distinctions between subject, cognition, and object.

Krama Mudra

The ultimate principle of consciousness that pervades and encompasses the twelve Kalis is known as Kala Sankarshini. This principle is revered as the highest metaphysical reality, often referred to as Maha Para Kali or Kala Akarshini. Maha Para Kali represents

the apex of subjective experience, embodying pure consciousness that is entirely free from any notions of duality and plurality. The process known as Kalana, which includes the five actions such as Kshepa and others, is deeply interwoven with the empirical mental processes and experiences. This concept is reflected in a cyclical succession, which is why the term Krama, meaning sequence, is applied to describe these phases. Each of these phases, represented by the twelve Kalis, manifests as a step in the cosmic and cognitive processes.

Kala Sankarshini, who brings about these processes of Kalana, plays a crucial role in the manifestation of the cosmos and the objects within it. She represents pure, unadulterated consciousness and has two primary aspects: one as the most transcendent form of subjective consciousness, characterized by an inner experience that is devoid of any external objectivity and duality; and the other as the active principle responsible for the creation and perpetuation of the cosmos, filled with the knowledge of objectivity and duality. In this sense, she is considered the causal principle behind the formation of the universe and also as the pure consciousness that underlies all of creation.

Kala Sankarshini transcends all forms of sequences and successions. She is not bound by the constraints of time and space. The realization of this principle brings about the dissolution of the concepts of space and time within the empirical individual. This realization allows one to experience the self as pure consciousness, which leads to the understanding of absolute unity where all multiplicities and dualities exist in perfect harmony. Moving from the stage of Srishti Kali to that of Maha Bhairava Chanda Ugra

Ghora Kali involves a gradual dissolution of patterns, successions, dualities, and the limitations imposed by space and time.

This principle, which represents ontological unity, is known as Kali or Kala Sankarshini. She is also referred to as Matrika Sadbhava because she constitutes the entire existence and encompasses the sum total of all objects within the cosmos and beyond. The awareness continually oscillates between the internal and external realms—a phenomenon described as Spanda. Krama Mudra involves consciously redirecting one's awareness inward from external objects. In this state, awareness withdraws from the external sensory experiences and remains anchored in a state of pure subjectivity, free from any constructs of thought. This profound inner awareness, which arises during Krama Mudra, leads to the ultimate recognition of Para-Shiva.

The term Krama signifies the cyclical processes inherent in consciousness, such as Kshepa and Jnana. By becoming aware of these eternal activities within the supreme consciousness, the individual transcends the limited self and recognizes their true nature as self-reflective consciousness. This realization dissolves all fetters, Malas, and the obscuring principles of Maya. The stage of Krama Mudra involves the dissolution of all thought processes, including emanation and sustenance, into an indeterminate state of consciousness. This awareness reveals an unlimited inner consciousness that remains untainted by any limited thoughts.

After attaining the pure state of consciousness in Krama Mudra, the adept understands that the entire universe exists within the divine consciousness and perceives the external world as an expression of this supreme consciousness. This realization leads to Jivan-Mukti,

or liberation, as previously discussed. The agitation within Shiva's seminal power (Bindu) initiates the cosmos and produces a cyclical movement of awareness between inward and outward, known as Spanda, which reflects the continuous flow and interaction between the inner and outer dimensions of consciousness.

Vikalpa Kshaya

Certainly! The concept of **Vikalpa Kshaya** and its associated practices delve deeply into the nature of thoughts and consciousness in spiritual traditions, particularly within the context of Shaivism and related philosophies. Here's a comprehensive exploration of Vikalpa Kshaya, including its process, significance, and associated practices.

In the context of Vikalpa Kshaya, it is crucial to explore the intricate process of how mental constructs dissolve. Our mental landscape is significantly shaped by our experiences, which encompass a myriad of thoughts, emotions, and feelings. The mind accumulates an endless array of thoughts, each moment giving rise to one or more new thoughts, many of which appear without our conscious awareness. These thoughts, like waves continuously rolling across the ocean, can either pass quickly or persist, shaping our actions and words.

The ceaseless flow of thoughts results from the agitation of the **Chit**, which is the essence of consciousness. This agitation, or **Spanda**, manifests as the ever-changing stream of thoughts that lead to experiences of pleasure, pain, happiness, anger, and anguish. By becoming aware of these fleeting thoughts or **Vikalpas**, individuals can gain control over their mental processes. This awareness enables

them to either eliminate these thoughts using specific techniques, such as **Mantras**, or to dissolve them back into the indeterminate state from which they originated. This process of dissolving thought constructs into an **Anakhya**—an indeterminate or unformed state of awareness—is referred to as **Vikalpa Bhavana Mudra**.

The spontaneous occurrence of **Vikalpa Kshaya** happens when the **Anugraha Shakti**, or the grace of the supreme divine, descends upon the adept. In such moments, the adept experiences a profound realization of their true self as divine and perceives the universe as resting entirely within their own awareness. The **Upayas**—methods or techniques previously discussed—can be employed to aid in the dissolution of these mental constructs. The more one engages with these methods, the more Vikalpas dissolve back into the foundational awareness, gradually expanding consciousness. This expansion continues until all limited thought constructs are eradicated, ultimately leading to liberation.

By observing thoughts and deeply analyzing their nature, the adept becomes increasingly conscious of their actions and thoughts. This heightened awareness facilitates the realization of the true self and can lead to the achievement of **Vikalpa Bhavana Mudra**. Contemplating the five actions of Shiva—creation, sustenance, destruction, hiding, and blessing—within oneself helps in recognizing the divine nature inherent in the self. Prolonged practice of this contemplation reveals that the god-consciousness, or **Chit**, represents the true nature of the self, furthering the realization of the divine self.

Another method involves meditating on the concept of **'Aham'**, which combines the first and last phonemes of Sanskrit letters. This

syllable represents the highest reality and aids in the dissolution of limited thoughts. Contemplation on **'Aham'** helps in recognizing one's true nature and achieving a profound understanding of the self. This practice illuminates the realization that the consciousness which underlies all knowledge is self-luminous and cannot be objectified or contemplated directly as it serves as the foundation for all manifestation.

In essence, the process of Vikalpa Kshaya involves a thorough understanding and dissolution of thoughts and mental constructs, leading to a clearer perception of the self and the universe. Through dedicated practice and contemplation, one can achieve a state where the duality of subject and object dissolves, revealing the self as the ultimate consciousness and attaining liberation.

Nada and Bindu

In discussing the five aspects of Kali, we have encountered the terms **Nada** and **Bindu**. It is now important to delve deeper into what these concepts represent. The term **Nada** literally translates to "sound." However, Nada encompasses more than just the physical sounds we commonly experience. It manifests in two primary forms: articulate and inarticulate sounds.

Articulate sounds are those that can be physically heard, such as when an animal makes a noise, a person speaks, or a musical instrument is played. These sounds, which are perceptible through our physical ears, fall under the category of **Vaikhari** or spoken sounds.

In contrast, **Nada** primarily refers to inarticulate sound. This inarticulate Nada is subtler and more profound than the physical

sounds we hear. It pervades all forms of sound and is the underlying essence that makes physical sound possible. Because of its subtle nature, Nada cannot be perceived through ordinary physical means. When one withdraws inwardly and achieves a deep state of inner silence, a very subtle hum or resonance may be sensed. This subtle hum is what is referred to as Nada.

Nada is described as an eternal and subtle sound that persists even when our conscious awareness of it fades. It is not a sound that is physically uttered but is the essence that pervades all physical sounds. Every articulated sound, whether a word or a sentence, exists as an extension of this imperceptible Nada before it becomes manifest in physical form. Saint Abhinava Gupta, in his seminal work **Tantra Aloka**, uses the term **Varna** to refer to Nada. He posits that all sounds are unified within this Varna or Nada, which continuously vibrates through all forms of existence. This Nada is also known as **Anahata**, or the "unstruck sound," because it is the source of all sounds without itself being struck or produced.

In certain meditative practices, when one's awareness is withdrawn from the external world and thoughts cease to arise, the inner awareness begins to expand, making the Nada naturally perceptible. Sometimes, it may be experienced as a faint, subtle hum or an "Ammmm" sound. Concentrating on the breath, specifically on the inhalation and exhalation, can facilitate the recognition of Nada. Abhinava Gupta suggests that awareness of Nada can also be attained by focusing on the interval between the **Srishti** (creation) and **Samhara** (destruction) bijas, a concept that will be explored further in the practical sections of this text.

The **Nada Bindu Upanishad** describes a practice where a yogi

sits with eyes open, disregarding external visual stimuli, and focuses on hearing. With prolonged practice, the yogi begins to perceive a faint, subtle sound that initially appears as a gentle hum and gradually intensifies to the quality of a drumbeat. Abhinava Gupta elaborates on ten states of Nada, which will be discussed in detail in the practical part of this work. In the Vedic tradition, this subtle sound is equated with the Pranava, or the sacred sound **AUM**, which is said to exist in nine stages, each representing a step towards spiritual illumination.

Bindu, on the other hand, is described as the seminal power of Shiva, concentrated into a single point before manifesting as the objective cosmos. Symbolically represented by a dot, Bindu embodies the concentrated essence from which the universe emerges. The detailed praxis of Nada, Bindu, and the sound **AUM** will be thoroughly examined in the practical sections of this book.

Bhasa

In this chapter, we encounter a term previously unexplored in this text: **Bhasa**. This term refers to the freedom or **Chit-Shakti** of **Parama Samvid**, representing the most transcendent aspect of the supreme subject, whether conceived as **Kala-Sankarshini** or **Para-Bhairava**. We have already discussed how the processes of manifestation and withdrawal are fundamentally unified with the supreme subject. The entire cosmos emerges due to the powers of **Para-Samvid**, and when it reflects the objective world, it does so without separating it from its own existence; the universe is in an eternal union with the supreme consciousness. Thus, the creator and the created are inherently one, and the substratum of manifestation,

the act of manifestation, and the object of manifestation are all intrinsically connected.

The processes of manifestation are represented by the **16 Kalas** or phases of the moon. The fifteen forms observed during the waxing phases signify emanation, while the fifteen forms during the waning phases signify withdrawal. The sixteenth form is believed to pervade all the sixteen forms and remains invisible. In Shaivism, there is also a seventeenth form known as **Baindhavi-Kala**, which is considered the eternal principle that remains unchanged and is the causative factor for the manifestation of all the Kalas. This Baindhavi-Kala is synonymous with supreme consciousness or **Para-Samvid** in its most radiant form. The evolution and involution of this principle correspond to the expansion and contraction of the thirty-six **Tatwas** and are represented by the fifty letters of the Sanskrit alphabet, which embody the principles constituting the cosmos.

In Shaivism, consciousness is referred to as **Anuttara**, the supreme and most transcended state. Saint Abhinava Gupta, in his work **Tantra Aloka**, uses the term **Pratibha** to describe Bhasa. This seventeenth Kala, **Anuttara**, and the causal factor of the cosmos, is explained as **"Svatma Paramarsha Matra"** or self-reflective consciousness. This ultimate, self-affirming consciousness is identified with **Kala-Sankarshini**. In more accessible terms, this principle is often referred to simply as **Kali**. It is all-comprehending, all-pervading, infinite, and eternal—a supreme light that encompasses all.

Sukshma

Apart from the four states of speech previously discussed, this chapter introduces an additional stage known as **Sukshma**,

which literally means "subtle." There are nuanced differences in interpretation between **Siddhanta Shaivism** (South Indian Shaivism) and the **Krama system** regarding Sukshma. For now, we will consider the Krama perspective. Siddhanta Shaivism holds that Sukshma pertains to the limited subject rather than the transcended principle. Conversely, Monistic Shaivism, which acknowledges **Para-Vak** encompassing **Pashyanti**, **Madhyama**, and **Vaikhari**, asserts that these stages are interpenetrated by the supreme light and that Sukshma is also one with the supreme consciousness.

Sukshma represents the stage that manifests immediately after **Para** begins to evolve and expand. The Will, Knowledge, and Action of the supreme subject align with **Pashyanti**, **Madhyama**, and **Vaikhari**. Sukshma is characterized by the unity of **Icha** (Will), **Jnana** (Knowledge), and **Kriya** (Action), corresponding to the unified state of the three stages of speech. It is associated with **Bliss** or **Ananda Shakti** of the supreme principle.

Kundalini And The Ultimate Subjectivity

This chapter will tackle a topic that is often misunderstood: **Kundalini** within the Shaivite traditions. As indicated by the title, this chapter will focus on the Agamic or classical perspective of Kundalini in Shaivism. The author will refrain from discussing the Chakras and other elements related to the subtle bodies, as these subjects are already well-explored in Western literature. Instead, the aim is to delve into the traditional Shaivite understanding of Kundalini. At this point, it is assumed that the reader has a basic familiarity with Shaivism, including fundamental concepts such as the triad of consciousness, the four stages of speech, and the seven subjective states. With this foundational knowledge in place, we will proceed directly to examine the concept of Kundalini.

The term **Kundalini** literally translates to "coiled one." It is traditionally depicted as a serpent coiled in three and a half turns, resting at the base of the spine or within the **Muladhara Chakra**. This image, while vivid, is more metaphorical than literal. In the classical Shaivite understanding, the awakened Kundalini is not merely a form of energy rising through the spinal column but represents the supreme subjective state of the individual.

The nature of Kundalini is intrinsically tied to the concept of **Para-Shiva**, which is characterized by self-awareness or self-reflective consciousness. Kundalini is a manifestation of this fundamental awareness. It plays a crucial role in illuminating every subjective

and objective experience. Thanks to the presence of Kundalini, individuals are capable of perceiving and assimilating knowledge in various ways. As discussed earlier, the objective world is merely a reflection of the subject. The processes of emanation, sustenance, withdrawal, and dissolution of all objective experiences from the subject are facilitated by the existence of Kundalini. To put it more clearly, Kundalini is the inherent power that allows the subject to reflect upon itself through the expressions and experiences of the external world.

Kundalini, being the innate power of awareness within Shiva, represents the two primary activities of **Para-Shiva**: the emanation and dissolution of the cosmos. This inherent power is often referred to as **Shakti**, the feminine principle that embodies the creative and transformative forces of the divine. Consequently, Kundalini is seen as the agent through which all manifestations occur, acting as the absolute will of **Para-Samvid** that brings the cosmos into being and dissolves it. Shiva represents the essence of consciousness, while Shakti signifies the inherent awareness associated with that consciousness. Therefore, Kundalini can be viewed as the ultimate subjective awareness of Shiva. The cosmos itself is a manifestation of this boundless awareness. Thus, Kundalini is considered the highest form of subjective awareness, which emerges spontaneously when both external and internal objective impressions are transcended. The fully awakened state of Kundalini is characterized by a profound awareness directed both inwardly towards the self and outwardly towards the supreme subject, embodying a state of complete realization and unity with the divine consciousness.

From a religious perspective, self-aware consciousness is

often depicted through the union of male and female principles, represented by the deities **Shiva** and **Parvati**, or as the androgynous figure of **Ardha-Narishvara**. This union symbolizes the essential oneness and interdependence of the masculine and feminine aspects of the divine. In the context of linguistic symbolism, vowels are associated with Shiva, while consonants, which emerge from the expansion of vowels, correspond to Shakti. The act of planting Shiva's seed into the womb of Shakti symbolizes the emission of the cosmos. This concept is further illustrated by how the Shiva **Tattvas** (principles) are reflected in Shakti through the **Malini** arrangement of phonemes, which has been previously discussed.

The ascent of Kundalini serves as a symbolic representation of the individual's evolution from a lesser state of subjectivity to the highest state of spiritual realization. In Shaivism, there are seven subjective states. The first state is **Sakala**, the gross state of subjectivity characterized by a profound ignorance of the self. In this state, there is a clear distinction between subject and object, and the empirical individual mistakenly identifies themselves with external objects. The highest state is the **Shiva Pramatr**, a state of subjectivity that transcends all dualities, where the object is perceived as inherently unified with the subject. This state of **Shiva Pramatr** is beyond verbal description; it represents the sensation of the supreme **'I'**, where the cosmos is experienced as the supreme self. It is a pure state of subjectivity, devoid of any objectivity. The symbolic journey of Kundalini rising through the six mystical wheels, or **Chakras**, culminating in the seventh wheel with a thousand spokes, the **Sahasrara**, represents the transcendence from the gross state of objectivity to the pure state of subjectivity.

Certain texts related to monistic Shaivism attribute the three primary **Nadis** or channels in the body—**Ida**, **Pingala**, and **Sushumna**—to the processes of preservation, creation, and withdrawal, respectively. In this framework, **Sushumna** represents the subject, **Pingala** corresponds to the process of cognition, and **Ida** symbolizes the object. These Nadis are also associated with celestial bodies: the moon, the sun, and fire. In Shaivism, Shiva is often depicted as a three-eyed deity, symbolizing the integration of these elements. The deity is described as **Soma Surya Agni Lochanaya**, meaning "one who has the moon, sun, and fire as his eyes." Here, fire corresponds to the subject and the **Sushumna** or central path, while the third eye represents this aspect of divine vision. The sun is associated with the process of cognition and the right path or right eye, while the moon is linked to the left path and the left eye, symbolizing the object and the action of **Para-Shiva**. This triadic correspondence underscores the dynamic interplay between the divine principles of subject, cognition, and object within the cosmic order.

In Shaivite doctrines, Kundalini is symbolically represented as a serpent coiled in three and a half turns. The three full turns represent the triad of subject, cognition, and object, which correspond to the three primary aspects of divine power: will (Icha), knowledge (Jnana), and action (Kriya-Shakti). The half turn is known as **Prama** or **Pramiti**, signifying pure consciousness that pervades and empowers the triadic forms of subject, cognition, and object. This half turn represents the ultimate power, manifesting in the triadic form and serving as the foundation for the entire process.

In Shaivite thought, the **Ida** Nadi is associated with the moon,

the **Pingala** Nadi is associated with the sun, and the middle path, or **Sushumna**, is linked with fire. Specifically, the Sushumna is often synonymous with subjectivity, while Ida and Pingala are associated with objectivity and cognition, respectively. The concept extends to how **Prana**, or awareness, interacts with these Nadis. When Prana enters the Ida channel, it is described as being in a state akin to a lunar eclipse, and when it moves to the Pingala channel, it is likened to a solar eclipse. This concept correlates with esoteric aspects of astrology, such as Rahu and Ketu, representing the north and south lunar nodes, though this aspect is beyond the immediate scope of our discussion.

When Prana, or awareness, is in the state of objectivity or engaged with the external world (the moon), it is said to be in the first coil of Kundalini. As awareness transitions to the cognitive state (the sun), it is attached to the second coil. When awareness shifts towards fire, or the subjective consciousness of the 'I,' it reaches the third coil. These three coils embody the triple emanation of Shakti. The final half coil, **Prama** or **Pramiti**, represents pure consciousness or illumination. Even at the level of subjective consciousness, where the 'I' still recognizes the outer world and its traces, some degree of objectivity persists. The state of Prama is characterized by the complete dissolution of all traces of objectivity. In this state, the 'I' is perceived in its pure form, devoid of any external reference or distinction.

According to the doctrines, the empirical individual is a contracted form of **Para-Shiva**, the supreme consciousness. In his works, such as the *Para Trishika Vivarana* and *Tantra Aloka*, the scholar **Abhinava Gupta** elaborates on the triple emanation of Kundalini and refers to

it as **Kauliki**. The concept of Kundalini holds significant importance among Kaula practitioners, which has its roots in Monistic Shaivism. The term "Kaula" has various meanings within Shaivite traditions and is sometimes misinterpreted as involving sexual rites related to Sri Chakra practices. However, foundational texts clarify that these practices are symbolic representations rather than literal enactments.

Kundalini in Shaivite traditions is much more than a mere metaphor for spiritual awakening. It embodies the dynamic interplay of divine will, knowledge, and action, culminating in the pure consciousness of Prama. The journey through the coils of Kundalini symbolizes the ascent from objectivity to the ultimate realization of pure subjective awareness, reflecting the profound depth of Shaivite metaphysical and spiritual teachings.

Abhinava Gupta, in his writings about Kaula practices, provides a nuanced understanding of Kundalini. He explains that the masculine principle is represented by the sun, while the feminine principle is associated with the moon, and their union is symbolized by fire. This union of male and female principles leads to the merging of the sun, moon, and fire, culminating in the awakening of Kundalini. The key insight here is that the Kundalini awakens when the empirical individual realizes the inherent union between subject and object. Unfortunately, later Western interpretations of Shaivism have distorted this sacred spirituality by introducing misguided sexual practices that misrepresent the essence of these teachings. Subsequently, Eastern works have often rehashed these distorted Western interpretations, further confusing the original spiritual concepts.

Let's delve into the significant interpretations of the term **Kaula**.

The term "Kaula" is derived from the word "Kula," and in Shaivite doctrines, it has several layers of meaning.

1. **Gross and Subtle Manifestations**: The first interpretation of Kula encompasses both gross and subtle manifestations. Gross refers to the physical body, sense organs, Prana, etc. The term Kaula signifies that the objective world is an expression of transcendent consciousness. In this view, objects manifest from the subject and always abide within the subject. Without the self-luminous light of consciousness, the objective world could not be realized. Thus, Kula represents the very awareness that brings objectivity into existence. It is the power of the subject to manifest the object.

2. **Subjective and Objective Experience**: The second interpretation describes Kaulika as the experience of both subjective and objective phenomena—expressed as 'I' and 'THIS.' In this context, 'THIS' represents the objective reality comprising numerous objects, while 'I' denotes the perceiver of these objects, which is the self, fundamentally consciousness. This interpretation points to the limited awareness of individuals, which is essentially the manifestation of Shakti herself.

3. **Self-Luminous Light**: The third interpretation suggests that Kauliki represents the form of Shiva and Shakti, or the self-luminous light inherent in everyone, which many are not consciously aware of. This view holds that Kauliki is the power responsible for liberation in every empirical individual, aligning with the concept of Anugraha or the grace of Shiva.

This aspect highlights another function of Kundalini.

4. **Blissful Power**: The fourth interpretation identifies Kula as the power of delight or bliss, known as Ananda-Shakti, associated with Shiva. It is through this bliss that the cosmos, with its myriad objects, manifests. The bliss experienced by Para-Shiva when he manifests the cosmos from himself is referred to as Kula-Shakti. This self-luminous light or self-aware consciousness, which brings the cosmos into manifestation, is also called Kula-Shakti.

These interpretations clarify why Kundalini is referred to as **Kauliki**. Kundalini is the power through which Shiva manifests the cosmos. Therefore, Kundalini should not be equated with the objective world; she transcends objectivity. Instead, she is the cause of objectivity and manifests it in the gross states of existence. The nature of Kundalini is self-revealing, and the ascent of Kundalini symbolizes the ascent of consciousness from the field of objectivity to pure subjectivity.

Let us now explore the different manifestations of Kundalini as described in Shaivite doctrines. Kundalini is classified into three major forms: Para-Kundalini, Chit-Kundalini, and Prana-Kundalini. Each form represents a distinct aspect of Shakti, the divine energy.

Para-Kundalini is the most transcendent aspect of Shakti. In this form, there is no distinction between subject and object. Para-Kundalini is the essence from which the cosmos emerges during the phase of emanation. This form is also referred to as the power of **Visarga**. Visarga is symbolized by two vertically arranged dots, representing Shiva and Shakti, with Shakti depicted as the lower dot

reflecting the upper dot of Shiva.

The interplay between these two dots illustrates the dual aspects of Shakti—the concealing and revealing nature of Para-Shiva. Para-Kundalini enables the contraction of the divine consciousness into empirical individuals and the subsequent realization of its true identity. While some scholars suggest that Para-Kundalini cannot be experienced in a living body and is only realizable at the time of physical death, it is also believed that the most potent grace, or Shaktipath, from Para-Shiva can facilitate the realization of this Kundalini while still embodied. When one reaches the level of Para-Kundalini, the cosmos is perceived as existing within the awareness of the supreme subject. This stage allows the total identification of the lesser subject with the supreme subject. At this point, a yogi may either choose to shed their physical body voluntarily or continue to engage with the physical world while maintaining this heightened awareness.

During its manifestation phase, Para-Kundalini is known as **Shakti-Kundalini**, reflecting the dynamic interplay between Shiva and Shakti in the creation of the limited cosmos. Para-Kundalini is always associated with **Icha-Shakti** or the will of the supreme lord, as the will to create is inherently united with the awareness of Para-Shiva. When Para-Kundalini transforms into Shakti-Kundalini, it manifests as **Pramana Tejas**, or the light of consciousness. This light signifies the knowledge acquired through the five senses— sound, touch, sight, etc. The experience of Para-Kundalini often occurs when a yogi meditates on the indeterminate state that precedes the emergence of thoughts in the mind. By focusing on this indeterminate state, a yogi can realize their true self and become

aware of the omnipresent consciousness, a direct manifestation of the Chit-Shakti of Shiva. Another approach to recognizing this Kundalini is through contemplation of the five actions of Shiva within oneself.

The next form is **Chit-Kundalini**, which is responsible for consciousness itself. This aspect of Kundalini enables the manifestation of unlimited consciousness into individual, lesser consciousnesses. Chit-Kundalini is recognized in an individual when they become aware of their inner nature. This recognition can be achieved through various practices, one of which involves meditating on the interval between inhalation and exhalation, known as **Sandhi**. Sandhi, meaning the gap or interval between two breaths, is a crucial practice in understanding and experiencing Chit-Kundalini. Further details on these practices will be elaborated in the practical section of the text.

The manifestations of Kundalini—Para-Kundalini, Chit-Kundalini, and Prana-Kundalini—represent different aspects of divine energy and consciousness. Each form plays a distinct role in the process of creation, awareness, and realization within the framework of Shaivite spirituality.

To deepen our understanding of Kundalini, let us explore various methods and concepts related to its manifestation and awakening.

Concentration on Thought and Awareness

One effective method for awakening Kundalini involves concentrating on a single thought and being acutely aware of the gap between successive thought forms. This practice requires a high degree of mental attention and mindfulness. By focusing on

the intervals between thoughts, an individual can gain insight into the underlying nature of consciousness. This practice is known as **Shakti Chakra Dhyana**, where "Chakra" refers to the cyclical nature of mental processes. These processes are periodic and are symbolized by the twelve forms of Kali, which represent various stages of mental activity.

The essence of this meditation is to realize the supreme 'I' by enkindling consciousness and becoming aware of it. This requires the individual to dispel all limited thoughts and impressions, thereby achieving a state of awareness focused solely on the inner self. By withdrawing awareness from external objects and concentrating on the internal self, a practitioner engages in **Vikalpa Kshaya**. Here, "Vikalpa" denotes limited thought constructs, and "Kshaya" refers to their dissolution. This process is central to the initiation into Hermetics as described by Franz Bardon, which emphasizes the importance of achieving Vikalpa Kshaya.

Once an individual has stirred their inner self with sparks of awareness, they realize their unity with **Virya**, which represents the creative power of Shiva. Contrary to popular misinterpretations, Virya in this context does not refer to sexual energy but to the supreme creative potential inherent in divine consciousness.

Chit-Kundalini

The next manifestation is **Chit-Kundalini**, which represents the power of consciousness itself. Chit-Kundalini is responsible for transforming unlimited consciousness into individual awareness. This form of Kundalini is recognized when a person becomes aware of their inner nature. Practical meditation techniques, such as

focusing on the interval between inhalation and exhalation (Sandhi), facilitate the recognition of Chit-Kundalini. Sandhi, meaning the gap or interval between breaths, is a key aspect of meditative practice aimed at experiencing this state of consciousness.

Prana-Kundalini

Prana-Kundalini is associated with the vital energy or awareness manifested through **Mantras**. In Shaivism, Devi or the divine feminine is referred to as **Malini**, meaning "garlanded with letters." The eight categories of letters in Sanskrit are embodied by the eight female goddesses known as the **Ashta Matrikas**. The awakening of **Mantra Virya**—the potential of Mantras within an individual—is a result of recognizing Prana-Kundalini. The letters of the Sanskrit alphabet, which are integral to Mantras, form the heart of Para-Shiva, symbolizing the center of awareness or Shakti. Thus, Prana-Kundalini is directly linked to the manifestation and understanding of Mantras.

Urdhwa-Kundalini and Adhah-Kundalini

In **Kaula practices**, two additional aspects of Kundalini are discussed: **Urdhwa-Kundalini** and **Adhah-Kundalini**.

1. **Urdhwa-Kundalini** represents the upward movement of awareness from objectivity to subjectivity. It signifies the ascent of consciousness from the material realm (Prthwi Tatwa) to the divine consciousness (Shiva Tatwa). This form of Kundalini is associated with the power of withdrawal and grace-bestowing in empirical individuals.

2. **Adhah-Kundalini** denotes the downward movement of awareness from the divine to the material realm. It involves the descent of consciousness from the higher, subjective state of Shiva to the lower, objective state of Prthwi. This power is responsible for both the concealment and manifestation of the cosmos.

Both Urdhwa-Kundalini and Adhah-Kundalini are crucial in the process of spiritual evolution. They embody the dual functions of withdrawal and manifestation and play significant roles in the bestowal of grace. Practical methods for experiencing these aspects of Kundalini will be elaborated in the practical section of this work, specifically in relation to the initiation process.

The Muladhara Chakra and Its Symbolism

The **Muladhara Chakra**, symbolically the seat of Kundalini, represents the convergence of the three primary channels: Ida, Pingala, and Sushumna. This union, known as **Triveni Sanghama**, signifies the integration of objectivity, cognition, and subjectivity. The Muladhara is also referred to as **Andhatamishra**, meaning "the darkest realm."

Some practitioners, due to ignorance or misunderstanding, may perceive the Muladhara Chakra and its associated objectivity as dark or evil. However, Shaivite doctrines clarify that this darkness refers to the phase of withdrawal of awareness from external and internal objective impressions. The night side or darkness symbolizes the transition from objectivity to subjectivity. This concept parallels the Kabbalistic mysticism, where the **Qliphotic Tree** represents the gradual withdrawal

of objective awareness, while the **Sephirotic Tree of Life** illustrates the emanation of divine awareness to actualize the objective world.

The various manifestations of Kundalini—Para-Kundalini, Chit-Kundalini, Prana-Kundalini, Urdhwa-Kundalini, and Adhah-Kundalini—each play a unique role in the process of spiritual evolution and realization. Understanding and practicing these concepts are essential for the advancement of spiritual knowledge and personal transformation.

Glossary of Terms

~ A ~

A: The first alphabet in Sanskrit, representing supreme consciousness.

Abhasa: Self-reflection or manifestation of the self as an object.

Adhwa: Refers to a path; in Monistic Shaivism, it denotes a dimension or sphere in cosmogony.

Aghora: Refers to the state of subjectivity where there is no distinction between object and subject; signifies the consciousness where the object is cognized as one with the subject.

Aham: The experience of pure 'I' or the pure ego self.

Ahamta: The experience of 'I' consciousness.

Ahamkara: The Tatwa in its impure state, giving the feeling of a lesser and limited ego or 'I'.

Ajnana: Absence of knowledge; in Shaivite schools, this refers to the ignorance of self or limited cognition characterized by the complete distinction between object and subject.

Akala: In some contexts, this refers to the supreme stage of subjectivity characterized by pure consciousness.

Akhyati: Primal nescience.

Akula: Literally 'That which is not Shakti'; refers to the supreme consciousness or Para-Shiva.

Amarsha: The reflection of the self.

Ananda: Eternal bliss resulting from inner awareness.

Ananda Shakti: One of the five powers of Para-Shiva, representing his blissful nature achieved through the realization of

the complete self and abiding in pure subjectivity.

Anashrita: State characterized by pure consciousness, free from any objectivity and not dependent on any external force to actualize the cosmos.

Anava Mala: The impurity causing limitations in will, knowledge, and action; leads to the sensation of a limited 'I'.

Anava Upaya: Inferior means adopted in Shaivism for self-realization, such as the use of idols, glyphs, Yantras, etc.

Anu: Refers to the contracted self in Shaivism; in Vaisheshika philosophy, it refers to atoms.

Anugraha: The grace of the supreme lord that removes the limited sensation of 'I'; one of the five functions of Para-Shiva.

Anuttara: The supreme, second to none; the most transcended.

Apana: The inhaled breath or the process of inhalation.

Ashuddha: Impure.

Atma: The self.

Atma Vishranti: Abiding in the self.

Atma Vimarsha: Reflection of the self.

~ B ~

Baindhavi: Related to Bindu, referring to the seminal power of the supreme lord; represents the power of subjectivity.

Bandha: Nescience or limited knowledge; the sensation of a limited 'I'.

Baudha Jnana: Supernal knowledge; identification of the self with the supreme lord.

Baudha: Supernal awareness.

Bhairava: A term representing the supreme lord. Bha denotes

Bharana (sustenance), Ra denotes Rava (withdrawal), and Va denotes Vamana (emanation).

Bhavana: Contemplation of the self as the supreme lord and identifying all objects as one with the self or supreme subject.

Bhoga: The experience of the cosmos or the Tatwas.

Bhokta: One who experiences objects; the experiencer.

Bhuchari: One of the powers inherent in the supreme feminine principle, representing the power to materialize objects from pure awareness.

Bhuta: The gross physical elements: Akasha (ether), air, fire, water, and earth.

Bhuvana: World, sphere, or dimension existing within the Tatwas.

Bija: Seed or seminal power; the concentrated power of Shiva or the supreme Shakti that manifests the cosmos in the form of Tatwas, Adhwas, and Bhuvanas.

Bindu: The seed or seminal power of the supreme subject; the concentrated power of Shiva before manifestation as cosmos; the supreme Shakti that brings the cosmos into existence.

Brahman: The supreme absolute principle in Vedanta doctrines and classical texts such as the Upanishads, Aranyakas, and Brahmanas.

Buddhi: One of the three internal sense organs that helps the limited empirical individual experience the objective world in reference to the limited 'I'.

~ C ~

Chaitanya: That which shines or sheds light on itself; another

term for the self or Atma. Refers to the supreme consciousness that pervades everything.

Chandra: Moon; in Shaivite context, represents objective knowledge and is associated with the left channel called Ida.

Chit: Pure consciousness devoid of objectivity; one of the five powers of the supreme lord.

~ D ~

Dik: Directions, space, or void.

Dik-Chari: That which moves in the void or space; the power of Supreme Kali that enables the experience of the cosmos through external sense organs.

~ G ~

Gandha: Smell or odor.

Go-Chari: Refers to sound; that which moves in sound. The power of Kali to manifest as phonemes and the four stages of speech.

Ghora: Literally means terrible. In the triadic form of Shakti, it refers to unity in diversity.

Ghora-Tara: Most terrible. Refers to objectivity and complete nescience of the self, characterized by the notion of duality.

Grahaka: Subject, the experiencer.

Grahya: Object of experience.

Guna: The properties inherent in Prakriti or root element.

~ H ~

Hridaya: Heart; in Shaivism, it refers to the core of the self or self-aware consciousness.

~ I ~

Icha: The divine will inherent in the supreme lord; one of the five powers of Para-Shiva.

Idam: This.

Indriya: Sense organs.

Ishwara: The fourth Tatwa in descending order of Shaivite cosmogony, predominant with Jnana-Shakti.

~ J ~

Jala: Water element.

~ M ~

Madhyama: The third stage of manifestation of speech, occurring before gross speech.

Maha-Maya: The supreme Shakti functioning above Maya Tatwa, responsible for the emanation and withdrawal of the seemingly objective universe.

Mala: Impurities enveloping the divine logos.

Manas: One of the three internal sense organs, serving as the locus of imagination, desire, etc., in limited individuals.

Mantra: Sacred sounds aiding self-realization. It also represents pure subjective experience at the level of Shuddha-Vidya Tatwa.

Mantra-Maheswara: Pure subjectivity at the level of Sada-Shiva Tatwa.

Mantreswara: Pure subjective experience in the Ishwara Tatwa.

Matrika: Phonemes or mother goddesses embodying groups of phonemes.

Maya: In non-dual Vedanta, refers to illusion caused by ignorance.

In Shaivite context, Maya denotes creative power and is derived from the word 'Maana' (to measure).

Mayiya-Mala: The impurity that veils the true nature of the self.

~ N ~

Nada: The supreme eternal sound or unstruck sound, existing in the background of every gross form of sound.

Nara: Limited individual in non-dual Shaivism.

Nigraha: One of the five actions of the supreme lord, referring to the self-limiting power of Para-Shiva.

Nimesha: Closing of the eyes, representing the withdrawal of awareness from objectivity.

Nirvikalpa: Free from limited thoughts or the notion of a limited 'I'.

Niyati: One of the five Kanchukas or veils of Maya, causing the notion of limitation in space and the concept of duality.

~ P ~

Paada: Organs of locomotion or legs.

Pada: Word.

Pancha: Pentad or refers to the number five.

Pani: Organs of action or hands.

Para: Supreme.

Parama: Most transcended.

Para-Shiva: Supreme Shiva.

Para-Samvid: Supreme consciousness.

Para-Shakti: Supreme Power, represented by the divine feminine.

Pancha-Vaktra: Five-faced.

Pancha Vaha Chakra: Five-fold wheels.

Paramarsha: Self-reflection, self-experience.

Parameswara: Supreme lord.

Para-Pramata: The supreme subjectivity.

Para-Vak: The supreme speech, usually identified with the supreme feminine principle.

Pasha: Literally means rope; in Shaivite contexts, used synonymously with the illusion of bondage.

Pashu: Fettered empirical souls.

Pashyanti: Second stage of the manifestation of speech. Refers to seeing, cognition, and the state of speech characterized by non-distinction between the observer and the observed or subject and object.

Paurusha-Ajnana: Primal nescience caused by impurities and the five veils of Maya.

Paurusha-Jnana: Awareness of the self.

Payu: Organ of excretion.

Prakasha: Light; in Shaivite context, self-reflective or self-affirming consciousness.

Prakriti: Manifestation of the supreme Shakti as limited under the influence of Maya and the five veils. The root principle for the manifestation of the cosmos.

Pralaya Kala: State of awareness characterized by the negation of objectivity; sensation of voidness.

Prama: The subject.

Pramana: The process of cognition.

Prameya: The object.

Prami: Pure consciousness.

Prana: Vital breath, also divine awareness.

Pratibha: Gnosis.

Pratyabhijnana: Recognition of self or realization of self.

Pratyavamarsha: Self-experience.

Prthwi: Earth element; the material universe.

Purna: Complete and perfected state.

Purna-Aham: The complete 'I'; the higher ego or the supreme subject.

Purusha: The limited subject, empirical souls.

Puryashtaka: The eight Tatwas representing the eight principles of the senses, including the five Tanmatras and Manas, Buddhi, and Ahankara.

~ R ~

Raga: One of the five veils of Maya, which causes attachment towards limited objectivity.

Rakta: Blood; in Shaivite context, it refers to the creative principle of the divine feminine.

Rajas: One of the three Gunas, representing dynamic motion.

Rasa: Taste or tactile sensation.

Rupa: Vision.

~ S ~

Sabda: The creative Monads as sound.

Sabda-Brahman: The supreme principle as sound.

Sada-Shiva: The third Tatwa in descending order, representing the divine subject in his full splendor.

Samana: The vital force that aids in digestion and assimilation

of food.

Samarasya: The inherent union of Shiva and Shakti.

Samavesha: The penetration of limited awareness into the supreme.

Samhara: The process of dissolution.

Samvid: Supreme consciousness; self-affirming consciousness.

Sandhana: Union of the limited subject with the supreme subject.

Sarvartha: All-pervading.

Shabda: Sound.

Shakta-Upaya: A mode of training involving contemplation on phonemes and Mantras to attain self-realization.

Shakti: The power inherent in the divine providence, represented by the divine feminine, considered as self-awareness in Shaivism.

Shaktiman: One who possesses Shakti.

Shaktipath: The descent of divine grace that removes impurities and brings about self-realization.

Shakti Tatwa: The second Tatwa in descending order, representing the self-reflective nature of the supreme consciousness.

Shambhava-Upaya: Training using the pure will of the aspirant.

Shiva: The first principle in cosmogony, representing the pure consciousness aspect of the supreme principle.

Shuddha: Pure.

Shuddha-Vidya: The fifth Tatwa representing the awareness moving towards the object.

Shunya: Void; negation of external objectivity.

Shunya Pramata: Lesser subject.

Soma: The divine elixir or lunar nectar; in Shaivite context, it refers to the ecstatic bliss experienced when penetrating into the

supreme consciousness. Also refers to the dynamic awareness of divinity or the divine feminine.

Spanda: The dynamic activity of the supreme consciousness.

Sphuranti/Sphurata: The self-illuminating or reflecting property of consciousness.

Sparsha: Touch.

Sukshma: Subtle.

Surya: Sun; representing the process of cognition.

Sushumna: The central channel or spine; also represents the aspect of Will.

Sushupti: The dreamless state of awareness.

Svachanda: Sovereign ruler of the cosmos; absolute authority.

Swapna: The state of dreams.

Swatantra: Total freedom to perform any action.

~ T ~

Tamas: One of the three properties of the root element, the primal cause of stagnation or stability.

Tanmatra: The five subtle elements associated with sense organs.

Tatwa: The primal principles that constitute the cosmos.

Tejas: The fire element.

Trika: A triadic form; a Monistic Shaivite school.

Trishula: The trident; represents will, knowledge, and action, as well as the triad of subject, cognition, and object.

Turiya: The final state of awareness characterized by the sensation of objectivity existing within the subject.

Turiyateeta: The state of awareness marked by the complete annihilation of all forms of duality and objectivity.

~ U ~

Ucchara: A practice in Anava Upaya where the individual becomes aware of Prana (vital breath) through deep contemplation.

Unata: To retract or withdraw.

Unmesha: The opening of the eyes; represents the dynamic movement of awareness towards objectivity and the phase of emanation.

Upastha: Reproductive organs.

~ V ~

Vaikhari: The gross state of speech; the manifest form of verbal expression.

Varna: A process in Anava-Upaya; also refers to mantras formed by the combination of letters.

Vayu: Air element.

Vijnana-Kala: The third subjective experience in the ascending order of subjects.

Vikalpa: Limited thought constructs or conceptual distinctions.

Vimarsha: Reflection, illumination, and self-awareness.

Visarga: The power to emanate, represented by two vertical dots.

~ Y ~

Yoni: Womb; also denotes the source or cause, and represents causal efficacy and reason.

The Crest Jewel of Supreme Bhairava

Book II :: Practice

Acknowledgements

I am profoundly grateful to the Great Para Bhairava, whose divine guidance has illuminated my path in understanding and decoding the sacred scriptures. It is through His immense grace and boundless wisdom that I have been able to unravel the depths of these ancient teachings and integrate them into my spiritual practice. His presence has not only clarified the intricate aspects of these texts but also empowered me to successfully engage in these profound spiritual practices. My deepest gratitude goes to Para Bhairava for making this journey of discovery and realization possible, and for enabling me to share these insights through this book.

I extend my heartfelt thanks to my father and mother, whose unwavering love and support have been the bedrock of my spiritual and personal growth. Their encouragement and belief in me have provided a nurturing foundation from which I have been able to explore and embrace these spiritual teachings. Their sacrifices, wisdom, and unconditional support have been instrumental in my journey, and for this, I am eternally grateful.

This book is a reflection of not only my personal journey but also of the collective support and love from those who have been my guiding lights. To my parents, your steadfast encouragement has been a beacon of strength, and to Para Bhairava, your divine intervention has transformed my understanding and practice. May this work serve as a testament to the profound impact of your support and divine grace, and may it offer guidance and insight to others who seek to embark on their own spiritual journeys.

With deepest appreciation and gratitude,
Dr. Shreeram Iyer

Introduction

Indian philosophy, deeply intertwined with religion, has always aimed not merely at theoretical understanding but at the practical realization of spiritual ideals. Unlike Western philosophical traditions that often emphasize abstract theorizing, Indian philosophy prioritizes lived experience and practical methods for achieving spiritual goals. This characteristic is particularly evident across various schools of Indian thought, each offering its own set of practices and disciplines. Everything that exists, spanning across all of time and even beyond, is essentially a single, infinite divine Consciousness. This Consciousness is both liberated and blissful, and within its vast awareness, it projects a multitude of seemingly distinct subjects and objects. Each object in this vast field is an actualization of a timeless potential that resides within the Light of Consciousness. Similarly, each subject represents not only this timeless potential but also a localized and limited sense of self-awareness.

This creation can be seen as a divine play, resulting from Consciousness's inherent desire to express the totality of its self-knowledge through action. This desire, which stems from a fundamental impulse of love, drives the unbounded Light of Consciousness to contract into finite forms of awareness according to its own free will. When these finite forms, or individual subjects, identify with the restricted and particular circumstances of their existence rather than recognizing their true nature as part of the expansive and transcendent pulsation of pure Awareness, they

experience what is termed "suffering."

In response to this suffering, some individuals are compelled to embark on a spiritual journey through gnosis and yogic practices. The aim of these practices is to disrupt their false sense of self and reveal directly within their immediate awareness that the divine powers of Consciousness—such as Bliss, Willing, Knowing, and Acting—comprise the entirety of individual experience. This realization leads to an understanding that one's true identity is that of the highest Divinity, a reflection of the Whole within every individual part.

This experiential knowledge, or gnosis, is deepened and solidified through various practices until it becomes the non-conceptual foundation of every moment of experience. Ultimately, this process eradicates the limited, contracted sense of self and the illusion of separation from the Whole. In this state of complete expansion into perfect wholeness, one's perception fully grasps the reality of a universe that moves and thrives in ecstatic celebration of its absolute and perfect divinity.

The essential aspect of Indian philosophy is its focus on **sadhana**, or spiritual discipline, which forms the core of its practice. Every major school, whether it adheres to Vedic, Agamic, or other traditions, has developed its unique methods to facilitate the realization of the ultimate spiritual goals. This focus on practical methodology is crucial for understanding the philosophical teachings of these traditions, as it connects abstract concepts with tangible practices.

Sadhana plays a central role in the **Agamic** traditions, which include schools like the Trika of Monistic Shaivism. The Agamic schools emphasize ritual, meditation, and other forms of spiritual practice over purely theoretical discourse. This is reflected in

their philosophical outlook, which often prioritizes methods and practices for attaining spiritual insight rather than solely debating metaphysical issues.

For a comprehensive grasp of Indian philosophy, it is essential to study both the metaphysical ideas and the practical sadhanas of each school. This dual approach helps in appreciating how these traditions not only articulate their visions of reality but also offer actionable paths for their realization. The Monistic Shaivism tradition, in particular, illustrates this well by giving precedence to practical disciplines over theoretical discussions.

To understand the philosophy of **sadhana** as articulated by the Saivācāryas of Kashmir, it is valuable to first trace its historical and conceptual development from the earliest Indian religious and philosophical texts.

In the earliest religious literature, such as the Upanishads, the focus is often on personal experiences of the divine or the ultimate reality rather than systematic philosophical arguments. The sages (ṛṣis) of this period shared their intuitive insights into the nature of the ultimate reality and provided practical guidance for spiritual realization. The Upanishads, foundational texts of Indian philosophy, document these insights. They are characterized by a vivid description of mystical experiences and visions of Truth rather than dialectical discourse. Here, **sadhana** is discussed implicitly, mainly through descriptions of meditation (yoga) and introspection.

For example, in the *Brihadaranyaka Upanishad*, sage Yajnavalkya speaks of the necessity of meditating on the Atman (the Self) to achieve complete knowledge and realization. His emphasis is on seeing, hearing, and meditating upon the Atman to gain a direct

and experiential understanding of the ultimate reality. Similarly, the *Chandogya Upanishad* emphasizes the pursuit of "great happiness" which is eternal and unchanging. This happiness is achieved through the realization of the unity between the individual self (Atman) and the universal reality (Brahman). The text suggests that true happiness comes from recognizing the omnipresence of the Infinite and understanding one's identity with it.

As philosophical schools began to emerge in India, each developed its own interpretation of **sadhana** based on its broader metaphysical framework. The diverse schools—ranging from Nyaya and Vaisheshika to Sankhya, Yoga, Mimamsa, and Vedanta—each offered specific methods and practices for spiritual realization. For example, the **Yoga** school of thought, particularly as developed by Patanjali, provides a detailed framework of sadhana that includes ethical precepts, meditation practices, and mental discipline aimed at attaining liberation (moksha). This approach represents a more systematic and methodical treatment of spiritual practice compared to the more intuitive and descriptive approaches of the earlier Upanishadic texts.

The Agamic traditions, which include the **Monistic Shaivism** school, place a strong emphasis on ritual and esoteric practices. These traditions developed sophisticated methods of sadhana, including elaborate rituals, meditation techniques, and mystical practices that are integral to their spiritual goals. Monistic Shaivism, for instance, highlights the importance of direct experiential knowledge of the divine through practices that go beyond mere theoretical understanding. It provides a comprehensive guide to various spiritual disciplines and their application, focusing on the

transformative power of these practices.

The philosophy of **sadhana** has evolved from its early expression in the Upanishadic literature, where it was closely tied to personal mystical experiences and direct realization of the ultimate reality, to more structured and diverse practices within later philosophical schools and traditions. Each tradition built upon the intuitive foundations laid by the Upanishads, developing unique methods and practices that reflect its metaphysical and spiritual goals. Understanding these historical developments helps to appreciate the richness and complexity of Indian spiritual practices and their philosophical underpinnings.

The *Mundaka Upanishad* advises that one should transcend verbal discussions about Reality and focus directly on the knowledge of the Atman, as this alone leads to immortality. It emphasizes the importance of meditating on the Atman using the symbol *Om*, which facilitates crossing the metaphorical ocean of darkness. Similarly, the *Kathopanishad* asserts that the Self cannot be realized through words, discursive thought, or scriptural study but is directly perceived through meditation by a purified mind.

The second trend in the development of the philosophy of sadhana emerges in later philosophical literature, where systematic and rational approaches were developed by various acaryas such as Kapila, Gotama Akṣapāda, Kanāda, and Patanjali. These figures provided a rational foundation for the religious experiences of their predecessors and organized them into distinct philosophical schools. During this period, Indian philosophy evolved into a more rationalistic framework, and the philosophy of sadhana also gained a structured rationale.

Each system outlined a specific goal for human life and prescribed methods to achieve this Supreme Goal.

It was during this time that the concept of **puruṣārthas**—the goals of life corresponding to the four stages of human existence (āśramas)—was developed. This phase recognized that a singular mode of sadhana could not suit everyone universally. Instead, different philosophical schools proposed various methods tailored to their respective Supreme Ideals.

For instance, schools like **Sankhya** and **Advaita Vedanta** viewed ignorance as the root cause of all suffering and therefore emphasized the acquisition of spiritual knowledge (**jñāna**) as the path to eradicate ignorance and attain the Supreme Goal. On the other hand, **Mimamsa** philosophers argued that action (**karma**), particularly as prescribed by scriptures, was essential for achieving the Supreme End. They contended that action could not be completely avoided while embodied, so it must be performed in a manner that aids in reaching the ultimate goal.

The *Bhagavad Gita* offers a practical approach known as **Karma Yoga**, which involves performing actions selflessly, without attachment to the results. This form of desireless action, dedicated to the Supreme Being, is presented as a viable path for individuals to achieve the ultimate goal while in the embodied state.

In contrast, the **Vaishnava** schools advocate **Bhakti** (devotion) as the highest form of sadhana. They emphasize loving devotion to a personal deity as the most effective way to attain spiritual fulfillment and reach the Supreme Goal.

Thus, the philosophy of sadhana has been richly developed across different schools of thought, each proposing distinct methods aligned

with their metaphysical perspectives and spiritual objectives.

During the later phase of development in Indian philosophical thought, there were efforts to synthesize various modes of sadhana by establishing a hierarchy among them. This synthesis sought to integrate the diverse approaches into a coherent framework, highlighting commonalities and underlying principles across different schools of thought.

A careful examination of the philosophy of sadhana reveals several shared traits among these schools. Firstly, all Indian philosophical and religious traditions place the human individual at the center of their sadhana practices. They view humanity as uniquely positioned within a complex creation that encompasses numerous levels of existence. According to traditional beliefs, there are a vast number of life forms, each with its own evolutionary potential.

Humans, however, are considered central due to their unique capacity for self-directed evolution or decline, influenced by their actions and personal efforts. Unlike other creatures, which possess bodies suited only for enjoyment and are thus incapable of purposeful action, humans alone have the potential to achieve the highest spiritual goals through deliberate effort and free will.

Secondly, except for Buddhists and the materialist Cārvākas, most Indian philosophical systems agree that humans, at their core, are pure and free. However, in their current state, individuals are ignorant of their true nature and thus experience suffering and bondage. From the perspective of these traditions, human suffering is seen as a fall from an original state of purity and perfection. The goal of sadhana in this context is to restore the individual to their true nature, which represents the essence of being.

Thirdly, the complexity of the human personality is a common theme across most Indian philosophical systems (with the exception of the materialist Cārvākas). These systems describe the self as being covered by multiple layers of gross and subtle matter, which obscure the true spiritual self. In the ordinary state of existence, individuals are unaware of their real nature due to these layers, leading to a false sense of ego and self-identification with the physical body and material experiences. The aim of sadhana is to transcend this false identification and ego-based perception, guiding the individual inward to recognize their true spiritual essence. This process is often metaphorically described as a journey from the external world to the innermost core of one's being.

While different schools of Indian thought offer various methods and approaches to sadhana, they share fundamental assumptions about the central role of the human individual, the nature of suffering and liberation, and the complexity of the self. These shared elements form a common foundation upon which diverse sadhana practices and philosophical systems are built.

While the Advaita Vedāntins recognize that the ultimate spiritual Self is beyond the reach of the finite mind (as indicated in some Upanishads), they also acknowledge that the veil of ignorance obscuring the Self must be lifted through intellectual understanding. The intellect, in this context, is crucial because it serves as the foundation for both ignorance and knowledge, which can counterbalance each other. Therefore, the intellect plays a significant role in removing ignorance and facilitating the realization of the Self.

In an embodied state, the intellect is often tainted by residual

impressions (samskāras) from past actions and desires (vāsanās), which accumulate over time. This contamination prevents a clear vision of the true Self. Thus, the first step towards self-realization involves purging the intellect of these impurities. This process of purification is essential for preparing the intellect to serve as an effective medium for experiencing the Self.

Ethical practices are pivotal in this purification process. Practices such as **śama** (control of internal sense-organs), **dama** (control of external sense-organs), **titikṣā** (tolerance), and yogic disciplines including **yama** (external disciplines), **niyama** (internal disciplines), and **āsana** (postures) form the initial stages of sadhana, which can be broadly termed as purgation.

These practices help cleanse the mind and intellect, making them more receptive to higher spiritual insights.

Before delving into the philosophy of sadhana as articulated by the various Śaivācāryas of Kashmir, it is useful to survey the rise and development of Saiva thought, particularly the Trika school in Kashmir. Saivism, as a significant religious and philosophical tradition, has ancient roots. Archaeological evidence suggests that it existed as a cult among aboriginal tribes in India even before the Aryan influence. Tradition connects Saivism with the Agamic tradition, believed to have developed alongside the Vedic tradition. However, no Agamic texts from the Vedic period have survived to confirm this traditional view.

Nevertheless, evidence indicates that Saivism was present during the Vedic era. For example, the *Rigveda* references a group of ascetics, possibly Saiva practitioners, described as wearing ochre-colored garments and living in a semi-naked state. This group, known

for their rigorous ascetic practices, is believed to have worshipped Rudra, an early form of Shiva. Their practices, including ritual consumption of substances like poison, align with the characteristics of early Saiva worship. This historical context provides insight into the deep and enduring nature of Saiva traditions and their evolution over time.

Although the name "Shiva" does not appear explicitly in the Vedic Samhitās, the term "Shiva" is used as an adjective for Rudra in several Vedic texts, notably in the *Vajasaneyi Samhita*. This usage has led scholars to identify Shiva with Rudra, a Vedic deity. The *Satarudriya* portion of the *Yajurveda* lists one hundred names of Rudra, among which "Shiva" is included, reinforcing this connection. Some scholars also link Shiva with Mahadeva mentioned in the *Vratya* hymns of the *Atharva Veda*, though this identification is debated. Notably, the Vratya hymns describe a particular religious practice involving yoga, suggesting a possible connection between the Vratyas and Saiva traditions.

There is scholarly debate regarding the relationship between phallus worshippers in the *Rgveda* and the Saiva cult. While some scholars argue that the disapproval of phallus worship in the *Rgveda* indicates a tribal nature of early Saiva practices, others, such as R. G. Bhandarkar, assert that linga worship was not prominent at the time of Patanjali or even in later periods. However, figures like F. Kittel and Barth trace linga worship to Greek influences.

Positive evidence of the Saiva cult appears in the *Svetasvatara Upanishad* (likely composed in the 3rd century BCE), where Shiva is prominently featured as a major deity with the epithet *Mahesvara*. This Upanishad's focus on Shiva marks a significant moment in the

development of Saivism as a distinct tradition. Furthermore, the *Ashtadhyayi* of Panini (circa 500 BCE) contains a sutra that provides evidence of Shiva worshippers, indicating that Shiva worship was well-established by this time.

The Trika school of Saivism, which systematized Saiva philosophy, was formally established by Vasugupta around 825 CE. This school is one of several within the broader Saiva tradition. The Saiva tradition is composed of various schools, each with its own approach and emphasis. For instance, the dualistic Saiva stream includes schools like the Pasupatas and Saiva Siddhanta, while the dualistic-cum-non-dualistic stream features schools such as the Lakulisa Pasupata and Virasaiva. The monistic stream includes traditions like Nandikeśvara Saiva, Rasasvara Saiva, Trika Saiva, and the Visistadvaita Saiva of Srikantha.

Historically, the Saiva tradition encompasses eight main schools of thought that developed in different regions and periods in India. These include the Pasupatas, Lakulisa Pasupata, Saiva Siddhanta, Virasaiva, Nandikeśvara Saiva, Rasesvara Saiva, Trika Saiva, and Visistadvaita Saiva of Srikantha. Each of these schools contributes uniquely to the diverse landscape of Saiva philosophy, reflecting various interpretations and practices within the broader Saiva tradition.

Of the eight schools of Saivism previously mentioned, the Pasupata school is historically the earliest. It is traditionally attributed to Srikantha Saiva, who is believed to have lived before Patanjali. Srikantha Saiva is recognized as the author of the *Pingalamata*, and his followers were referred to as *Siva Bhagavatas*. The Lakulisa Pasupatas emerged later, around the 2nd century CE, with Lakulisa

being a significant figure in this later development.

The Trika school of Saivism, known for its rich philosophical literature, represents a notable development in the Saiva tradition. This school, which espouses a monistic philosophy, emerged in Kashmir around the 8th century CE. Despite its popular name, "Kashmir Saivism," this term is somewhat misleading, as the Trika system evolved through three distinct phases in Kashmir before coalescing into what is now recognized as the Trika system. The Trika system, as described in Agama Shastras, is considered to have an eternal existence.

Among the foundational texts of this school is the work of Somananda, who laid the groundwork for the Trika tradition. His pupil, Utpaladeva, wrote the *Pratyabhijna-Karika* around 970 CE, summarizing Somananda's philosophy. Although shorter than Somananda's works, Utpaladeva's text became highly influential, and the system became widely known by his name. This text was extensively commented upon, with notable commentaries including those by Abhinavagupta, who wrote the *Vimarshini* and the more comprehensive *Vivriti Vimarshini*. Abhinavagupta's contributions are substantial, including his extensive works such as the *Paramarthasara*, *Tantrasara*, and the voluminous *Tantraloka*. The *Tantraloka* is particularly significant, being a comprehensive encyclopedia of the Trika system. Jayaratha, in the 12th century CE, produced a detailed commentary on the *Tantraloka*.

Another key figure in the Trika tradition is Ksemaraja, a prolific writer who contributed commentaries on essential texts like the *Siva Sutra* and *Spanda-Karika*. His works include the *Pratyabhijna-Hrdaya* and various commentaries on the Agamas, reflecting his

deep engagement with the Trika philosophy.

Overall, the Trika school stands out for its profound philosophical depth and extensive literary contributions, with Abhinavagupta and Ksemaraja being among its most influential scholars.

Guru-The Universal Teacher

The concept of Divine Grace, or *Anugraha*, within the context of Saivism, is deeply rooted in the understanding of divine functions and the nature of spiritual transmission. This grace is regarded as one of the Supreme Lord's (Paramesvara's) essential and ever-operating functions, reflecting the divine freedom and autonomy in bestowing spiritual blessings. It is an aspect of the divine will that flows from the Supreme Source, embodying an eternal and independent process.

However, this Divine Grace is not universally accessible to all beings. Its direct influence is typically experienced by those who are entirely free from impurity and material constraints. In the context of Saivism, this includes:

1. **Unembodied Souls**: These are souls in their pre-creational state, existing in a form untouched by physical matter. They are naturally receptive to Divine Grace because they are not encumbered by the impurities of material existence.
2. **Disembodied Beings (Vijnanakalas)**: These beings, not bound by material bodies, also receive Divine Grace directly. Their lack of material encumbrance allows them to be in direct communion with the Supreme Source.

In contrast, once individual beings enter into creation and assume physical bodies composed of impure matter, their capacity to receive Divine Grace directly is impeded. The presence of material impurities in their embodied state prevents them from withstanding

the direct transmission of grace from the Supreme Lord. As a result, they require an intermediary or medium through which Divine Grace can be imparted.

This medium typically takes the form of a spiritually realized and purified individual—an *Acarya* or *Guru*. The role of such a spiritual guide is twofold:

1. **Relay Center**: The Guru acts as an intermediary, channeling the Divine Grace from the Supreme Lord to the embodied seeker. By virtue of their own spiritual purity and realization, the Guru is capable of transmitting divine blessings and guidance to those who are otherwise unable to receive them directly.

2. **Agent of Divine Will**: The Guru also serves as an executor of the Supreme Lord's divine will on a more accessible level of existence. They impart divine knowledge and spiritual teachings to seekers who are on the path of realization. Through their guidance, seekers can navigate their spiritual journey and progressively purify themselves to become receptive to Divine Grace.

While Divine Grace emanates freely from the Supreme Source, its direct reception is limited to those beings who are free from material constraints. For embodied beings, the grace is mediated through spiritually advanced individuals who act as channels and guides, facilitating the transmission of divine knowledge and blessings.

In the Agamic tradition, Divine Teachers are categorized into three classes based on their nature and the degree of spiritual purity

they possess.

Celestial Teachers, or Deva Gurus, are divine beings who dispense Grace to aspirants who have attained a high level of spiritual perfection through their personal efforts. These aspirants may have transcended the impurities of material existence and achieved profound contemplation. The Deva Gurus are often the presiding deities of various divine realms, such as Rudra, Vishnu, and Brahma. While their primary role is to govern their respective regions, when acting as Divine Teachers, they become instruments of the Supreme Lord's will rather than their own, dispensing Divine Grace to spiritually prepared individuals. This Grace is usually received unconsciously by the aspirants, though conscious reception is also possible.

Superhuman Teachers, or Siddhas, are beings who, while still embodied, are highly advanced and possess great spiritual purity. They are considered superior to ordinary human teachers due to their greater connection with the Divine Will and their elevated spiritual status. They guide those aspirants who have a lesser degree of purity in their receptivity. Although they are not as exalted as the Deva Gurus, their role is vital for assisting aspirants who cannot yet receive Grace directly from celestial beings.

Human Teachers, or Purusas, are embodied beings who hold a superior spiritual position due to their divine connection and representation of the Supreme Lord. They serve as conduits for transmitting Divine Grace to aspirants whose bodies are heavily influenced by impurities.

These teachers act as representatives of the Supreme Lord on a more accessible level, facilitating the spiritual journey of their

disciples. Divine Grace transmitted through human teachers can be experienced in various forms—whether through physical touch, speech, vision, or thought. The effectiveness of these methods may vary, but the essence of the Grace remains consistent.

Overall, the transmission of Divine Grace in the Agamic tradition involves different levels of spiritual beings, each playing a crucial role in guiding and uplifting aspirants according to their degree of spiritual readiness and purity. The nature of the Grace received may differ based on the teacher's status and the aspirant's receptivity, but its fundamental quality remains unchanged.

From the observations above, it is evident that there are two primary ways through which Divine Grace can descend upon individuals from the Highest Source. The first method involves direct Grace to the aspirants, a process that applies to unembodied and some disembodied beings. These beings, free from material impurities, receive Grace directly from the Supreme Source without any intermediary. The second method involves the transmission of Divine Grace through pure, embodied mediums, such as divine or enlightened teachers.

These mediums act as intermediaries, relaying Grace from the Supreme Source to the embodied aspirants.

Despite these two approaches appearing distinct, they fundamentally represent different facets of the same process. Both methods share the underlying principle that Divine Grace, whether direct or mediated, leads to the same ultimate goal of self-realization for the aspirant. The principle of the guru remains central in both scenarios. In the direct transmission method, the abstract principle of Divine Grace itself functions as the guru. In the mediated

approach, the Divine Grace operates through a concrete medium—an embodied teacher—who then assumes the role of guru.

Thus, in theory, the guru is seen as an embodiment of the Supreme Principle of Compassion. The Supreme Lord, being omnipresent and transcendent, may sometimes choose a specific, embodied individual to act as a conduit for dispensing Grace. Such an embodied being, while functioning as a guru, embodies the divine qualities necessary for guiding the aspirant. This role can be temporary, based on the individual's spiritual merits and the Supreme Will. Once these merits are exhausted, the role of guru may pass to another suitable individual, maintaining the continuity of the spiritual guidance.

The guru, therefore, may be human or divine-human, depending on the nature of the medium chosen by the Supreme Lord. This flexibility underscores the importance of treating all forms of gurus—whether human, superhuman, or celestial—with the highest respect and veneration. Even secondary teachers, regardless of their classification, should be regarded as divine embodiments due to their role in channeling Divine Grace.

Among embodied beings, there are two distinct types of sadhakas. The first type experiences an immediate awakening of latent divinity through Divine Grace, leading to instantaneous self-realization and transformation. Such individuals do not require external guidance to achieve spiritual enlightenment, as their realization is complete and self-sustaining. They are considered masters of all spiritual phases and can impart knowledge to others when needed. These individuals are termed Akalpita Gurus, as they are their own teachers and possess innate understanding and mastery without the need for external interpretation.

Not all aspirants have the capacity for immediate and complete self-realization from within. Those with a lesser degree of spiritual perfection require external guidance to fully awaken their latent divine knowledge and achieve integral self-realization. Such aspirants depend on an external guru to assist them in refining their understanding and removing imperfections, referred to as malas, from their inner self. While Divine Knowledge may be awakened within them, this initial awakening does not equate to full self-realization. Achieving integral self- realization necessitates additional effort and practices, such as japa (chanting), dhyana (meditation), and pranayama (breathing exercises). These individuals are known as Akalpita Gurus, as they require external aid to reach full spiritual enlightenment.

When Divine Grace is transmitted by the guru to an aspirant, the impurities obscuring the aspirant's true nature are removed, and the latent knowledge of Divinity is activated. This process, known as dikṣā, involves the guru infusing pure knowledge into the aspirant and dismantling their limited self-conception. Abhinavagupta defines dikṣā as a process where pure knowledge is bestowed upon the sadhaka, leading to the dissolution of their limitations. Dikṣā is a crucial step toward integral self-realization, whether the Grace is received directly from the Divine Source or through a guru. It is not merely a series of external rituals; rather, it is a profound internal process where the guru purifies the aspirant's receptacle and ignites the latent divine knowledge, paving the way for complete self-realization.

From a ceremonial perspective, dikṣā is categorized into two types according to the Agamas: Samaya Dikṣā and Putraka Dikṣā.

Samaya Dikṣā is performed at the beginning of the aspirant's spiritual journey and aims at purifying and preparing the aspirant for spiritual discipline. This purificatory process involves various ceremonies performed at specific life stages, totaling forty-eight, as outlined in the Agamas. These ceremonies renew the aspirant's spiritual life and instill a desire for ultimate self-realization, making it a crucial preliminary step.

Putraka Dikṣā is conducted after the completion of Samaya Dikṣā, when the aspirant's body and mind are sufficiently purified to receive Divine Illumination from the guru. During this rite, the guru awakens the latent essence of the disciple by transmitting Grace from the Highest Source. As a result, the aspirant is elevated to a higher spiritual realm, though they may still appear to live in the mundane world. This higher state of being signifies their transition from a state of impurity to one of spiritual enlightenment, despite their outward existence.

Before performing Putraka Dikṣā, the scriptures advise that the guru should consider the inclination of the disciple. Since individual inclinations vary, and not all aspirants are immediately inclined towards achieving the highest state of Siva-rasa (Divine Bliss), it is important for the guru to tailor the dikṣā process accordingly. Aspirants generally fall into two broad categories based on their inclinations: those driven by **bhoga-vāsana** (desire for enjoyment) and those focused on **mokṣa** (salvation). The former are called **bhogī** (desirous of enjoyment), and the latter are known as **mumukṣus** (seekers of liberation). The scriptures stipulate that the guru should provide the appropriate mantra to each disciple to help them achieve their specific goals.

Bhogī sadhakas are further classified into two types: **Siva-dharma bhogīs** and **Loka-dharma bhogīs**, based on their particular desires for enjoyment. Siva-dharma bhogīs aspire to attain a high position, such as that of a Presiding Deity (Adhikarika-pada) of a particular realm, from which they can both govern and enjoy. For these sadhakas, the guru provides a suitable mantra and performs the corresponding form of Putraka Dikṣā, which destroys the accumulated fruits of their past, present, and future actions, allowing them to enjoy their elevated position. They remain in this state of enjoyment until their desires are satisfied or cosmic dissolution occurs, after which they can attain their ultimate goal of Siva-rasa.

In contrast, **Loka-dharma bhogīs** do not seek elevation but prefer to remain in the world as enlightened beings (jñānis), moving among ordinary mortals. The guru performs Putraka Dikṣā for them in a way that eliminates the accumulated fruits of their past and present actions while leaving the seeds of future actions intact. This allows them to continue performing good deeds in their lifetime until their physical bodies naturally expire, after which they realize their Supreme Goal, Siva-rasa.

For **mumukṣus**, who seek liberation, there are two types of Putraka Dikṣā: **Sabhijā mumukṣa Dikṣā** and **Nirbījā mumukṣa Dikṣā**. Those receiving Sabhijā Dikṣā have their karmic seeds (karmabīja) partially removed and are able to remain in embodied form for a time. They live like ordinary individuals but are always conscious of their true Self, though they do not achieve complete self-realization until their physical body eventually perishes. The Nirbījā Dikṣā, on the other hand, involves a more profound purification process, leading to the complete removal of all karmic seeds, allowing the

aspirant to attain liberation more directly.

Thus, the appropriate form of Putraka Dikṣā is carefully chosen based on the aspirant's inclination, ensuring that their spiritual path aligns with their personal desires and ultimate goals.

The **bhubukṣu** sadhakas can again be classified under two heads, viz. the **Siva-dharma bhubukṣus** and the **Loka-dharma bhubukṣus**, according to the difference in their **bhoga- vāsana**. The Siva-dharma bhubukṣu sadhakas aspire to attain the elevated position of a Presiding Deity (Adhikarika-pada) of some order, such as **mantra, mantra-maheṣvara**, etc., from which they can govern and enjoy (bhoga) as well. To such sadhakas, the guru gives the appropriate mantra and performs the suitable form of **Putraka Dikṣā**, whereby the accumulated fruits of their past, present, and future karmas are automatically destroyed (purified). This enables them to enjoy their elevated position uninterruptedly and to satisfy their **bhoga-vāsana** (desire). These aspirants can continue to remain in this elevated position until their desires are fulfilled or cosmic dissolution occurs, whichever comes first, after which they attain their Supreme Goal, **Siva-rasa**.

The **Loka-dharma bhubukṣus**, on the other hand, do not desire elevation but prefer to remain in this world as enlightened beings (jñānis), moving about like ordinary mortals. Therefore, the guru gives them the appropriate mantra and performs the suitable form of Putraka Dikṣā, ensuring that the accumulated fruits of their past and present karmas are destroyed. However, the seeds of their karma (karmabīja), which are the roots of future actions, are allowed to remain as they were. This arrangement allows them to continue living in the world, performing meritorious deeds until their physical body

is naturally destroyed.

Afterward, they achieve their Supreme Goal, Siva-rasa.

Even among the **mumukṣu** sadhakas, the scriptures prescribe two different kinds of **Putraka Dikṣā**: the **Sabhijā mumukṣu Dikṣā** and the **Nirbījā mumukṣu Dikṣā**. The mumukṣu sadhakas who receive the **Sabhijā Putraka Dikṣā** are able to remain in embodied form for some time, as their karmabījas are not entirely destroyed in Dikṣā. They live in the world like ordinary mortals, performing essential karma to sustain their embodied form. Unlike the bhoga-dharma bhubukṣus, they do not possess any **bhoga-vāsana**. They are always conscious of their real Self, although they do not achieve integral self-realization at that stage. Their existence in the world corresponds roughly to that of the **jīvan-muktas**. When their physical body is eventually destroyed, they are automatically established in their true nature, Siva-tva.

The **mumukṣu** sadhakas who receive the **Nirbījā Putraka Dikṣā**, on the other hand, realize their Supreme Goal instantaneously with the Dikṣā because their karmabījas are entirely destroyed during the process. Their dissociation from the physical body and integral self-realization occur simultaneously with the Dikṣā.

This classification of Dikṣā is based on the external ceremonies performed during the process. However, Dikṣā also has an inner aspect. It is not merely an external ceremonial act; it is an inner process in which the guru transmits Divine Grace to the aspirant in an intense form, corresponding to their capacity to receive it. Accordingly, four distinct forms of Dikṣā are recognized by the **Trika** system: **Anupāya Dikṣā**, **Sambhava Dikṣā**, **Śakti Dikṣā**, and **Aṇuṣṭhāna Dikṣā**. When the descending Divine Grace is

extremely powerful, **Anupāya Dikṣā** follows naturally, allowing the sadhaka to realize their Goal immediately. If the descending Grace is relatively less powerful, **Sambhava Dikṣā** is performed. When the Grace is still less powerful, **Śakti Dikṣā** is prescribed. In both these forms of Dikṣā, external kriyās (rituals) to supplement the Grace are not considered necessary. However, when the Grace is very weak, as in the case of sadhakas receiving **Aṇuṣṭhāna Dikṣā**, external kriyās for self-purification become imperative.

Descent of Divine Grace

In the previous section, we discussed how the Trika system views the descent of Divine Grace (Anugraha) from the highest reality, known as Parama Shiva, as crucial for an individual's spiritual progress towards their ultimate goal, Sivatva. This Divine Grace marks the start of the aspirant's transformation into the divine. It's worth noting that the concept of Divine Grace is not unique to the Trika system; it also plays a significant role in other Indian philosophical traditions inspired by the Agamas.

For example, in various branches of Saiva, Sakta, and Vaisnava traditions, receiving Divine Grace from the highest reality is considered essential for achieving the Supreme Goal.

Similarly, the Mahayana school of Buddhism holds that aspirants cannot reach the highest state of perfection, Buddhahood, without Divine Grace. Medieval Christian mystics also acknowledged the importance of Divine Grace in self-realization. They suggested that before experiencing Divine Illumination, one must go through a stage of purification, which involves the reception of Divine Grace.

Although this discussion does not aim to compare how different philosophical systems view Divine Grace, it highlights that the importance of Divine Grace in self-realization is recognized across various traditions, including those unrelated to the Trika system.

To understand the crucial role of Divine Grace (Anugraha) in spiritual practice (sadhana), we need to examine how far an individual aspirant, according to the Trika system, can progress towards their ultimate goal of complete self-realization (Sivatva)

through personal effort alone. This inquiry can be approached from two perspectives: first, considering the aspirant's position as a being within creation, and second, examining their intrinsic nature.

In the Trika view, creation is divided into two realms or planes of existence, known as the Adhvas. These are the Impure Order (asuddha adhva) and the Pure Order (suddha adhva). The Impure Order corresponds to the material plane, while the Pure Order corresponds to the spiritual plane. Importantly, these realms are not external or separate from individuals but are intrinsic to every person, who is also composed of all thirty-six tattvas. This means that what applies to the individual (the microcosm) also applies to the cosmos (the macrocosm).

Typically, humans are considered to inhabit the Impure Order, being deeply connected to the material world due to their physical bodies. Their ultimate goal—achieving the realization of their true self, Sivatva—lies within the spiritual plane. Therefore, the first step toward this goal involves detaching from the material world and cultivating non-attachment (vairagya) to transient things. This process of detachment involves turning inward and focusing on one's pure Self (Suddha svarupa) through introspection. The journey of this introspection is often likened to traveling through various levels or tattvas of the Impure Creation.

An embodied human being, according to the Trika view, has the potential to evolve through the vast realms of Prakriti and Maya through dedicated effort. However, this effort alone can only take him to a certain point: the highest level he can achieve through his own efforts is to transcend Prakriti and Maya, reaching liberation from the constraints of material association. Beyond this limit, an

individual cannot advance solely by their own efforts.

Once the individual surpasses Prakriti, they encounter the realm of Maya, which overwhelms them with ignorance. At this stage, their physical form dissolves into Maya, leading to a loss of their distinct individuality or ego-consciousness, which arises from a mistaken identity with the material world. This state, where the individual's ego-consciousness is lost, is referred to as the 'pralayakala' state. In this state, progress is not possible until the individual is again associated with a physical body and their ego-consciousness is reawakened.

However, even with the reawakening of ego-consciousness, progress is minimal because this ego is still based on false identification and does not represent the Real Self. This false ego-consciousness is merely a conceptual image of the true Self, hidden behind ignorance.

Therefore, the individual must wait for the descent of Divine Grace (Anugraha) from the highest level. Without this Divine Grace, the individual remains trapped in the Impure Creation. The arrival of Divine Grace awakens the individual's latent consciousness of the Real Self (svarupa Aham or buddha aham), enabling entry into the pure spiritual realm (caitanya) and crossing into the Pure Order.

From another perspective, examining the individual's constitution, the Trika view posits that each being is covered by two types of veils of self-ignorance. The primary veil (mūla-ajñāna) is the deepest form of ignorance, arising from the individual's limited, atomistic nature. This basic self-ignorance is inherent in all beings and forms the root of secondary ignorance. It is described as conceptual because it merely covers the pure essence of the individual and has

no existence apart from them.

The secondary veil (bauddha ajñāna) arises from the individual's association with their physical body and results from false identification of the self with the body and other external factors. This veil is considered to be conceptual and serves as an outer shell of ignorance. It stems from the intellect (buddhi) and is a result of the mistaken identification of the self with the material body and external aspects.

Among the two types of self-ignorance that envelop every individual, an aspirant can only eliminate the outermost veil, known as bauddha ajñāna, through intense personal effort. This involves detaching from the material self (the body) and dissolving the false identifications created in the intellect (buddhi). However, the innermost veil, known as Pauruṣa ajñāna, cannot be destroyed by personal effort alone because it is rooted in the inherent, atomic nature imposed by the Nigraha aspect of Divine Shakti.

The destruction of this self-imposed limitation (saṅkoca) can only be achieved through the Amṛta aspect of Divine Shakti. Therefore, Pauruṣa ajñāna is instantly removed with the descent of Divine Grace (Anugraha). Once Pauruṣa ajñāna is eliminated, the greatest obstacle to the emergence of Pauruṣa jñāna (knowledge of the Real Self) is removed. This knowledge, which is the awareness of one's divine nature (svarūpa), is latent in every being and naturally illuminates the individual once the Pauruṣa ajñāna is destroyed.

Although the destruction of Pauruṣa ajñāna and the arising of Pauruṣa jñāna occur simultaneously with the arrival of Divine Grace, the eradication of bauddha ajñāna (the outer layer of ignorance) does not always happen instantly. In some cases, as will be discussed

later, the aspirant must continue their sādhanā (spiritual practice) to fully eradicate bauddha ajñāna and experience Pauruṣa jñāna in their intellect as intellectual knowledge.

Upon a critical examination of Saktipāta (the descent of Divine Grace) and the subsequent process of divinization, three distinct phases become evident. Although the Trika texts do not explicitly outline these stages, they can be discerned through the effects of Saktipāta:

1. **Mala-ksaya**: The destruction of the bonds formed by malas (impurities).
2. **Pratibha-jñānodaya**: The awakening of Pratibha (intuitive knowledge).
3. **Sivatva-prāpti**: The attainment of the integral realization of the Self (Sivatva).

These stages correspond to the traditional phases of Purgation, Illumination, and Divine Union described by medieval Christian mystics.

The first stage of Saktipāta, known as **Mala-ksaya**, is crucial for the aspirant. It focuses on purging the aspirant's body (adhāra) of the malas (impurities), specifically **āṇava-mala** and **māyā-mala**, preparing them to receive Divine knowledge. The term **Mala-ksaya** in the Trika system is used specifically for the destruction of āṇava-mala, which is the fundamental impurity. Other malas, like māyā and karma, are secondary and can be removed through the aspirant's own efforts.

Once the adhāra is purified from fundamental self-limitation,

Divine knowledge, known as **Pratibha-jñāna**, emerges from within and illuminates the aspirant's being. This innate knowledge of one's true essence (svarūpa) is latent in every individual and needs only a spark of Divine Shakti, through Saktipāta, to awaken.

The manifestation of Pratibha-jñāna can vary among aspirants. For some, it occurs immediately and spontaneously with Saktipāta, while for others, it may require the intervention of an external agent. This is particularly true if the intensity of Saktipāta is insufficient or if the aspirant's adhāra is not sufficiently pure. In such cases, the aid of an external agent, such as a guru or the study of scriptures, becomes necessary to awaken the latent Pratibha-jñāna. This process is known as **dikṣā** (initiation).

In the final stage, Pratibha-jñāna culminates in **Puruṣa-jñāna** or Supreme Knowledge, which is the complete realization of the Self (Sivatva). This marks the end of the aspirant's spiritual journey, corresponding to the stage of Divine Union described by Christian mystics.

However, despite the immediate rise of Pratibha-jñāna following the purgation of malas, the full realization of Sivatva may not be immediate for all aspirants. This delay is often due to the remaining māyā and karma malas that persist even after the destruction of āṇava-mala, particularly if the Divine Grace received was not intense enough. In such cases, aspirants must continue their efforts to eliminate these residual malas and purify their adhāra to achieve complete self-realization during their lifetime. If they do not strive to remove these last impurities, their experience of Pratibha-jñāna may be incomplete. Nevertheless, complete self-realization is ultimately inevitable after the physical body dies.

When exploring the conditions that lead to the descent of Divine Grace (Anugraha) on individual aspirants within the Trika system, we face a complex issue that can be examined from two main perspectives: the standpoint of the individual aspirant and that of the Supreme Reality, Parama Shiva, who dispenses Divine Grace.

From the perspective of the individual aspirant, Abhinavagupta outlines several potential causes or conditions for the descent of Divine Grace, evaluating each one critically:

1. **Karma-Based Explanation**: If we propose that Divine Grace is conditioned by the aspirant's meritorious karma (actions), we must address a fundamental issue: what causes these karmas? The common belief is that present karma is influenced by past actions and their residual impressions (saṃskāras). This creates an endless regress, where each present karma is connected to prior karmas, leading to an infinite chain. This cyclical explanation falls into the logical fallacy of *regressus ad infinitum*, meaning it does not provide a satisfactory ultimate cause and thus is considered logically untenable.

2. **Divine Will Explanation**: Another view is that the awakening of *buddha-jñāna* (knowledge of the Real Self) following Divine Grace is the result of the Divine Will of the Supreme Lord. However, this assumption presents a problem: aspirants would need to be aware of *buddha-jñāna* before it is awakened in them to justify the belief in Divine Will as the cause. Since they cannot have this awareness prior to the awakening, this assumption is also logically problematic.

3. **Partiality of the Supreme Lord**: If we assume that the Supreme Lord's Divine Grace is dispensed according to Divine Will, there's a potential issue of perceived partiality (rāga-dveṣa) — that is, the notion that the Supreme Lord might show favoritism or bias in granting Divine Grace. This raises ethical and philosophical concerns about the fairness and impartiality of Divine Grace.

While there are various explanations for the descent of Divine Grace, each faces significant logical and philosophical challenges. The issue of determining the precise conditions for Divine Grace involves complex considerations of karma, divine will, and the nature of divine impartiality.

The issue of what leads to the descent of Divine Grace (Anugraha) is intricate and multifaceted. Various potential factors, such as the development of intense non-attachment (vairāgya), self-purification, or the worship of a deity, have been considered. However, each of these factors faces significant objections:

- **Non-Attachment and Self-Purification**: While these practices are important, they do not consistently account for Divine Grace, as they may not be universally applicable or sufficient on their own.
- **Discriminatory Knowledge**: The rise of knowledge through personal effort does not guarantee Divine Grace, as it may not address the deeper, more fundamental causes of its descent.
- **Worship of Deities**: The effectiveness of worship in attracting Divine Grace can be questioned, as it may not be universally effective or sufficient.

Abhinavagupta concludes that no single explanation can universally account for the descent of Divine Grace. This aligns with the Trika system's principle of **Svātantrya** (Divine Freedom), which holds that Divine Grace is an act of absolute freedom and is not bound by specific conditions.

From the Supreme Lord's perspective, Divine Grace is a manifestation of divine freedom and is therefore unconditional. Imposing specific causal conditions would contradict the principle of Svātantrya. Despite this, humans, driven by rationality, struggle to accept that Divine Grace is entirely unrelated to the recipient's actions or state. The concept of Divine Grace being beyond logical comprehension challenges the human instinct for reason and explanation.

In addressing the paradox of seeking causal conditions for the descent of Divine Grace, which is inherently an act of divine freedom, the Trika system offers a perspective that satisfies our rational instincts. It suggests that certain conditions within the individual recipient are most favorable for receiving Divine Grace. Specifically, the maturation (paripāka) of the aspirant's malas, known as mala-paripāka, is considered a key factor conducive to the descent of Divine Grace.

However, while mala-paripāka is a widely accepted explanation, it does not apply in all cases. This is because mala-paripāka describes the state of the aspirant's adhāra (body or substratum) rather than being a direct cause of Divine Grace. The maturation of malas is seen as making the aspirant's adhāra more suitable for receiving Divine Grace, but the actual descent of Grace itself involves the exercise of Divine Freedom.

The Trika system acknowledges that Divine Grace can descend in any of the three states of existence: sakala (manifest), pralaya (dissolution), and vijñāna (knowledge). This possibility underscores the idea that while mala-paripāka can prepare the recipient, the ultimate cause of Divine Grace lies beyond these preparatory states and involves the direct intervention of divine freedom.

The maturation of malas is compared to the ripening of fruits, where time plays a role but is not the sole factor. Just as fruit ripening involves heat and other conditions, the maturation of malas is influenced by various experiences and sufferings encountered over time. These vicissitudes and sufferings, which are closely linked to the passage of time, contribute significantly to the maturation process, thereby making the individual more receptive to Divine Grace.

In the context of the Trika system's understanding of Divine Grace, the distinction between the states of vijñāna-kala and pralaya-kala, where individuals lack a physical body and thus do not experience worldly suffering, raises a pertinent issue. According to the Trika perspective, the prolonged duration spent in these states is precisely due to the slow maturation of the āṇava-māla (the fundamental mala) in such states. This slow maturation process necessitates a longer period in these states, reflecting the unique nature of āṇava- māla.

The maturation of malas is not uniform across all individuals. It varies qualitatively as well as temporally, which accounts for differences in the intensity of Saktipāta (the descent of Divine Grace). This variation reflects both the imminent arrival of Divine Grace and the individual's preparedness to receive it. The Trika system, therefore, acknowledges that while Saktipāta is fundamentally

a unified act of Divine Freedom, it manifests differently across individuals based on their level of mala maturation.

To categorize these differences, the Trika system classifies Saktipāta into three principal types based on intensity: Tīvra (intense), Madhya (medium), and Manda (mild).

Abhinavagupta further elaborates this classification into nine sub-categories, each denoting varying degrees of intensity. This classification highlights the different levels of receptivity among aspirants and provides a framework for understanding the variation in their experiences of Divine Grace.

It is crucial to note that this classification of Saktipāta, based on its intensity, pertains to the individual's experience. From the perspective of the Supreme Lord, Divine Grace is uniform and unconditioned by qualitative differences. The apparent variation in intensity is a reflection of the aspirants' varying capacities to receive and integrate the Divine Grace due to their differing degrees of mala maturation.

Thus, the Trika system uses the concept of mala-paripāka to explain the differences in Saktipāta intensity among individuals. This approach allows for a nuanced understanding of how Divine Grace operates in relation to the individual's spiritual development, while acknowledging that the essence of Saktipāta remains consistent and undifferentiated from the Supreme Lord's perspective.

Cakrodaya Pranayama

Breath can vary significantly in its spatial presence. For instance, when the breath is extended to seventeen units (known as *tuṭis*), it occupies a smaller space. Conversely, when it extends over fewer units, it occupies more space. This variation becomes evident in urgent situations—like when fleeing from danger, where rapid breathing increases the breath's spatial extent, creating a more pronounced presence.

In the practice of Cakrodaya Pranayama, the inhalation and exhalation processes should be performed slowly. Despite this slow pace, the breath must be audible to others around you. Ensure that your breathing is long and audible, so that someone nearby can hear it.

There are two methods for practicing Cakrodaya Pranayama:

1. **Through the Throat:** This method involves both exhaling (prāṇa) and inhaling (apāna) through the throat. It is essential for thinning out the breath and maintaining consistent awareness during practice.
2. **Through the Heart:** This method, while also effective, should be avoided. It tends to generate excessive heat in the system and can lead to severe health issues, including heart failure, if practiced incorrectly or excessively. It is notably difficult and risky.

The recommended practice for Cakrodaya Pranayama is through

the throat. The breath should be made extremely subtle and practiced with constant awareness. If you maintain awareness, you will avoid falling into a state of slumber. The breath becomes so thin that it reaches a point between sleep and wakefulness. Successfully maintaining awareness at this point leads to experiencing the fourth state, known as *turya*. In this state, you are not affected by sleep, nor do you experience dizziness.

As you continue in this practice, impurities known as *kārma-mala* are purified. During Cakrodaya Pranayama, your body remains still, and there is no movement or change in position. Your limbs stay as they were at the start of the practice. The organs of action (karmendriyas) become inactive, and only your eyes can move. However, even when your eyes see, there is no attachment or concern.

Your perception becomes detached from the external world, akin to noticing a minor blade of grass without any thought or concern. Similarly, during practice, the yogi remains unconcerned by external stimuli. Whether in a hall with sounds or surrounded by activity, the practitioner hears but does not react or pay heed. This detached awareness continues through the states of waking, dreaming, and sleeping, embodying the essence of Cakrodaya Pranayama.

In the Upanishads, it is emphasized that the internal journey of pranayama—an advanced practice of controlling the breath—is likened to walking on a razor's edge. This comparison highlights the difficulty and danger of this path, which is why it is described as a 'hard path,' an 'uphill task,' and 'very trying.' This journey is challenging because, during pranayama, the practitioner—referred to as a yogi—may experience various divine phenomena.

In the practice of advanced Yoga, it is crucial to maintain a disciplined focus. The yogi must avoid becoming entangled in any emotional responses or sensory experiences, even if they seem divine or profound. According to the Upanishads, one should disregard any distractions from divine sensations like touch, taste, or sight. These sensory experiences, though captivating, are not to be attended to during meditation and should be set aside.

The adept yogi,do not get caught up in spiritual distractions or temptations. They understand that even seemingly spiritual experiences can be misleading. There is a stage in which the yogi's journey where the self-realized individual perceives Para-Bhairava, the Supreme Self, in everything around them. At this stage, the yogi sees their own essence reflected in the entire universe and remains unaffected by external thoughts or distractions. The yogi reaches a state of profound bravery and awareness.

However, at this advanced level, the yogi may encounter divine forces or deities that attempt to divert them from their path. These entities, known as superintending deities (*sthaniya devatas*), try to mislead the practitioner as they enter this stage of Para-Bhairava. Even though the process of inhaling and exhaling continues, the yogi must remain focused and not be swayed by these divine distractions. They continue their journey through the state of *turya*, the fourth state of consciousness.

The next phase of the journey involves the practice of *dhyana* or concentration. The yogi advances beyond the qualities of the intellect, focusing on an objectless object. As this concentration matures, the movement of vital airs ceases. The yogi then seeks to enter the *sushumna dham*, the central channel of the nervous

system,which is a metaphorical description of the profound inner awareness that the yogi develops,the awareness is towards the dimension of subjectivity. When concentration is firmly established, this process happens naturally.

In the advanced stage of this practice, vital airs—*prana* and *apana*—merge into the *sushumna*, rising to a state of universal consciousness or *urdhva kundalini*.

When the awakened yogi firmly grasps the essence of *spanda tattva* (the pulsation or vibration of consciousness,the dynamic awareness), they resolve to follow the divine will. As they rest in this experience, *Surya* (prana) and *Soma* (apana) converge in the *sushumna*, moving towards higher consciousness. The yogi must remain vigilant, or they risk being overcome by sleep or inertia.

In this state, the yogi reaches a point where no further effort is required. The process of vital airs ceases, leaving only the life current—*pranapana*. This transition of awareness from Pramana and Prameya to Pramiti to signifies a form of metaphorical death, or *crossing the abyss*.

As the yogi engages in this inner journey, they may perceive divine sounds, sensations, and visions as they traverse different layers of the inner worlds and inner realities. They might see celestial beings of extraordinary beauty, taste divine flavors, and smell heavenly fragrances. Despite these experiences being intensely vivid and compelling, they are considered distractions rather than aids on the path of Yoga. These sensory experiences can divert the yogi's focus from the true objective of their practice. Therefore, the yogi is advised not to become attached to or distracted by these divine sensations, even though they may seem captivating.

Instead, the yogi should recognize these experiences as signs that they are progressing on their path. If the yogi remains aware of the ultimate reality—referred to as the Supreme Self—these experiences can be useful indicators that they are on the right track. However, if the yogi becomes ensnared by these sensory delights, they risk falling into difficulties and distractions. Hence, while it is important to acknowledge these experiences, the yogi must remain focused and not let them derail their practice.

The key to navigating this internal journey is awareness. Maintaining awareness is crucial for staying on course and overcoming the challenges encountered.

Following this, we move to the concept of *pratyahara*, which involves withdrawing the mind from external distractions and refocusing it on its source, the mind gathers knowledge through the five senses—touch, taste, hearing, sight, and smell. These sensory inputs relate to objects of enjoyment, which can cause pleasure or pain. During spiritual practice, one must give up attachment to these sensory experiences, a process known as pratyahara. This practice helps in breaking free from the bondage of existence.

To achieve this, one must be diligent and sincere. One must fully engage in their practice with dedication. The divine experiences—touch, taste, hearing, sight, and smell—should be perceived directly through the higher intellect, which is unified with the Supreme Self. This emphasizes the necessity of being aligned with Supreme Consciousness.

In Vedanta and Yoga philosophy, this higher intellect is called *stambhara prajna*, which translates to the highest, most refined form of intellect. This pure intellect, often described as magnetic,

allows one to recognize the Supreme Self. This aptly describes this refined intellect as it helps in breaking the cycle of birth and death, or samsara (or the self imposed illusion of Avidya).

As the yogi progresses, the nature of the life current undergoes significant transformations. This life current, which is not a static entity but a dynamic force, operates in various profound ways. In his *Tantraloka*, the philosopher Abhinavagupta refers to one such advanced practice as *vedha-diksha*, or "initiation with penetration." This elevated form of initiation is granted to a highly advanced disciple who has met all necessary qualifications and whose intellect is perfectly pure.

To receive this initiation, the disciple must have completed all preliminary practices and demonstrated readiness for this advanced stage. Only a true and skilled master can perform this initiation, which involves a deep, transformative process similar to how an auger creates a hole with precision. The master effectively "bores" into the disciple's vital air (prana), leading to a profound internal transformation. This process aligns with the Upanishadic teaching that "prana is the Self," highlighting the essential nature of prana in realizing the Self.

The *vedha-diksha* or initiation with penetration manifests in six distinct forms, each providing unique experiences of elevated consciousness:

1. **Sakta Vedha**: This form was described previously and involves specific divine experiences.
2. **Bindu Vedha**: This initiation provides an experience of pleasure that surpasses any earthly sensation. It is described

as a joy multiplied infinitely beyond the pleasure of sexual union. The disciple feels this immense pleasure during the initiation, even though they may not be consciously aware of the process.

3. **Bhujanga Vedha**: Combining elements of *vedha-diksha* and *bindu vedha*, this initiation causes the disciple to perceive themselves as having the shape of a serpent. This experience is accompanied by a boundless sense of joy.

4. **Bhramara Vedha**: Here, the initiation induces sensations akin to the buzzing of bees. This sound represents a deep, internal experience of vibration.

5. **Nada Vedha**: This form of initiation is experienced as an inner sound. The yogi perceives subtle, inner auditory sensations that are integral to their spiritual journey.

6. **Mantra Vedha**: This involves the realization or direct experience of the essence of a mantra. The yogi gains a profound understanding of the vibrational power and significance of specific sounds or syllables.

Beyond these six types of initiation, there is a seventh form called **Para Vedha**. In this state, the yogi transcends the need for concentration and meditation. The yogi's experience culminates in the realization that there is only Supreme Consciousness, with no distinction between prana and apana, or any form of concentration. At this ultimate stage, the yogi fully embodies the Supreme Self, experiencing pure consciousness without the intermediary processes.

After completing the journey through the various stages of vital forces, we arrive at the practice of *dharana*, or meditation.

According to the Netra Tantra (VI.16), *dharana* is the essence of the Supreme Self, maintained consistently across all states of consciousness: wakefulness, dreaming, and sleep. This meditative state, as described by the great sages, liberates one from the intricate web of limitations—known as *bhavabandhavi-mocika*—and leads to spiritual freedom.

In this advanced stage, after successfully navigating the four processes related to the vital forces (*prana* and *apana*), the yogi can either keep their eyes open or closed while meditating. To recap, the four stages of this journey are:

1. **External Pranayama (Cakrodaya)**: This involves practicing pranayama (breath control) in the states of wakefulness, dreaming, and sleep.
2. **Internal Pranayama**: Here, the yogi experiences the divine nature of the five senses from within.
3. **Internal Pranayama in the Turya State**: This involves practicing pranayama within the fourth state of consciousness, known as *turya*.
4. **Entering the Susumna**: This stage involves guiding the vital force down into the central channel of the sushumna.

Once the yogi has mastered these stages, they achieve a state of meditation even when their eyes are open. In this state, the yogi's actions are performed from the perspective of Supreme Consciousness. Every action is carried out with the awareness of absolute, self-eternal Consciousness. This ultimate realization is referred to as *jagadananda*, which means the bliss of universal existence.

Ajapa Gayatri

In Pranayama, the three phases of the breath cycle are:

1. **Puraka** is the act of inhaling deeply and slowly through the nose, filling the lungs completely and expanding the abdomen and chest. Focus on the sensation of the breath entering your body and the expansion it brings.
2. **Kumbhaka** involves retaining the breath. After inhalation (Antar Kumbhaka), hold the breath in for a comfortable count. Similarly, after exhalation (Bahir Kumbhaka), you might hold the breath out for a period.
3. **Rechaka** is the process of exhaling gently and completely through the nose, releasing all the air from your lungs while contracting the abdomen slightly.

In practice, you start with Puraka, hold with Kumbhaka, exhale with Rechaka, and then hold again with Kumbhaka before repeating the cycle.

In your meditative practice, focus on the central breath, the pause between inhaling and exhaling. This pause, known as kumbhaka, is a natural stillness where you should center your awareness on the Supreme Self. This central breath is not merely about physical posture but about maintaining awareness at this pivotal point.

As you deepen your practice, remember that true asana is not the physical postures like bhadrāsana or svastikāsana. Instead, it's the state of constant awareness of the Supreme Self at the junction of

your breaths. This inner state represents the real asana, transcending external positions.

To achieve a truly pure mind, cultivate perfect awareness of the Supreme Consciousness. This means avoiding negative thoughts or actions like speaking ill of others, harboring hatred, or being greedy. Instead, focus on treating each other with love, sympathy, and support. A clean mind, free from ego and prejudice, is essential for spiritual progress.

When you can maintain awareness at the point between inhaling and exhaling, you are engaging in anusandhana, or constant assimilation of the Supreme Self. This is the true conquest of the Asana. Practice this diligently.

Pranayama, the control of breath, follows a similar principle. It is not just about the physical act of breathing but involves subtle, internal control. Initially, you might notice the breath's movement, but with practice, the breath becomes finer and more refined. The goal is to reach a state where the breath is so subtle and quiet that it merges seamlessly with the awareness of the Supreme Self.

In the practice of Ajapā Gayatri-Pranayama, the breath should be so refined that it is imperceptible to you and to others around you. The movement of the breath should be so subtle that you yourself are unaware of it, leaving only awareness of the Supreme Consciousness. This represents the ultimate achievement in pranayama

Ascend gradually and steadily towards the realization of God-consciousness. Embrace the understanding that "He am I," maintaining this awareness with unwavering focus.

It is crucial to maintain continuous and consistent practice in your japa, or sacred chant. This means that the Ajapa Gayatri Pranayama,

which involves synchronizing breath with constant awareness, must remain uninterrupted. The practice should be seamless and steady, ensuring that every breath is infused with awareness of the Supreme Consciousness.

The practice involves transcending the gross movement of the breath. When you reach a state where the prana, or vital air, becomes extremely subtle and refined, you achieve the movement-without-movement, or the universal movement of prana. This represents the true essence of pranayama, or breath control. Once you attain this level of practice, you break free from the cycle of birth and death, entering a superior state of existence. This mastery of breath and awareness is considered the true Asana (āsana).

However, practicing Ajapa Gayatri Pranayama is challenging and requires dedication. An alternative practice is Cakrodaya, which also involves maintaining awareness but in a different manner. Mastery of Cakrodaya is another significant achievement in pranayama, reflecting a commendable Asana

To truly master the subtlety of awareness, practice diligently and consistently. This subtle awareness, known as *sūksmaparimarśana*, requires continuous and vigilant effort. I've shared insights on *cakrodaya* from personal experience and the teachings of the Śāstra.

Cakrodaya involves a nuanced practice that requires deep focus and constant vigilance. This technique, as outlined in sacred texts, is essential for advancing in pranayama. The goal is to achieve a high level of awareness and control over the breath, which will set a solid foundation for more advanced practices.

Comparing Ajapa Gayatri and Cakrodaya:

Ajapa Gayatri Pranayama is more challenging and demands a

higher level of practice. During this process, you might find yourself falling into drowsiness or losing focus as you attempt to grasp the central force. The practice requires extraordinary discipline and concentration.

Given its difficulty, it is advisable to first establish yourself in Cakrodaya. This practice is more accessible and serves as a preparatory stage for Ajapa Gayatri. Mastering Cakrodaya will make the transition to Ajapa Gayatri smoother and more effective, ensuring that your efforts are not in vain. Ajapa Gayatri is an advanced practice, and its mastery, as achieved by great yogis signifies a high level of spiritual attainment.

In practice, you should focus on conquering the mind before attempting Ajapa Gayatri. It is advised that the yogi control their mind by physically engaging the body.

The Right Asana for Pranayama:

Before engaging in Ajapa Gayatri, the adept should have mastered Cakrodaya. This preparatory stage is crucial for setting the right foundation for pranayama. Once established in the correct Asana, you can move on to more advanced pranayama practices.

Pranayama, when done correctly, involves overcoming the gross movements of the vital airs. You achieve this by refining the breath, making it more subtle. Through this process, you reach a state where the breath becomes so refined that you experience the movement without movement, or the universal flux of Divine unity. This subtle state of prana represents the highest level of pranayama, where inhalation and exhalation are performed with extreme slowness and complete awareness, revealing the finest and most universal

movement. This is the essence of *sparida*, the movement without movement.

If you are not yet capable of adopting this Asana, all your efforts in practicing pranayama might go in vain, even if you continue for an extensive period. Without achieving the proper

Asana, your efforts may seem fruitless, and you might feel as if nothing has been accomplished.

To truly master this Asana, you need both the grace of a master and your own sincere efforts. Individual effort is crucial. The grace of the master alone will not suffice without your dedicated practice. As stated in the Yoga Vasistha:

"Neither the sacred texts (Śāstras) nor the master can help unless the intellect of the practitioner (sādhaka) has become serene, clear, and sharp. This intellect must be established in the state of pure subtlety, or suddha sattva guna."

This means that your intellect must be purified and serene to fully grasp and establish this Asana. A pious and sharp intellect is essential for understanding and practicing the true essence of pranayama.

The real pranayama involves entering and maintaining the Middle Path (madhya-dhama or madhya-bhave). This concept is profound and not easily explained but is crucial for your practice. As expressed by Śrī Śaṅkarācārya:

"When the experience of beingness, occurring at the boundary between sleep and wakefulness, becomes stable, one experiences the bliss of non-duality."

This point is where sleep transitions into wakefulness and vice versa. It represents a pure and pious state free from the clutter of thoughts and impressions (vāsanās). Capturing and maintaining this state, even briefly, represents true pranayama. If you can hold this state consistently, it leads to the unparalleled joy of non-duality, known as advayānanda.

True pranayama is about achieving and maintaining a state of thoughtlessness and purity that bridges the transition between sleep and wakefulness. This state, once firmly established, leads to a profound and joyful realization of non-duality. If you persist in your efforts and manage to stabilize this state, you will transcend the cycle of birth and death, achieving a superior form of pranayama.

This concept can be expressed poetically:

"There is a point between sleep and waking where you must remain alert without wavering. Enter this space where transient forms fade away. Endure the distractions and remain steadfast, closing all openings to maintain this state."

This reflection captures the essence of maintaining awareness at the threshold between different states of consciousness, emphasizing the importance of persistence and focus.

Visualization: The Creative Will of Yogi

A fundamental factor contributing to the swift and significant progress of a tantric practitioner is the elaborate and nuanced process of inner visualization, as meticulously outlined in tantric sadhana. This process, which centers on imaginative and creative visualization, is far from arbitrary; it is intricately linked to the symbolic universe of the psyche. This symbolic world serves as a gateway to ideas that extend beyond the limits of rational thought, yet maintain an intrinsic connection to the deep, structural aspects of human experience.

In the contemporary world, heavily shaped by Western intellectual traditions and philosophies, there is a strong emphasis on knowledge derived from factual evidence and objective experience. This preference for empirical validation has led to a widespread focus on observable and measurable phenomena. Nevertheless, there are numerous aspects of human experience that lie beyond the reach of empirical scrutiny. These are realms that cannot be assessed through laboratory experiments or objective analysis but can only be explored through personal introspection and the subjective depths of the mind. Despite the inherently subjective nature of such exploration, the transformative impact of these inner experiences is undeniable and significant.

To fully develop and enhance these inner visions, it is essential to tap into and expand your creative imagination and visualization capacities. Imagination is not merely a passive mental exercise but a dynamic and active process that allows the thinker to create

and experience dimensions of reality that are inaccessible through logical reasoning alone. The more expansive and uninhibited your imagination, the broader and more profound your experiential horizons become.

While every individual has some level of imaginative capability, this basic form of imagination is often insufficient for achieving deeper, more transformative visionary states. Ordinary imagination tends to operate within the confines of what is probable and acceptable according to societal norms and conventional thought patterns. It rarely ventures beyond the boundaries of everyday experience and seldom evolves into genuine visionary insight. In contrast, a true seer—someone who has significantly refined their imaginative faculties— experiences knowledge as vivid, symbolic patterns that convey deeper truths. This enhanced ability allows the seer to access and interpret realms of understanding that are both dynamic and universal, using the same imaginative capacity that everyone possesses but in a far more profound and comprehensive manner.

Imagination: The Source of Creative Power

Imagination is a fundamental source of creative power, and its strength is a key determinant in the ability to create. It is a potent mental force that can be harnessed in myriad ways. By constructing an inner world rich with visions and symbols, you empower the forces of your mind, which are drawing from the deep reservoir of potential inherent within you, represented by archetypes. As these mental forces gain the ability to shape and manifest the images you conceive, they naturally develop the capacity to achieve whatever

goals or aspirations you set.

Recent developments in the application of inner visualization techniques have demonstrated their effectiveness, particularly in the realm of medical treatment. Notably, the work of Dr. Ainslie Meares from Australia and Dr. Simonton from the United States has showcased the efficacy of this approach in treating cancer patients. Their methods involve guiding patients through a series of visualizations where healthy cells are imagined as actively combating diseased ones, akin to an army engaging in battle. The success of these treatments heavily relies on the patient's ability to focus, concentrate, and vividly imagine this healing process. The results have been promising, underscoring the transformative potential of inner visualization.

The use of such visualization techniques in modern therapeutic practices has its roots in the ancient traditions of Shaivism and yoga. In Shaivism, visualization and creative imagination serve as a bridge between the objective world and the subjective realm. While your imagination may draw from objective experiences, the images you create are fundamentally subjective and internally generated.

This is why Shaivism has developed the sophisticated art of iconography. Icons provide a structured foundation, guiding the aspirant's imagination by offering a focal point and a medium for concentration. Although abstract imagination holds great potential, it is challenging for most individuals to harness effectively in a way that produces beneficial outcomes. Most people require structured guidance to channel their imagination constructively, as the untrained mind is prone to distraction and loss of control. In cases where imagination is directed towards destructive outcomes,

it can be particularly perilous. This is precisely why the disciplines of yoga are essential; they ensure that the mind remains disciplined and focused, even as it explores higher realms of thought.

To utilize imagination as a true creative force, it is necessary to initiate a thought, visualize it vividly, and maintain concentrated focus until the idea reaches its full development or resolution. Only through this disciplined approach does the mind gain true power. The challenge lies in overcoming the difficulties and distractions that arise during this process, which often leads to disappointment and frustration for the average person. Mastery of the creative power of imagination requires perseverance and a well-developed ability to channel and sustain mental focus.

In the practice of *tattwa shuddhi*, you are invited to delve deeply within yourself, engaging in a process that encourages exploration of your inner world. This practice provides you with the opportunity to create and interact with colors, sounds, and images, and to contemplate abstract ideas by transforming them into tangible forms within your mind. You encounter a diverse range of images, from the grotesque to the pleasing, and while there are specific guidelines to steer your journey, you are also given the freedom to explore and push the boundaries of your imagination as far as you wish.

Initially, the images you conjure may only exist as vague thoughts or abstract notions. However, as you persist in your practice and your mind becomes increasingly concentrated, these initial thoughts gradually evolve into clearly defined and vivid pictures. This transformation occurs as you focus more deeply on the images you are creating, leading to subtle and nuanced experiences that might otherwise go unnoticed. Through this focused and sustained

practice, you cultivate a heightened awareness and insight into the more intricate layers of your inner experience.

Imagination Must Follow Guidelines

The practice of imagination and visualization is a potent method for developing profound inner experiences and enhancing the powers of the mind. It is crucial to approach this practice with an understanding that it is not merely a form of brainwashing, as some critics might claim. Instead, in *tattwa shuddhi*, imagination and visualization serve as sophisticated tools for spiritual growth and mental development. The symbols and images used in this practice have been chosen for their deep, universal significance. These symbols are not arbitrary but are rooted in both subjective experiences and objective validation, representing eternal archetypes that evoke significant spiritual insights across diverse cultural and religious contexts.

These archetypal symbols have been meticulously examined by individuals with profound inner vision, and they are considered crucial in bridging the gap between the individual and the eternal spirit they seek to connect with. Tantric imagery often extends beyond conventional rational limits. Some images may depict figures with multiple arms and eyes, others might be shown in provocative or extreme states, such as drinking blood or carrying destructive weapons. For instance, Kali is illustrated with a necklace of skulls, while Shiva is shown with serpents coiled around his body. These diverse and sometimes unsettling images underscore the tantric principle that life cannot be confined to a single, uniform perspective. Instead, Shaivism embraces the complexity and variety

of life, acknowledging that a full experience of existence involves recognizing and integrating its inherent contradictions.

Today, Shaivism remains a distinctive spiritual tradition that actively preserves and applies these practices as a scientific approach to exploring the human mind and consciousness. It upholds the belief that imagination and inner experiences should not be subject to random moods or transient whims but should be guided and controlled by the practitioner's will.

Mastery in this area involves the ability to create a thought, develop and visualize it, and then intentionally let it go. This disciplined approach is foundational not only to spiritual growth but also to achieving material success and fulfillment.

To effectively utilize imagination within tantric practices, strict adherence to established rules and guidelines is necessary. Shaivism provides comprehensive instructions on not only the symbols and images to be used but also on the precise manner in which the practice should be conducted. This includes specific guidance on posture, breathing techniques, the lighting and environment of the practice space, and the timing for introducing particular symbols. All of these aspects are to be carried out under the careful supervision of a knowledgeable master.

This structured approach ensures that the practice is both effective and transformative, helping the practitioner to achieve the desired spiritual and personal outcomes.

Tatwa Shuddhi and Papa Purusha

In the practice of tattwa shuddhi, one encounters a range of unusual and symbolic imagery, with perhaps the most striking being that of Papa Purusha, the embodiment of sinful tendencies. This figure represents the various causes of personal suffering—such as ego, attachment, jealousy, and pride—that plague our lives. During tattwa shuddhi meditation, you are guided to envision a complete transformation of Papa Purusha within your own being.

This inner transformation reflects a broader process of self-transformation, where you work to reconcile and harmonize conflicting inner energies.

Understanding this transformation requires recognizing that it symbolizes the inner struggle between opposing forces. These forces include the negative and positive energies that, when properly balanced, lead to the awakening of a third, neutral force. This balance is essential for achieving harmony and stability within oneself. The transformation of Papa Purusha thus represents a profound inner process where the clash between these energies—often seen in the physiological and psychological realms—seeks resolution.

It is crucial to see this transformation not merely as a moral or ethical purification, but as a deep-seated process of restoring equilibrium between opposing forces within us. The conflict and disharmony that create errors in our personality and behavior are both physiological and psychological in nature. The forces of ida and pingala, which symbolize the sun and moon, as well as the vital and mental energies inherent in each person, continually interact

and influence each other. Any imbalance in these forces inevitably affects our mental and psychological state, and conversely, our mental state can impact the balance of these energies.

Thus, the transformation of Papa Purusha is far more complex than simply addressing moral failings or sins. It is not a matter of mere confession or superficial acts of cleansing. If resolving our inner conflicts were as simple as confessing our sins, life would be far less challenging. Instead, this process requires a deep, transformative effort to harmonize and balance the internal forces that shape our experiences and actions.

Papa Purusha, contrary to what might be suggested by traditional ethical or religious interpretations as merely a "sinful man," actually represents a broader concept within tantra. He symbolizes the inherent conflict, disharmony, and imbalance present within us and the universe. In tantra, these elements are not merely obstacles but are seen as essential components of the process of achieving harmony. The philosophy of tantra underscores the importance of experiencing and understanding conflict as a means to attain a deeper sense of balance and integration.

Tantra posits that duality and opposing forces are fundamental aspects of existence. At the highest level of this dualistic framework are Shiva and Shakti, who embody the dynamic interplay of cosmic forces. This principle of duality is not confined to a single realm but permeates all levels of creation and experience. For example, concepts like day and night, sun and moon, heat and cold, love and hate all illustrate this interplay. Each aspect of duality gains meaning and significance through its opposite; we recognize night because of our experience of day, and we understand cold through the contrast

of heat.

This principle of duality is also reflected in the concept of ida and pingala, the two vital energies in tantric practice. Ida, associated with the moon, represents mental or lunar energy, which is cool and calming. Pingala, associated with the sun, represents pranic or vital energy, characterized by warmth and activity. The interaction between these opposing energies creates a dynamic tension or 'pull,' which is crucial for the evolution and progression of life. This tension is not something to be avoided but rather embraced as it fuels growth and development.

Without this tension and conflict, we would stagnate, remaining at a state of inertia and complacency, known as tamas. It is through the ongoing struggle to balance these opposing forces that we are driven to seek spiritual growth and evolution. This quest for balance propels us forward, pushing our development to higher levels of consciousness and understanding. Thus, the process of transformation, symbolized by Papa Purusha, is integral to our spiritual journey, emphasizing that conflict and imbalance are necessary catalysts for evolution and self-realization.

The grotesque figure of Papa Purusha, created within our bodies during meditation, serves as a powerful symbol of the energy imbalances present within our entire system—encompassing both mind and body. This figure should not be understood as the Devil or Satan in a literal sense. Instead, it is a symbolic representation intended to address the deeply ingrained imbalances that influence our behavior and thought patterns. The concept of sin and moral wrongdoing, which Papa Purusha embodies, is rooted in the collective unconscious shaped by our ancestral past and evokes a

visceral, often uncomfortable response.

In tantric practice, Papa Purusha is introduced at a crucial stage when you have adopted the role of an objective witness. At this point, you are detached from certain parts of your mind, observing your thoughts and actions from a distance. This detachment allows you to assess your reactions and behaviors with clarity and objectivity. It is only through this impartial view that you can uncover various facets of your personality that were previously hidden by your ego. These facets are often aspects of yourself that you may have been reluctant to acknowledge or confront due to embarrassment or shame.

Tantra insists on the importance of confronting yourself with honesty. It challenges you to see yourself as you truly are, rather than as you would like to believe you are. This process requires immense strength and willpower to face both your weaknesses and strengths directly. A superficial glance is insufficient; instead, you must engage in a deep, penetrating examination of your inner self. This profound self-reflection reveals the true nature of your being and provides the inner knowledge necessary for personal growth and transformation.

To facilitate this deep self-exploration, specific practices have been developed. One such practice involves the use of mandalas, which are intricate geometric designs that serve as focal points for meditation. Mandalas are believed to have the power to draw forth and reveal aspects of the subconscious and unconscious mind. By placing these mandalas before your inner vision, you can access and confront the hidden elements of your psyche.

Tattwa shuddhi, a key practice in this tradition, utilizes mandalas to represent both the transcendental and the gross aspects of your personality. As you engage with these mandalas, you are prompted

to make a conscious choice regarding which aspect of yourself you wish to unite with or integrate. This practice helps you navigate the complexities of your inner world, guiding you toward a deeper understanding of your true self and facilitating your spiritual evolution.

Detailed Technique for Tattwa Shuddhi Practice

To begin the practice of tattwa shuddhi, it is crucial to first establish a calm and focused state of mind. This can be achieved through preliminary practices like trataka (concentrated gazing) or pranayama (controlled breathing exercises). Spend about ten to fifteen minutes on these practices to steady your mind and deepen your internal focus. Once you feel adequately prepared, close your eyes to transition into the meditative phase.

1. Find a Comfortable Posture

Adopt a comfortable and stable seated posture to facilitate prolonged meditation. The preferred asanas for this practice include Siddhasana (Accomplished Pose), Siddha Yoni Asana (Perfected Yoni Pose), or Padmasana (Lotus Pose). Ensure that your seated position supports a steady and comfortable alignment, helping you maintain focus and stillness throughout the practice.

2. Visualization of the Guru

Begin by visualizing the form of your guru, whether they are a physical teacher or an abstract embodiment of spiritual wisdom. In your mind's eye, offer your respects and reverence to this figure, acknowledging their role in guiding and inspiring your practice.

This act of paying homage helps align your intentions with the higher spiritual guidance represented by your guru.

3. Meditate on the Mantra Hamsa

In your meditative state, focus on the mantra "Hamsa" and synchronize it with your breath. As you inhale, mentally chant "Ham" while visualizing the energy flowing downward through the Sushumna Nadi (the central energy channel). As you exhale, mentally chant "So," visualizing the energy rising within this channel. This synchronization of mantra and breath helps in deepening your connection with the supreme consciousness, Brahman.

4. Visualize the Tattwas

a. Prithvi Tattwa (Earth Element)

Direct your awareness to the area between your toes and knees. Visualize a yellow square in this region, symbolizing the Prithvi Tattwa, which represents the earth element. The square's yellow color embodies the solidity and stability associated with the earth. As you focus on this yellow square, repeat the bija mantra "Lam" mentally. This repetition helps to reinforce the grounding and stabilizing qualities of the earth element within your being.

b. Apas Tattwa (Water Element)

Move your attention to the area between your knees and navel. Here, visualize a crescent moon with two lotuses at its ends, encircled by a circle of water, and imbued with a white color. This imagery

represents the Apas Tattwa, symbolizing the fluidity and adaptability of the water element. As you concentrate on this crescent moon, mentally repeat the bija mantra "Vam." This repetition reinforces the fluid and nurturing qualities of the water element.

c. Agni Tattwa (Fire Element)

Shift your focus from the navel to the heart area. Visualize an inverted triangular yantra made of fire, surrounded by a Bhupura (protective boundary) adorned with three swastika marks.

This represents the Agni Tattwa, associated with the transformative and energetic properties of fire. As you visualize this fiery yantra, mentally repeat the bija mantra "Ram." This repetition strengthens the transformative and dynamic aspects of the fire element.

d. Vayu Tattwa (Air Element)

Move your awareness from the heart to the center of the eyebrows. Here, imagine six grey- blue dots arranged in a hexagonal shape. This represents the Vayu Tattwa, symbolizing the air element with its smoky, ethereal quality. As you visualize this hexagonal formation, mentally repeat the bija mantra "Yam." This repetition enhances the qualities of movement and subtlety associated with the air element.

e. Akasha Tattwa (Ether Element)

Finally, bring your awareness from the center of the eyebrows to the crown of your head. Visualize the circular form of the Akasha Tattwa, clear and radiant, representing the ether or space element. As you focus on this circular form, mentally repeat the bija mantra "Ham." This repetition reinforces the expansive and infinite nature

of the ether element.

5. Dissolution of the Tattwas

To conclude the practice, visualize the dissolution of the tattwas in a sequence that symbolizes their return to a unified state. Imagine the Prithvi Yantra (earth element) dissolving into the Apas Yantra (water element), the Apas Yantra dissolving into the Agni Yantra (fire element), the Agni Yantra dissolving into the Vayu Yantra (air element), and finally, the Vayu Yantra dissolving into the Akasha Yantra (ether element). This process signifies the merging and integration of the elements, restoring a sense of balance and unity within your consciousness.

Detailed Technique for Advanced Tattwa Shuddhi Practice

1. Preparation and Initial Visualization

Begin by centering yourself through preliminary practices such as trataka (concentrated gazing) or pranayama (breath control). Spend ten to fifteen minutes on these practices to stabilize your mind. Once prepared, close your eyes and settle into a comfortable, steady seated posture, such as Siddhasana, Siddha Yoni Asana, or Padmasana.

Visualize the form of your guru and mentally offer your respect and gratitude for their guidance. This act aligns your intention with higher spiritual support.

Visualize the Elements

a. Prithvi Tattwa (Earth Element)

Direct your awareness to the area between your toes and knees. Visualize a yellow square representing the Prithvi Tattwa. Repeat the bija mantra "Lam" to solidify the grounding and stability of the earth element.

b. Apas Tattwa (Water Element)

Move your focus to the area between your knees and navel. Imagine a crescent moon with two lotuses at its ends, surrounded by a circle of water. This symbolizes the Apas Tattwa. Mentally repeat the bija mantra "Vam" to enhance the fluid and nurturing qualities of water.

c. Agni Tattwa (Fire Element)

Shift your awareness from the navel to the heart. Visualize an inverted triangular yantra made of fire, surrounded by a Bhupura with three swastika marks. This represents the Agni Tattwa. Repeat the bija mantra "Ram" to invoke the transformative power of fire.

d. Vayu Tattwa (Air Element)

Focus from the heart to the center of the eyebrows. Visualize six grey-blue dots forming a hexagonal shape, representing the Vayu Tattwa. Repeat the bija mantra "Yam" to engage the dynamic and subtle qualities of air.

e. Akasha Tattwa (Ether Element)

Direct your attention from the center of the eyebrows to the crown of your head. Visualize a clear and radiant circular form representing the Akasha Tattwa. Repeat the bija mantra "Ham" to invoke the

expansive and boundless nature of ether.

3. Transformation of Papa Purusha

a. Dissolution of Elements

Imagine the Akasha Tattwa dissolving into Ahamkara (the sense of individual self). Then, visualize Ahamkara dissolving into Mahat Tattwa (the great principle or cosmic intelligence), and Mahat Tattwa dissolving into Prakriti (the primordial nature). Finally, see Prakriti dissolving into Purusha (the supreme self or pure consciousness). Consider yourself as the highest knowledge, pure and absolute.

b. Visualization of Papa Purusha

Shift your awareness to the left side of your abdomen. Visualize Papa Purusha, a small, grotesque figure about the size of your thumb. His appearance is dark and menacing, with black skin, fiery eyes, and a large belly. He holds an axe and a shield, embodying the imbalances and negative aspects you aim to transform.

c. Transformation Process

- **Inhalation and Purification:** Close your right nostril with your right thumb. Inhale deeply through the left nostril while repeating the bija mantra "Yam." Visualize Papa Purusha being cleansed and transformed into a figure of pure, white light.
- **Breath Retention and Burning:** Close both nostrils and hold your breath. Repeat the bija mantra "Ram" while visualizing

Papa Purusha being consumed by fire and reduced to ashes.

- **Exhalation and Reformation:** Exhale the ashes through the left nostril while repeating the bija mantra "Vam." See the ashes forming into a ball and merging with the nectar from the moon in the water yantra. Then, repeat the bija mantra "Lam" and visualize this ball transforming into a golden egg.
- **Expansion and Integration:** Repeat the bija mantra "Ham" and watch as the golden egg grows and radiates, eventually filling your entire body. You become the golden egg itself, symbolizing the purified and balanced state.

4. Recreation of the Elements

In reverse order, visualize the elements being recreated:

- **From the Golden Egg:** Revert to the state of Purusha (supreme self), then Prakriti, then Mahat Tattwa, and finally Ahamkara.
- **Reconstruction of the Tattwas:** From Ahamkara, see the Akasha Yantra emerge. From Akasha, visualize Vayu; from Vayu, Agni; from Agni, Apas; and from Apas, Prithvi. Place each element in its respective position, represented by their bija mantras as described earlier.

5. Final Meditation

- **Separation of Souls:** Repeat the mantra "Soham" while visualizing the separation of the Jivatma (individual soul)

from the Paramatma (cosmic soul). Locate the Jivatma in the heart region, where it resides.

- **Vision of Prana Shakti:** Finally, direct your awareness to the Chidakasha (inner space). See before you a vast red ocean with a large red lotus floating on it. Seated on this lotus is Prana Shakti, the vital life force. Her form is radiant like the rising sun, adorned with beautiful ornaments. She has three eyes and six hands, each holding sacred symbols: a trident, a bow made of sugarcane, a noose, a goad, five arrows, and a skull dripping with blood. This vision embodies the dynamic and potent aspects of Prana Shakti, completing the advanced practice.

Mastering the Phonemes

In the vast tapestry of human knowledge, certain practices have remained shrouded in secrecy, guarded by esoteric traditions and cloaked in layers of mysticism. One such practice is the meditative use of phonemes, a sacred art that has been quietly practiced within the confines of closed, clandestine sects for centuries. This ancient methodology, until now, has been revealed only to a select few within these esoteric circles. Today, for the first time, this profound practice is being shared openly, offering a rare glimpse into its transformative power and its potential to deepen our understanding of both sound and self.

At its core, phoneme meditation is a practice that integrates sound, color, and the physical body to achieve heightened states of awareness and resonance. Phonemes—the distinct units of sound that constitute the building blocks of speech—are not merely tools for communication but also vessels of profound vibrational energy. In the ancient traditions that have preserved this practice, each phoneme is imbued with unique properties that influence both the mind and body. The secrets of this practice were carefully guarded, passed down through generations within secluded sects that viewed these techniques as sacred rites.

Origins and Secrecy

The origins of phoneme meditation are as elusive as the practice itself. Its roots are deeply embedded in the esoteric traditions of the East, particularly within the non-dual cults of Shaivism, where sound

and mantra play pivotal roles. In these traditions, sound is considered a fundamental force that shapes reality and consciousness. Phoneme meditation emerged as a sophisticated method of harnessing this force, integrating it with the body's own energy systems and Psycho spiritual elements to achieve a profound state of harmony.

Historically, the practice was reserved for initiates who underwent rigorous training and demonstrated a deep commitment to the esoteric path. The teachings were transmitted through oral traditions, often in secretive gatherings away from the prying eyes of the outside world. These clandestine sects believed that revealing the practice to the uninitiated could diminish its potency or, worse, lead to its misuse. This veil of secrecy ensured that the practice remained pure and potent, safeguarded from the distractions and distortions of the outer world.

For the first time, the practice of phoneme meditation is being revealed explicitly to the Western world and beyond. This unveiling offers an unprecedented opportunity for individuals outside these guarded circles to explore and experience this ancient art. The practice involves a holistic approach that combines sound, color, and bodily awareness to tap into the vibrational essence of each phoneme.

To begin, practitioners create a serene, distraction-free environment. They sit or lie comfortably, ensuring their bodies are fully supported and relaxed. The process starts with the selection of a phoneme, which is associated with a specific color and tone. Each phoneme is believed to carry distinct vibrational qualities, which are visualized and internalized during meditation.

Practitioners first engage with the phoneme on a whole-body

level. They visualize the chosen color enveloping their entire body as they vocalize the phoneme in its assigned tone. This whole-body approach allows them to experience the phoneme's resonance in a comprehensive manner, feeling its vibrations throughout their being. For example, if practicing the vowel sound /a/ with a blood-red color, practitioners imagine this color radiating from their entire body and produce the sound, experiencing a full-bodied resonance.

After becoming familiar with the phoneme on a whole-body level, practitioners then focus on specific body parts associated with each phoneme. This involves visualizing the phoneme's color and letter concentrated on a targeted area, such as the top of the head or the throat. They vocalize the phoneme, paying attention to how the resonance is localized and felt in that specific area. This focused practice enhances their awareness of the phoneme's vibrational qualities and its impact on different parts of the body.

The Ultimate Goal: Self-Realization

The ultimate goal of phoneme meditation extends beyond mere practice and into the realm of profound spiritual transformation. This practice is not merely an exercise in sound and color but a path toward self-realization and the recognition of one's inherent oneness with the divine.

In the ancient traditions that guard this practice, phoneme meditation is viewed as a means to achieve a direct experience of unity with the self and, ultimately, with God. By deeply engaging with the vibrations of each phoneme and integrating them into the body and mind, practitioners are guided toward an experiential realization of their true nature. This journey through sound and

resonance is a pathway to experiencing the divine essence within oneself, a state where individual identity merges with universal consciousness.

The introduction of phoneme meditation to a broader audience marks a significant moment in the history of spiritual and meditative practices. The methodology, once veiled in secrecy, offers profound insights into the interplay between sound, color, and bodily awareness. By exploring these connections, practitioners can achieve enhanced states of consciousness and greater alignment with their inner selves.

Phoneme meditation provides a unique approach to personal growth and self-awareness. It offers a method for individuals to explore the vibrational qualities of sound and its effects on the body and mind. By integrating colors and tones with phonemes, practitioners engage in a practice that harmonizes internal and external elements, leading to a deeper understanding of themselves and their surroundings.

Moreover, the practice of phoneme meditation has the potential to bridge cultural and spiritual divides. By sharing these ancient techniques with a global audience, there is an opportunity for cross-cultural exchange and a deeper appreciation of the rich traditions from which these practices originate. This integration can foster greater understanding and respect for diverse spiritual paths and methodologies.

The revelation of phoneme meditation represents a ground breaking moment in the dissemination of ancient wisdom. Once guarded fiercely by clandestine sects, this practice is now accessible to a wider audience, offering a chance to explore its transformative

potential. By combining sound, color, and bodily awareness with the profound resonance of anusvara, practitioners can tap into the ultimate goal of self-realization. This practice not only enriches lives but also deepens our connection to the fundamental forces that shape our existence and our intrinsic oneness with the divine

Meditational Praxis with Phonemes

To practice phonemes as per the classical shaivite doctrines,use the method described below, it is an approach that integrates the whole body, colors, tones, and anusvara.

Begin by creating a calm, distraction-free environment. Sit or lie comfortably, ensuring your body is fully supported and relaxed.

Start with each phoneme across your entire body. Choose a specific color and tone that represent the phoneme, and visualize this color enveloping your whole body as you vocalize the phoneme in the assigned tone. Allow the tone to resonate throughout your body, feeling the vibrations and qualities comprehensively. For example, if practicing the vowel sound /a/ with a blood-red color, imagine this color radiating from your entire body and produce the sound, experiencing its full-bodied resonance. It is better to practice the phonemes in proper order,initially with vowels followed by consonants starting with ka.

Once you have established this whole-body practice, shift your focus to the specific body parts associated with each phoneme. Visualize the color and letter of the phoneme concentrated on the targeted body part. For instance, if practicing the vowel sound /a/, focus on the top of your head. Envision the color blood-red at this location and vocalize the sound, paying close attention to how the

resonance and vibrations are localized.

Incorporate Anusvara into Your Practice:

To include anusvara, apply it to each phoneme, modifying the sounds to include nasal resonance. Here's how to integrate anusvara into your practice:

1. Add Anusvara:

- **Practice with Nasal Resonance:** For each phoneme, incorporate anusvara to create a nasalized sound. For example, practice the phoneme /ka/ as "kam" and /kha/ as "kham." This modification adds a nasal resonance to each phoneme.

- **Vocalize with Anusvara:** As you vocalize each phoneme with anusvara, visualize the anusvara symbol (•) and feel its nasal resonance throughout your body. This adds a nasal quality to the sound, enriching the vibrational experience.

2. Practice Whole-Body with Anusvara:

- **Phoneme with Anusvara:** Begin with the nasalized phoneme across your entire body. For instance, practice "kam" (from /ka/) by imagining the color and nasal resonance enveloping your whole body. Feel the vibrations and nasal quality throughout.

3. Localized Practice with Anusvara:

- **Specific Body Part:** After practicing the whole-body approach, focus on specific body parts. For example, for the nasalized phoneme "kam," concentrate on the area around your throat and nasal cavity. Visualize the anusvara effect and the color associated with the phoneme at this location. Vocalize the sound with anusvara and feel the nasal resonance in this targeted area.

Examples of Practice with Anusvara:

Vowels:
- अ (a) - "am"
- इ (i) - "im"
- उ (u) - "um"

Consonants:
- क (ka) - "kam"
- ख (kha) - "kham"
- ग (ga) - "gam"

Practice Steps:

1. **Whole-Body Practice:** Begin by vocalizing each phoneme with anusvara, such as "kam" for /ka/. Visualize the color and nasal resonance throughout your entire body.
2. **Localized Practice:** Shift to focused body part practice. For each nasalized phoneme, concentrate on the specific body part associated with the sound and visualize anusvara's effect

there. Vocalize the nasalized phoneme, feeling the resonance and vibrations locally.

3. **Reflection:** After completing your practice, reflect on the experience and adjust as needed. Observe how the nasal resonance affects your perception and physical sensations.

By integrating anusvara with each phoneme and practicing both whole-body and localized vibrations, you deepen your connection to the nasalized sounds and enhance their effects on your body. Regular practice will improve your awareness of each phoneme's qualities, including its nasal resonance, and enrich your phoneme practice

Note:Incorporation of Anuswara with phonemes during practice is mandatory.

Vowels:

1. अ (a) - Blood Red - Top of Head
- **Visualization**: Imagine the lettter in a blood-red colour at the top of your head.
- **Tone**: C

2. आ (ā) - White - Forehead
- **Visualization**: Visualize the letter in pure, white light gently illuminating your forehead.
- **Tone**: C

3. इ (i) - Dark Blue - Right Eye
- **Visualization**: Picture the letter in a deep, dark blue colour illuminating your right eye, like the midnight sky.
- **Tone**: C

4. ई (ī) - Yellow - Left Eye
- **Visualization**: Imagine the letter in bright yellow colour illuminating your left eye.
- **Tone**: C

5. उ (u) - Black - Right Ear
- **Visualization**: Envision the letter in a deep black colour inside your right ear, like the vast cosmos.
- **Tone**: C

6. ऊ (ū) - Dark Blue - Left Ear
- **Visualization**: Picture the letter in dark blue colour inside your left ear, resembling twilight.
- **Tone**: C

7. ऋ (ṛ) - Yellow - Right Nostril
- **Visualization**: Visualize the letter in bright yellow colour inside your right nostril, like the morning sun.
- **Tone**: C

8. ॠ (ṝ) - Dark Blue like Collyrium - Left Nostril
- **Visualization**: Imagine the letter in a dark blue hue inside your left nostril, similar to traditional collyrium.
- **Tone**: C

9. ऌ (ḷ) - White - Right Cheek
- **Visualization**: Picture the letter in a snow white light on your right cheek..
- **Tone**: C

10. ॡ (ḹ) - Blood Red - Left Cheek
- **Visualization**: Envision the letter in a vibrant blood-red hue on your left cheek.
- **Tone**: C

11. ए (e) - Yellow - Upper Lip
- **Visualization**: Visualize the letter in a warm yellow light at your upper lip.
- **Tone**: C

12. ऐ (ai) - Crystalline White - Lower Lip
- **Visualization**: Imagine the letter in crystalline white light at your lower lip, sparkling like a Quartz Crystal.
- **Tone**: C

13. ओ (o) - Luminous White - Upper Teeth
- **Visualization**: Picture the letter in a luminous white hue around your upper teeth.
- **Tone**: C

14. औ (au) - Snow White - Lower Teeth
- **Visualization**: Envision the letter in a snow-white colour around your lower teeth.
- **Tone**: C

15. अं (aṁ) - Blood Red - Upper Palate
- **Visualization**: Visualize the letter in a deep blood-red energy at the upper palate.
- **Tone**: C

16. अः (aḥ) - Blood Red - Tongue
- **Visualization**: Picture the letter in a vibrant blood-red colour on your tongue.
- **Tone**: C

Consonants
1. क (ka) - Yellow - Right Shoulder
- **Visualization**: Envision the letter in bright yellow hue

radiating from your right shoulder.
* **Tone**: D

2. ख (kha) - Milky White - Right Elbow
* **Visualization**: Picture the letter in a milky white glow around your right elbow.
* **Tone**: D

3. ग (ga) - Blood Red - Right Wrist
* **Visualization**: Visualize the letter in deep blood-red aura around your right wrist.
* **Tone**: D

4. घ (gha) - Pearly Grey/White - Right Palm
* **Visualization**: Imagine the letter in a pearly grey colour emanating from your right palm.
* **Tone**: D

5. ङ (ṅa) - Black - Right Hand Fingers
* **Visualization**: Picture the letter in a deep black hue around your right hand fingers.
* **Tone**: D

6. च (cha) - Black like Collyrium - Left Shoulder
* **Visualization**: Envision the letter in a pitch black hue around your left shoulder.
* **Tone**: E

7. छ (chha) - Deep Blue Hue like Lapis Lazuli - Left Elbow
* **Visualization**: Visualize the letter in a deep blue colour around your left elbow, like lapis lazuli.
* **Tone**: E

8. ज (ja) - Blood Red - Left Wrist
* **Visualization**: Picture the letter in a vibrant blood-red

colour around your left wrist.

- Tone: E

9. झ (jha) - Dark Blue - Left Palm

- **Visualization**: Envision the letter in a dark blue hue in your left palm.
- Tone: E

10. ञ (ña) - Dark Yellow - Left Hand Fingers

- **Visualization**: Visualize the letter in a dark yellow colour around your left hand fingers.
- Tone: E

11. ट (ṭa) - Blood Red - Right Hip

- **Visualization**: Picture the letter in a vibrant blood-red colour in your right hip.
- Tone: F

12. ठ (ṭha) - Lunar White - Right Knee

- **Visualization**: Visualize the letter in a gentle lunar white colour around your right knee.
- Tone: F

13. ड (ḍa) - Yellow - Right Ankle

- **Visualization**: Imagine the letter in a bright yellow colour around your right ankle.
- Tone: F

14. ढ (ḍha) - Blue - Right Sole

- **Visualization**: Picture it in a Sky blue colour in your right sole.
- Tone: F

15. ण (ṇa) - Blood Red - Right Toes and Tips

- **Visualization**: Envision the letter in a vibrant blood-red

colour at your right toes and tips.
- **Tone**: F

16. त (ta) - White - Left Hip
- **Visualization**: Visualize the letter in a pure white colour in your left hip.
- **Tone**: G

17. थ (tha) - White like Jasmine - Left Knee
- **Visualization**: Picture the letter in a delicate white light, reminiscent of jasmine, around your left knee.
- **Tone**: G

18. द (da) - Dark Blue - Left Ankle
- **Visualization**: Envision the letter in a deep dark blue light around your left ankle.
- **Tone**: G

19. ध (dha) - Yellow - Left Sole
- **Visualization**: Imagine the letter in a bright yellow light around on left sole.
- **Tone**: G

20. न (na) - Crystalline White - Left Toes
- **Visualization**: Picture the letter in a crystalline white light on your left toes
- **Tone**: G

21. प (pa) - Milky White - Right Flank
- **Visualization**: Visualize a soft milky white light around your right flank.
- **Tone**: A

22. फ (pha) - White - Left Flank
- **Visualization**: Picture the letter in a bright white colour

around your left flank.
  * **Tone**: A

23. ब (ba) - Yellow - Sacrum
  * **Visualization**: Envision the letter in a warm yellow light at your sacrum.
  * **Tone**: A

24. भ (bha) - Blood Red - Navel/Umbilicus
  * **Visualization**: Visualize the letter in a vibrant blood-red light at your navel.
  * **Tone**: A

25. म (ma) - Dark Blue - Pelvis
  * **Visualization**: Picture it in a deep dark blue hue on your pelvis.
  * **Tone**: A

26. य (ya) - Black - Heart
  * **Visualization**: Envision the letter in a profound black colour in your heart.
  * **Tone**: B

27. र (ra) - Blood Red - Right Lung
  * **Visualization**: Visualize the letter in a blood-red light in your right lung.
  * **Tone**: B

28. ल (la) - Yellow - Throat
  * **Visualization**: Imagine the letter in a warm yellow colour surrounding in your throat.
  * **Tone**: B

29. व (va) - Conch Shell White - Left Lung
  * **Visualization**: Picture the letter in a conch shell white

colour in your left lung.

- **Tone**: B

30. श (sha) - Golden Yellow - A Nadi Carrying Prana from Heart to Right Arm

- **Visualization**: Visualize the letter in a golden yellow light flowing through the nadi from your heart to your right arm.
- **Tone**: C

31. ष (ṣa) - Blood Red - A Nadi Carrying Prana from Heart to Left Arm

- **Visualization**: Imagine the letter in a vibrant blood-red light flowing through the nadi from your heart to your left arm.
- **Tone**: C

32. स (sa) - Blood Red - A Nadi Carrying Prana from Heart to Right Leg

- **Visualization**: Picture the letter as a blood-red light flowing through the nadi from your heart to your right leg.
- **Tone**: C

33. ह (ha) - Crystalline White - A Nadi Carrying Prana from Heart to Left Leg

- **Visualization**: Visualize the letter as a crystalline white light flowing through the nadi from your heart to your left leg.
- **Tone**: C

34. क्ष (kṣa) - Milky White - Solar Plexus/Epigastric Fossa

- **Visualization**: Imagine the letter in a milky white light radiating from your solar plexus or epigastric fossa.
- **Tone**: C

The revelation of phoneme meditation, a practice once confined to the hidden corridors of ancient sects, marks a monumental shift in spiritual and meditative exploration. This intricate method, blending sound, color, bodily awareness, and the sacred resonance of anusvara, offers a profound pathway to self-realization and spiritual unity. As these esoteric techniques are shared with a global audience for the first time, they present an unprecedented opportunity to explore the depths of human consciousness and the divine essence within.

Phoneme meditation is not merely an exercise in vibrational awareness but a transformative journey towards recognizing one's inherent oneness with the divine. By engaging with the distinct qualities of each phoneme, practitioners are invited to experience a holistic resonance that integrates mind, body, and spirit. This practice facilitates a deeper connection to the self, leading to an experiential understanding of unity with the universal consciousness.

As this ancient art becomes accessible to a broader audience, it bridges the gap between diverse spiritual traditions, fostering greater understanding and respect for the rich tapestry of human spiritual experience. The practice of phoneme meditation holds the promise of not only enhancing personal growth but also enriching the collective spiritual consciousness.

In embracing this practice, individuals are called to embark on a journey of profound inner exploration. Through the integration of sound, color, and bodily awareness, and by experiencing the resonance of Anusvara, practitioners move closer to the ultimate goal of self-realization. This journey reveals the divine presence within each of us, reaffirming our intrinsic connection to the universal and eternal. The unfolding of phoneme meditation thus stands as

a testament to the enduring power of ancient wisdom, offering new pathways to enlightenment and self-discovery in the modern world.

PS: Whatever the author has mentioned in this chapter is the most basic and primary training regimen in the sacred science of Phonemes or Matrika. There are advanced practices with phonemes as per the Bimba Pratibimba theory which the author has mentioned in the first part of this work.

Vowels
- अ (a) - Blood Red - Top of head
- आ (ā)- White - Forehead
- इ (i) – Dark Blue – Right Eye
- ई (ī) – Yellow – Left Eye
- उ (u) –Black – Right Ear
- ऊ (ū)- Dark blue – Left Ear
- ऋ (ṛ) – Yellow – Right Nostrill
- ॠ (ṝ) – Dark blue like collyrium – Left Nostrill
- ऌ (ḷ) – White – Right Cheek
- ॡ (ḹ) – Blood red – Left Cheek
- ए (e) –Yellow – Upper Lip
- ऐ (ai) – Crystalline white – Lower Lip
- ओ (o) – Luminous white – Upper Teeth
- औ (au) – Snow white – Lower Teeth
- अं (aṁ) – Blood red – Upper Palate
- अः(aḥ)- Blood red - Tongue

Consonants

- क (ka) – yellow –Right Shoulder
- ख (kha) – Milky White – Right Elbow
- ग (ga) – Blood Red – Right wrist
- घ (gha) – Peraly grey/white – Right Palm
- ङ (ṅa) – Black – Right Hand Fingers
- च (cha) - Black like collyrium – Left Shoulder
- छ (chha) – Deep blue hue like lapis lazuli – Left Elbow
- ज (ja) – Blood red – Left wrist
- झ (jha) – Dark Blue – Left palm
- ञ (ña) – dark Yellow – Left hand fingers
- ट (ṭa) – Blood red – Right Hip
- ठ (ṭha) – lunar White – Right Knee
- ड (ḍa) – Yellow – Right Ankle
- ढ (ḍha) – Blue – Right sole
- ण (ṇa) – Blood red – Right toes and tips
- त (ta) – White – Left hip
- थ (tha) – white like Jasmine – Left knee
- द (da) – Dark Blue – Left ANkle
- ध (dha) – Yellow – Left sole
- न (na) - Crystalline white – Left toes
- प (pa) – Milky White – Right Flank
- फ (pha) – White – Left Flank
- ब (ba) – Yellow - Sacrum
- भ (bha) – Blood Red – Navel/Umbilicus

- म (ma) – Dark Blue - Pelvis
- य (ya) – Black - Heart
- र (ra) – Blood Red – Right Lung
- ल (la) – Yellow - Throat
- व (va) – Conch shell white – Left Lung
- श (sha) – Golden Yellow – A nadi which carries prana from Heart right arm
- ष (ṣa) – Blood red – A nadi which carried prana from heart to left arm
- स (sa) – Blood Red – A nadi which carries prana from heart to right leg
- ह (ha) – Crystalline white – A nadi which carries prana from heart to left leg
- क्ष.- (kṣa) – Milky White – Solar plexus/Epigastric fossa

Initial Congress with Para Devi

In Non-Dual Shaivism, achieving union with the divine or realizing the divine within is the ultimate goal. This pursuit often begins with foundational practices that prepare the practitioner for more advanced spiritual endeavors, such as the conquest of Tatwas—the fundamental principles of the universe. One crucial preliminary exercise is inner alchemy, a practice that involves transforming the inner self through meditation and visualization. This step-by-step guide will walk you through the essential aspects of this inner alchemical practice, providing a structured approach to prepare your mind and spirit for deeper spiritual exploration.

Begin by finding a serene and quiet space where you can practice undisturbed. Choose a comfortable posture, whether seated on a chair or on the floor in a lotus position, ensuring that your position is stable and conducive to meditation.

To start, engage in a relaxation routine to calm your mind and prepare for the practice. You can use deep breathing or Pranayama. For a specific technique, use the Nadi Shuddhi Pranayama method as follows:

1. Sit comfortably and close your eyes.
2. Take a few deep breaths to settle in.
3. Close your right nostril and inhale through your left nostril for six seconds. Retain the breath for three seconds.
4. Close your left nostril and exhale through your right nostril. Retain the breath for three seconds.

5. Inhale through your right nostril, retain for three seconds, then close the right nostril and exhale through the left nostril. Retain for three seconds.
6. Repeat this cycle for five to six rounds to achieve a relaxed state.

Stage One: Initial Practice

1. **Preparation:** Start by setting up a quiet and comfortable space where you can practice without interruptions. Choose a posture that allows you to remain still and focused, whether sitting on a chair or the floor in a lotus position.
2. **Relaxation and Breathing:** Begin with the Nadi Shuddhi Pranayama technique to achieve relaxation and mental clarity. Practice the breathing cycle as described:
3. Sit comfortably and close your eyes.
4. Take a few deep breaths to center yourself.
5. Perform the Nadi Shuddhi Pranayama: Close the right nostril, inhale through the left for six seconds, retain for three seconds, close the left nostril, exhale through the right, retain for three seconds, then inhale through the right nostril, retain for three seconds, and exhale through the left nostril. Repeat this cycle for five to six rounds.
6. **Visualization and Chanting:** Shift your focus to the heart Chakra. Visualize a pure snow-white lotus with eight petals. Begin by mentally chanting the mantra "SAUH" and visualizing the syllables in a white hue at the center of the lotus.

7. **Mastery of Stage One:** Practice these steps consistently for a few days. Ensure you are comfortable with the breathing techniques and the visualization of the lotus. The goal is to achieve a calm and focused state, where the visualization of the lotus and chanting become fluid and effortless.

Stage Two: Intermediate Practice

1. **Enhanced Visualization:** Once you are comfortable with Stage One, begin to expand your visualization. As you chant the mantra "SAUH", start to visualize the syllables transforming into the goddess Para. Focus on the details of her appearance: the color of the full moon, snow-white garments, garland of white pearls, long dark hair, three eyes, two arms, a rosary in her right hand, a book in her left, and the crescent moon in her hair.

2. **Goddess Visualization:** Continue with the mantra while immersing yourself in the visualization of Para. Observe her features in detail and try to integrate her essence into your meditation.

3. **Mastery of Stage Two:** Practice these enhanced visualizations and chanting for a few days until you can consistently and vividly visualize the goddess Para. Ensure that your mental image of Para is clear and detailed, and that the chanting becomes more natural and synchronized with the visualization.

Stage Three: Advanced Practice

1. **Union Visualization:** In this final stage, deepen your practice by visualizing the goddess Para chanting the mantra "SAUH" from the heart center. As you continue your mental chanting, imagine yourself gradually transforming into the goddess. Embody her form, sensations, and presence fully.

2. **Embodiment:** Focus on the sensation of being the goddess Para, and experience the mantra and the visualization as a unified whole. Ensure that you feel a deep connection with the divine essence of Para, and that your entire meditation experience reflects this transformation.

3. **Mastery of Stage Three:** Practice this advanced stage until you have mastered the experience of embodying the goddess. This stage requires a high level of concentration and visualization. Ensure that you are completely comfortable with this practice before moving on to more advanced spiritual work.

Mastery of each stage is crucial before proceeding to the next. Take your time with each phase, ensuring that you have fully integrated the practices and achieved a deep level of understanding and comfort. The success of your subsequent spiritual practices, including the conquest of Tatwas, relies on the solid foundation built through these stages. Regularly reflect on your progress and make adjustments as needed to ensure that each stage is fully mastered before advancing.

By methodically working through these stages, you will cultivate a strong and effective inner alchemical practice, preparing yourself for deeper spiritual exploration and realization.

Conquest of The Gross Elements

Once the practitioner has been purified through initiation and gained mastery in invoking the goddess as previously mentioned, they should start their yoga practice with a specific ritual. First, they should focus on the seed-mantra, the sacred sound, and project it into their hands. By performing the Great Gesture—moving their hands from bottom to top—they should visualize an energy like fire rising from their feet to their head.

With their hands placed in reverence at their heart level, they should hold their breath and visualize the seed-mantra (Sauh) in its most brilliant form. Next, they should imagine the three syllables (Sa,au,h) of the seed-mantra traveling through their central channel and reaching three empty spaces in their head. If the adept has mastered the prvious exercise this will be rather easy to master will lead to immersion in the practice, and even those with no previous experiences in any other mystical practice will succeed after a few days of daily practice.

Once the practitioner's body has been empowered by the goddess through this ritual, they should continue with the specific rites mentioned earlier. If the practitioner has already been guided through this process by a teacher at the beginning of their spiritual journey, they can then move forward by revisiting and activating the impressions from the possession experience.

Starting with the principle of earth, which serves as the foundation for higher stages of realization, the practitioner should focus on specific properties of earth, such as its yellow color and heaviness.

The practice involves concentrating on fourteen distinct qualities, each of which is complex and requires personal teaching. Therefore, detailed instructions on these practices are not included here but should be learned directly from a qualified teacher.

Now let us master the Tattvas:

Meditation on the Earth Element

Preparation:
- Find a quiet and comfortable place where you will not be disturbed.
- Sit in a comfortable meditation posture, ensuring your back is straight and your body is relaxed.

Centering and Grounding:
- Close your eyes and take a few deep, calming breaths.
- As you breathe in, imagine drawing in calmness and focus. As you breathe out, release any tension or distractions.

Visualization of the Earth Element:
- Begin by visualizing the earth element as a yellow square. Picture this square clearly in your mind's eye. Ensure the yellow is a vibrant and radiant hue.
- Surround the yellow square with vajras (symbolic thunderbolts or lightning bolts). Visualize these vajras as golden, emanating powerful energy and creating a protective and energizing aura around the square.

Integration with the Earth Element:

- As you continue to visualize the yellow square with vajras, imagine yourself becoming one with this element. Picture yourself gradually merging into the yellow square, feeling yourself transforming into the very essence of this element.
- Sense the sensation of yourself being surrounded entirely by the yellow square. Feel the yellow color enveloping you completely, creating an environment where nothing exists except this specific element.

Deepening the Experience:

- Focus on the sensations and feelings that arise as you immerse yourself in the yellow square. Notice any physical or emotional changes as you fully integrate with the earth element.
- If any distractions arise, gently bring your focus back to the yellow square and the vajras surrounding it.

Affirmation and Immersion:

- Mentally affirm your connection with the earth element. You might use a phrase like, "I am one with the earth element; I am surrounded by its energy and light."
- Continue to meditate on this feeling of unity until you experience a profound sense of being transformed into the earth element, surrounded solely by its yellow energy.

Conclusion of Meditation:
- Gradually begin to withdraw from the visualization. Picture yourself slowly separating from the yellow square and returning to your usual state of awareness.
- Take a few deep breaths and gently stretch your body to bring yourself back to the present moment.

Reflection:
- Spend a few moments reflecting on the experience. Notice any insights or sensations that may have arisen during the meditation.
- Write down any observations or feelings if you find it helpful.

Completion:
- Conclude your practice by expressing gratitude for the experience and for the opportunity to connect deeply with the earth element.
- Resume your daily activities with the awareness and energy you have gained from the meditation.

Meditation on the Water Element

Preparation:
- Find a quiet, comfortable space where you won't be disturbed.
- Sit in a relaxed meditation posture with your back straight and your body at ease.

Centering and Grounding:
- Close your eyes and take several deep, calming breaths.
- As you inhale, imagine drawing in tranquility and focus. As you exhale, release any tension or distractions.

Visualization of the Water Element:
- Visualize the water element as a crescent-shaped conch shell, colored in a soothing, water-like hue. This crescent is a symbol of the water element, which embodies fluidity and purity.
- Picture the conch shell with its graceful, curved shape, and imagine it glowing with a soft, calming blue or translucent color that resembles the clarity of water.

Integration with the Water Element:
- As you maintain the visualization of the conch shell, imagine yourself merging with this water element. Visualize yourself gradually blending into the crescent shape, feeling yourself becoming one with the flowing, fluid essence of water.
- Sense the sensation of being completely surrounded by this water element. Visualize the environment around you being filled with the soft, blue light and fluidity of the conch shell.

Deepening the Experience:
- Focus on the sensations and feelings that emerge as you immerse yourself in the water element. Pay attention to

any physical or emotional responses, such as a sense of fluidity, smoothness, or relaxation.

- If distractions arise, gently bring your focus back to the crescent-shaped conch shell and the sensation of being enveloped by its water-like quality.

Affirmation and Immersion:

- Mentally affirm your connection with the water element. Use a phrase such as, "I am one with the water element; I am surrounded by its fluidity and calm."
- Continue to meditate on this feeling of unity until you experience a profound sense of transformation into the water element, surrounded solely by its soothing blue light.

Sensation of Wetness:

- With prolonged practice, you may start to feel a sensation of wetness. This is a natural outcome of deeply connecting with the water element. Embrace this feeling as a sign of your successful meditation and integration with the water element.

Conclusion of Meditation:

- Gradually begin to withdraw from the visualization. Picture yourself gently separating from the crescent-shaped conch shell and returning to your usual state of awareness.
- Take a few deep breaths and gently stretch your body to help transition back to the present moment.

Reflection:
- Spend a few moments reflecting on your experience. Notice any insights or sensations that emerged during the meditation.
- If it helps, write down your observations and feelings to track your progress and experiences.

Completion:
- Conclude your practice by expressing gratitude for the experience and the opportunity to connect deeply with the water element.
- Resume your daily activities with the refreshed sense of calm and fluidity you've gained from the meditation.

Meditation on the Fire Element

Preparation:
- Choose a quiet, comfortable space where you will not be interrupted.
- Sit comfortably with your back straight and your body relaxed. You can sit in a cross- legged position or on a chair with your feet flat on the ground.

Centering and Grounding:
- Close your eyes and take several deep, calming breaths.
- As you breathe in, imagine drawing in clarity and focus. As you breathe out, let go of any tension or distractions.

Visualization of the Fire Element:
- Begin by visualizing the fire element as a red blazing

inverted triangle. Picture this triangle clearly in your mind. Ensure it appears vibrant and intense, radiating a deep red color with the energy of flames.

- The inverted triangle should appear dynamic and powerful, symbolizing the transformative and purifying qualities of fire.

Integration with the Fire Element:

- As you maintain the visualization of the red inverted triangle, imagine yourself merging with this element. Visualize yourself gradually becoming one with the blazing triangle, feeling yourself transformed into the very essence of fire.
- Sense the sensation of being entirely surrounded by the fiery energy. Visualize the intense red flames enveloping you, creating an environment where nothing exists except the fiery essence.

Deepening the Experience:

- Focus on the sensations and feelings that arise as you immerse yourself in the fire element. Notice any physical or emotional responses such as warmth, energy, or a sense of power.
- If any distractions arise, gently refocus your attention on the red blazing triangle and the sensation of being surrounded by its fiery energy.

Affirmation and Immersion:

- Mentally affirm your connection with the fire element. Use a phrase like, "I am one with the fire element; I am surrounded by its transformative energy and light."

- Continue to meditate on this feeling of unity until you experience a deep sense of transformation into the fire element, surrounded entirely by its blazing red energy.

Sensation of Heat:

- With extended practice, you may start to feel a sensation of heat. This is a natural outcome of deeply connecting with the fire element. Embrace this warmth as a sign of successful meditation and integration with the fire element.

Conclusion of Meditation:

- Gradually begin to withdraw from the visualization. Picture yourself slowly separating from the red blazing triangle and returning to your usual state of awareness.
- Take a few deep breaths and gently stretch your body to help transition back to the present moment.

Reflection:

- Spend a few moments reflecting on your experience. Notice any insights, sensations, or changes that occurred during the meditation.
- If it helps, write down your observations and feelings to track your progress and experiences.

Completion:

- Conclude your practice by expressing gratitude for the experience and for the opportunity to connect deeply with the fire element.
- Resume your daily activities with the renewed energy and power you've gained from the meditation.

Meditation on the Air Element

Preparation:
- Find a quiet and comfortable place where you will not be disturbed.
- Sit in a comfortable meditation posture with your back straight and your body relaxed. You can choose a cross-legged position or sit on a chair with your feet flat on the floor.

Centering and Grounding:
- Close your eyes and take several deep, calming breaths.
- As you inhale, imagine drawing in clarity and focus. As you exhale, release any tension or distractions.

Visualization of the Air Element:
- Begin by visualizing the air element as a dark blue hexagon. Picture this hexagon clearly in your mind. Ensure it appears deep and vibrant, with a color reminiscent of the vastness of the night sky or the deep ocean.
- The hexagon should have a sense of depth and expansiveness, symbolizing the boundless and ever-moving quality of air.

Integration with the Air Element:
- As you maintain the visualization of the dark blue hexagon, imagine yourself merging with this element. Visualize yourself gradually blending into the hexagon, feeling yourself becoming one with the expansive and fluid nature of air.
- Sense the sensation of being completely surrounded by

this air element. Picture the environment around you being filled with the dark blue hue and the feeling of openness and lightness.

Deepening the Experience:
- Focus on the sensations and feelings that emerge as you immerse yourself in the air element. Notice any physical or emotional responses such as a sense of lightness, freedom, or expansiveness.
- If any distractions arise, gently refocus your attention on the dark blue hexagon and the sensation of being enveloped by its airy quality.

Affirmation and Immersion:
- Mentally affirm your connection with the air element. Use a phrase like, "I am one with the air element; I am surrounded by its expansive and free-flowing energy."
- Continue to meditate on this feeling of unity until you experience a profound sense of transformation into the air element, surrounded entirely by its dark blue essence.

Sensation of Lightness:
- With continued practice, you may start to feel a sensation of lightness and freedom. This is a natural outcome of deeply connecting with the air element. Embrace this feeling as a sign of successful meditation and integration with the air element.

Conclusion of Meditation:
- Gradually begin to withdraw from the visualization. Picture yourself gently separating from the dark blue hexagon and returning to your usual state of awareness.

- Take a few deep breaths and gently stretch your body to help transition back to the present moment.

Reflection:

- Spend a few moments reflecting on your experience. Notice any insights or sensations that arose during the meditation.
- If it helps, write down your observations and feelings to track your progress and experiences.

Completion:

- Conclude your practice by expressing gratitude for the experience and for the opportunity to connect deeply with the air element.
- Resume your daily activities with the renewed sense of lightness and expansiveness you've gained from the meditation.

Meditation on the Element of Akasha (Ether)

Preparation:

- Choose a quiet and comfortable space where you will not be disturbed.
- Sit in a relaxed meditation posture, ensuring your back is straight and your body is at ease. You may sit cross-legged on the floor or in a chair with your feet flat on the ground.

Centering and Grounding:

- Close your eyes and take several deep, calming breaths.
- As you inhale, imagine drawing in serenity and focus. As you exhale, release any tension or distractions.

Visualization of the Akasha Element:
- Begin by visualizing the element of Akasha as a black collyrium-hued circle. Picture this circle clearly in your mind. The color should be deep and rich, resembling the dark, limitless expanse of the night sky or the void of space.
- Ensure the circle embodies the qualities of all-pervasiveness and vacuity, representing the boundless and infinite nature of Akasha.

Integration with the Akasha Element:
- As you maintain the visualization of the black circle, imagine yourself merging with this element. Visualize yourself gradually blending into the circle, feeling yourself becoming one with the vast, all-pervading emptiness.
- Sense the sensation of being surrounded by this infinite void. Visualize the environment around you being filled with the profound stillness and expansiveness of the black circle.

Deepening the Experience:
- Focus on the sensations and feelings that emerge as you immerse yourself in the Akasha element. Notice any physical or emotional responses such as a sense of boundlessness, infinite space, or profound stillness.
- If distractions arise, gently bring your focus back to the black circle and the sensation of being enveloped by its all-pervading quality.

Affirmation and Immersion:
- Mentally affirm your connection with the Akasha element.

Use a phrase like, "I am one with the element of Akasha; I am surrounded by its infinite expanse and profound emptiness."

- Continue to meditate on this feeling of unity until you experience a deep sense of transformation into the Akasha element, surrounded entirely by its all- pervading and vacuous nature.

Sensation of Vastness and Emptiness:

- With prolonged practice, you may begin to feel a sensation of vastness and emptiness. This is a natural outcome of deeply connecting with the Akasha element. Embrace this feeling as a sign of successful meditation and integration with the element of Akasha.

Conclusion of Meditation:

- Gradually begin to withdraw from the visualization. Picture yourself gently separating from the black collyrium-hued circle and returning to your usual state of awareness.
- Take a few deep breaths and gently stretch your body to help transition back to the present moment.

Reflection:

- Spend a few moments reflecting on your experience. Notice any insights or sensations that emerged during the meditation.
- If helpful, write down your observations and feelings to track your progress and experiences.

Completion:

- Conclude your practice by expressing gratitude for the experience and for the opportunity to connect deeply with

the Akasha element.
- Resume your daily activities with the renewed sense of vastness and profound stillness you've gained from the meditation.

As you conclude your meditations on the five elements—Earth, Water, Fire, Air, and Akasha—reflect on the profound journey you've undertaken through each elemental experience. Each element represents a unique aspect of the natural world and of ourselves, providing a gateway to deeper self-awareness and spiritual insight.

- **Earth** grounds us, offering stability and a sense of being rooted. By visualizing the yellow square and feeling the solidity of the earth element, you connect with the fundamental support and nourishment that sustains all life.
- **Water** embodies fluidity and adaptability. Through the conch shell-shaped crescent and the sensation of wetness, you've tapped into the flowing and nurturing qualities of water, embracing its ability to cleanse and transform.
- **Fire** signifies transformation and energy. By visualizing the red blazing inverted triangle and experiencing the warmth of fire, you have engaged with the dynamic force of change and purification that fuels growth and creativity.
- **Air** represents freedom and expansiveness. Through the dark blue hexagon and the feeling of lightness, you've aligned with the boundless and ever-moving nature of air, which inspires openness and clarity.
- **Akasha (Ether)** signifies the all-pervading and the void. By

focusing on the black collyrium-hued circle and the sensation of vast emptiness, you have connected with the infinite space and profound stillness that underlies all existence.

As you integrate these elemental meditations into your daily life, carry with you the qualities and insights gained from each practice. Allow these experiences to enrich your understanding of yourself and the world around you. The balance and harmony of these elements within you can guide you towards a more centered, aware, and harmonious existence.

Conquest of the Sense Organs

Meditation on the Sensory Medium of Scent

Preparation:
- Choose a quiet, comfortable space where you will not be disturbed.
- Sit in a relaxed posture with your back straight. You can sit cross-legged on the floor or in a chair with your feet flat on the ground.

Centering and Grounding:
- Close your eyes and take several deep, calming breaths.
- As you inhale, draw in a sense of calm and focus. As you exhale, release any tension or distractions.

Visualization of the Sensory Medium of Scent:
- Visualize the sensory medium of scent as a yellow square. Picture this square clearly in your mind, ensuring it is vibrant and glowing with a deep yellow hue.
- The yellow square should be detailed with joints and adorned with vajra (thunderbolt) emblems, which symbolize the power and clarity of scent.

Focus on the Tip of the Nose:
- Unlike previous meditations where the focus might be on the heart, direct your concentration to the tip of your nose. Imagine the yellow square with its vajra emblems located precisely at the tip of your nose.

- Picture this square as a part of your sensory experience, integrating it with the sense of smell.

Intensifying the Sensory Experience:

- As you meditate, focus on the scent becoming increasingly perceptible. Begin by imagining a faint scent that gradually intensifies. This scent should start to become extraordinarily perceptible as you maintain your concentration.
- Over time, visualize this scent as becoming two-fold and then evolving into many kinds, reflecting the richness and variety of olfactory experiences.

Experiencing the Pure Scent:

- With continued meditation, envision the pure scent becoming firm and stable. As you practice consistently, this scent will grow more defined and distinct.
- Aim for a point where, within approximately two months, you can experience the pure scent clearly and firmly.

Attaining the Nature of Scent:

- After about six months of dedicated practice, focus on integrating the nature of scent into your being. Visualize yourself becoming one with the essence of the scent, embodying its characteristics.
- Cultivate the ability to produce desired smells rapidly, reflecting mastery over the sensory medium of scent.

Conclusion of Meditation:

- Gradually withdraw from the visualization. Picture the yellow square and the scent slowly fading away, returning to your usual state of awareness.

- Take a few deep breaths and gently stretch your body to help transition back to the present moment.

Reflection:

- Spend a few moments reflecting on your experience. Notice any changes or insights regarding your sense of smell or your ability to perceive and produce scents.
- If helpful, write down your observations and feelings to track your progress and experiences.

Completion:

- Conclude your practice by expressing gratitude for the experience and for the opportunity to deepen your connection with the sensory medium of scent.
- Resume your daily activities with a renewed sense of awareness and sensitivity to scents.

This step-by-step guide aims to help you engage deeply with the sensory medium of scent, enhancing your ability to perceive and integrate scents through focused visualization and meditation.

Meditation on the Sensory Medium of Taste

Preparation:

- Choose a quiet and comfortable place where you will not be disturbed.
- Sit in a relaxed meditation posture with your back straight. You can sit cross- legged on the floor or in a chair with your feet flat on the ground.

Centering and Grounding:
- Close your eyes and take several deep, calming breaths.
- As you inhale, imagine drawing in peace and focus. As you exhale, let go of any tension or distractions.

Visualization of the Sensory Medium of Taste:
- Visualize the sensory medium of taste as a bubble of water. Picture this bubble clearly in your mind. It should resemble a delicate, transparent sphere filled with water, reflecting the subtlety and purity of taste.
- Ensure that your focus is on the property of taste, rather than the appearance of the bubble itself.

Focus on the Tip of the Tongue:
- Direct your attention to the tip of your tongue. Imagine the water bubble located precisely at this point.
- Visualize the bubble of water as being delicately poised at the end of the royal nerve (rājanādī), which is believed to be the conduit for sensory experiences related to taste.

Concentration on Taste:
- As you meditate, focus on the sensory experience of taste associated with the water bubble. Imagine the bubble releasing a variety of flavors, reflecting the full spectrum of taste experiences.
- Let the sensation of taste become more vivid and distinct as you maintain your concentration on the bubble.

Experiencing the Flavors:
- Allow yourself to experience a range of flavors emanating from the water bubble. Visualize the bubble producing different tastes, from sweet to salty, sour to bitter, and beyond.

- Cultivate an internal awareness of how these flavors interact and manifest on your tongue.

Attaining the Knowledge of the Water Realm:

- As you deepen your meditation, contemplate yourself as the bubble of water. Envision yourself embodying its properties and the esoteric knowledge associated with the water realm.
- By identifying with the bubble, you gain a profound understanding of taste and the sensory medium of water.

Conclusion of Meditation:

- Gradually begin to withdraw from the visualization. Picture the water bubble and the sensations of taste gently fading away, bringing you back to your usual state of awareness.
- Take a few deep breaths and gently stretch your body to help transition back to the present moment.

Reflection:

- Spend a few moments reflecting on your meditation experience. Notice any new insights or changes in your perception of taste.
- If helpful, write down your observations and feelings to track your progress and experiences.

Completion:

- Conclude your practice by expressing gratitude for the experience and the opportunity to connect deeply with the sensory medium of taste.
- Resume your daily activities with a refreshed sense of awareness and sensitivity to flavors.

This step-by-step guide is designed to help you deeply engage with the sensory medium of taste through focused visualization and meditation, allowing you to experience and understand its full range of flavors.

Meditation on the Auspicious Form-Contemplation

Preparation:
- Find a quiet and comfortable place where you can meditate without interruption.
- Sit in a relaxed posture with your back straight. You can sit cross-legged on the floor or in a chair with your feet flat on the ground.

Centering and Grounding:
- Close your eyes and take several deep, calming breaths.
- As you inhale, draw in peace and focus. As you exhale, release any tension or distractions.

Initial Visualization:
- Close your eyes to external perceptions and bring your awareness inward.
- Visualize an indistinct, cloud-like form with a lustrous quality, akin to clouds during autumnal twilight. This form should be soft and diffuse in your inner vision.

Focus on Subtle Drops:
- As you continue focusing on this indistinct form, begin to notice subtle drops (bindū) appearing within it. These drops may be white, red, yellow, or blue.
- Concentrate on these drops, letting them become the sole

focus of your attention. Observe their colors and shapes without distraction.

Recognition of Shapes:
- As you maintain your concentration, you will gradually start to perceive various shapes emerging from the drops.
- Allow these shapes to become more distinct and varied as your meditation deepens. Embrace the shapes as they reveal themselves.

Enhancing Brilliance:
- Over time, the shapes you perceive will begin to blaze with brilliance. They will grow more vivid and steady in their appearance.
- Focus on the increasing luminosity and stability of these shapes, allowing them to become a central part of your visual experience.

Perception of Orbs:
- As your practice continues, the shapes will begin to transform into orbs. These orbs will manifest with clarity and presence in your inner vision.
- Immerse yourself in the experience of these orbs, letting them become the focal point of your meditation.

Experience of Formless Light:
- With further practice, the orbs will gradually merge into a formless light. This light will appear as a radiant, omnipresent presence in your meditation.
- Observe this formless light and its qualities, embracing its pure, unstructured essence.

Transformation to Pervasive Light:

- The formless light will begin to expand, becoming a pervasive light that fills your entire inner vision.
- Experience this pervasive light as it reaches into every corner of your awareness, enveloping you completely.

Realization of Universal Presence:
- As the pervasive light continues to expand, it will eventually reach everywhere, becoming an all-encompassing presence.
- Feel yourself as part of this universal light, sensing its boundless and all- encompassing nature.

Achievement of Divine Vision:
- With consistent practice, you will achieve divine vision and the rewards contained in the form-realm. This vision will arise naturally, free from discursive thought.
- Embrace this divine vision and the insights it brings, recognizing it as a culmination of your dedicated contemplation.

Final Reflection:
- Conclude your meditation by reflecting on your experience. Notice any new insights or changes in your perception.
- If helpful, write down your observations and feelings to track your progress and experiences.

Completion:
- Finish your practice by expressing gratitude for the experience and the opportunity to connect with the auspicious form-contemplation.
- Gently transition back to your daily activities with a renewed sense of clarity and spiritual insight.

This step-by-step guide is designed to help you gradually progress through the meditation on the sensory medium of form, leading to the attainment of divine vision and the realization of the auspicious form-contemplation.

Meditation on the Sensory Medium of Touch

Preparation:
- Find a quiet and comfortable space where you can meditate without interruptions.
- Sit in a relaxed posture with your back straight. You can sit cross-legged on the floor or in a chair with your feet flat on the ground.

Centering and Grounding:
- Close your eyes and take several deep, calming breaths.
- As you inhale, draw in a sense of calm and focus. As you exhale, let go of any tension or distractions.

Visualization of the Hexagonal Diagram:
- Visualize yourself seated within a hexagonal diagram. This hexagon should be clear and defined in your inner vision.
- The diagram symbolizes the sensory medium of touch, representing the structure within which you will meditate.

Contemplation of the Sensory Medium:
- Imagine yourself as dry, black, and experiencing a sensation of twitching throughout every part of your body.
- Focus on this sensation of being dry and black, and allow the feeling of twitching to become prominent in your awareness.

Perception of Crawling Sensation:

- As you concentrate, you will start to experience a crawling sensation similar to that of ants moving across your skin. This sensation should cover your entire body.
- Allow this crawling sensation to become the central focus of your meditation. Notice how it spreads and how it feels across different areas of your skin.

Contemplation of the Sensation:

- Deepen your focus on the sensation of the crawling ants. Embrace this feeling as part of your meditation, and let it fully occupy your awareness.
- Contemplate this sensation deeply, recognizing it as a manifestation of the sensory medium of touch.

Attainment of the Adamantine Body:

- Through sustained meditation on this sensation, you will gradually attain an adamantine body, characterized by its firmness and resilience.
- Visualize and embody this adamantine quality, feeling its strength and stability within yourself.

Realization of Touch-Realm Knowledge:

- As you progress, recognize that you are achieving esoteric knowledge of the touch-realm. This knowledge is the deeper understanding and mastery of sensory touch experiences.
- Meditate on this understanding, integrating it into your perception and practice.

Advanced Contemplation Without the Diagram:

- Move beyond the hexagonal diagram and focus solely on

the sensation of touch itself.

- Contemplate the self in its pure form, without reliance on any visual aids or diagrams. This advanced stage helps in achieving sovereignty over the reality- level of touch.

Reflection and Integration:
- Conclude your meditation by reflecting on your experience. Notice any new insights or changes in your perception of touch.
- If helpful, write down your observations and feelings to track your progress and understand the advancements in your practice.

Completion:
- Finish your practice by expressing gratitude for the experience and the insights gained into the sensory medium of touch.
- Gently transition back to your daily activities, carrying forward the sense of resilience and enhanced sensory awareness.

Meditation on the Sensory Medium of Sound

Preparation:
- Find a quiet and comfortable space where you can meditate without disturbance.
- Sit in a relaxed posture with your back straight. You can sit cross-legged on the floor or in a chair with your feet flat on the ground.

Sealing the Sense Apertures:

- Close both ears gently by pressing your fingers against them to block out external sounds.
- Close your eyes to further minimize external distractions.
- This sealing of the senses helps induce a state of introversion and prepares you for deeper meditation.

Initial Focus on Sound:
- Begin by directing your focus inward and listen for the initial great noise (mahāghoṣa). This is a prominent, underlying sound that you may perceive as a kind of internal hum or vibration.
- Concentrate your mind on this sound, allowing it to become the primary focus of your meditation.

Awakening Abdominal Fire:
- As you focus on the great noise, you may notice an awakening of internal energy or heat in your abdominal area, often referred to as abdominal fire. This signifies the activation of internal energies.

Perception of Faint Resonance:
- With continued practice, the sound you perceive will start to diminish into a faint resonance (dhvani). This sound may be less distinct but can be perceived at its end.
- Contemplate this faint resonance as the Sakala-soul. By maintaining focus on this resonance without distraction, you will gain esoteric knowledge of remote hearing.

Sound Resembling Conch Blowing:
- Focus on a sound that resembles the blowing of a conch. This sound should become your central point of meditation.

- This sound indicates the merging of the experient into nature, and meditating on it helps in realizing its rewards.

Intensity of Sound:
- As you progress, the sound will become extremely intense and may start to drown out all other sounds.
- Contemplate this intense sound as the experient isolated by awareness, where the sound becomes all-encompassing.

Delightful Sound at Cessation:
- Observe a delightful sound that is heard as it ceases. This sound is known as the Mantra-experient and is associated with those eager for spiritual progress and yoga.
- Meditate on this sound to deepen your understanding and connection with the Mantra-experient.

Sound Resembling Silenced Bell:
- Focus on a sound that resembles the reverberation of a silenced bell. This sound represents the Mantra-regent.
- Contemplating this sound will help you achieve success in all Perfections associated with the sound-realm.

Sound Like a Stick-Zither Tone:
- The final stage involves meditating on a sound similar to the tone emanating from a stick-zither struck by the wind.
- This sound represents the level of Śiva and symbolizes the ultimate realization and Perfection within the sound-realm.

Sequential or Separate Practice:
- You may choose to practice these sounds either separately or in sequence, depending on your focus and goals.
- Each sound represents a different level of realization and

Perfection in the sound-realm, leading to comprehensive spiritual attainment.

Reflection and Integration:
- Conclude your meditation by reflecting on your experiences with each stage of sound. Notice any new insights or changes in your perception.
- If helpful, record your observations to track your progress and understand the advancements in your practice.

Completion:
- Finish your meditation by expressing gratitude for the experience and the insights gained into the sensory medium of sound.
- Gently transition back to your daily activities, carrying forward the sense of heightened awareness and spiritual achievement.

This step-by-step guide is designed to help you progressively explore and master the sensory medium of sound, leading to profound spiritual insights and Perfections within the sound- realm.

Conquest of the Organs of Action

Meditation on the Organ of Speech

Preparation:
- Find a quiet and comfortable place where you can meditate without interruptions.
- Sit in a relaxed posture with your back straight. You can sit cross-legged on the floor or in a chair with your feet flat on the ground.

Centering and Grounding:
- Close your eyes and take several deep, calming breaths.
- As you inhale, draw in a sense of calm and focus. As you exhale, let go of any tension or distractions.

Initial Focus on the Sound of the Void:
- Direct your attention inward and focus on the sound of the void (nabhah Svarūpa-śabda) within your own mouth.
- Listen to this inner sound carefully, allowing it to become the central focus of your meditation. This sound is associated with the emptiness within.

Silent Contemplation:
- Practice remaining silent during this meditation. Allow yourself to fully immerse in the inner sound without external distractions or vocal expression.
- By maintaining silence, you align yourself with the mastery of speech and deepen your connection with the sound within.

Voice Expansion:

- As your meditation deepens, you may start to experience your voice moving and resonating without obstruction. This signifies that your speech is becoming more fluid and powerful.
- Contemplate the expanding reach of your voice, envisioning it as traveling everywhere freely.

Attainment of Knowledge:

- With continued practice, you will gain knowledge of the meaning of all sciences. Your voice will become adorned with poetic figures of speech, reflecting a profound understanding and eloquence.

Becoming a Composer:

- Over time, you will develop the ability to compose sciences yourself. This represents the culmination of your mastery over speech and your deep knowledge of various fields.

Contemplation of the Body in the Mouth:

- Shift your focus to contemplating your own body within the space of your mouth. Visualize your body in this context and integrate it into your meditation practice.

Visualization of the Body as White and Shining:

- Visualize your body as being white and faintly shining with light. This represents purity and enlightenment within the context of speech.

Perception of Flavors and Light:

- Contemplate the series beginning with a lunar orb filled with flavor (rasa) and ending with all-pervasive light.

This progression signifies the enrichment and expansive quality of speech.

Attainment of Speech-Realm Rewards:
- By following this sequence, you will attain all of the rewards associated with the speech-realm. This includes mastery over speech, profound knowledge, and the ability to influence and inspire through your voice.

Reflection and Integration:
- Conclude your meditation by reflecting on your experiences and insights gained from the practice. Notice any changes or advancements in your understanding and use of speech.
- If helpful, record your observations to track your progress and integrate the lessons learned into your daily life.

Completion:
- Finish your meditation by expressing gratitude for the insights and growth achieved through this practice.
- Gently transition back to your daily activities, carrying forward the enhanced mastery of speech and understanding of the speech-realm.

This step-by-step guide provides a structured approach to meditating on the organ of speech, facilitating a gradual and profound mastery of speech and its associated realms.

Meditation on the Organs of Grasping (Hands)

Preparation:
- Find a quiet and comfortable space where you can meditate

without interruptions.

- Sit in a relaxed posture with your back straight. You can sit cross-legged on the floor or in a chair with your feet flat on the ground.

Centering and Grounding:

- Close your eyes and take several deep, calming breaths.
- As you inhale, draw in a sense of calm and focus. As you exhale, release any tension or distractions.

Initial Focus on the Hands:

- Direct your attention to your hands. Visualize them clearly and vividly in your mind.
- Fix your mind on the sensation and presence of your hands, establishing a strong mental connection with them.

Grasping Remote Objects:

- With practice, begin to visualize yourself being able to grasp objects that are remotely located.
- As you develop this ability, expand your focus to grasp objects even if they are on the far shore of an imagined ocean.

Contemplation of the Fourteen Stages:

- Carefully contemplate the fourteen stages within your hands. Begin with visualizing your hands in an anthropomorphic form, appearing lotus-hued.
- Explore both the vibrating and static aspects of these stages. This involves understanding how your hands can be in dynamic motion or in a static, stable state.

Realization of Rewards in the Hand-Realm:

- As you progress through these stages, you will begin

to obtain all of the rewards inherent in the hand-realm. These rewards include increased dexterity, precision, and the ability to influence and interact with distant objects.

Advanced Practice and Integration:
- Continue practicing and integrating the contemplation of these stages into your meditation. Notice the gradual enhancement of your abilities related to grasping and manipulating objects.
- Reflect on how these abilities translate into practical skills and spiritual insights in your daily life.

Reflection and Completion:
- Conclude your meditation by reflecting on the experiences and insights gained from this practice. Recognize the advancements in your grasping abilities and their impact.
- If helpful, record your observations and experiences to track your progress and reinforce the skills developed.

Transition and Application:
- Gently transition back to your daily activities, carrying forward the enhanced mastery and understanding of the organ of grasping.
- Apply the insights gained from your meditation to improve your practical skills and spiritual growth.

This step-by-step guide provides a structured approach to meditating on the organs of grasping, helping you gradually develop mastery over the abilities and rewards associated with your hands.

Meditation on the Organs of Locomotion (Feet)

Preparation:
- Find a quiet and comfortable space where you can meditate without interruptions.
- Sit in a relaxed posture with your back straight, or you can lie down if that is more comfortable.

Centering and Grounding:
- Close your eyes and take several deep, calming breaths.
- As you inhale, draw in a sense of calm and focus. As you exhale, let go of any tension or distractions.

Initial Focus on the Feet:
- Direct your attention to your feet. Visualize them clearly and vividly in your mind.
- Fix your mind on the sensation and presence of your feet, establishing a strong mental connection with them.

Visualization of Traversing Great Distances:
- Begin to visualize yourself walking across vast distances. Imagine traversing the entire earth, bounded by oceans, in a remarkably short period without tiring.
- See yourself moving effortlessly and swiftly, covering great distances with ease and energy.

Integration of Walking Abilities:
- As you continue to practice this visualization, you will develop enhanced abilities related to walking and movement.
- Notice how these abilities translate into real-life skills, such as increased stamina, speed, and endurance.

Attainment of Rewards in the Foot-Realm:
  - By meditating on the feet and practicing the visualization, you will attain all the rewards inherent in the foot-realm. These rewards include the ability to travel quickly and tirelessly over long distances.

Reflection and Application:
  - Conclude your meditation by reflecting on the experiences and improvements in your walking abilities. Recognize the advancements and their impact on your daily life.
  - If helpful, record your observations to track your progress and reinforce the skills developed.

Transition and Practice:
  - Gently transition back to your daily activities, carrying forward the enhanced abilities and understanding gained from the meditation.
  - Apply the insights and skills from your meditation to improve your practical experiences and overall well-being.

This step-by-step guide provides a focused approach to meditating on the organs of walking, helping you develop enhanced abilities and rewards associated with your feet.

Meditation on the Anus as an Organ of Excretion

Preparation:
  - Find a quiet and comfortable space where you can meditate without interruptions.
  - Sit in a relaxed posture with your back straight. You can

sit cross-legged on the floor or in a chair with your feet
flat on the ground.

Centering and Grounding:

- Close your eyes and take several deep, calming breaths.
- As you inhale, draw in a sense of calm and focus. As you
  exhale, release any tension or distractions.

Focus on the Anus:

- Direct your attention inward to the area of the anus.
  Visualize this region clearly and vividly in your mind.
- Imagine the anus as a powerful organ of excretion, capable
  of assimilating and releasing various forms of matter.

Assimilation Process:

- Visualize the anus as a central processing unit for physical,
  mental, and emotional elements.
- Picture it absorbing and processing physical waste, as
  well as metaphorical waste such as unhelpful thoughts
  and negative emotions.

Release of Physical, Mental, and Emotional Waste:

- Meditate on the process of releasing these assimilated
  elements. Imagine the anus efficiently expelling physical
  waste and simultaneously letting go of mental clutter and
  emotional baggage.
- Visualize this release as a cleansing and rejuvenating
  process, bringing a sense of relief and renewal.

Enhanced Functioning and Well-Being:

- Contemplate how this process of assimilation and
  release enhances your overall well-being. Notice any
  improvements in physical health, mental clarity, and

emotional balance.
- Reflect on the sense of lightness and freedom that comes from effectively managing and releasing these various elements.

Reflection and Integration:
- Conclude your meditation by reflecting on the experiences and benefits gained from this practice. Recognize any changes in your physical, mental, and emotional state.
- If helpful, record your observations to track progress and reinforce the positive outcomes of your practice.

Application in Daily Life:
- Gently transition back to your daily activities, carrying forward the improved sense of balance and well-being.
- Apply the insights from your meditation to continue assimilating and releasing unhelpful elements in your life, maintaining a healthier and more harmonious state.

This step-by-step guide provides a structured approach to meditating on the anus as an organ of excretion, focusing on the assimilation and release of physical, mental, and emotional elements for overall well-being.

Meditation on the Genitals as an Organ of Procreation and Creativity

Preparation:
- Find a quiet and comfortable space where you can meditate without interruptions.

- Sit or lie down in a relaxed posture, ensuring your body is supported and comfortable.

Centering and Grounding:
- Close your eyes and take several deep, calming breaths.
- As you inhale, draw in a sense of calm and focus. As you exhale, release any tension or distractions.

Focus on the Genitals:
- Direct your attention to the genitals. Visualize this area clearly in your mind.
- Understand the genitals as not only an organ of physical procreation but also as a center of higher creativity and divine power to create in the physical world.

Contemplation of Creative Power:
- Meditate on the genitals in their own form, recognizing their capacity for creativity and generation.
- Visualize this area as a powerful source of creative energy and divine potential. Imagine it radiating with creative force and vitality.

Mastery of Senses:
- Contemplate the influence of this creative power on your sensory experiences. Visualize mastering your senses through the energy and creativity emanating from the genitals.
- Envision yourself gaining control over sensory perceptions and experiences, leading to enhanced awareness and pleasure.

Experience of Sexual Enjoyment:
- Focus on the ability to experience sexual enjoyment

according to your desires. Visualize this enjoyment coming effortlessly and fulfilling your wishes.

- Imagine this pleasure as a natural and harmonious expression of your creative and divine power.

Integration of Creativity:

- Reflect on how this creative and generative energy extends beyond physical procreation to manifest in other areas of your life.
- Contemplate the ways in which this energy contributes to your overall creativity, productivity, and ability to bring forth new ideas and projects.

Reflection and Benefits:

- Conclude your meditation by reflecting on the benefits gained from recognizing and harnessing the creative power of the genitals.
- Notice any improvements in your sense of creativity, control over senses, and overall satisfaction.

Application in Daily Life:

- Gently transition back to your daily activities, applying the enhanced sense of creativity and control to your tasks and interactions.
- Continue to harness this creative energy to enrich your life and manifest your desires.

This step-by-step guide provides a structured approach to meditating on the genitals, emphasizing their role as an organ of both physical procreation and higher creativity.

Meditation on the Legs as a Divine Instrument of Movement

Preparation:
- Find a quiet and comfortable space where you can meditate without interruptions.
- Sit or lie down in a relaxed posture, ensuring your body is well-supported and comfortable.

Centering and Grounding:
- Close your eyes and take several deep, calming breaths.
- As you inhale, draw in a sense of calm and focus. As you exhale, release any tension or distractions.

Focus on the Legs:
- Direct your attention to your legs. Visualize them clearly in your mind.
- Understand the legs as not just physical organs of movement but as divine instruments that embody the dynamic and evolutionary aspects of the cosmos.

Contemplation of Divine Movement:
- Meditate on your legs as symbols of divine movement and dynamic energy. Visualize them as conduits of cosmic power and evolution.
- Imagine your legs moving with grace and purpose, reflecting the fluid and transformative nature of the divine force that governs the cosmos.

Symbol of Evolution and Resolution:
- Contemplate how the movement of your legs represents the process of cosmic evolution and resolution. Visualize

each step as a contribution to the ongoing creation and dissolution of the universe.

- Envision your steps guiding the progression and harmonization of cosmic energies, participating in the divine dance of creation and resolution.

Alignment with Divine Dynamics:
- Focus on aligning your movements with the divine rhythm of the cosmos. Visualize your legs moving in harmony with the flow of universal energy.
- Contemplate how your dynamic actions and movements reflect and contribute to the greater evolutionary processes of the universe.

Integration and Benefits:
- Reflect on how recognizing the divine nature of your legs enhances your sense of purpose and connection to the cosmic order.
- Notice any improvements in your awareness of movement, alignment with divine energy, and overall sense of harmony with the universe.

Reflection and Application:
- Conclude your meditation by reflecting on the insights and benefits gained from this practice. Recognize how your movements can embody and influence cosmic evolution and resolution.
- Transition back to your daily activities with a renewed sense of purpose, integrating the dynamic and divine aspects of your movement into your actions and interactions.

- **Ongoing Practic0.25**
- This guide provides a structured approach to meditating on the legs, focusing on their role as divine instruments of movement that contribute to the cosmic evolution and resolution.

Conquest of the Tanmatras

**Meditation on the Tongue as an
Organ of Divine Sensation**

Preparation:
- Find a quiet and comfortable space where you can meditate without disturbances.
- Sit or lie down in a relaxed posture, ensuring that your body is well-supported.

Centering and Grounding:
- Close your eyes and take several deep, calming breaths.
- As you inhale, draw in a sense of calm and focus. As you exhale, release any tension or distractions.

Focus on the Tongue:
- Direct your attention to your tongue. Visualize it clearly in your mind.
- Imagine your tongue having the color of the moon, radiant and luminous.

Contemplation of Tongue Sensation:
- Begin by contemplating the sensation of the tongue as it would be if it were absent. Imagine experiencing the absence of the tongue, sensing the subtlety and expanded perception that arises from this state.
- Gradually, focus on your ability to taste sensations from distant sources, as if your sensory perception extends beyond the physical boundaries of your tongue.

Experience of Supreme Nectar:
- Meditate on the experience of directly savoring the supreme nectar. Visualize this nectar as a divine, life-enhancing essence that transcends ordinary taste.
- Contemplate how this nectar frees you from the limitations of aging and death, providing a profound sense of rejuvenation and immortality.

Integration of Transformative Qualities:
- Reflect on how this practice allows you to transcend ordinary sensory experiences and engage with higher divine sensations.
- Visualize integrating this transformative quality into your life, noticing any enhancements in your sensory perception and overall sense of well-being.

Application and Reflection:
- Conclude your meditation by reflecting on the rewards gained from this practice. Recognize the enhancements in your sensory experiences and the profound sense of divine connection achieved.
- Carry this awareness into your daily life, applying the heightened perception and rejuvenation gained from this meditation.

Continued Practice:
- Incorporate this meditation into your regular practice to deepen your connection with the divine sensations of the tongue and experience ongoing benefits.

This guide outlines a gradual progression for meditating on the

tongue, focusing on its divine sensory qualities and the rewards of this transformative practice.

Meditation on the Nose as an
Organ of Divine Perception

Preparation:
- Find a quiet and comfortable space where you can meditate without interruptions.
- Sit or lie down in a relaxed posture, ensuring your body is well-supported.

Centering and Grounding:
- Close your eyes and take several deep, calming breaths.
- As you inhale, draw in a sense of calm and focus. As you exhale, release any tension or distractions.

Focus on the Nose:
- Direct your attention to your nose. Visualize it clearly in your mind.
- Imagine your nose as having the radiant and pure color of gold, symbolizing its divine qualities.

Contemplation of Sensory Absence:
- Meditate on the sensation of having no nose. Visualize the absence of the nose and the subtle shift in perception that comes from this state of sensory detachment.

Extended Scent Perception:
- Gradually expand your awareness to include the ability to smell distant scents. Visualize your sense of smell extending far beyond the physical reach of your nose, allowing you to detect scents from far-off places.

Divine Scent Experience:
- Contemplate the attainment of a divine scent. Imagine experiencing a unique, transcendent fragrance that signifies divine presence and purity.
- Reflect on how this divine scent endows you with freedom from old age and death, elevating you to a state of divine worthiness.

Integration and Application:
- Reflect on the transformative qualities of this practice. Recognize how the enhanced sense of smell connects you to higher realms and divine perceptions.
- Visualize integrating these newfound abilities into your daily life, applying the insights gained from this meditation.

Continued Practice:
- Incorporate this meditation into your regular practice to deepen your connection with the divine perception of the nose and experience ongoing benefits.

This guide provides a structured approach to meditating on the nose, focusing on its divine perception qualities and the transformative rewards of this practice.

Meditation on the Eyes as a Divine Instrument of Perception

Preparation:
- Find a quiet and comfortable space where you can meditate

without interruptions.
- Sit or lie down in a relaxed posture, ensuring your body is well-supported.

Centering and Grounding:
- Close your eyes and take several deep, calming breaths.
- As you inhale, draw in a sense of calm and focus. As you exhale, release any tension or distractions.

Focus on the Eyes:
- Direct your attention to your eyes. Visualize them clearly in your mind.
- Imagine your eyes as resembling the rising sun, radiating with a bright and transformative light.

Contemplation of Sensory Perception:
- There might be a sensation of blood through from your eyes. Visualize this sensation as part of a deep transformation process, acknowledging any discomfort as a sign of progress.
- Understand that this sensation, though intense, is a necessary step in unlocking higher levels of perception.

Divine Vision Development:
- Shift your focus to developing divine vision. Visualize your ability to perceive the physical world, from its deepest, densest aspects (symbolized by the Earth or Prithvi Tattwa) to the highest heavens.
- See your vision expanding beyond the Earth, ascending through the realms until it reaches the divine presence of Shiva Tattwa, the highest, most transcendent level of consciousness.

Expansion of Perception:

- Contemplate your vision reaching the highest divine realms associated with Shiva Tattwa. Visualize perceiving the pure, all-encompassing light and consciousness of Shiva.
- Imagine yourself moving through and understanding the highest celestial realms, achieving a direct connection with the divine essence of Shiva.

Integration and Application:

- Reflect on the transformative qualities of this practice. Recognize how this enhanced divine vision connects you to the highest spiritual realms and the ultimate consciousness of Shiva.
- Visualize integrating these newfound abilities into your daily life, applying the profound insights and wisdom gained from this meditation.

Continued Practice:

- Incorporate this meditation into your regular practice to deepen your connection with divine perception and experience ongoing spiritual benefits.
- Maintain your focus and determination, understanding that persistence is key to fully realizing the rewards of this practice.

Concluding Reflection:

- As you complete this meditation, acknowledge the profound insights and perceptions gained. Recognize that achieving such divine vision, extending from the Earth to the highest realms of Shiva, is a testament to your

spiritual progress and connection to the ultimate divine consciousness. Embrace the clarity and wisdom gained, and let it guide your journey forward.

This guide provides a structured approach to meditating on the eyes, emphasizing their role as a divine instrument of perception and the transformative journey from the earthly realms to the highest divine consciousness associated with Shiva Tattwa.

Meditation on the Skin for Attaining the Adamantine Body

Preparation:
- Find a quiet, comfortable space where you can meditate undisturbed.
- Sit or lie down in a relaxed posture, ensuring your body is well-supported.

Centering and Grounding:
- Close your eyes and take several deep, calming breaths.
- As you inhale, draw in a sense of calm and focus. As you exhale, release any tension or distractions.

Focus on the Skin:
- Direct your attention to your skin. Visualize it clearly in your mind.
- Imagine your skin taking on a pale grey color, similar to the hue of Hanumat, the son of Anjanā. Visualize this transformation as a divine and protective quality.

Contemplation of Protection:

- Meditate on the sensation of your skin becoming impervious to harm. Visualize your skin as a shield that cannot be cut, burned, or injured by external forces.
- As you deepen this practice, imagine your skin resisting intense heat, sharp objects, and any form of physical damage.

Attaining the Adamantine Body:

- Visualize your body gradually becoming adamantine—strong, unbreakable, and impervious to harm. Understand that this transformation is a result of intense and sustained practice.
- Contemplate your body as unaging and immortal, free from the effects of aging, injury, and external threats.

Integration and Application:

- Reflect on the significance of this transformation. Recognize that attaining an adamantine body is a symbol of profound spiritual and physical strength.
- Visualize integrating this strength into your daily life, applying the insights and resilience gained from this meditation.

Continued Practice:

- Incorporate this meditation into your regular practice to maintain and deepen the qualities of the adamantine body.
- Understand that persistent and intense practice is essential for fully realizing and embodying this transformation.

Concluding Reflection:

- As you complete this meditation, appreciate the progress you have made in achieving an adamantine body.

Recognize the strength and resilience gained through your dedicated practice, and let it inspire your ongoing spiritual journey.

This guide provides a structured approach to meditating on the skin, focusing on its transformation into an adamantine form through dedicated and intense practice.

Meditation on the Ears for Attaining Esoteric Knowledge of Hearing

Preparation:
- Choose a quiet and comfortable space where you will not be disturbed.
- Sit or lie down in a relaxed posture, ensuring your body is fully supported.

Centering and Grounding:
- Close your eyes and take several deep, calming breaths.
- With each inhale, draw in a sense of calm and focus. With each exhale, release any tension or distractions.

Focus on the Space in the Ears:
- Direct your attention to the inner space of your ears. Visualize this space clearly in your mind.
- Imagine this space as a vast, open expanse, free from any physical constraints.

Contemplation of Remote Hearing:
- Meditate on the sensation of hearing sounds from far away. Visualize yourself extending your auditory perception

beyond the immediate environment.

- Imagine your hearing becoming so acute that you can perceive distant sounds with clarity and precision.

Attaining Esoteric Knowledge:

- Visualize yourself achieving the esoteric knowledge of hearing, which allows you to hear all that is spoken within the egg of Brahmā. This represents a profound level of auditory perception.
- Contemplate how this heightened sense of hearing connects you to a greater understanding of the cosmos and the divine.

Integration and Application:

- Reflect on the transformative nature of this practice. Recognize how this advanced auditory perception enhances your spiritual awareness and connection.
- Visualize integrating these newfound abilities into your daily life, applying the insights and understanding gained from this meditation.

Continued Practice:

- Make this meditation a regular part of your practice to deepen and sustain the esoteric knowledge of hearing.
- Understand that consistent and focused practice is key to fully realizing the rewards of this meditation.

Concluding Reflection:

- As you complete this meditation, acknowledge the progress you have made in achieving advanced auditory perception. Appreciate the enhanced awareness and understanding gained through dedicated practice.

Conquest of the Internal Senses, Prakrti and Purusha

**Meditation on the Manas for
Attaining All Perfections**

Preparation:
- Find a quiet and serene space where you will not be disturbed.
- Sit or lie down comfortably, ensuring that your posture supports relaxation and focus.

Centering and Grounding:
- Close your eyes and take several deep, calming breaths.
- With each inhale, draw in a sense of calm and concentration. With each exhale, release any tension or distractions.

Focus on the Manas:
- Direct your attention to the area of your heart. Visualize the Manas as a half- moon facing downwards, located at this central point.
- Imagine this half-moon as a radiant symbol of divine insight and intuitive power.

Contemplation of Intuitive Insight:
- Meditate on the Manas as a source of intuitive insight. Visualize yourself gaining spontaneous, intuitive knowledge and understanding.
- Imagine experiencing perceptions and insights without

logical reason, as if you are receiving direct, unfiltered knowledge from the universe.

Development of Sensory Cognition:
- Gradually expand your awareness to include the sensory cognition of each of your senses. Visualize these senses becoming more acute and clear.
- Contemplate the clarity and precision of your sensory experiences, recognizing the heightened state of perception that arises from deep meditation.

Attaining Perfections:
- Visualize yourself achieving the Perfection of Soma (Saumya), which represents the ultimate realization and mastery over the Manas and senses.
- Reflect on how this perfection connects you to divine qualities and liberates you from ordinary limitations.

Integration and Application:
- Reflect on the transformative power of this meditation. Recognize how the enhanced Manas and sensory perception elevate your spiritual awareness and understanding.
- Visualize integrating these advanced abilities into your daily life, applying the insights and clarity gained from this practice.

Continued Practice:
- Incorporate this meditation into your regular practice to deepen your connection with the divine insight of the Manas.
- Understand that ongoing practice is key to fully realizing the rewards and perfections associated with this meditation.

Concluding Reflection:
- As you complete this meditation, acknowledge the progress you have made in attaining profound insight and perception. Appreciate the heightened awareness and divine connection achieved through dedicated practice.

This guide provides a structured approach to meditating on the Manas, focusing on attaining intuitive insight and the ultimate perfection of spiritual awareness.

Meditation on Ahankara (Divine Ahankara)

Preparation:
- Find a quiet, comfortable space where you can meditate without interruptions.
- Sit or lie down in a relaxed posture, ensuring your body is well-supported.

Centering and Grounding:
- Close your eyes and take several deep, calming breaths.
- As you inhale, draw in a sense of calm and focus. As you exhale, release any tension or distractions.

Focus on the Wheel:
- Visualize yourself as a wheel with sixteen spokes, contained within your own physical body. Picture this wheel clearly in your mind.
- Imagine this wheel as a symbol of divine Ahankara, representing the highest form of introspection.

Contemplation of Self as the Wheel:

- Meditate on the wheel as an embodiment of your own essence. With full attention and without distraction, think to yourself: "I am this wheel."
- Cultivate the sense of being invulnerable and realize that everything is a manifestation of your essence.

Identification with the Hub:

- Contemplate your body as the hub of the wheel. Reflect on the idea: "I am everything; all resides in me."
- Recognize that this identification with the hub signifies the esoteric knowledge of Ahankara (Ahankara), where you perceive yourself as the center of all existence.

Attainment of Divine Pride:

- Visualize yourself as the embodiment of divine pride, represented by the wheel in the heart region. Embrace the sense of supreme self-assurance and accomplishment.
- Reflect on the rewards arising from the realization of this divine Ahankara, including a profound sense of self-empowerment and control.

Integration of the Levels of Ahankara:

- Contemplate each level of Ahankara in a structured manner, starting with the orb and visualizing it in various colors, such as blue-red or purple.
- As you progress through these levels, integrate the qualities and insights gained from each stage into your understanding of divine Ahankara.

Continued Practice:

- Incorporate this meditation into your regular practice to deepen your connection with Ahankara and to experience

the full range of its divine rewards.
- Recognize that sustained practice will enhance your sense of divine pride and realization of the fifty-six Perfections of the Prajāpatis.

Concluding Reflection:
- As you finish this meditation, appreciate the elevated state of self-awareness and divine pride that you have attained. Acknowledge the transformative impact of this practice on your perception and spiritual development.

This guide provides a structured approach to meditating on Ahankara, focusing on the attainment of divine pride and the realization of profound self-empowerment through dedicated introspection.

Meditation on the Lotus of Intellect/Buddhi

Preparation:
- Find a quiet and comfortable space where you can meditate without interruptions.
- Sit or lie down in a relaxed posture, ensuring your body is well-supported.

Centering and Grounding:
- Close your eyes and take several deep, calming breaths.
- As you inhale, draw in a sense of calm and focus. As you exhale, release any tension or distractions.

Focus on the Lotus:
- Visualize a lotus flower in your heart. Picture it with the

radiant color of the rising sun, symbolizing purity and enlightenment.

- The lotus should have eight petals, each representing one of the eight essential qualities or virtues (such as dharma and buddhi).

Contemplation of the Lotus:

- Contemplate the lotus in your heart, focusing on its structure and vibrant color.
- Reflect on the significance of the lotus's petals and pericarp, and how they represent different aspects of your intellect and spiritual growth.

Stabilizing Intellect:

- As you meditate on the lotus, notice how your intellect and mental clarity become steadier and more focused.
- Embrace the transformation as your mental state aligns with the purity and strength of the lotus.

Gaining Knowledge:

- Through continued meditation, perceive how your understanding deepens. Begin to feel a connection with the ancient wisdom of the scriptures ('Sruti).
- Recognize how this insight leads you to become well-versed in sacred knowledge and eventually to author new spiritual or philosophical works.

Integration of Intellect:

- Contemplate your own physical form within the lotus in your heart. Reflect on how this visualization helps you perceive the principle of intellect more clearly.
- Integrate the understanding gained from this practice into your daily life and spiritual pursuits.

Continued Practice:
- Maintain this meditation practice regularly to deepen your connection with the lotus of intellect and to enhance your spiritual and intellectual capacities.
- Recognize that sustained practice will continually refine your understanding and contribute to your personal and spiritual development.

Concluding Reflection:
- As you conclude the meditation, appreciate the clarity and insight you have gained from focusing on the lotus in your heart.
- Reflect on the transformative impact of this practice on your intellect and spiritual journey.

This structured meditation guide focuses on visualizing and contemplating the lotus of intellect in the heart, aiming to enhance intellectual steadiness and spiritual insight.

Meditation on the Disc of the Sun and Moon (Prakriti)

Preparation:
- Find a quiet, comfortable space where you can meditate without interruptions.
- Sit or lie down in a relaxed posture, ensuring your body is well-supported.

Centering and Grounding:
- Close your eyes and take several deep, calming breaths.

- As you inhale, draw in a sense of calm and focus. As you exhale, release any tension or distractions.

Focus on the Disc:
- Visualize a disc of the sun within your heart. Imagine this disc as radiant and powerful, symbolizing divine light and energy.
- Inside this sun-disc, visualize a disc of the moon, which represents cool, serene, and nurturing qualities.

Contemplation of Divine Vision:
- Meditate on the interplay of the sun and moon discs in your heart. Reflect on how their combined energies enhance your perception and spiritual vision.
- As you focus on this vision, allow yourself to experience the awakening of divine sight, gaining clarity and insight into the unseen realms.

Achieving Perfection:
- With sustained practice, recognize how your efforts lead to the attainment of spiritual perfection. Embrace the sense of completion and fulfillment that arises from this deep meditation.

Understanding Unmanifest Matter:
- Contemplate your own physical form within the context of the sun and moon discs. Reflect on how this visualization reveals the nature of unmanifest matter, a fundamental principle underlying existence.

Sovereignty Over the Liṅga:
- Visualize the shape of a blazing liṅga (symbol of divine energy) within the sun-moon disc. Contemplate

your mastery and control over this powerful symbol, symbolizing your sovereignty over transformative energies.

Exploring the Decad:

Meditate on the ten-fold aspects of the unmanifest realm, beginning with the orb of divine light. Visualize each aspect and integrate its qualities into your understanding.

Recognize the ten-fold rewards associated with these contemplations and how they enhance your spiritual and material existence.

Continued Practice:

Incorporate this meditation into your regular practice to deepen your connection with the divine discs of the sun and moon and to gain the benefits of mastering unmanifest matter.

Understand that consistent practice will continue to reveal the deeper principles of existence and enhance your spiritual growth.

Concluding Reflection:

As you conclude the meditation, appreciate the divine vision and understanding you have gained. Reflect on how the interplay of the sun and moon discs has expanded your perception and spiritual awareness.

This structured meditation guide focuses on visualizing and contemplating the discs of the sun and moon in the heart, aiming to achieve divine vision, mastery over unmanifest matter, and deeper spiritual insight.

Meditation on Purusha Tattva
(Divine Person Principle)

Preparation:
- Find a quiet and comfortable space where you can meditate without interruptions.
- Sit or lie down in a relaxed posture, ensuring your body is well-supported.

Centering and Grounding:
- Close your eyes and take several deep, calming breaths.
- As you inhale, draw in a sense of calm and focus. As you exhale, release any tension or distractions.

Visualize the Purusha:
- Imagine the Purusha (the divine principle of Person) seated on a white lotus. Visualize this lotus as radiant and pure, floating in the center of a triad of mandalas.
- Contemplate the Purusha as the essence of existence, beyond the physical body, embodying the ultimate reality.

Contemplation of Purusha:
- Focus on the Purusha seated on the lotus. Recognize that, beyond the physical body, there is nothing else in ultimate reality.
- Allow this contemplation to steady your mind and deepen your understanding of the divine essence.

Experiencing Freedom and Knowledge:
- With consistent practice, observe how this meditation leads to the liberation from all forms of disease and physical limitations.

- As your practice deepens, you gain esoteric knowledge of all that exists on the surface of the Earth.

Realization of Immortality:
- Continue meditating on the Purusha to transcend old age and achieve a state of eternal youth.
- Recognize how this realization leads to an understanding of the principle of Person, embodying the highest state of existence.

Contemplation in the Heart Region:
- In the heart region, visualize your own body as a lotus with six digits, ending with the heart, located below this lotus.
- Contemplate this form as being aligned with the Purusha, aiming to conquer the cycle of death and achieve immortality.

Attainment of Divine Equality:
- With persistent practice, you will find yourself attaining equality with the ruler of the Purusha principle, embodying divine qualities and insights.

Continued Practice:
- Incorporate this meditation into your regular practice to further align with the Purusha and to experience ongoing benefits.
- Acknowledge that sustained practice will continue to reveal deeper aspects of the Purusha and enhance your spiritual development.

Concluding Reflection:
- As you conclude the meditation, reflect on the profound

realization of the Purusha and the transformation it brings to your perception of existence.
- Appreciate the elevated state of awareness and the divine rewards achieved through this practice.

This structured meditation guide focuses on visualizing and contemplating the Purusha Tattva, aiming to achieve a deep understanding of the divine Person principle and its transformative effects on spiritual and physical existence.

Conquest of The Five Veils of Maya

Contemplation on Raga Tatwa

1. Preparation:
- Find a quiet and comfortable space where you can sit undisturbed.
- Sit in a relaxed position with your back straight and hands resting comfortably on your lap or knees.

2. Initial Relaxation:
- Close your eyes and take a few deep breaths. Inhale slowly through your nose, hold for a moment, and exhale gently through your mouth.
- Allow your body to relax with each breath, letting go of any tension.

3. Visualization (Starting Point):
- Begin by visualizing your own body. Imagine it as a mass of autumnal twilight clouds.
- Picture these clouds as being above a full cloud, gently glowing with a reddish hue.

4. Contemplation (Early Stage):
- As you continue with this visualization, see your body as red and located above the full cloud.
- Focus on the concept of desirelessness. Let go of any desires or attachments that arise.

5. Deepening the Practice:
- Gradually deepen your contemplation by seeing the body

as a red form that starts six digits below the heart and extends up to your heart.

- Visualize this red form encased in a red lotus located in the heart region.

6. Enhancing Awareness:

- As your practice evolves, enhance your focus on overcoming pairs of opposites. Strive to achieve a state of equanimity and mastery over desires.
- Continue to observe how your sense of detachment from aging and death develops.

7. Integration:

- Regularly practice this visualization and contemplation. Reflect on the progress you make towards wisdom and freedom from the cycle of aging and death.

8. Closing:

- Gently bring your awareness back to the present moment.
- Open your eyes slowly, take a deep breath, and stretch if needed.
- Carry the sense of calm and desirelessness with you throughout your day.

Contemplating the Vidya Tatwa

1. Preparation:

- Find a quiet and comfortable space where you can sit undisturbed.
- Sit in a relaxed position with your back straight and hands resting comfortably on your lap or knees.

2. Initial Relaxation:

- Close your eyes and take a few deep breaths. Inhale slowly through your nose, hold briefly, and exhale gently through your mouth.
- Allow your body to relax with each breath, letting go of any tension.

3. Visualization of the Divine Lotus:

- Begin by visualizing a white, divine lotus in your heart center.
- Imagine this lotus as made up of ambrosia, with sixteen petals and the vidyā moon at its center as the pericarp (central part).

4. Focused Contemplation:

- Fix your mind on this visualization of the lotus, ensuring your focus remains unwavering.
- Maintain this contemplation with full attention until you naturally begin to fall asleep.

5. Dream and Reality Connection:

- As you fall asleep, the intention is for your dreams to reflect the reality of your meditation practice.
- Observe how the visions or experiences in your dreams align with or manifest aspects of your meditation.

6. Integration and Reflection:

- Upon waking, reflect on the experiences from your dreams and how they relate to the meditation on the lotus.
- Understand that this practice helps in achieving all the rewards associated with the lotus of intellect.

7. Contemplation of the Body:

- In your ongoing practice, also contemplate your body and other aspects as measuring four digits, integrating this understanding into your meditation.

8. Closing:
- Gently bring your awareness back to the present moment when you finish your meditation.
- Open your eyes slowly, take a deep breath, and stretch if needed.
- Carry the clarity and sense of connection with you throughout your day.

Feel free to adapt these steps to suit your personal meditation practice and experiences.

Contemplating the Three Successive Wheels of Kala, Kaala and Niyati

1. Preparation:
- Find a quiet and comfortable space where you can sit undisturbed.
- Sit in a relaxed position with your back straight and hands resting comfortably on your lap or knees.

2. Initial Relaxation:
- Close your eyes and take a few deep breaths. Inhale slowly through your nose, hold for a moment, and exhale gently through your mouth.
- Allow your body to relax with each breath, letting go of any tension.

3. Visualization of the Three Successive Wheels:
- Visualize three successive wheels located half a digit above the heart, moving upwards.
- Contemplate each wheel in the following order:
  - The first wheel is red.
  - The second wheel is dark blue.
  - The third wheel is black.
- See these wheels clearly and distinctly in their respective colors and positions.

4. Contemplation of the Person:
- In the same location where the wheels are visualized, also contemplate the Person.
- Visualize the Person measuring three digits in size, with the same red, dark blue, and black colors corresponding to the wheels.
- Ensure the Person is clearly visualized in alignment with the colors and location of the wheels.

5.Contemplation of the Sixteen Spokes:
- Extend your visualization to include sixteen spokes connected to the wheels.
- See these sixteen spokes radiating out from the wheels, enhancing the clarity and structure of the wheels' visualization.

6. Reflection:
- Reflect on the great triad of principles you have visualized—the wheels, the Person, and the sixteen spokes.
- Understand the interconnectedness and significance of

these elements in your meditation practice.

7. Integration and Closing:
- Gradually bring your focus back to the present moment.
- Open your eyes slowly, take a deep breath, and stretch if needed.
- Carry the insights and clarity gained from this practice with you throughout your day.

Mastering the Pralaya Kala

1. Preparation:
- Find a quiet and comfortable space where you can sit undisturbed.
- Sit in a relaxed position with your back straight and hands resting comfortably on your lap or knees.

2. Initial Relaxation:
- Close your eyes and take a few deep breaths. Inhale slowly through your nose, hold briefly, and exhale gently through your mouth.
- Allow your body to relax with each breath, letting go of any tension.

3. Visualization of the Self:
- Visualize your own self as having blazing eyes. Imagine these eyes are radiant and full of light, symbolizing inner wisdom and perception.

4. Pericarp of the Lotus:
- Picture this radiant self seated on the pericarp (central part) of a lotus with five petals.

- Visualize the lotus in the region of the cavity of your throat, with its five petals clearly defined.

5. Contemplation of the Lotus:
- Focus on the lotus with its five petals. Each petal represents a different aspect of your consciousness or principles.
- Contemplate the beauty and significance of the lotus as a symbol of purity and spiritual awakening.

6. Mastering the Tatwas in dimension of objectivity:
- Reflect on the principles from the basic elements (earth) to the principle of time.
- Recognize that understanding these principles provides insight into the nature of existence and time.

7. Mastery Over Time:
- Contemplate how mastering the understanding of these principles—from earth to time—enables you to transcend the limitations imposed by time.
- Realize that, with this mastery, you are not overpowered by the constraints of time.

8. Reflection and Integration:
- Reflect on the interconnectedness of your radiant self, the lotus, and the Tatwas.
- Embrace the insight that achieving mastery over these elements allows you to transcend temporal limitations.

9. Closing:
- Gently bring your awareness back to the present moment.
- Open your eyes slowly, take a deep breath, and stretch if needed.
- Carry the sense of clarity and mastery gained from this practice with you throughout your day.

Overcoming Maya, the principle of Limitation
(Conquest of Vijnana Kala)

1. Preparation:
- Find a quiet and comfortable space where you can sit undisturbed.
- Sit in a relaxed position with your back straight and hands resting comfortably on your lap or knees.

2. Initial Relaxation:
- Close your eyes and take a few deep breaths. Inhale slowly through your nose, hold briefly, and exhale gently through your mouth.
- Allow your body to relax with each breath, letting go of any tension.

3. Visualization of the Moon and Rahu:
- Visualize yourself resembling the moon that is partially devoured by the eclipse-causing demon Rahu.
- Imagine this moon as having the color described in the procedure related to the cavity of your throat. See the moon's light being obscured by the demon.

4. Contemplation of the Eclipse:
- Contemplate how this moon, obscured by Rahu, represents your own self. Focus on the image of the moon being partially covered, symbolizing a state of being influenced or obscured by external forces.
- Reflect on the idea that by recognizing and meditating on this state, you are not subject to the illusions and evolutes of Māyā.

5. Visualization of Freedom from the Eclipse:
- Next, visualize the moon as though freed from the eclipsing demon Svarbhānu.
- Imagine the moon regaining its full brilliance and light, symbolizing liberation and clarity.

6. Contemplation of Bodies of Light:
- Expand your contemplation to include the bodies of light and other luminous forms.
- Visualize these radiant bodies as embodiments of supreme clarity and sovereignty.

7. Achieving Supreme Sovereignty:
- Reflect on how this meditation and visualization lead to the attainment of supreme sovereignty.
- Recognize that by overcoming the obscuring influences of Rahu and Svarbhānu, you align yourself with a state of ultimate power and control.

8. Reflection and Integration:
- Reflect on the interconnectedness of your visualization of the moon, the eclipse, and the bodies of light.
- Embrace the insight gained from this practice and the sense of sovereignty and liberation it brings.

9. Closing:
- Gently bring your awareness back to the present moment.
- Open your eyes slowly, take a deep breath, and stretch if needed.
- Carry the clarity and sense of empowerment from this practice with you throughout your day.

In their practice, the yogi now focuses on two distinct forms of introspection at the level of the Pralayākala. They understand these forms not merely as the Pralayākala and his Shakti, which are typically differentiated by the presence or absence of vibration. Instead, they distinguish between the Savedya-Pralayākala and the Apavedya-Pralayākala.

When the yogi engages with the Savedya-Pralayākala, they are aware of a limited power of desire directed towards external objects. Conversely, the Apavedya-Pralayākala, which they contemplate separately, represents a state of awareness devoid of external objects of desire.

Their introspection also includes a focus on the limited capacity for knowledge, or vidyā, which they center on in the heart region. They visualize this knowledge as white in color. This form of introspection is distinct from the previous ones primarily in its location and color.

The yogi understands that in the eleven-fold introspection, two key realities are the Savedya-Pralayākala and the Apavedya-Pralayākala. According to Abhinavagupta, when they perceive the reality of Māyā, they also recognize the dormancy of the veils since Māyā represents the unity of these veils. As they experience this, they embody the Vijñānakala, free from veils. The same comprehension applies to the second Pralayākala when it merges with Māyā, forming the Apavedya-Pralayākala.

In their introspective practice, the yogi realizes that the object of contemplation is not confined to any particular Tattva. Instead, they focus on the Vijñānakala, the experiencer situated in the interstice between Māyā and Śuddhavidyā. As Abhinavagupta notes, when the

yogi perceives the Vijñānakala, who is entirely free from veils, this awareness transforms their experience.

At this stage, the yogi recognizes that the experiencers they engage with are in the Mantra Pramātra form, on the brink of awakening. This realization indicates that they are approaching a state of higher awareness and insight.

In their journey of introspection, the yogi understands that this level of Vijñānakala is part of the conquest of the tattvas, representing an experiential stage rather than an ontological one. This understanding marks the conclusion of their contemplation of the principles in the dimensions of objectivity.

Contemplating Suddha Vidya and Reaching the State of Mantra Pramatr

1. Preparation:
- Find a quiet and comfortable space where you can sit undisturbed.
- Sit in a relaxed position with your back straight and hands resting comfortably on your lap or knees.

2. Initial Relaxation:
- Close your eyes and take a few deep breaths. Inhale slowly through your nose, hold briefly, and exhale gently through your mouth.
- Allow your body to relax with each breath, letting go of any tension.

3. Visualization of the Eight-Spoked Wheel:
- Visualize an eight-spoked wheel located at the back of

your hard palate. See this wheel clearly in your mind, with each of the eight spokes vividly defined.

- Each spoke represents a different category of phonemes. Picture these phonemes as active and vibrating, contributing to the wheel's dynamic form.

4. Contemplation of the Phonemes and Wheel:

- Focus on the phonemes vibrating within each spoke. As they vibrate, imagine them forming and energizing the wheel.
- Visualize the phonemes' vibrations merging into the wheel, creating a powerful, unified structure that represents the essence of the mantras.

5. Integration of the Sounds:

- Contemplate how the phonemes and their vibrations not only form the wheel but also become the wheel itself. Feel how the sounds and the wheel are interconnected and harmoniously integrated.
- Experience the wheel as a living, dynamic entity, pulsating with the energy of the phonemes.

6. Contemplation of the Combined Wheel:

- Shift your focus to the combined form of all mantras, visualizing this as a single wheel. Imagine it appearing like the midday sun, radiating intense light and energy.
- Place this combined wheel in the uvula at the back of your throat. Visualize its brilliance and power illuminating this area.

7. Reaching the State of Mantreswara:

- As you continue to meditate, allow yourself to embody

the state of Mantresswara. This is a level where you are fully immersed in and empowered by the essence of the mantras.

- Embrace the realization that you have become a Mantra experient, deeply connected to the transformative power of the combined wheel and its phonemes.

8. Reflection and Integration:
- Reflect on the significance of reaching the state of Mantresswara. Understand how this level represents a profound mastery and insight into the mantras.
- Integrate this awareness and empowerment into your daily life, carrying the clarity and energy from this practice with you.

9. Closing:
- Gradually bring your awareness back to the present moment.
- Open your eyes slowly, take a deep breath, and stretch if needed.
- Carry the sense of mastery and the insight gained from this practice with you throughout your day.

The Ultimate Subjectivity

**Mṛityuñjaya Yoga of Trika (Conquest of Death)
and the Sada´siva Tatwa**

1. Preparation:
- Find a quiet, comfortable place where you can sit undisturbed.
- Sit in a relaxed position with your back straight and hands resting comfortably on your lap or knees.

2. Initial Relaxation:
- Close your eyes and take a few deep breaths. Inhale slowly through your nose, hold briefly, and exhale gently through your mouth.
- Allow your body to relax with each breath, releasing any tension.

3. Visualization of the Eight-Petalled Lotus:
- Visualize an eight-petalled lotus with a white pericarp, emerging from the vacuum above your head. Imagine this lotus as crystalline and sparkling like frost.
- See the lotus vividly in your mind, with its petals delicately unfolding and shimmering.

4. Center of the Lotus:
- In the center of this lotus, visualize the moon disc. Picture the moon as radiant and cool, situated amidst the lotus.
- Understand that the lotus is firmly rooted, with the stem extending down through your spinal cord.

5. Self-Visualization:
- Visualize yourself as having a crystalline form, glittering like frost. See this form in alignment with the lotus and moon disc above you.

6. Contemplation of Devī Parā:
- Within the moon disc, visualize Devī Parā, a divine figure of clear complexion. Picture her sending down a stream of nectar.
- Focus on the mantra associated with Devī Parā, which is the single syllable "sauH."

7. Nectar Flow:
- As you meditate, see the nectar flowing from Devī Parā through the brahmarandhra (the crown of the head) and descending through the amṛitavāhinī nerve.
- Visualize this nectar filling the cavity of your heart, bringing clarity and purification.

8. Repeating the Mantra:
- While visualizing this process, repeatedly chant or mentally focus on the mantra "sauH," associated with Devī Parā.
- Maintain a steady and focused practice, allowing the mantra to resonate deeply within you.

9. Mṛityujit or Conquest of Death:
- Continue this practice regularly, focusing on the visualization and mantra for six months.
- As you sustain this meditation, you will progressively attain the state of Mṛityujit, overcoming the power of death and achieving spiritual victory.

Contemplation on the Ishwara Tatwa

1. Preparation:
- Find a quiet and comfortable place where you can sit undisturbed.
- Sit in a relaxed position with your back straight and hands resting comfortably on your lap or knees.

2. Initial Relaxation:
- Close your eyes and take a few deep breaths. Inhale slowly through your nose, hold briefly, and exhale gently through your mouth.
- Allow your body to relax with each breath, letting go of any tension.

3. Visualization of the Blazing Flame:
- Focus your attention on the forehead, visualizing a great flame of light. Imagine this blaze composed of distinct colors.
- Visualize the colors in the following order:
  - Lustre of sapphire
  - Lustre of a peacock's throat
  - Color resembling lapis lazuli
  - Color similar to a cat's-eye gem
  - Topaz
  - Coral
  - Ruby
  - The moon

4. Contemplation of the Colors:

- Contemplate each color of the blaze in sequence, allowing yourself to fully experience the unique qualities and energies of each hue.
- Feel the vibrant energy and transformative power of these colors as they blend into the overall blaze.

5. Experience the Supreme Moonlight:

- As you continue to visualize the blaze, focus on the supreme moonlight within it. This divine light represents the highest form of illumination and insight.
- Allow this moonlight to fill your mind, bringing clarity and a sense of divine knowledge.

6. Arising of Divine Knowledge:

- From this supreme moonlight, let divine knowledge arise within you. Recognize that this knowledge encompasses everything, starting from the immobile to the mobile aspects of existence.

7. Contemplation of Pervasiveness:

- Contemplate how this divine knowledge and moonlight pervade both upwards and downwards. Visualize this illumination extending throughout your being and beyond.
- Understand that this pervasiveness signifies the complete integration and mastery of this knowledge.

8. Sustaining the Experience:

- Maintain your focus on the blaze and the divine knowledge it represents. This practice will help you remain steadfast at this elevated level of awareness and insight.

9. Reflection and Integration:

- Reflect on the profound effects of this meditation. Integrate the insights and clarity gained into your daily life.
- Carry the sense of divine knowledge and illumination with you throughout your day.

10. Closing:

- Gradually bring your awareness back to the present moment.
- Open your eyes slowly, take a deep breath, and stretch if needed.
- Reconnect with your surroundings while maintaining the inner sense of calm and realization achieved through the meditation.

Contemplation of Ishwara Tatwa, a Further Understanding

1. Preparation:

- Find a quiet and comfortable place where you can sit undisturbed.
- Sit in a relaxed position with your back straight and hands resting comfortably on your lap or knees.

2. Initial Relaxation:

- Close your eyes and take a few deep breaths. Inhale slowly through your nose, hold briefly, and exhale gently through your mouth.
- Allow your body to relax with each breath, letting go of any tension.

3. Visualization of the Eight-Colored Blaze:

- Focus your attention on the forehead and visualize a great blaze of light. Imagine this blaze as composed of eight distinct colors, each representing a different state of subjectivity.

4. Contemplation of the Eight States of Subjectivity:

1. **Lustre of Sapphire:** Visualize this color representing the **Sakala Pramatr** state, where consciousness is engaged with the sensory and physical realm.

2. **Lustre of a Peacock's Throat:** See this hue as the **Pralaya Kala** state, where there is a deeper contemplation and dissolution of forms.

3. **Color Resembling Lapis Lazuli:** Contemplate this color as the **Vijnana Kala** state, signifying the level of refined, intellectual insight and awareness.

4. **Color Similar to a Cat's-Eye Gem:** Imagine this color representing the **Mantra Pramatr** state, where one is deeply connected to the power of mantras and their transformative effects.

5. **Topaz:** Visualize this color as the **Mantreswara Pramatr** state, denoting a profound mastery over mantras and their subtle influences.

6. **Coral:** See this hue as the **Mantra Maheswara Pramatr** state, reflecting an even deeper level of mantra mastery and divine authority.

7. **Ruby:** Contemplate this color as the **Shakta Pramatr** state, representing a supreme connection to the divine feminine energy and power.

8. **The Moon:** Visualize the moonlight as the **Shiva** state, the ultimate realization of pure consciousness and the unconditioned self.

5. Experiencing Divine Knowledge:

- Allow the divine knowledge associated with each state to arise within you as you focus on the corresponding colors.
- Understand that this progression leads to the supreme realization of pure consciousness.

6. Contemplation of the Divine Illumination:

- Focus on how the supreme moonlight within the blaze signifies the culmination of all these states, representing the highest level of divine consciousness.
- Feel this supreme illumination integrating and transcending all states of subjectivity.

7. Pervasiveness of Consciousness:

- Visualize this ultimate consciousness pervading both upwards and downwards, sensing its all-encompassing presence throughout your being and beyond.
- Recognize that this divine illumination represents the complete mastery and integration of all states of consciousness.

8. Sustaining the Experience:

- Maintain your focus on the blaze and the supreme consciousness it represents. Allow yourself to remain in this elevated state of awareness.

9. Reflection and Integration:

- Reflect on the insights and profound awareness gained from this meditation. Integrate this higher understanding

into your daily life.
- Carry the sense of divine illumination and ultimate consciousness with you throughout your day.

10. Closing:
- Gradually bring your awareness back to the present moment.
- Open your eyes slowly, take a deep breath, and stretch if needed.
- Reconnect with your surroundings while maintaining the inner sense of calm and realization achieved through the meditation.

Beyond this point, no further Tattvas can be contemplated, as the Shiva-Shakti principle embodies the ultimate state of subjectivity and is not an object of contemplation.

Kali - A Further Exposition on Kalas

Kali Bhagavati is intimately connected with the concept of *Matrsadbhava*, which can be understood as the perception or realization that emerges from taking refuge in her divine presence. This idea implies that by aligning oneself with Kali, one gains insight into the fundamental nature of existence and reality. Kali's role in this process is to make known or reveal the true essence of the world and consciousness.

In her manifestation as *Vamesvari* or *Tripurasundari*, Kali transforms from her traditionally fierce and terrifying form, known for her destructive power, into a more benevolent and blissful aspect. This transformation reflects her shift from a form characterized by wrath and fear—*raukdra*—to one that embodies grace and delight. As *Vamesvari*, Kali is seen as the embodiment of joy and fulfillment, bestowing blessings and harmony upon her devotees.

Kali Bhagavati is described as having two distinct states. The first is a state of contraction, termed *Anakhyaripa*, which translates to "the form of the inexplicable." In this state, Kali's divine essence is contracted to such an extent that no duality or differentiation can exist. This state is also known as *Visvottirna*, meaning "Transcendent to the world." It represents a realm beyond the ordinary boundaries of experience and perception, where the multiplicity of the material world dissolves into a unified, indescribable essence.

The second state of Kali Bhagavati is characterized by the expansion of her self-form. This state is referred to as *Visvamaya*, meaning "Immanent in the world." Here, Kali's divine essence

manifests in the diverse and differentiated forms of the world, allowing the continued existence of variety and subdivision within the universe. Despite the inherent multiplicity of this state, it is still a reflection of her divine presence and power.

While both states are seen as manifestations of the same fundamental reality, there is a philosophical distinction between them. The state of immanence (*Visvamaya*) is often considered superior by certain *Saivacaryas*, or scholars of Saivism, because it represents the active engagement of the divine in the world and its phenomena. This state reflects the goddess's ongoing influence and presence within the realm of worldly experience, demonstrating her ability to sustain and enliven the multiplicity of existence.

When discussing the contraction and expansion of Kali Bhagavati's self-form, the text addresses profound metaphysical principles. In the state of contraction, Kali's self-form becomes so abstract and ineffable that it transcends the usual means of description or perception. This state is beyond the scope of speech and thought, existing in a realm where conventional categories and distinctions, like name and form, do not apply. It is described as unmentionable and far removed from the ordinary processes of cognition and expression.

Conversely, when Kali's self-form expands, it becomes accessible and perceivable to her devotees. In this expanded state, Kali manifests in a way that allows her followers to directly encounter and experience her divine essence. This expansive form is known as *Visvamaya*, and it is divided into twelve distinct manifestations. Each of these twelve forms represents an aspect of Kali Bhagavati's presence and power, illuminating various aspects of the world and

its governing principles. From these twelve forms, one can infer Kali's nature as encompassing innumerable forms and aspects.

The question arises: Why are there specifically twelve forms associated with Kali Bhagavati, and not thirteen or eleven? The resolution offered by the texts is based on the division of world-form-ness into four distinct categories:

1. **Pramiti-varga**: This category pertains to the highest state of perception, beyond both the act of perceiving and the perceived. It is the realm of pure potential and result, free from agitation or differentiation. This state, sometimes referred to as *caturdala-cakra* (the four-petaled wheel), represents the first emergence of world-form-ness. In this state, the distinctions between the perceiver and the perceived dissolve into pure knowledge.

2. **Pramatr-varga**: This is related to the perceiver and involves the interaction between the perceiver and the perceived, yet it remains distinct from the result of that interaction.

3. **Pramana-varga**: This involves the means of knowledge or the process of perceiving.

4. **Prameya-varga**: This refers to the object of knowledge or the content of perception.

According to the text, the pramiti-varga, or the realm of pure potential, is further subdivided into four components: Devi traya (the triad of goddesses—Para, Parapara, and Apara) and *Matrsadbhava*.

In this state, these goddesses are seen as forms of divine power or *Sakti*.

Alongside them is Parapramata (a form of Siva), who, in this state, embodies the nature of

Sakti rather than his usual form. Because this state represents the essence of divine potential without the full manifestation of power, it is also referred to as *Andkhya* (the unmanifested state).

The twelve forms of Kali Bhagavati, therefore, correspond to the division of the world into these fundamental categories and are seen as reflecting different aspects of divine presence and power within the structure of the world. The specific number of twelve is thus linked to the metaphysical framework that organizes the divine and cosmic principles rather than an arbitrary choice.

Pramatr Varga

In the context of the metaphysical and philosophical framework described, the concept of *Pramatr-varga* or "the Section of the Knower" is a crucial component in understanding the nature of divine perception and the manifestation of worldly experiences.

Pramatr-varga refers to the aspect of reality associated with the perceiver or the knower, contrasting with the previous discussion of *Pramiti-varga* (the section of pure potential or essence). This section is characterized by its manifestation at a macrocosmic level, where it interacts with the world-form-ness described by the pramiti-varga.

In this framework, the Pramatr-varga is symbolized by the *Astaracakra* or *Eightfold Cycle* (also known as *Samharaa-cakra*).

This cycle is comprised of two key groups:

1. Triad of Devis and Kulesvari:
- **Para**: The highest or transcendent goddess.
- **Parapara**: The goddess representing the intermediate state.
- **Apara**: The goddess embodying the manifest or material state.
- **Kulesvari**: A form associated with the divine feminine power or *Sakti*, also referred to as *Matrsadbhava*.

2. Triad of Bhairavas and Kulesvara:
- **Para**: The supreme Bhairava, representing the highest aspect of divine consciousness.
- **Parapara**: The Bhairava representing the intermediate aspect.
- **Apara**: The Bhairava associated with the material world.
- **Kulesvara**: The divine form associated with the principle of lordship or rulership, corresponding to the male counterpart of the goddesses.

When the Pramatr-varga emerges in the broader context of world-form-ness, it appears together with the Pramiti-varga, from which it derives. In this state, the entire ensemble of *pramata* (the knower) experiences worldly enjoyments through the five senses: sound (*sabda*), touch (*sparsa*), form (*rupa*), taste (*rasa*), and smell (*gandha*). The Pramatr-varga is symbolically represented by *Agni*

(fire), highlighting its role as an essential transformative and perceptual force.

In this context, *Agni* is not only a physical element but also a metaphorical representation of the self-form of the *pramata*. There is no distinction between *Agni* and *pramata*; both are considered manifestations of the same underlying reality. From the perspective of the *kalas* (aspects or phases), *Agni* is divided into eight *kalas*, which are viewed as components of the *pramata*. These eight *kalas* are integral to the Pramatr-varga and are associated with the process of *samhara* (dissolution or transformation).

To summarize, the **Pramatr-varga** consists of the eight key forms represented by the *Astaracakra* and includes:

1. Devi Traya:
- **Para**
- **Parapara**
- **Apara**
- **Kulesvari** (also known as *Matrsadbhava*)

2. Bhairava Traya:
- **Para**
- **Parapara**
- **Apara**
- **Kulesvara**

These forms are intricately connected to the eight *kalas* and

are essential to understanding the divine structure and perceptual dynamics within this metaphysical system.

Pramana Varga

The concept of *Pramana-varga* or "the Section of Knowledge" is a pivotal part of the metaphysical framework described. It relates to the means and processes of acquiring knowledge and the ways through which the divine interacts with the world. This section is embodied in the *Dvadasaracakra* or *Solar Twelvefold Cycle* (also known as *Sthiti-cakra*), which is intricately connected to the principle of knowledge and perception.

The *Dvadasaracakra* integrates various aspects of divine and perceptual reality, combining elements from different cycles:

1. **Anakhya-cakra**: This is a foundational aspect, also referred to as the Non-expressed Triad of Devis (Para, Parapara, Apara) and *Matrsadbhava*. It represents the unmanifest or abstract forms of divine power and essence.
2. **Samharaa-cakra**: This includes the Four Kalas (phases) associated with the Triad of Bhairavas (Para, Parapara, Apara) and *Kulesvara*. These are aspects of divine perception and authority.
3. **Sthiti-cakra**: This cycle combines the expressed and non-expressed forms of the Triad of Devis (Para, Parapara, Apara) and *Matrsadbhava*, signifying the divine's active presence and sustenance within the world.

In the context of *Pramana-varga*, which is concerned with

knowledge and its means, the *Dvadasaracakra* integrates twelve key components. These components are associated with the various ways through which knowledge and perception manifest:

Indriyas: The means of sensory perception and action, divided into twelve categories:

- **Five Jñanendriyas** (organs of cognition): Ears, eyes, nose, tongue, and skin.
- **Five Karmendriyas** (organs of action): Feet, hands, anus, genitals, and mouth.
- **Manas** (mind or imagination).
- **Buddhi** (intellect).

These indriyas are responsible for experiencing and interacting with the world through the senses and actions. In this context, the Sun is symbolically identified with *pramana* (knowledge) because it represents illumination and the source of perceptual clarity. The Sun is considered to possess twelve *kalas*, which are integral to its nature and role in sustaining and expanding knowledge.

The integration of the twelve *kalas* in *Pramana-varga* is as follows:

1. **Four Kalas of Pramiti-varga (Anakhya-cakra)**: These include the Non-expressed forms of the Triad of Devis and *Matrsadbhava*, representing the abstract potential of knowledge.
2. **Four Kalas of Pramatr-varga (Samharaa-cakra)**: These include the Triad of Bhairavas and *Kulesvara*, reflecting the

perceptual and authoritative aspects of knowledge.

3. **Four Kalas of Pramana-varga (Sthiti-cakra)**: These consist of the expressed and non-expressed forms of the Triad of Devis and *Matrsadbhava*, indicating the dynamic and sustaining aspects of knowledge.

By combining these aspects, the total number of twelve *kalas* is achieved, highlighting the comprehensive nature of knowledge and perception within the framework. Thus, the *Sthiti- cakra* or *Dvadasaracakra* represents the Solar Twelvefold Cycle, embodying the essence of knowledge and the means through which it manifests and operates in the world.

Prameya Varga

The concept of *Prameya-varga* or "the Section of the Known" delves into the nature of the objects of knowledge and their manifestation within the cosmic and perceptual framework. This section is symbolized by the *Sodasaracakra* or *Lunar Sixteenfold Cycle* (also known as *Srsti-cakra*), which represents the cycle of creation and the expression of divine forms in the material world.

Structure of Prameya-varga

Components of Sodasaracakra:

- **Andakhya-cakra:** This includes the foundational aspects from the earlier *Anakhya- cakra*, which is the Non-expressed Triad of Devis (Para, Parapara, Apara) and *Matrsadbhava*. It represents the non-manifested or

abstract potential forms.

- **Four Kalas of Samhara-cakra:** These are the components related to the Triad of Bhairavas (Para, Parapara, Apara) and *Kulesvara*, reflecting the perceptual and authoritative aspects of knowledge.
- **Four Kalas of Sthiti-cakra:** These include the expressed and non-expressed forms of the Triad of Devis (Para, Parapara, Apara) and *Matrsadbhava*, indicating the divine's sustaining and active role in the world.
- **Sthiti-cakra:** This cycle represents the expressed forms of the Triad of Devis and *Matrsadbhava*, highlighting the active manifestation of divine forms.

In *Prameya-varga*, the focus is on the objects of knowledge, known as *prameya*. This section encompasses all the sensory experiences and substances perceived through the organs of cognition. The objects of knowledge (*visayas*)—such as sound (*sabda*), touch (*sparsa*), form (*rupa*), taste (*rasa*), and smell (*gandha*)—are integrated into this framework, allowing for the comprehensive experience of the material world.

Lunar Nature and the Concept of Kalas:

The *Prameya-varga* is considered lunar in nature, symbolized by the Moon, which is associated with sixteen *kalas*. This is reflected in the concept of *Sodasaracakra* (the Sixteenfold Cycle), indicating the completeness and fullness of the manifested forms of knowledge.

The sixteen *kalas* in *Prameya-varga* are detailed as follows:

- **Four Kalas from Pramiti-varga (Anakhya-cakra):** These are the Non-expressed forms of the Triad of Devis and *Matrsadbhava*, representing the abstract potential.
- **Four Kalas from Pramatr-varga (Samhara-cakra):** These correspond to the Triad of Bhairavas and *Kulesvara*, reflecting perceptual and authoritative aspects.
- **Four Kalas from Pramana-varga (Sthiti-cakra):** These include the expressed and non-expressed forms of the Triad of Devis and *Matrsadbhava*, signifying the divine's role in sustaining and manifesting knowledge.
- **Four Additional Kalas from the Expressed Forms:** This adds to the total, reflecting the complete manifestation of divine forms and the objects of knowledge.

Thus, the total number of sixteen kalas in Prameya-varga captures the complete range of the known and perceptible aspects of the universe.

The distinction among the *Pramiti-varga* (fourfold cycle), *Pramatr-varga* (eightfold cycle), *Pramana-varga* (twelvefold cycle), and *Prameya-varga* (sixteenfold cycle) relates to their respective roles in the expansion and manifestation of the self-form of the divine, specifically Kali Bhagavati.

- **Pramiti-varga**: Considered the initial stage of the divine's expansion, representing potential without manifest world-form-ness.
- **Pramatr-varga**: Represents the perceiver's engagement with the world, involving the eightfold cycle.

- **Pramana-varga**: The twelvefold cycle signifies a higher stage of world-form-ness where knowledge and perception are more fully integrated.
- **Prameya-varga**: The sixteenfold cycle represents the most complete and detailed expression of the known world, embodying the fullness of manifestation.

The reason the twelvefold cycle (in *Pramana-varga*) is highlighted, despite the sixteenfold cycle (in *Prameya-varga*) being more comprehensive, lies in the specific role each cycle plays. The twelvefold cycle represents a more direct and accessible manifestation of the divine's world-form-ness, making it a pivotal stage in understanding the world and divine interaction. The sixteenfold cycle encompasses this and extends further, providing a more detailed and expansive view of the world.

In essence, while all cycles contribute to the overall understanding of divine manifestation and knowledge, the twelvefold cycle of *Pramana-varga* serves as a critical point in experiencing and integrating the divine presence within the material realm

The process by which a Saiva yogi attains the state of unfolding of the self, characterized by the bhava (state of being) of Para-pramatr, and navigates through the maya (illusion) of differentiated objects and creatures, involves a profound spiritual journey and practice. The Saiva tradition describes this journey in intricate detail, emphasizing the transition from internal realization to external perception. Here is an elaboration of the process and concepts involved:

In the Saiva tradition, the state of the self known as *Para-pramatr* represents the ultimate reality or consciousness that is beyond the dualistic distinctions of perceiver and perceived. Achieving this

state involves transcending ordinary experiences and realizing the fundamental nature of the self. The *samsara-cakra* (cycle of worldly existence) and its corresponding self-forms, such as the twelve Kalis described in texts like the *Kramastotra*, are crucial for this process.

Maya, the illusory force that creates the appearance of duality and differentiation, affects how the world is perceived. Even when a yogi reaches a state of profound internal realization (samadhi), the external world still appears as differentiated and agitated due to the influence of maya. This state of agitation involves the interplay of objects and creatures, presenting a challenge to the yogi who aims to maintain the inner realization of non-differentiation while interacting with the external world.

Samadhi and Vyutthana:

- **Samadhi**: In the state of samadhi, the yogi experiences a deep, unified state of consciousness where the self is fully realized in its pure, undifferentiated form. This state transcends ordinary perceptions and dualities.
- **Vyutthana**: Upon emerging from samadhi and engaging with the external world (vyutthana), the yogi encounters the world in its apparent differentiated state, which seems contrary to the non-differentiated state experienced in samadhi.

The Concept of Vikasa-samadhi:

Acharya Utpaladeva highlights that the ultimate state of realization, where the yogi maintains the experience of non-

differentiation even in the midst of worldly activity, is known as *Vikasa-samadhi*. This state represents a union of deep meditation (samadhi) and active engagement with the world (vyutthana). It is characterized by the ability to experience the self's true nature in all states of consciousness, whether in profound meditation or in everyday activities.

Jagadananda and Nirvyutthana-samadhi:

- **Jagadananda**: This term refers to a state of bliss or joy that surpasses ordinary states of delight, such as *Cidananda* (the bliss of consciousness) and others. Jagadananda is seen as superior because it integrates both the ecstatic union of samadhi and the active, dynamic engagement of vyutthana.
- **Nirvyutthana-samadhi**: The state of Nirvyutthana-samadhi is described by the ancient sages as the highest realization where the yogi achieves a seamless experience of the divine and self, regardless of external conditions. In this state, the yogi does not lose the self-awareness of Para-pramatr even when interacting with the differentiated world. It represents a state of perfect integration where the yogi transcends the illusions of duality while remaining active in the world.

The *Para-pramatr* state is marked by the realization that the perceived differentiation of objects and experiences is an illusion created by maya. The yogi, adorned with *Parabhakti* (supreme

devotion), can overcome this illusion not through mere intellectual or meditative practices but through the deep, transformative realization that integrates both the highest meditative state and the active engagement with the world. This realization is said to break through the "mountain" of differentiation, revealing the underlying unity of all existence.

In essence, a Saiva yogi attains the state of unfolding of the self of the nature of Para-pramatr by deeply engaging in practices that reveal the non-differentiated nature of reality. Through *Vikasa-samadhi* and ultimately *Nirvyutthana-samadhi*, the yogi transcends the illusions of maya and integrates profound meditative experiences with active worldly engagement. The realization of this state is marked by the ability to see the divine presence in both internal contemplation and external interactions, achieving a harmonious balance between the two.

The state described is one where the self is unbounded and fully manifest, revealing its divine essence without any limitations. In this state, the miracle of the self is perceptible everywhere, creating an experience that is immersed in the *Ananda-rasa* (the blissful essence) of *Para-Ananda* (Complete Bliss). This state is marked by its completeness and unity, where traditional spiritual practices such as *dhyana* (meditation), *dharana* (concentration), and *samadhi* (profound meditation) are no longer necessary. It is characterized by an inherent, spontaneous realization of the divine and the self, without the need for deliberate effort or techniques.

This profound state is referred to as *Jagadananda*, a term bestowed by Gurudeva Sri Sambhunatha. Achieving this state requires not only a deep self-experience but also the grace of a

Guru. The guidance and blessings of the Guru are essential for reaching this level of spiritual realization. Thus, maintaining sincere adoration and devotion towards the Guru is crucial for experiencing and understanding this exalted state.

Kali and Her Twelve Expansions

According to the established understanding, the Para-pramatr-rupa Samvid Devi, who represents the supreme consciousness, expands her self-form across various cakras within the Prameya, Pramana, and Pramatr sections. Specifically, she takes shelter in the **Srsti, Sthiti, Samhara**, and **Anakhya** cakras. By multiplying these three sections (Prameya, Pramana, and Pramatr) with the four cakras, a total of twelve distinct states are obtained. This multiplication reflects the integration of these cakras into the broader framework of the divine manifestation:

Varga	Srsti-dasa	Sthiti-dasa	Samhara-dasa	Anakhya-dasa
Prameya-varga	1. Srstikali	2. Raktakali	3. Sthitinasakali	4. Yamakali
Pramana-varga	5. Samharakali	6. Mrtyukali	7. Bhadrakali	8. Martandakali
Pramatr-varga	9. Paramarkakali	10. Kalagnirudrakali	11. Mahakalakali	12. Mahabhairav-aghoracandakali

1. **Srsti-dasa (Creation state)**
2. **Sthiti-dasa (Preservation state)**
3. **Samhara-dasa (Destruction state)**
4. **Anakhya-dasa (Transcendental state)**

Thus, in each section, the Devi's self-form is realized in these twelve states, representing a comprehensive view of divine presence and action across different phases of existence

Although the supreme consciousness, Maha Para, pervades all activities such as creation, preservation, and dissolution, worldly beings often remain unaware of these divine processes due to ignorance. As a result, they miss the profound experience of the bliss (dnanda) inherent in these states of divine self-form. To become aware of and elevated in these states, one must understand and integrate the principles governing these cosmic processes.

For a person to truly experience the gain of self-form and stay elevated in these divine states, they must transcend ordinary awareness and recognize the twelve forms of Para-sthiti. This realization is essential for anyone who aspires to be considered a true yogi. Without this understanding, even those who practice yoga diligently may not fully grasp the essence of these states.

Conversely, someone who comprehends these twelve states precisely can become a master of their own world. By reflecting on the **Srsti** (creation), **Sthiti** (preservation), **Samhara** (destruction), and **Anakhya** (transcendence) cakras, such a yogi perceives the radiant form of light that is equivalent to Shiva. This profound realization allows the yogi to fully understand their own self-form, distinguishing themselves from others who may not reach this depth of understanding.

Human effort alone is insufficient to attain this elevated state; it is trivial compared to the divine intervention required. The intense grace (Tivra saktipata) of Paramesvara (Supreme Lord) and the blessings of the Guru are crucial for experiencing and comprehending this

state. The Guru's grace facilitates the realization of the self-form and enables the yogi to achieve the ultimate state of consciousness.

In subsequent sections, the descriptions of the twelve Kalis will be provided, starting with those related to the prameya pada (known) and concluding with those pertaining to the pramatr pada (knower).

Additionally, before delving into the specifics of the twelve Kalis, it is important to understand why the Advaitavada of Trikasastra is referred to as the **Antararthavada** (doctrine of inner meaning). This term signifies that, according to the Trika philosophy, what appears as external substances in the world is, in reality, an assembly of substances that reflects the inner essence of *Svātma-samvid* (self-awareness). Therefore, for the Saiva yogi, the experience of external phenomena such as sound (sabda) is actually an expansion of internal *Samvit-sakti* (divine energy). This internal expansion aligns with the Advaitavada's emphasis on the inner meaning and essence of reality.

First Expansion

The first expansion of Paramesvari Samviddevi, or the supreme consciousness, occurs in the **Srsti dasa** of the **Prameya pada**. This phase is critical for understanding the nature of perception and its divine implications. To clarify, when an individual begins to perceive any object through the senses—such as sound, touch, form, taste, and smell—the initial experience of the object is in its pure, undifferentiated form. This initial perception is known as **nirvikalpa**, which means without distinction or conceptualization.

In simpler terms, when an object is first encountered, it appears

in a state of pure, formless awareness, devoid of specific attributes like name and form. This state of **nirvikalpa samvid** represents the primordial and purest level of observation. It is the experience where the intellect (pramatr) first engages with the object without any added conceptualization or differentiation. At this stage, there is no "I see" or "I eat"—the perception is simply an undivided awareness of the object.

This **nirvikalpa** state is essentially the initial phase of what the ancient sages describe as the commencement of observation. Here, the aspects of the object and the senses involved in perception are not yet distinct; they are merely part of an undifferentiated awareness. This pure awareness is referred to as **Kaalsankarsini Devi** by the sages, highlighting its role as the primordial consciousness that precedes differentiation.

Kalacakra (the cycle of time) integrates into this state, and the **Kaalsankarsini Devi** embodies the essence of this initial observation. The yogi who deeply contemplates and investigates this state of commencement of observation experiences the divine essence of **Para Bhagavati**—the ultimate meaning and consciousness. In this first wave of perception, the Devi represents the primal vibration or **Spanda**, a dynamic force that combines both **unmesa** (emergence) and **nimesa** (dissolution), signifying the continuous flow of divine consciousness.

This primordial form of **Kaalsankarsini** is revered and reflected upon, as it represents the entrance into a higher state of consciousness. It embodies the initial undivided experience of reality, before it becomes segmented into distinct perceptions.

The **Srsti dasa** within the **Prameya pada** thus concludes with

an understanding of this divine initial observation. It sets the stage for the subsequent expansions and deeper realizations of the divine presence and consciousness that permeate all levels of existence.

Second Expansion

In the second expansion of **Para Bhagavati**, attention shifts to the **Prameya pada** in the **Sthiti dasa**. After the emergence of **Srstikali Devi**, the supreme consciousness (Para Samvid) begins to turn its focus towards the external world of objects, such as pot, garment, and other substances. This transition signifies a shift from the initial pure perception to a more engaged interaction with the world.

As **Kali Devi** manifests in the **Sthiti dasa** within the **Prameya** section, she engages with the substances through the senses. This is marked by an affectionate delight towards these substances, described as **Raga** or **Rakti**. This affection represents a deeper enjoyment of the sensory experiences associated with the substances. The divine consciousness (Samvid) experiences this delight in a state of **nirvikalpa bhava**—a state beyond conceptual differentiation, where the essence of the objects and the perceiving consciousness merge seamlessly.

In this state, the divine essence of Kali Devi, filled with the experience of substance and delight, becomes manifest. She embodies the **Vikasa dasa**, a state of unfolding or expansion, where every substance is perceived as an expression of divine bliss. This state is likened to being filled with an elixir or divine wine, symbolizing the profound satisfaction and intoxication derived from the experience of divine presence.

This second expansion is known as **Raktakali** in the esoteric texts **"matrcakra"** refers to the assembly of **Karanesvari**, which relates to the senses and their divine aspects. The term **"virendraka"** suggests the highest yogis, who, imbued with the divine bliss of **suddhavidya** (pure knowledge), are absorbed in the divine play of the **Karanesvari**. These yogis experience profound states of bliss and spiritual delight as they connect with the divine feminine principles. The highest yogis here refer to the subjective state of Mantra Pramatr.

This indicates that the highest yogis, in their state of profound pleasure and divine experience, come into contact with the **Mahasiddha-yogini** (great perfected beings) and experience a divine union. During this time, **Para Samvid** is ready for the **Maha-Lila** (great divine play) in the assembly of Siddhas and Yoginis. This divine play involves activities like **havana** (ritual offerings) and **japa** (recitation of mantras), which are performed by **Bhagavati** herself, radiating in the assembly.

Moreover, **Raktakali Bhagavati** is lauded as embodying the essence of dissolution and appearance in the world. This form of Kali Devi represents the divine essence in a state of **nirvikalpa bhava**, continuing to manifest as the world itself.

Thus, the second expansion of **Para Bhagavati** in the **Sthiti dasa** within the **Prameya pada** reflects a deeper engagement with the external world and its sensory experiences, revealing the divine delight and consciousness inherent in every aspect of reality.

Third Expansion

The third expansion of **Para Bhagavati** concerns the **Samhara dasa** within the **Prameya** context. This phase is characterized by the divine activity of **Sthitinasakali** in the realm of **Prameya**.

When the **Sthitinasakali** form arises, it signifies the culmination of the experience and enjoyment of various substances, wherein the divine essence engages deeply with these experiences. This stage follows the complete satiation of the **Raktakali** aspect, where the sensory activities reach their zenith, and the divine presence embodies the final phase of absorption and dissolution.

Para-pramatr Samvit—the supreme consciousness in the state of perceiving—realizes the essence of substances, expressed as: "I have understood this substance." This understanding comes after a thorough engagement with the external world, transitioning from an active experience of objects to a state of internal reflection and integration.

In this state, **Sthitinasakali** represents the divine consciousness's immersion in the inward aspects of perception and reality. The **Karanesvari** goddesses, having exhausted their activities related to sensory enjoyment, merge with the consciousness of **Bhairava Natha**. They embody the level of interiority, reflecting a state where the senses, having fulfilled their purpose, rest in a contemplative embrace with the divine essence. This signifies a state devoid of desire, where the senses and consciousness align in a serene and unified form.

The **Sthitinasakali** form symbolizes a state where the indriyas

(senses) and prameya (objects) are united within the knower (pramatr) in a tranquil and void state of **nirvikalpa**—a state of pure, undifferentiated consciousness. This state is characterized by a profound calm, representing the end of agitation and the dissolution of distinctions between prameya (the known) and pramadi (the knower).

Sthitinasakali is likened to a void or the essence of stillness, where the agitation of **pramana** (knowledge) and **prameya** (objects) is transcended. This state is akin to the quietude found in the cosmic breath, where the processes of **prana** and **apana** (inhaling and exhaling) align in harmony. Here, the divine essence is represented by **Sivardatri** (the Night of Siva), embodying the ultimate stillness and radiant bliss.

In summary, the third expansion of **Para Bhagavati** in the **Samhara dasa** reveals the profound state of stillness and unity achieved after the completion of sensory engagement.

Fourth Expansion

The divine form **Sthitinasakali** encapsulates this state of serene void, merging all sensory activities and consciousness into a unified, blissful state. This expansion reflects the divine victory and the ultimate realization of the self in its pure, unmanifest form

In the context of the **Rakta kali** and **Sthitinasakali** expansion, it is important to distinguish between the two related concepts of **Karanesvari goddesses** and **indriyas** (senses), as they function differently in the process of perception and consciousness.

1. Karanesvari Goddesses:

- These are the **divine embodiments** of the senses when they are oriented towards **interiority**. In this state, the senses are not just functional organs but are seen as divine manifestations that embody deeper spiritual principles.
- **Karanesvari** goddesses represent the **sublime aspect** of the senses, emphasizing their role in internal, contemplative, or meditative processes. They are connected to the **inward focus** of consciousness, reflecting an elevated state of perception and awareness.
- These goddesses are associated with the **face of interiority**, where sensory activities are aligned with deeper spiritual insights and integration within the self.

2. Indriyas:

- The term **indriyas** refers to the senses in their more **ordinary, external** roles. They are the faculties through which sensory experiences are perceived and interacted with in the material world.
- These senses are primarily engaged with **external objects** and phenomena, functioning within the realm of ordinary perception and action.

The distinction lies in the orientation and state of the senses:

- **Karanesvari goddesses** embody the **internal** and **sublime** aspect of sensory faculties, emphasizing their spiritual and contemplative dimensions.
- **Indriyas**, on the other hand, are concerned with **external** perception and interaction with the physical world.

In summary, while both terms refer to the senses, **Karanesvari goddesses** highlight their divine and internal dimensions, whereas **indriyas** denote their functional and external aspects. This distinction reflects the different roles the senses play in spiritual and everyday contexts

The term **Dvadasanta**, which translates to "the end of twelve," refers to a specific concept in the context of breath control and spatial awareness within certain spiritual and yogic traditions. It denotes two distinct but related points of focus:

1. Internal Dvadasanta:

- **Location**: This is situated inside the body, specifically **twelve finger-breaths** away from the tip of the nose, which corresponds to a point near the **heart center**.
- **Function**: It is the point within the body where the **inhalation** phase of breathing transitions into the **exhalation** phase. This internal dvadasanta represents the boundary or turning point in the breath cycle within the body, marking the area where breath changes direction during inhalation.

2. External Dvadasanta:

- **Location**: This point is found in the outer space, **twelve finger-breaths** away from the tip of the nose, located near the **sternum**.
- **Function**: It is the external boundary where the **exhalation** phase of breathing transitions back into **inhalation**. This external dvadasanta represents the outer limit of breath

movement, signifying the turning point in the breath cycle outside the body.

Dvadasanta:
- **Internal Dvadasanta**: Located inside the body, near the heart center, marking the turning point of inhalation to exhalation.
- **External Dvadasanta**: Located outside the body, near the sternum, marking the turning point of exhalation to inhalation.

Understanding and focusing on these points can be integral in practices like pranayama (breath control), meditation, and certain yogic exercises, where awareness of breath transitions and spatial boundaries is essential for achieving deeper states of consciousness and control over the breath

In the described expansion, the focus is on the **Anakhya dasa** within the **prameya pada**. This expansion is characterized by the following aspects:

Anakhya Dasa:

1. Dual Aspects of Anakhya Dasa:
- **Face of Exteriority**: This represents the covering up or obscuring of self- form-ness.
- **Face of Interiority**: This involves the visibility or revelation of self-form- ness.

These aspects can only be experienced by a Saiva-yogi who has advanced in their practice.

2. Experience of Sthitinasakali:
- After experiencing the Sthitinasakali state, where opposites such as prana and apana or pramana and prameya are resolved within Para-citi (the supreme consciousness), the yogi enters into the Anakhya dasa.
- If the yogi becomes lax in their self-reflection at this stage, they risk entering into **Mahāmaya**, a state characterized by the covering of self-form, rather than remaining in the true Anakhya dasa.

3. Two Potential States:
- **Mahāmaya**: When the yogi becomes nonplussed and immersed in doubts, moving towards the face of exteriority.
- **Cidakasa**: If the prana and apana (symbolized as Sun and Moon) or pramana and prameya dissolve into the Cidakasa (the sky of consciousness), then the uninformed yogi may fall into a state resembling sleep, which is characterized by Mahāmaya.

4. Role of Self-Reflection:
- The potential for falling back into Mahāmaya highlights the importance of self-reflection. The yogi must remain vigilant and focused on the self to avoid this lapse.

5. Yamakali:
- **Mahāgrāsa and Mahāvilāsa**: Yamakali is described as embodying both Mahāgrāsa (Great Devouring) and

Mahāvilāsa (Great Sport). In this state, vikalpa (conceptual differentiation) is managed through mutual reasoning of forms and substances, holding together limited form-ness, and expanding the limited pramata (knower).

Yamakali helps in subduing the world and is celebrated for her role in the transformation and expansion of the pramata's experience.

Yamakali's Dual Actions: Through her unbounded svātantrya (autonomy), the Para Devi assimilates the world's mandala in the form of Yama (conceptual differentiation) and, simultaneously, engages in Mahāvilāsa, expanding the limited form-ness.

The description of the four Kālīs—**Sṛṣṭikālī**, **Raktakālī**, **Sthitinasakālī**, and **Yamakālī**— within their respective stages (Sṛṣṭi, Sthiti, Samhāra, and Andākhyā) in the prameya context concludes in this fourth expansion. Each Kālī represents a different facet of the cosmic functions and states of consciousness, emphasizing the depth of experience and practice required for a Saiva-yogi to attain mastery over these profound states.

Fifth Expansion

In this fifth expansion, the focus shifts to the Srsti Dasa within the Pramana Pada. The Srsti Dasa within the Pramana Pada involves the stage where the yogi, after experiencing the Anakhya Dasa related to the prameya, engages deeply with the nature of both concealment and revelation of self-form. With the help of the Guru's grace, the yogi overcomes the illusion or the covering (concealment) that obscures the true nature of self-form. This process is akin to

dissolving the external appearance of self-forms through a profound internal realization.

Initially, the yogi deals with the external layer of perception, which hides the true essence of self-form. This is the state where worldly existence and its coverings obscure the true nature of self-form. With the Guru's guidance, the yogi transcends this concealment and merges into the Srsti Dasa, which is a stage where the true nature of self-form is revealed without external distractions. This stage is characterized by a direct and effortless realization of the true self.

In this advanced state, the yogi experiences nirvikalpa bhava—a state of non-differentiated awareness—where distinctions between self and object dissolve. The svayama-samvitti (intellect of the self) provides the yogi with a deep understanding of the true nature of self, revealing a state of unmana (transcendental awareness).

The process described involves the slaying of bhava, which means the dissolution of all illusory forms and differentiations that pertain to self and objects. This leads to a state where the yogi experiences pure being without the distortions of external appearances.

The state of slaying bhava is poetically described in the Kramastotra as a state where all distinctions, like those between pot and garment, dissolve into a singular, pure awareness. This state is praised as Sri Samharakali in various secret scriptures. Samharakali represents the goddess who embodies the power of dissolution and is characterized by the ability to eliminate all forms of differentiation and illusion.

The goddess Samharakali is seen as a divine force that maintains the equilibrium by dissolving the multiplicity of forms into a singular essence. Her nature is one of profound purity and clarity,

where all forms and distinctions are resolved into unity. The yogi, upon reaching this state, experiences a blissful awareness free from the limitations imposed by duality and differentiation. This bliss is akin to the clear sky where clouds dissolve, leaving only the vast expanse of clarity.

The fifth expansion under Pramana Pada describes the process where the yogi, through the grace of the Guru and the realization of their own self-form, enters a state of pure awareness and dissolution of all illusory forms. This stage, known as Sri Samharakali, represents a pinnacle of spiritual experience where the limitations of self-form and external appearances are transcended, leading to an exalted state of unity and bliss.

Sixth Expansion

In the sixth expansion, we explore the concept of Sthiti-Cakra within the Pramana-Dasa, focusing on how the goddess Mrtyukali operates within this stage. After the destruction of the prameya (the known object) by Samharakali, which represents the power of dissolution, there remains an underlying attribute called samskara (mental impression). This samskara continues to exist even after the apparent dissolution of the prameya.

In this stage, the goddess Samharakali, who embodies the power of destruction, reflects upon herself and experiences the essence of non-differentiation. This self-reflection reveals that even the residual samskara, which is an imprint or residue left behind, must also be dissolved. As a result, the goddess Mrtyukali arises as the sixth expansion. Mrtyukali is known for her ability to consume or

absorb death (mrtyu) and dissolution (samhara), thus representing a further stage of transcending previous limitations.

The essence of Mrtyukali is her ability to consume even the remaining subtle residues of differentiation and samskara, leading to a state where the previously mentioned Samharakali is also transcended. This process involves ingesting and eliminating the final remnants of individuality and differentiation, resulting in a state of pure non-dual awareness.

In this stage, the yogi experiences a form of awareness where even the subtleties of self- identity and distinctions are removed. The goddess Mrtyukali, through her supreme power, consumes and integrates these final remnants, thus embodying the ultimate state of dissolution and unity.

This state of Mrtyukali is characterized by a profound realization of unity beyond any remaining forms of differentiation. The key aspect of this stage is the complete absorption of all previous forms and distinctions into the divine essence, leading to a state of pure, undifferentiated consciousness.

The process involves not just the physical or apparent forms but extends to the very subtle impressions left by previous experiences. The goddess Mrtyukali represents the culmination of this process, where all forms and differentiations are fully absorbed and transcended.

In this exalted state, the yogi achieves a level of awareness that is free from all previous limitations and distinctions. This includes the subtle mental impressions and residues that persisted even after the destruction of the physical forms. The yogi, upon reaching this stage, experiences an intense and perpetual state of craving or desire,

symbolizing the endless pursuit of the ultimate reality. Even when physically satisfied, the yogi remains spiritually hungry, reflecting a deep and continuous quest for the realization of the self.

This description highlights the final stage of the Pramana-Dasa, where the goddess Mrtyukali embodies the ultimate state of dissolution and unity, transcending all forms and residues. This state represents the culmination of the yogi's journey through various stages of realization, leading to a profound understanding of the true nature of consciousness and existence.

Seventh Expansion

In the seventh expansion, the focus is on the state of Parapramatr-ripa Cinmahesvari, or Bhadrakali, within the Pramana-Dasa. This stage follows the dissolution of prameya (the known) by Samharakali. Even after this dissolution, there remains an underlying attribute, samskara, which is a residual mental impression or tendency. This samskara can cause existential doubts about the nature of existence, leading to a tendency to return to the cycle of samsara (worldly existence).

Despite the initial dissolution, the divine principle of Parapramatr-Samvit has the inherent power to reawaken these doubts. However, in this state of Bhadrakali, the doubts arising from samskara are both immediately and effortlessly resolved. Bhadrakali embodies the fusion of differentiations and the subsequent integration of these forms back into the self.

The name Bhadrakali derives from "bhad" meaning "to split" or "to differentiate" and "dra" meaning "to fuse" or "to unite."

This reflects Bhadrakali's role in managing the dual aspects of differentiation and integration. She is characterized by her ability to simultaneously reveal and resolve the doubts and differentiations, integrating them into the self without the yogi needing to exert effort.

In this state, Bhadrakali's influence allows the yogi to experience doubts and their resolution in a simultaneous manner. This means that the doubts that arise about what should and should not be done are resolved effortlessly. Unlike the previous stages where the yogi needed to actively manage doubts and differentiate between various states, Bhadrakali's presence ensures that these doubts are resolved naturally and instantaneously.

This expansion of Bhadrakali represents a state where the yogi, under her influence, experiences both the emergence and dissolution of doubts as part of a seamless process. The yogi is absorbed in this state of Bhadrakali, experiencing the rise and immediate resolution of doubts with ease.

Bhadrakali's role highlights the transition from a state of active effort in resolving doubts to a state where doubts are naturally and effortlessly dissolved. This represents a significant shift in the yogi's experience, moving towards a more profound realization of the self and the nature of existence.

The state of Bhadrakali also illustrates the removal of obstacles and doubts that previously bound the yogi. These doubts, according to the teachings, are akin to impurities or barriers that restrict spiritual progress. By embodying Bhadrakali, the yogi transcends these barriers, achieving a state of purity and unity.

The seventh expansion through Bhadrakali describes a

transformative state where existential doubts are resolved effortlessly, reflecting a significant advancement in spiritual realization. The yogi, under the influence of Bhadrakali, moves beyond previous limitations, experiencing a direct and natural dissolution of doubts and differentiations, leading to a deeper understanding of the self and existence.

Eighth Expansion

In this eighth expansion, we delve into the state of Paramesvari Devi as she manifests in the Pramana-Dasa, specifically focusing on the Anakhya dasa.

Even after the dissolution of prameya (the known) described in the seventh expansion, the twelve indriyas—comprising the five sensory organs (jnanendriyas), the five action organs (karmendriyas), the mind (mana), and intellect (buddhi)—remain subtly present. These indriyas are crucial as they are seen as solar in nature, akin to the twelve Suns, and they continue to exist in a latent form.

In this expansion, Paramesvari Devi, embodying the supreme consciousness, uses her inherent power (svatantrya) to assimilate these twelve indriyas into their place of origin, which is the ahamkara (the ego or sense of self). This process transforms the indriyas into their true form within the level of ahamkara. This state of assimilation and transformation is known as Martandakali.

Martandakali, derived from "Martanda" meaning "Sun" and "kali" referring to the goddess, signifies the state where these solar aspects, or the indriyas, are absorbed and ultimately dissolved into their source, which is the ego. The process is akin to an insect (patanga)

flying into a flame, willingly giving up its life as it is consumed. This imagery reflects the intense and complete dissolution of the indriyas and their impressions.

When a yogi reaches this Anakhya dasa, they encounter Martandakali's influence, which illuminates and ultimately absorbs all indriyas and their associated impressions. The indriyas, along with their past experiences and tendencies, are brought into the self-form of the goddess and lose their separate existence. This process ensures that the indriyas cease to function independently, merging into the divine consciousness.

In essence, Martandakali's role is to eradicate the subtle remnants of the indriyas and their samskaras (mental impressions) that persist despite the previous dissolution. Her presence allows for the complete integration of these elements, ensuring that they are assimilated into the higher self.

This state represents a profound realization where the yogi experiences the indriyas' dissolution and the complete absorption of their tendencies into the divine essence. This process highlights the transition from the subtle forms of existence to a state of unified consciousness.

Thus, the eighth expansion describes the culmination of the dissolution process, where Martandakali, through her divine grace, ensures that all remnants of the indriyas are fully absorbed and transformed within the self. This marks a significant step towards the realization of the ultimate state of consciousness and unity.

Ninth Expansion

In this ninth expansion, we explore the state of Parapramatr-rupa Samvidisvari within the srsti-cakra under the pramatr. This

expansion describes a pivotal phase in the dissolution process where the four Kalis, skilled in tasting the pramatr, play a crucial role.

Previously, in the eighth expansion, the Solar assembly, represented by the twelve indriyas, was completely dissolved into the Paramdditya named ahamkara. This dissolution marked the absorption of these indriyas into their source. However, the thirteenth Paramdditya, which represents the ahamkara itself, also needs to be dissolved in its turn. This state of dissolution is characterized by the presence of a blazing limited pramatr, known as Bhagavati Paramarkakali.

This state of pramatr is distinct from ordinary limited pramatr as it operates under a different intensity and quality. In ordinary terms, limited pramatr is detached from the objects of perception (visaya) and the attributes (upadhi) of the indriyas. However, in this expanded state, a remnant of the visaya and the upadhi remains, though the light of pramatr is present in its purest, undifferentiated form.

Acarya Abhinavagupta refers to this specific limited pramatr as Kalagnirudra, highlighting its role in both creating and destroying the worldly realm. Kalagnirudra is described as a fiery entity, embodying both the differentiation and limitation inherent in time (past, present, future). This entity causes the creation and dissolution of the worldly realm through processes of impedance (rodhana) and assimilation (drdvana), thus earning the designation of Rudra.

In the Kramastotra, this state is described as Paramarkakali. The Paramarkakali is characterized by a state of tranquil radiance where the twelve indriyas, each representing a different aspect of perception and action, are absorbed into her self-form. Here, the supreme radiance of Paramdditya, which is the crest of all radiance, is also

dissolved and assimilated into the infinite light of Paramarkakali.

This dissolution process is crucial because it represents the complete integration of the differentiated aspects of consciousness (represented by the indriyas and ahamkara) back into the undivided, supreme consciousness. The state of Paramarkakali signifies the culmination of this assimilation process, where the pramatr's light becomes pure and undifferentiated, embodying the ultimate state of unity.

This ninth expansion concludes the description of the srsti dasa under pramatr. It describes the final integration of the indriyas and ahamkara into the supreme radiance of Paramarkakali, highlighting the transition from a state of differentiation and limitation to one of pure, undivided consciousness.

Tenth expansion

In the tenth expansion of Jagadisvari, we explore the sthiti dasa, or state of preservation, under the pramatr. This stage reveals how the limited pramatr, known as Kalagnirudra, transitions into a higher state of consciousness.

Kalagnirudra, having previously assimilated the twelve indriyas and the Paramdditya named ahamkara, now begins to transcend its own limitations. This pramatr, through its inherent power, starts merging with the nature of ahamtd, the sense of "I-ness," beyond its own limitations. As Kalagnirudra, adorned with the unity of the differentiated world and boundless expansion, dissolves into the Parapramatr, it becomes one with Mahakali, the embodiment of complete and unending awareness.

This state of integration is recognized as the revered realm of Jagadamba Kalika Bhagavati. It represents the culmination of the dissolution process, where Kalagnirudra's limited form is absorbed into the infinite Parapramatr, symbolizing the ultimate state of consciousness.

The revered nature of this state is highlighted in a verse that praises Jagadamba Kalika Bhagavati for her boundless willpower, which enables the creation of the universe from the highest deity to the smallest insect. This power signifies that attaining this state allows the yogi to engage in the five primary actions (pancakrtya) of creation, preservation, dissolution, blessing, and concealment, similar to how Paramasiva inherently performs these acts.

The name Kalagnirudrakali reflects the essence of this state. It denotes how the limited pramatr, Kalagnirudra, merges into the higher Parapramatr, embodying the ultimate form of consciousness. The transformation is depicted in the Kramastotra, which describes how Kalagnirudra, with its fiery essence, annihilates the pramatr mandala consisting of the twelve indriyas, representing the five functions of Kala (creation, preservation, dissolution, blessing, and concealment). By assimilating this mandala into its own blazing radiance, Kalagnirudra dissolves into the supreme form of Parapramatr, known as Kalagnirudrakali. This process signifies the final dissolution of the individual pramatr into the supreme consciousness.

Thus, the tenth expansion concludes with the description of the sthiti dasa under pramatr, showcasing how the state of preservation culminates in the ultimate unity with the supreme radiance, embodying the highest form of consciousness.

Eleventh expansion

In this expansion, the self-form of Parakali Devi in the samhara-cakra of pramatr pada is discussed.

In the tenth expansion, the Parapramatr-rupa svatma-samvitti is depicted as radiant and imbued with the miracle of Pairndhamta. In this state, the yogi experiences the Alamgrdasa (total devouring) of Bhairava. The entire section of bhava is pacified, resulting in the svatma- samvitti becoming full and visible. However, Mahakali, even in this elevated Parapramatr state, remains inclined toward entering the realm of Akula. Consequently, this leads to the eleventh expansion.

In this eleventh expansion, the yogi transcends Ad/a and its acts of impelling to reach the abode of Samana, becoming Akalakalita forever. In the Samana dasa, time loses its distinct existence, meaning that an infinite duration of time feels like an instant to the yogi. Acarya Utpaladeva captures this state in his verse, which describes a state beyond the regular perception of time—neither eternal nor transient.

The Kramastotra further elaborates this state:
During the great night of void, where the differentiation of light dissolves, the five Mahabhutas (elements) and various pramatr states (deha, prana, puryastaka, and sañyapramatr) are consumed. In this cremation ground (smashana), represented by the heart filled with light, the Cinmahesvari Devi, along with Khecari energies, ingests even Mahakala, signifying her immense power. She is thus named Mahakadalakali, embodying the infinite greatness and consuming

all with her boundless energy.

This eleventh expansion concludes with the depiction of Parabhagavati, situated in the samhdra-cakra of pramatr, through the compassion of the mother of the world.

Twelfth expansion

In the final expansion of Kali Devi, endowed with the miracle of citta, the highest state of the Anakhya-cakra within the pramatr-varga is described.

In this state, the Parapramatr Kali Devi, having reached the Anakhya residence, fully blossoms and reaches its ultimate form of expansion. The miracle of Parapramatr, abundant in this state, generates the previously mentioned states and absorbs them within her self-form, serving as their ultimate shelter. The devis presiding over the cakra-mandala in the states of pramatr, pramàna, prameya, and their creation rise and set here. When these states rise, this Paradevi is known as Parapramatripa, and when they are absorbed within her, she is known as Aysrapa, the accomplisher of the difficult.

In this Anakhya-cakra state, only Kalasankarsini kala remains. This state has been described as a place where the twelve forms of samvitti are unified into one, transcending any mention of krama (order) or akrama (simultaneity).

The name Mahabhairavaghoracandakaii for this Kalika Devi reflects her full manifestation in the cakras related to pramatr, pramàna, and prameya. She both brings about their dissolution and their manifestation within her self-form. This Mahabhairavaghoracandakali, endowed with all characteristics, is

lauded for her role. I dissolve the deha-prana-puryastaka and the stinya of pramatr pada within her self-form and enter into her blissful and rasa-filled self- form beyond limitations.

This concludes the brief description of the twelve Kalis, through the boundless compassion of Samvit Devi.

Decoding Some Basic Mantras

Aum

The journey to understanding one's core essence, which is inherently unified and indivisible, reaches its peak by moving through the diverse expressions of energy. This process is guided by kriya-shakti, the force of realization, which evolves through multiple stages until it fully matures, symbolized by the phoneme 'āu'. This phoneme represents the culmination of realizing one's true nature, signifying a state where all distinctions dissolve into a single, unified essence.

The phoneme 'āu' captures the essence of complete realization and embodies a deep awareness of both the undifferentiated, empty consciousness and the diverse manifestations of the material world. It stands as the pinnacle of recognition and understanding, often referred to as the trident of power. Within this framework, knowledge is conceptualized as kriya-shakti, which integrates the forces of will (iccha-shakti) and knowledge (jnana-shakti). As iccha-shakti matures into jnana-shakti, it further evolves into kriya-shakti, illustrating that kriya-shakti encompasses both the will and knowledge aspects.

In this context, the phonemes 'i' and 'u', having reached their full evolution and merged into the essence of anuttara, transcend their individual variations and come together in the state represented by 'ṃ'. This bindu denotes a fundamental, non-conceptual understanding of reality as pure consciousness. When the primal

consciousness (Shiva) is illuminated by the recognition of its unity with dynamic awareness (Shakti), this unity manifests as Mahabindu. This represents a stage where internal expressions are absorbed into anuttara, symbolizing a comprehensive, undivided knowledge of the universe.

At this stage, the expression of anuttara-chit, which had previously been manifested through various phonemes up to 'āu', achieves a state where all these manifestations converge and dissolve into a single essence. This essence, denoted by 'ṃ', represents the fundamental reality in its aspect of knowledge, distinct from its initial stage of self-manifestation. The bindu 'ṃ' stands as the most potent self-expression of anuttara-chit, setting the stage for further emanations on a new level.

'hūṃ'

The concept of para-vak, represented by the phoneme 'ha', involves recognizing its indivisible nature across all manifestations. As it integrates with various aspects such as air, touch, and other sensory experiences, denoted by the phonemes 'u', 'ḷ', 'ṛ', 'i', and 'a', it ultimately settles into a state of non-discrimination symbolized by the bindu 'ṃ'. This bindu represents the pure consciousness that underlies the nature of reality.

In the context of Shaivism, the restoration of the great seed of Para Bhairava —an archetype that represents supreme subjectivity,is achieved through this process. Initially, the phoneme 'ha' emerges from the visarga-kalā, or the abundant stage symbolized by 'ḥ' (':'), which unfolds into the phoneme 'ha'. This stage represents the

external manifestation of consciousness, associated with the Shiva-Shakti tattva, and relates to the ultimate principle of para-vach.

The experience of this state of consciousness is beyond temporal and spatial limitations and is described as the existential affirmation, "I am." Attaining the state of 'ha' leads to the manifestation of a multitude of categories, denoted by 'k'-phonemes and others. This second stage is characterized by a sense of self-sufficiency and pleasure, reflecting a dynamic, creative consciousness that embodies undividedness. Within the realm of division, para-vach manifests as Prakriti, which balances all gunas (elements), and its dynamic nature unfolds into various sensory principles, such as touch and the air element, as well as the associated organs of action.

The phoneme 'ū' signifies jnana-shakti, or the power of knowledge. In this context, 'ū' represents the aspect of the Shiva-Shakti-tattva expressed through the phoneme 'ha', acting as a principle of negation. Here, Shakti negates the objective aspects of experience within Shiva, leading to a state of emptiness where only the subjective experience of undivided oneness remains.

At the stage denoted by the bindu 'ṃ', there is a dissolution of internal manifestations into anuttara, representing the unified knowledge of the cosmos. At this point, anuttara-chit, having expressed itself through various phonemes up to 'āu', achieves a state where all these expressions dissolve back into the primordial 'a'. This final state, marked by the bindu 'ṃ', reflects a profound unity and essence of reality in its aspect of knowledge. The bindu 'ṃ' symbolizes the most potent self-expression of anuttara-chit,

signifying a higher level of understanding and integration of reality's essence.

hrīṃ

This profound syllable representing the immense power of Para-Samvid is known as Raudri- bija or Mahamaya-bija or Shakti-bija. This specific bija, or seed sound, is integral to Shakti, the dynamic force that governs all occurrences within the universe. Therefore, no significant magical practice can be performed without it. To elucidate the meaning of 'hrīṃ', we must examine how the Matrikas interpret it.

In this context, 'hrīṃ' can be understood through the concept of vyoma, the primordial consciousness of the Supreme Reality, which is boundless and infinite. This expansive consciousness realizes its own freedom and limitless nature through an external manifestation, denoted as 'h'. This process is rooted in the principle of limitation and finiteness, where the sphere of knowledge—represented by 'ra'—reflects the limitations of the knower, the known, and the methods of knowing.

By expressing the world of multiplicity from an indivisible singularity, and by experiencing one's own undivided essence through various limited forms, one eventually reaches the state represented by 'ṃ'. This state signifies pure, non-discriminatory knowledge of the nature of reality itself.

This interpretation highlights that the Kaulic tradition does not perceive Maya as a mere illusion or as something detrimental. Instead, Maya is viewed as a manifestation of absolute freedom and

as a crucial tool in achieving spiritual goals.

The manifestation of the great seed of omnipotence unfolds in a specific manner. The phoneme 'ha' (apara-visarga) corresponds to the stage where 'ḥ' (parapara-visarga) emerges due to its inherent abundance, thereby transforming into an aspect of 'ha', which denotes external manifestation. Attaining the state of 'ha' leads to the emergence of a multitude of categories, symbolized by phonemes such as 'k', among others.

The phoneme 'ra' is the result of the condensation of 'ṛ'. When the primordial impulse of spanda (the dynamic force of desire) disrupts the equilibrium of mahabindu (the seed of creation), it causes a fragmentation of the unity between the two principles, Shiva and Shakti. At this moment of disruption, the impulse appears as two forms of light, conventionally referred to as 'the lightning' and 'the flash', representing the pre-cognitive impulses of expansion and emergence ('ṛ' and 'ḷ'). This indicates that the capacity for 'knowing' is based on two fundamental, dynamic factors:

1. The impulse that initiates the beginning of any process or phenomenon. This beginning or moment contains the potential for limitation and finiteness, manifesting in various aspects.
2. The duration or continuation of any phenomenon, which is understood as a sequence of changing moments perceived as 'space/time' by empirical consciousness.

The absence of either factor implies the absence of both and results in the inability to be aware.

The phoneme 'ṝ', derived from the unchanging and indestructible vyoma, symbolizes the light form of iccha-shakti (the desire power), expressed as a 'flash' or a point of origin. This flash signifies the beginning of the fragmentation of the whole. Vyoma, the empty space of consciousness, is responsible for the manifestation of the universe's four states of consciousness during its unfolding (sristi) and their dissolution during its contraction (samhara). Thus, 'ṝ' embodies the potential for limitation and finiteness, particularly in the context of knowledge limitations, as represented by the vidya kanchuka 'ra'. Simultaneously, 'ra' symbolizes the limitation of the sphere of knowledge for the empirical knower, while also containing the potential to achieve the primal, limitless source of all limitations, embodying the very principle of cognition and knowledge.

Consequently, 'ra' signifies the fire of awakening, and the bija 'ram' represents the seed bija of the fire of knowledge (pramana-tejas).

The phoneme 'i' stands for iccha-shakti, the primal impulse of spanda (dynamic energy) in its drive towards manifestation. The term "iccha" lacks a direct equivalent in European languages, but it can be understood as the pre-cognitive impulse. Iccha-shakti disrupts the equilibrium of the parabindu (the seed of creation), splitting the unity of the Shiva and Shakti principles. This disruption is metaphorically described as 'the one who pushes' and 'the one who is pushed', representing the prototypes of cause and effect. Iccha-shakti thus brings forth the primal consciousness space of the Supreme Reality, demonstrating infinite diversity. It also contains the principle of identity within the distinctions it creates. Recognizing

the differences among phenomena simultaneously reveals their shared root. Therefore, iccha- shakti is the source of understanding one's original nature (anuttara).

The bindu 'ṃ' corresponds to the dissolution of internal manifestations into anuttara, representing a state of undivided universal knowledge.

krīṃ

The bija 'krīṃ' is associated with Dakshinakali and other manifestations of Kali. To understand the nature of 'krīṃ', we need to explore how it unfolds according to the Matrika tradition.

In this tradition, the bija 'krīṃ' reveals its essence through the process of divine energy manifesting as earth (prithvi). At the final stage of the universe's full manifestation, the supreme divine energy transforms into the form of 'ka'. Here, 'ka' symbolizes the culmination of the world of objects and the embodiment of the principle of separation. This principle is a fundamental expression of the dynamic and creative consciousness.

The phoneme 'ka' represents the pinnacle of the principle of separation, where the divine energy, through the fire of knowledge, marks the beginning of a process of integration or absorption into the primal essence denoted by bindu 'ṃ'. This bindu symbolizes the awareness of the nature of reality, which is pure consciousness.

The unfolding of the seed of Shmashanakali, represented by 'krīṃ', follows a specific sequence:

1. **'ka' as the Mystical Name of the Unknowable God**: The phoneme 'ka' encompasses the entirety of all spheres of existence. It originates from 'a', which symbolizes anuttara, the supreme, undivided state of consciousness. As 'a' descends to the level of 'ha' (apara-visarga), which represents the realm of Shakti, Maya, and Prakriti, it evolves into 'ka' (prithvi), the sphere of earthly manifestation. Despite this transformation, the essence of 'ka' remains unchanged. It continues to embody the supreme divine energy, characterized by its undivided and void nature.

2. **Dynamic Creative Consciousness**: The nature of 'ka' is both dynamic and creative. It represents the principle of undividedness and the void, reflecting the highest level of divine energy.

3. **Subsequent Phonemes in 'krīṃ'**: The remaining phonemes in the bija 'krīṃ' are interpreted in a manner analogous to those in the bija 'hrīṃ'. This means that each phoneme in 'krīṃ' contributes to a deeper understanding of the divine energy and its manifestations, aligning with the principles already established in the earlier bija.

The phoneme 'ṛ', which arises from the eternal and immutable vyoma, signifies a form of iccha-shakti (the force of desire) manifesting as a 'flash' or initial point. This flash marks the onset of the division of the whole. Vyoma, the boundless expanse of consciousness, facilitates the emergence of the universe's four states of consciousness during its expansion (sristi) and their dissolution

during contraction (samhara). Consequently, 'ṛ' embodies the concept of limitation and finiteness, especially regarding the constraints of knowledge, as highlighted by the vidya kanchuka 'ra'. At the same time, 'ra' represents the boundaries of the knower's sphere of knowledge, while also containing the potential to access the primal, boundless source of all limitations, thus representing the fundamental principle of cognition.

In this framework, 'ra' symbolizes the awakening flame, and the bija 'ram' signifies the seed bija of this fire of knowledge (pramana-tejas).

The phoneme 'i' denotes iccha-shakti, the primary force of spanda (dynamic energy) that drives the process of manifestation. Although "iccha" does not have a direct equivalent in European languages, it can be understood as the pre-cognitive impulse. Iccha-shakti disturbs the equilibrium of the parabindu (the seed of creation), leading to a division between the principles of Shiva and Shakti. This division can be seen as 'the one who initiates' and 'the one who responds', representing the fundamental concepts of cause and effect. Iccha-shakti, therefore, brings forth the primordial consciousness of the Supreme Reality, which showcases infinite diversity while also holding the principle of unity within its distinctions. Recognizing these differences reveals their common origin. Thus, iccha-shakti is the source of understanding one's original nature (anuttara).

The bindu 'm' reflects the dissolution of internal manifestations into anuttara, representing a state of unified, universal knowledge 'krīm' is a profound bija associated with Kali in general. It represents the process of divine energy's transformation and integration, beginning with the manifestation of 'ka' as the highest expression of

the principle of separation and culminating in a unified awareness symbolized by bindu 'ṃ'. This unfolding process highlights the dynamic and creative nature of the supreme divine energy and its continuous interaction with the cosmic principles of Shakti, Maya, and Prakriti.

Sauh

To grasp the secret of the heart of Bhairava, one must understand the profound essence that defines this deity. At the core of Bhairava's essence is the three-fold power, which consists of Ichā, Jñāna, and Kriyā—these represent will, knowledge, and action, respectively. These powers are fundamental aspects of cosmic existence and are intricately intertwined in the nature of Bhairava.

Ichā, or will, signifies the inherent drive behind all creation. It is the divine intention that initiates the process of manifestation. Jñāna, or knowledge, represents the profound understanding and wisdom that perceives the true nature of reality. It is through this knowledge that one comprehends the essence of existence and the underlying principles that govern it. Kriyā, or action, embodies the force that actualizes the will and the knowledge, translating them into tangible outcomes and bringing about the cosmos into immanent existence.

The syllable "SAH" plays a crucial role in this context. It is associated with the thirty-second Tattva, which encompasses all that exists, from Prthvi (earth) to Māyā (illusion). This Tattva symbolizes a universal essence that integrates and binds these diverse elements into a cohesive whole. The sound "AU," when combined with "SAH," reflects the unity of the three powers—Ichā,

Jñāna, and Kriyā—within the divine framework of Suddhavidyā (pure knowledge), Īśvara (Supreme Lord), and Sadaśiva (Eternal Shiva). This sacred sound thus represents a comprehensive synthesis of these divine aspects.

The final component,the visarga "h," signifies the ultimate cosmic principles of Shiva and Shakti. Shiva represents the absolute consciousness, the unchanging and eternal reality, while Shakti embodies the dynamic energy and the force of creation and manifestation. Together, these principles represent the complete spectrum of divine reality.

When combined into "SAUH," these elements form a powerful expression of unity. The term "SAUH" signifies the merging of objective consciousness—the external, perceptible reality— with subjective consciousness—the internal, experiential reality. This union is considered the supreme sound or vibration that is believed to have brought the entire cosmos into existence. In essence, "SAUH" represents the profound synthesis of all these spiritual and cosmic principles, encapsulating the true essence of Bhairava and the fundamental nature of reality itself.

Bija of Dissolution of Objectivity and The Five Fold Manifestation

'khphreṃ'

The five-syllable bija 'khphrēṃ' represents the concept of destruction and illustrates the process of transitioning from the limited state of the 'experiencer' (sakala) to the ultimate state of the supreme 'experiencer', which is the undivided Absolute 'I-consciousness'.

Sakala, which encompasses both external (physical body) and internal (antahkarana) aspects, with the influence of the awakening fire (symbolized by the phoneme 'ra'), descends inward to the realm of ahamkara—the constrained 'I-consciousness' denoted by 'pha'.

According to the Matrika code, the phoneme 'ha' is associated with vidyatattva. Vidya-tattva is essentially the condensation of the vowel 'ṛ', reflecting a state akin to experiencing emptiness with a hint of luminosity (unstable vyoma-samadhi). In this void, where the four elements—earth, water, fire, and air (both subtle and gross)—are dissolved during the universe's contraction (samhara), a faint, indistinct sound of 'r' can be heard. The bija 'rāṃ' represents the seed of the fire of knowledge (pramaṇa-tejas).

The phoneme 'pha' corresponds to ahamkara-tattva, which is formed through the densification of the vowel 'u'—unmesha. This densification results in a state that serves as a foundation prior to differentiation: a point where all knowable objects are contracted back during the phase of samhara. The densification of unmesha

progresses through five stages, each linked to panchashakti.

Ahamkara-tattva is associated with the stage of jnana-kriya, which is the development of the phoneme 'o'. This stage is characterized by the processes of identification, connection, and separation. Consequently, ahamkara acts as a bridge between empirical and absolute consciousness.

The state attained through this process is experienced as akasha, or emptiness, represented by the phoneme 'kha'. This experience of emptiness, which traverses through the triad of energies embodied in the yoni-bija 'e', ascends to the level of 'the supreme experiencer', represented by bindu 'ṃ'. Ultimately, it merges into the essence of absorption itself.

The phoneme 'kha' encompasses all spheres of existence. It originates from the phoneme 'a' (anuttara), which, when descending to 'ha' (apara-visarga—the realm of Shakti, Maya, and Prakriti), transforms into 'ka' (prithvi—the sphere of earth) while retaining its essential nature. Both 'ha' and 'kha' signify mutual interpenetration and correspond to the tattva of Shiva-Shakti, pertaining to the pure level of para-vach. This level is experienced by Shiva- pramati, who exists beyond temporal limitations and separation, and is described as 'I am'. It represents the dynamic, creative consciousness characterized by unity and emptiness. Thus, 'kha' conveys meanings such as 'Brahman', 'chit', 'sky', or 'emptiness'.

The vowel 'e' (a/ā + i/ī—'yoni-bija') embodies three energies: iccha, jnana, and kriya. It represents an implicit (indefinite) force of activity (kriya-shakti). As a short vowel, it signifies Shiva in isolation from Shakti. In the state where the male and female principles (vowels and consonants) are not in active union and where there is

no external manifestation, the nature of kama-tattva is highlighted—the creative potency in itself.

Knowledge of any object reflects kriya-shakti, while knowledge of this fact relates to jnana- shakti. Without iccha (the direction of attention), no knowledge is possible. Thus, kriya- shakti encompasses both iccha and jnana.

To elucidate the mechanism of bindu 'ṃ', iccha (ishana—'i', 'ī') and unmesha (unata—'u', 'ū') are integrated into the essential nature of anuttara. They then discharge variations of these energies, rising to a state of non-discrimination and merging into bindu 'ṃ', which represents the awareness of reality's essence as pure consciousness. In this context, the bindu 'ṃ' signifies a state of unified, universal knowledge.

The phoneme 'kha' represents the state associated with the experience of emptiness or the vastness of space. This state emerges from the equilibrium achieved between inhalation and exhalation, as it exists in the space between these two acts and is what brings them into being.

The interval or pause that occurs between inhaling and exhaling is known as kumbhaka. This pause is a foundational state from which all empirical experiences originate. By engaging in the natural rhythm of breath (inhale-exhale) while maintaining a state of inner purity—free from desires and attachments—and cultivating a subtle, mental devotion (bhakti), one brings the experience of emptiness to the level of ahamkara, which is symbolized by the phoneme 'pha'.

Through this process of breath control, the 'fire of knowledge', denoted by vidya-tattva and symbolized by the phoneme 'ha', should be ignited. This inner fire of knowledge clears all subtle

channels and states of consciousness, eliminating distinctions and differences. The divine consciousness then infuses the universe as subtle energies, represented by the vowel 'e'.

All forms of 'creations' and phenomena arise from the delusions of the mind (manas) and are purely mental constructs. When one attains the state of pure, non-discriminating absolute consciousness, as symbolized by the phoneme 'ṃ', all creations and phenomena dissolve.

This state of pure consciousness transcends and nullifies any concept of creation or differentiation.

This stage of anuttara 'a', which incorporates all expressions within itself in unity, differs from the previous 'a', which was the initial stage of self-manifestation. This distinction, expressed in terms of knowledge, is captured by the use of bindu 'ṃ' to convey the essence of reality in the knowledge aspect. Typically, the construction of this bija involves combining the phonemes 'kha', 'pha', and 'ra', followed by adding the yoni-bija 'e' and bindu 'ṃ'. This results in the bija 'khphrēṃ'.

The bija mantra 'khphrēṃ' is esteemed as the ultimate five-syllable seed of Vyomeswari, or Kala Shankarshini, who epitomizes the zenith of ultimate subjectivity and divine consciousness. This sacred syllable encapsulates the very essence of her transcendental and cosmic nature, representing the most profound depths of her spiritual embodiment.

This sacred mantra encompasses the essence of the Pancha Vaha Chakra, a pivotal energy center representing the confluence of the five states of Para-Samvid. Each of these states weave the fabric of cosmic creation, and 'khphrēṃ' acts as the key to accessing and

harmonizing these states of awareness.

Furthermore, 'khphrēṃ' represents the embodiment of all kalas, which are the fragments of Para-Samvid that manifest the various facets of cosmic and spiritual wisdom. As the embodiment of these kalas, this mantra holds the profound capability to unlock and integrate the multifaceted aspects of divine knowledge and creative potential.

The book provides a comprehensive introduction to the practice of this mantra, laying a solid foundation for aspiring practitioners. The guidance and instructions offered within its pages are well-suited for initiating and progressing in the practice, facilitating the attainment of essential gnosis and spiritual insight.

Within the pages of this book, valuable insights and subtle clues have been provided to help the practitioner begin their journey into the meditative contemplation of Vyomeswari's five divine aspects. These foundational teachings serve as a robust starting point, enabling aspirants to begin their exploration and achieve the essential gnosis required for deeper spiritual advancement. With the instructions and guidance offered herein, the practice of the mantras can be safely undertaken and will foster significant progress on the path of spiritual realization.

However, it is important to recognize that the practice of these mantras, especially at advanced levels, entails a complex and nuanced process. The full realization of the bija 'khphrēṃ' and the associated advanced rituals involves a sophisticated understanding that goes beyond what can be fully detailed within the confines of a book. Such practices culminate in the dissolution of all tattvas into a state of pure consciousness and require precise, individualized

guidance.

To fully grasp and effectively engage in these advanced mantras and their intricate rituals, personal instruction from an experienced guru is essential. While the text provides a solid foundation and preliminary instructions, the deeper, more esoteric aspects of the practice are best learned through direct, in-person mentorship. Thus, the book serves as an excellent introduction, but for the advanced stages of practice, seeking a knowledgeable teacher is crucial to ensure authentic and transformative spiritual progress.

Uccāra

Abhinava Gupta's practice of uccāra under the āṇava-upāya is a refined and intricate method that places primary importance on prāṇa, or vital energy. To understand his version, it's useful to first explore the traditional Tantrik approach to uccāra.

In classical Tantrik practice, uccāra involves raising a seed-syllable (bīja-mantra) up the central channel of the practitioner's body to the crown of the head. This practice is a key component of daily yoga sādhanā for many Tantrikas. It integrates mantra, mudrā, and visualization, with a central focus on the movement of prāṇa.

Consider the example of the seed-syllable HRĪM. The practice begins at the mūlādhāra (located at the base of the spine or perineum). The practitioner enunciates the sound H, which is barely audible, and raises it along with the corresponding mudrā and a visualization of brilliant light. As the sound ascends through the central channel, it transitions to the navel where the R sound is introduced, then to the base of the heart where it changes to the Ī vowel. The sound

then moves up to the throat, becoming more nasalized, and finally reaches the palate where it vibrates intensely as a pure nasal sound. The audible sound diminishes as the vibration continues to rise to the crown of the head and beyond. This process is typically performed with a single breath and repeated multiple times—3, 5, 7, 9, 12, or 108 times. The same method applies to other bīja-mantras like HAUṂ, where the sounds ascend through the corresponding energy centers.

In traditional practice, the prāṇa's role is crucial, guiding the seed-syllable through the central channel and aligning it with the practitioner's energetic and spiritual centers.

This is the basic outline of the standard form of uccāra. Note that practicing this effectively is unlikely without a teacher's guidance. In his Tantra-Sara , Abhinava Gupta divides uccāra into two practices: one focuses on prāṇa flow and doesn't explicitly require a mantra, while the other (varṇa-uccāra) does require a mantra. We will discuss the first practice here, as the second cannot be taught through a book. Abhinava's prāṇa-uccāra differs from mainstream Tantrik uccāra in two key ways: it uses all five prāṇa-vāyus (aspects of vital energy), not just the exhale, and it is interpreted in terms of liberative spiritual concepts. We will now explore this form of uccāra, developed in the gnostic Trika, which was the most enduring form of Tantra in Kashmīr.

The uccāra described in the Tantra-Sara might seem similar to the Firewheel dhyāna mentioned earlier, as both aim to realize every object of experience as a vibration of divine Consciousness, which is the same as your innate awareness. However, while visualization is central in the dhyāna, this uccāra practice focuses on the sensation

of the rhythmic flow of breaths. For some, this approach may be easier and more effective, whereas others who prefer visual methods might find the dhyāna more suitable.

Classical works outlines six steps in his uccāra practice, which include the five prāṇa-vāyus plus an initial step of centering and opening to grace.

1. In this practice, someone aiming to elevate the vital energy first rests in the space of the Heart.

Meditating on the self-revealing Light of Consciousness that is present in all aspects of reality as the power of awareness that is your own Heart. It's the eternal self that has remained constant through all experiences: the dimension beyond thoughts or feelings. It's the core of your being. We might describe it as a present self-awareness, independent of any particular content. Words can only direct you to this inner space, hoping you will look where they point and intuit its meaning. You are already familiar with this inner place, though you may not have paid as much attention to it as you are learning to now; or you might have allowed certain concepts to obscure it and now need to recognize its pure essence. It is your Heart, which is and always has been a reflection of the universal Heart.

2. Next, as you exhale [prāṇa], your awareness flows through the sense faculties and focuses on an external object.

The initial step of the practice involves directing your awareness outward through the "solar" exhale that highlights a specific object. Beginners should use a physical object, such as something on your

altar, while more advanced practitioners may use a subtler object. As you direct your exhale toward the object, feel your consciousness's energy flowing through your sense channels and manifesting the object before you.

3. **Next, as you inhale [apāna], infusing yourself with the "moon" and drawing in the object, you will see yourself reflected in everything and thus free yourself from desires for external things.**

During the "lunar" inhale, let the vibration or "energy signature" of the object accompany your breath and enter your heart center. Feel the inhale as invigorating, bringing the awareness that the object has always been a part of you. This explains why Abhinava states that seeing yourself in all things frees you from longing for the other—since you cannot covet what you perceive as a part of yourself. In this practice, you come to understand any object as an expression of your true essence.

While starting with beautiful symbolic items on your altar, including deity forms, is ideal, you can eventually advance to the more challenging practice of using objects that represent difficult people or situations in your life. By recognizing these individuals or circumstances as expressions of your own essence, you can transform your relationship with them in a more constructive way.

4. **Following this, the emergence of the equalizing vital energy [samāna] within the heart leads to a sense of unity.**

In this step, which is crucial to Tantrik yoga, the focus is on extending, balancing, and equalizing the inhalation and exhalation,

incorporating breath retention between them. At its most basic level, this involves extending both the inhale and exhale to, for instance, nine counts each, making them equal in rate and smoothness, with a breath retention pause that is comfortably manageable. A more advanced approach involves holding the breath for the same number of counts as the inhalation and exhalation (e.g., 9-9-9). Advanced techniques might include adding a pause after the exhale (e.g., 9-9-9-9) or using a 1-4-2 ratio (e.g., inhaling for 4 counts, holding for 16, and exhaling for 8).

The purpose of this practice is that, with sufficient time, the two breaths (prāṇa and apāna) will naturally merge into samāna. You will recognize this fusion when, without any conscious effort, the breath becomes extremely subtle, barely perceptible, and then spontaneously enters a state of stillness for an infinite moment, free from thought-forms. This state is what Abhinava describes as repose in unity. Both Tantrik and haṭha-yoga texts highlight the "unification" of the in-breath and out-breath, underscoring its importance. After achieving this, your breathing will continue smoothly and effortlessly balanced. It's worth noting that samāna arises in the heart; interpreting "heart" as the "core" refers to the union of inhalation and exhalation or the awareness being absorbed in inner self by uniting the dimensions of object and cognition.

5. Next, as the fire of the up-breath [udāna] rises, the practitioner absorbs the functions of the perceiver, the perceived, and the process of perception.

There are two approaches here. After the breath and mind have spontaneously settled, you can either visualize the prāṇa ascending

through the central channel on an exhale, using focused awareness and vivid imagination to encourage its actual rise (which will be effective if these skills are well-developed), or you can wait for the rise to occur naturally. When samāna fusion is complete, the prāṇa-śakti will ascend forcefully up the central channel as udāna, also known as kundalinīśakti. At this moment, Abhinava describes how the three elements of consciousness—the knower, the act of knowing, and the known—merge into unity, dissolving into the fire of the Supreme Knower, the foundation of all three. This results in a spontaneous ascent to the highest spiritual center, where Śiva eternally resides.

6. **When the fire that absorbs them diminishes and the pervasive vital energy [vyāna] emerges, one shines or vibrates, free from all limitations.**

The final stage of prāṇa-uccāra cannot be practiced but only experienced. As the fire of reabsorption ascends the central channel, it reaches the Sky of Consciousness (cidākāśa) at the crown center, where it merges with transcendent Śiva. There, the fire extinguishes in the boundless space of limitless stillness, which is nonetheless filled with infinite potential. If your practice is sufficiently advanced and you remain aware in this infinite Void, the vyāna or pervasive vital energy will overflow from the crown center, filling every aspect of your being with the blissful essence of the Absolute. This energy permeates every cell, flows from every pore, and illuminates the entirety of reality with its radiant light. What was previously experienced as the transcendent Core of your own identity now

reveals itself as the totality of all things. Abhinava describes this as sphurati—he vibrates and shines, free of all limitations, having become one with everything. The stabilization of this state, known as Mahāvyāpti or the Great Pervasion (also referred to as turyātīta), represents liberation and the ultimate awakening. Additionally, uccāra can be practiced with bīja-mantras or seed-syllables, as Abhinava describes: "This is the key to performing uccāra with the seed-syllables of creation and dissolution; by integrating them with the breath, one can refine, purify, and perfect one's mental constructs until they are perfectly aligned with, and thus dissolve into, the highest nondual nature of reality."

Varna Uccāra

In the context of the 'upward movement' (uccāra) of the vital energy, there is a sound (dhvani) that continuously resonates, seemingly imitating the unmanifest. This sound is referred to as 'syllabic sound' (vārṇa). The essential features of this syllable include the seed mantras of creation, "sa," and dissolution, "ha." By practicing these mantras, one can attain supreme consciousness.

The primary syllables are "ha" (representing apāna, or inspiration) and "sa" (representing prāṇa, or the expiration). These syllables are essential for attaining supreme consciousness. Integrate them diligently into the practice of Uccāra.

For instance, when letters starting with "ka" and ending with "ma," either with or without vowels, are merged into the core of the vital energy or simply recalled, one experiences a balanced state of conscious vibration. This balance is achieved because the 'word'

or mantra transcends conventional relationships (samaya) and is complete in every aspect. Even words dependent on convention can convey their meanings according to the imagination of the mind.

Once supreme consciousness is experienced through these practices, one should align the heart, throat, lips, and the two 'ends of the twelve' (dvādaśānta), and unify them in the 'core of consciousness' (hrdayam). This unification is the esoteric secret of the syllable (vārṇa). Some traditions explain that from the 'reflective consciousness' vibrating in the 'core of the heart,' white- and yellow-colored syllables emerge('sa' should be visualised in white and 'ha' in yellow hue). This meditation enables a yogi to realize consciousness.

By experiencing vibrating consciousness in the absence of any specific object and by controlling the movements of the moon (indu, representing apāna) and the sun (arka, representing prāṇa), a person, by entering the realm of balanced consciousness, achieves perfection.

For some individuals, discursive thought (vikalpa) reaches completeness without any external means, while for others, it is purified through specific practices. The efficiency of this system manifests in the intellect (buddhi), the vital energy (prāṇa) within the body, and in external objects. Although these elements are described as limited, once the result is attained, distinctions between them dissolve.

Dharana of the Tri-Ishika or the Triadic Shakti

Find a comfortable seated position, with your spine straight and your eyes gently closed. Take a few deep breaths to center yourself and prepare for the meditation.

Visualize a trident in front of you, with its three prongs and a long, solid staff. Imagine the middle prong extending from the crown of your head, the right prong extending from your right temple, and the left prong extending from your left temple. See the staff of the trident running down your spine, from the crown of your head to your coccyx.

Focus on the sacral area, visualizing the Adhara Shakti residing there as a vibrant, creative energy. Move your attention to your heart center, where the great Huhuka Bhairava dwells, capturing the delights of the senses. Picture this energy as a warm, radiant light.

As you continue, see the three prongs of the trident meeting at your forehead, where the Penta Cephalic Para Shiva is in a state of restful slumber. The middle prong represents Para, the essence of pure consciousness. The right prong signifies Para-Apara, integrating both higher and lower aspects of existence. The left prong represents Apara, grounded in material reality.

Now, visualize the divine manifestations associated with each prong:

1. **Aghora/Para:** Appears in a peaceful, beautiful form with a white body. She embodies positive, serene energy and represents the subject in the triad of consciousness. See her as a calming presence, filling you with peace and tranquility.
2. **Ghora/Para-Apara:** Manifests with a red body, combining both passionate and wrathful qualities. She represents the cognitive space and the process of cognition. Visualize her as dynamic and intense, with a presence that is both compelling and powerful.
3. **Ghoratari/Apara:** Appears in a fearsome form with a black body, embodying both sexuality and wrath. She represents the object in the triad of consciousness and the universe. See her as a powerful, awe-inspiring force, with an energy that is intense and transformative.

Seated above these three goddesses, envision the ultimate goddess, Kalasankarshini (Maha Para). She is the ineffable, ultimate goddess who transcends the manifestations of the triad.

Visualize her as a radiant, boundless presence, enveloping and integrating the energies of Aghora, Ghora, and Ghoratari.

Allow yourself to absorb the balanced energy of the trident and the divine manifestations, feeling a deep sense of unity and integration within your being. Sit with this sensation for a few moments, experiencing the harmony and completeness of these energies.

When you're ready, gently bring your awareness back to your surroundings. Wiggle your fingers and toes, open your eyes, and take a moment to reflect on the meditation.

Acknowledge the sense of alignment and peace you've cultivated.

Here are step by step instructions to make it clearer:

Trident Meditation with Divine Manifestations

1. Prepare Your Space:
- Find a quiet, comfortable space where you can sit undisturbed.
- Sit in a comfortable position with your spine straight. You may sit cross- legged on the floor or in a chair with your feet flat on the ground.

2. Center Yourself:
- Close your eyes and take a few deep breaths, inhaling through your nose and exhaling through your mouth. Allow yourself to relax and become present in the moment.

3.Visualize the Trident:
- Imagine a majestic trident in front of you with three distinct prongs and a long staff.
- Visualize the middle prong extending from the crown of your head. See this prong moving downward through the center of your body.
- Picture the right prong extending outward from your right temple.
- Picture the left prong extending outward from your left temple.
- Envision the staff of the trident running along your spine, extending from the crown of your head to your coccyx.

4. Focus on Key Areas:
- **Sacral Area (Adhara Shakti):** Visualize this area as a vibrant source of creative energy. Feel this energy

radiating from your sacral region.

- **Heart Center (Huhuka Bhairava):** Move your attention to your heart center, picturing it as a warm, radiant light where the Huhuka Bhairava dwells, capturing the delights of your senses.

5. Unite the Prongs:

- See the three prongs of the trident meeting at your forehead.
- Visualize this point as where Penta Cephalic Para Shiva rests in a state of restful slumber.
- **Middle Prong (Para):** Represents pure consciousness. Feel its essence as calm and transcendent.
- **Right Prong (Para-Apara):** Represents the integration of higher and lower aspects of existence. Visualize it as dynamic and powerful.
- **Left Prong (Apara):** Represents grounded reality. See it as embodying material presence.

6. Visualize the Divine Manifestations:

- **Aghora/Para:** The goddess, resplendent in crystal white, is truly magnificent. With three radiant eyes, she holds a string of beads, a sacred text, a kapala, and a trident in her six hands. Her remaining two hands display the varada mudra and the abhaya mudra.She represents the subject in the triad of consciousness
- **Ghora/Para-Apara:** The red goddess, Ghora, is formidable with her three gleaming eyes and tongues that flash like lightning. Her body is somewhat coarsely built and is adorned with great snakes. She possesses

terrifying fangs and a wide-open mouth, exuding a fearsome presence. Her frowning eyebrows are joined, and she wears a garland of human corpses, a necklace of a massive snake, and earrings made from human hands. In her hands, Ghora (also known as Parapara) holds a trident, a staff decorated with skulls, a kapala filled with blood, and a jar. One of her hands is positioned in the vajrapataka mudra. She represents the cognitive space and process of cognition.

- **Ghoratari/Apara:** The black goddess, Ghoratari, is equally fearsome with three radiant eyes and tongues like lightning. Her body is savagely built and similarly adorned with great snakes. She has terrifying fangs and a wide-open mouth, contributing to her dread-inspiring appearance. Her eyebrows are frowning and joined, and she is adorned with a garland of human corpses, a necklace of a large snake, and earrings made from human hands. Ghoratari (also known as Apara) wields a trident, a staff embellished with skulls, a butcher's knife, a kapala, a damaru drum, and a sword.. She represents the object in consciousness and the universe.

7. Visualize the Ultimate Goddess:

- Above the three goddesses, envision Kalasankarshini (Maha Para) as the ultimate, ineffable goddess. She transcends the manifestations of the triad and represents boundless presence.

8. Absorb and Integrate:

- Feel the energies of the trident and the divine manifestations merging and harmonizing within you. Experience a deep sense of unity and integration.

9. Return to the Present:
- Gently bring your awareness back to your physical surroundings.
- Wiggle your fingers and toes to reawaken your body.
- Slowly open your eyes and take a moment to reflect on the meditation.

10. Reflect and Ground:
- Notice any shifts in your energy or state of mind.
- Take a deep breath and ground yourself, acknowledging the sense of balance and peace you have cultivated.

The meditation described above is a foundational practice designed to introduce you to the visualization and harmonization with the divine energies associated with the trident and its deities. It is important to note that each deity involved has their own intricate internal and external rites, including specific mantras and detailed techniques. These advanced practices are complex and cannot be fully detailed in this book. For a comprehensive understanding and proper guidance, personalized, in-person instruction is essential.

Sonic Body of The Para Samvid

Before beginning this practice, it is essential to ensure you have sufficient experience with foundational spiritual training depicted in this book. This practice should only be undertaken once you have gained considerable knowledge and proficiency in the preliminary aspects of spiritual development in the Shaiva Yoga. The advanced nature of this practice requires a deep understanding of the spiritual principles and experiences that come from prior training.

The concept of God in Non-Dual Shaivism is fundamental to this practice. According to this tradition, the supreme god, Para-Shiva, is considered to be pure consciousness. This pure consciousness is both the source and the essence of the cosmos, manifesting as a self- illuminating light. In this perspective, Para-Shiva assumes two principal forms: in the aspect of manifestation, Para-Shiva becomes the cosmos and all the myriad objects within it. In his transcendent aspect, however, Para-Shiva is the supreme subjective consciousness that manifests as the objective universe. The supreme consciousness's ability to manifest independently is referred to as Swatantra Shakti, with 'Swatantra' meaning sovereign power. Para-Shiva is believed to have five primary attributes and performs five core functions.

Consequently, anthropomorphic images of Para-Shiva are depicted with five heads, each representing one of these attributes, forms, and actions.

To understand and effectively practice the mantra, one must familiarize themselves with these five attributes and their associated

actions. The first attribute is Chit, which translates to Consciousness. Chit is the divine power through which Para-Shiva reveals himself and shines forth as the ultimate subject experiencing himself as the pure "I" (Aham). The action related to Chit is Anugraha, or grace. This action liberates limited objects and helps empirical souls recognize their true selves within the supreme consciousness. The face representing Chit is called Ishana, and Sadashiva, a manifestation of this power, corresponds to the element of Akasha. This dimension of awareness is described as pure illumination or Bhasa.

The second attribute, Ananda, signifies Bliss. This attribute reflects the profound satisfaction derived from the infinite and complete nature of Para-Shiva. Ananda involves the divine power to conceal his true nature during manifestation, allowing the finite and seemingly limited universe to appear. The face representing Ananda is Tat-Purusha, and Maheswara, a manifestation of this power, corresponds to the air element.

The third attribute is Icha, or Will. Icha Shakti is the divine power that drives the desire to create. This will represents the creative potential inherent in Para-Shiva. The action associated with Icha is Srishti, or creation. Para-Shiva, through his own will, manifests the cosmos from his mental dimension, limiting himself into finite objects and subjects. The face representing this power is Aghora, and Rudra, a manifestation of Icha, corresponds to the fire element.

The fourth attribute is Jnana, which translates to Knowledge. Jnana Shakti encompasses the power through which countless objects are created and brought into consciousness.

Everything in the objective world is a manifestation of Para-

Shiva's own self, and nothing exists outside his consciousness. The action related to Jnana is Stithi, or sustenance. The face representing Jnana is Vamadeva, and Vishnu, a manifestation of this attribute, corresponds to the water element.

The fifth attribute is Kriya, or Action. Kriya Shakti represents the power to actualize and manifest the universe. It involves the creation of all forms and the subsequent withdrawal of the universe back into Para-Shiva. The face representing Kriya is Sadyojatha, and Brahma, a manifestation of this power, corresponds to the earth element.

In the spiritual doctrines of Shaivism, the traditional functions of creation, preservation, and destruction are reinterpreted as emanation, sustenance, and withdrawal. This reinterpretation reflects the view that the supreme god is the ultimate subject experiencing everything; thus, creation and destruction are seen as processes within the self-awareness of Para-Shiva.

Emanation involves the outward flow of consciousness into the objective world, while withdrawal signifies the return to the subjective dimension, realizing the inherent oneness of subject and object.

To engage in the practice of the five-syllabled mantra, it is crucial to understand its significance and correct usage. The mantra "Na Ma Shi Va YA" represents the embodiment of the five divine attributes and their functions. Each syllable of the mantra corresponds to a specific divine power and should be vibrated in a particular location and color to align with the corresponding attribute.

The mantra "Na Ma Shi Va YA" embodies the five divine attributes and their corresponding functions. It serves as a sonic representation

of the supreme godhead and is essential for realizing these attributes within oneself.

Syllable Vibrations:

- **Na**: Represents Kriya Shakti. Visualize and vibrate this syllable in yellow within the sacro-coccygeal region, focusing on its power of manifestation and action.
- **Ma**: Represents Jnana Shakti. Vibrate this syllable in white in the organs of procreation, akin to the color of a conch shell, emphasizing divine knowledge and sustenance.
- **Shi**: Represents Icha Shakti. Visualize this syllable in bright red in the heart, focusing on the divine will and creative potential.
- **Va**: Represents Ananda Shakti. Vibrate this syllable in black at the mouth, reflecting the bliss and concealment of the divine nature.
- **Ya**: Represents Chit Shakti. Vibrate this syllable in smoky grey at the crown of the head, embodying divine consciousness and self-awareness.

Start with the basic technique of vibrating each syllable in its designated color and location. This foundational practice helps in aligning yourself with the divine attributes and qualities. Once you are comfortable with the basic practice, explore advanced variations of the mantra, such as "Shi Va Ya Na Ma," which focuses specifically on Icha Shakti. These variations should be approached after mastering the basics and achieving control over the five elements.

    Maintain a regular practice schedule to deepen your attunement to the divine attributes. Consistent practice helps in internalizing the divine qualities and integrating them into your being.

Uniting the Triune

This chapter delves into the profound spiritual practice of achieving union with the Godhead, particularly through meditation on the triadic attributes as articulated by Indian spiritual traditions. The focus here is on the Shaivite school of thought, which provides a unique perspective on this union. According to this tradition, the supreme Godhead is understood through a triadic representation, embodied by the divine triad of Brahma, Vishnu, and Rudra. These deities symbolize different facets of the ultimate reality and offer a structured approach to understanding and meditating on the divine.

Understanding the Divine Attributes

In Shaivism, the Godhead is described as having five essential attributes and performing five fundamental actions, each represented by a distinct divine form:

1. **Chit (Consciousness)**: The term "Chit" translates to consciousness. In this context, God is perceived as pure consciousness—an all-pervading, self-aware, and self-affirming presence. This aspect emphasizes the divine's fundamental nature as an ever-present and omnipresent awareness that underpins all existence.

2. **Ananda (Bliss)**: Ananda signifies bliss or ultimate joy. Here, God is not merely aware but is also imbued with the quality of bliss. This indicates that the supreme Godhead is perfect and complete, embodying an infinite capacity for joy and

fulfillment. The divine's blissful nature reflects its ability to accomplish and manifest anything effortlessly.

3. **Icha (Will)**: Icha represents the will or power to create. The supreme Godhead possesses an inherent will to manifest the cosmos out of its own consciousness. This attribute highlights the dynamic aspect of the divine, capable of shaping and bringing forth the universe through its will.

4. **Jnana (Knowledge)**: Jnana stands for knowledge, particularly the omniscient aspect of the divine. This includes the knowledge of the entire objective universe and the multitude of objects within it. It reflects the divine's profound understanding of all aspects of existence.

5. **Kriya (Action)**: Kriya denotes action or the ability to act freely. This attribute is associated with the divine's omnipotence in manifesting creation. It represents the active aspect of the Godhead, responsible for the actual process of creation and the ongoing actions that sustain the universe.

These attributes are personified in five deities: Brahma (the creator), Vishnu (the sustainer), Rudra (the destroyer), Ishwara, and Sada-Shiva. The supreme Godhead, embodying these attributes, is referred to as Para-Shiva, Parama-Shiva, or in some contexts, Para-Bhairava.

The Triadic Forms and Their Spiritual Significance

In Shaivism, the triadic forms of Brahma, Vishnu, and Rudra are pivotal. These forms represent the active principles of the Godhead and are crucial in spiritual practice. Brahma symbolizes creation and

cognition, Vishnu represents sustenance and the objective world, and Rudra signifies the subjectivity or the self.

Meditation on the Triadic Attributes

Traditional Shaivite practices involve meditation on these divine attributes to achieve a deeper awareness of the Godhead within and without. Here's a practical approach to this meditation:

1. **Contemplation on the Cognitive Self**: Begin by sitting comfortably and focusing on your cognitive faculties and the five sense organs. Recognize these as representations of Brahma, the creator. Brahma's role in cognition highlights how divine awareness manifests through our perception and understanding of the world.

2. **Reflection on Objective Knowledge**: Next, consider the objective knowledge gained through your senses as embodied by Vishnu. Vishnu represents the sustaining power of the objective reality. Reflect on how this knowledge sustains and organizes your understanding of the external world.

3. **Meditation on the Self**: Finally, direct your attention to the self as Rudra, the ultimate subject and observer. Rudra, associated with destruction in this context, symbolizes the dissolution of false distinctions between subject and object, leading to a deeper realization of the unity of all existence.

By integrating these contemplations, you align with the divine triad's attributes and deepen your connection to the supreme

Godhead. This practice fosters a profound sense of unity and awareness, ultimately guiding you toward spiritual enlightenment and union with the divine.

Realization of Unity Through Contemplation

Prolonged practice of the meditation exercise described earlier aims to lead to a profound realization of the unity between subject and object. The essence of this practice is to dissolve the illusory distinction between the two, revealing that the objective reality arises, abides, and ultimately rests in the supreme subjective awareness of the Godhead. This insight underscores the interconnectedness of all things, illustrating that the perceived differences between subject and object are mere illusions.

Contemplation of Individual Deities

Franz Bardon, in his work "Initiation into Hermetics," provides methods that closely align with these contemplative practices, emphasizing the importance of concrete union with the divine. Let's explore the iconography and symbolic attributes of Lord Vishnu and Brahma, and how these symbols facilitate deeper spiritual understanding.

Lord Vishnu's Iconography and Attributes

Lord Vishnu, one of the principal deities in the Hindu pantheon, is often depicted with a blue or dark hue and four arms. Each of his attributes—the conch, mace, lotus, and discus—holds significant symbolic meaning:

1. **The Mace (Gada)**: The mace represents the primordial knowledge and the principle of time. It symbolizes the cyclical nature of creation and destruction within the cosmos. From a theurgical perspective, this mace, while representing the limitations imposed by time, also functions as a conduit connecting individual souls with the divine. It embodies the knowledge that governs both the emergence and dissolution of the universe.

2. **The Conch Shell (Shankha)**: The conch shell, known as Panchajanya, signifies the dynamic activity of the divine that leads to the manifestation of the physical cosmos. It is also associated with the origin of the five elements (Earth, Water, Fire, Air, and Akasha), essential for the formation of the material world. The conch's sound is believed to awaken the divine presence and represents the primordial vibration that pervades all existence.

3. **The Discus (Sudarshana Chakra)**: The discus represents the principle of Manas, or mind. It is associated with the locus of perception and cognition provided by the five senses. While the conch pertains to the elements and sense organs, the discus pertains to the mental faculties that process sensory information and generate knowledge. This attribute symbolizes the divine intellect and the power to discern and understand the cosmos.

4. **The Lotus (Padma)**: In this context, the lotus symbolizes both the physical world and its inherent illusions. While in Buddhist traditions the lotus represents purity, here it also

represents the physical realm's splendor, its inherent inertia, and the illusions that separate subject and object. The lotus highlights the attachment to the external world and the false distinctions between self and the external reality.

Meditative Integration with Vishnu: To achieve a union with Vishnu, meditators are advised to focus on these attributes, internalize their meanings, and visualize themselves embodying these divine qualities. By deeply contemplating Vishnu's symbols, practitioners aim to align with the attributes represented by this deity, such as sustaining and maintaining the cosmos through divine principles.

Lord Brahma's Iconography and Attributes

Lord Brahma, the creator deity in the triad, is depicted with four heads and four arms, holding distinct items that represent various aspects of divine creativity and knowledge:

1. **The Four Heads**: The four heads of Brahma represent the four states of consciousness: the wakeful state, the state of dreams, the dreamless state, and the supreme awareness characterized by the recognition of self with the supreme God. Each head signifies Brahma's ability to perceive and understand these different states of consciousness, encompassing the entire spectrum of divine awareness.
2. **The Rosary (Mala)**: The rosary, consisting of 51 beads, symbolizes the fifty-one letters of the Sanskrit language or Devanagari script. These letters are considered the creative potential of the supreme Godhead in the form of sounds. The

rosary thus represents the divine creative force manifested through verbal expression and cosmic order.

3. **The Lotus (Padma)**: In Brahma's iconography, the lotus represents the pure awareness of divinity as creative potential. Previously, in Vishnu's context, the lotus symbolized the material world and the densification of supreme awareness into matter. Here, the lotus denotes the pure, unmanifest potential of divine creativity.

4. **The Book (Pustaka)**: The book symbolizes omniscience and the potential to bring the cosmos into the light of knowledge. It represents the divine wisdom and the creative ability to illuminate the universe with understanding and order.

5. **The Nectar of Immortality (Amrita)**: The elliptical vessel containing the nectar of immortality represents the immortal nature of the self. It signifies the eternal essence of the soul and the ultimate goal of spiritual realization, transcending the cycle of birth and death.

To achieve a union with Brahma, practitioners should meditate on these symbols and their meanings. By aligning with Brahma's attributes of creation and omniscience, meditators aim to embody the divine creative force and gain a deeper understanding of the cosmos.

In the meditative practice described, the adept should deeply contemplate the attributes associated with each deity in the triad, condensing these attributes into the image of the respective godhead. The goal is to unite one's awareness with the imagined deity, meditating until achieving a perfect union and embodying the qualities represented by that godhead.

Here's a closer look at how this applies to Rudra and the final stage of the spiritual exercise.

Contemplation of Rudra

Rudra, often identified with Shiva, represents a unique and profound aspect of the divine triad. The term "Rudra" translates to the destruction of limited light or awareness, with "Ru" meaning limited awareness and "Dra" meaning dissolution. This encapsulates Rudra's role in transcending the duality between subject and object.

1. **Trident (Trishula)**: The trident symbolizes the triple powers of will, knowledge, and action. In Indian spiritual philosophy, it is believed that during dissolution, Brahma and Vishnu are absorbed back into Rudra. This signifies the inherent unity of knowledge (Brahma), action (Vishnu), and will (Rudra). The trident thus represents the integration and oneness of these three divine faculties.
2. **Bowl of Fire**: This symbolizes the transformative fire of subjectivity. It ignites the adept's awareness, psyche, and astral and mental bodies, facilitating a deeper inner illumination and understanding. This fire represents the divine force that burns away illusions and reveals the true nature of reality.
3. **Drum (Damaru)**: The drum represents the rhythm of creation and destruction. Its sound is associated with the cosmic heartbeat, marking the cycles of time and the dynamic processes of the universe.
4. **Deer (or Antelope)**: The deer, often linked with the constellation Orion, symbolizes the hunter's precision in

capturing the essence of divine consciousness. The antelope also represents the agile and elusive nature of spiritual insight, suggesting the need for keen perception in recognizing the unity of self and divine providence.

Meditative Integration with Rudra: To unite with Rudra, practitioners should actively contemplate these symbols and their meanings. By embodying the attributes represented by Rudra—the trident's union of will, knowledge, and action; the transformative fire; and the celestial symbolism of the deer—practitioners aim to dissolve the illusory distinctions between subject and object and integrate the divine will into their own awareness.

Final Stage: Contemplation of the Triad Within the Body

The final stage of this spiritual exercise involves integrating the contemplation of the triadic deities—Brahma, Vishnu, and Rudra—within the body. This advanced practice aims to internalize the divine attributes and achieve a profound realization of the unity of these attributes within oneself.

1. **Internal Visualization**: Visualize the triadic forms of Brahma, Vishnu, and Rudra within the subtle body. See Brahma's creative energy, Vishnu's sustaining power, and Rudra's transformative force operating harmoniously within your own being.
2. **Embodiment of Attributes**: Meditate on embodying the

attributes of each deity. Imagine Brahma's creative potential, Vishnu's sustaining presence, and Rudra's transformative will as integral aspects of your own consciousness.

3. **Unified Awareness**: As you meditate, focus on the seamless integration of these attributes. Recognize the unity of creation, sustenance, and transformation within your own awareness, reflecting the triadic nature of the divine.

4. **Achieving Union**: Strive to achieve a state of perfect union with the divine triad. This involves transcending individual identity and experiencing the divine attributes as fundamental aspects of your own self.

By achieving this final stage, practitioners aim to fully embody the divine qualities represented by the triadic deities and realize their own inherent unity with the Godhead.

The advanced meditation practice described involves a sophisticated and nuanced approach, integrating the attributes of the divine triad—Rudra, Brahma, and Vishnu—into various aspects of the body and consciousness. It is essential for practitioners to have mastery over prior exercises before embarking on this meditation, as it builds upon earlier achievements and requires a deep familiarity with the spiritual processes involved.

The method begins by visualizing and internalizing the attributes of Rudra, Brahma, and Vishnu, each associated with different regions of the body. This process involves a meticulous and focused approach to aligning these divine qualities with the respective areas of one's being. In Shaivite doctrines, the triad is often symbolically linked to cosmic elements: fire, sun, and moon. Although delving

into these associations could lead us away from our current topic, it's helpful to understand that each deity corresponds to a specific element and its associated energy in the human body.

In this practice, the adept starts with the region of the moon, located at the glabella (the space between the eyebrows) and the area behind it. Here, the attributes of Vishnu, associated with sustenance and preservation, are meditated upon and solidified. The practitioner visualizes Vishnu's qualities of sustaining and maintaining balance being concentrated and energized within this region, thereby integrating these divine attributes into this part of the body.

Next, the focus shifts to the heart center, which is considered the region of the sun. This area is associated with Brahma, the deity representing creation and omniscience. The adept should meditate on Brahma's qualities of creative power and knowledge, infusing these attributes into the heart center. This process involves visualizing Brahma's creative energy and wisdom as residing within the heart, enhancing one's capacity for spiritual insight and creative expression.

The final region to be focused on is the base of the spine, including the coccyx, perineum, and genitals, which are associated with the element of fire. This area corresponds to Rudra, the deity linked to transformative power and the destruction of illusions. The practitioner should concentrate on Rudra's attributes of fiery will and transformative energy, channeling these divine qualities into this foundational part of the body.

After successfully integrating the attributes of Vishnu, Brahma, and Rudra into their respective regions, the adept should contemplate themselves as one with these three aspects of the supreme God. This

involves an intense meditation on the unity of these divine forms, culminating in a profound realization of their interconnected nature within the practitioner's own being.

To further solidify this union, the adept should engage in repeated practice of this meditation until it becomes a deeply ingrained and unwavering conviction. The goal is to reach a state where the practitioner can dynamically manifest any of these divine attributes—sustenance, creation, and transformation—within and outside themselves at will.

For those seeking to deepen their practice even further, advanced methods include meditating on the mantras associated with each of the three deities and energizing these mantras within the respective body regions. Each mantra embodies the essence of the divine qualities associated with Vishnu, Brahma, and Rudra, and focusing on these mantras can enhance the practitioner's connection with these attributes.

Another advanced technique involves contemplation of the three phases of breath—inhale, retention, and exhale—as metaphors for the divine attributes. Inhalation corresponds to Rudra, representing the withdrawal of awareness from the objective world. Retention symbolizes Vishnu, reflecting the sustenance and balance within. Exhalation aligns with Brahma, signifying the emanation and creation of awareness towards the objective reality.

Additionally, practitioners may engage in a method called Sandhia Vandhana, which focuses on the interval or gap between thoughts. By cultivating awareness of this interval between thoughts or breaths, practitioners develop a heightened inner awareness and an understanding of the subjective principle represented by Rudra.

This technique helps in recognizing the unity of cognition and the object of thought with the self.

Through these advanced practices, the adept aims to realize and embody the divine attributes of Rudra, Brahma, and Vishnu within themselves, leading to a profound spiritual awakening and a deeper connection with the supreme Godhead.

Conquest of The Varna Adhwa, Internalising the Fifty-One Divinities

1. **अ (a) - Top of the Head**
   - श्रीकान्त (shrIkaNTha) = पूणोदरी (pUrNodarI)

2. **आ (ā) - Forehead**
   - अनन्त (ananta) = ववरजा (virajA)

3. **इ (i) – Right eye**
   - सूक्ष्म (sUkShma) = शाल्मली (shAlmalI)

4. **ई (ī) – Left Eye**
   - वमूिवती (trimUrti) = लोलाक्षी (lolAkShI)

5. **उ (u) – Right Ear**
   - अमरेश्वर (amareshvara) = वततिलाक्षी (vArtulAkShI)

6. **ऊ (ū) – Left Ear**
   - अघीश (arghIsha) = दीगगिहन (dIrgaghoNa)

7. **ऋ (ṛ) – Right Nostril**
   - भावभूत (bhAvabhUti) = सतदीघमितखी (sudIrghamukhI)

8. **ऋ (ṝ) – Left Nostril**
   - वतवथ (tithi) = गौमतखी (gomukhI)

9. **ल (ḷ) – Right Cheek**
   - सथानत (sthAnu) = दीघविजवहहका (dIrghajihvikA)

10. **लृ (ḹ) – Left Cheek**
    - हर (hara) = क्ळण्डोदरी (kuNDodarI)

11. **ए (e) – Upper Lip**
    - वझवन्तष (jhiNTIsha) = ऊर्धवकिे शी (Urdhvakeshi)

12. **ऐ (ai) – Lower Lip**
    - भौवतक (bhautika) = ववकृ तमतखी (vikR^itamukhI)

13. **ओ (o) – Upper teeth**
    - सदयोजात (sadyojAta) = ज्वालामतखी (jvAlAmukhI)

14. **औ (au) – Lower teeth**
    - अनतग्रेश्वर (anugraheshvara) = उल्कामतखी (ulkAmukhI)

15. **अं (aṁ) - Palate**
    - अकृ र (akrUra) = श्रीमतखी (shrImukhI)

16. **अः(aḥ) - Tongue**
    - महासेन (mahAsena) = ववदयामतखी (vidyAmukhI)

17. **क (ka) – Right Shoulder**
    - क्रोधीश (krodhIsha) = महाकाली (mahAkAlI)

18. **ख (kha) – Right Elbow**
    - चान्देश (chaNDesha) = सरस्वती (saravatI)

19. ग (ga) – **Right Wrist**
    - पञ्चान्तक (pa~nchAntaka) = सर्वसिर्व (sarvasiddhi)

20. घ (gha) – **Right Palm**
    - शिवोत्तम (shivottama) = गौरी (gaurI)

21. ङ (ṅa) – **Right Hand Fingers**
    - एकरुद्र (ekarudra) = त्रैलोक्यविद्या (trailokyavidyA)

22. च (cha) – **Left Shoulder**
    - कूर्म (kUrma) = मन्त्रात्मशक्ति (mantrAtmashaktI)

23. छ (chha) – Left **Elbow**
    - एकनेत्र (ekanetra) = भूतामाता (bhUtamAtA)

24. ज (ja) – **Left Wrist**
    - चतुर्मुख (chaturmukha) = लंबोदरी (lambodarI)

25. झ (jha) – **Left Palm**
    - अजेय (ajesha) = द्राविणी (drAviNI)

26. ञ (ña) – **Left Hand Fingers**
    - शर्व (sharva) = नागरी (nAgarI)

27. ट (ṭa) – **Right Hip**
    - सोमेश्वर (someshvara) = वैखरी (vaikharI)

28. ठ (ṭha) – **Right Knee**
    - लाङ्गली (lA~NgalI) = मञ्जरी (ma~njarI)

29. ड (ḍa) – Right Ankle
   - दारुका (dAruka) = रूवपणी (rUpiNI)

30. ढ (ḍha) – Right Sole
   - अधनिारीश्वर (ardhanArIshvara) = वीररणी (vIriNI)

31. ण (ṇa) – Right toes
   - उमाकान्त (umAkAnta) = कोटरी (koTarI)

32. त (ta) – Left Hip
   - आशाढी (AshADhI) = पततना (pUtanA)

33. थ (tha) – Left Knee
   - दवण्डन (danDin) = भद्रकाली (bhadrakAlI)

34. द (da) – Left Ankle
   - अद्री (adri) = योवगनी (yoginI)

35. ध (dha) – Left Sole
   - मीन (mIna) = शङ् वखनी (sha~NkhinI)

36. न (na) – Left toes
   - मेष (meSha) = गरवजनी (garjinI)

37. प (pa) – Right Flank
   - लोवहता (lohita) = कालरार्व (kAlarAtrI)

38. फ (pha) – Left Flank
   - वशवखन (shikhin) = क्तवजजनी (kubjinI)

39. **ब (ba)** - Sacrum
   - चागलाण्ड (ChagalaNda) = कपवदनिी (kapardinI)

40. **भ (bha)** - Umbilicus
   वदव्राण्ड (divraNDa) = महावज्रा (mahAvajrA)

41. **म (ma)** - Pelvis
   - महाकाल (mahAkAla) = जया (jayA)

42. **य (ya)** - Heart
   - कपावल (kapAll) = सतमतखेश्वरी (sumukheshvarI)

43. **र (ra)** – Right Lung
   - भतजङ्गेश (bhuja~Ngesha) = रेवती (revatI)

44. **ल (la)** - Throat
   - वपनाकी (pinAkI) = माधवी (mAdhavI)

45. **व (va)** – Left Lung
   - खड्गीश (khaDgIsha) = वारुणी (vAruNI)

46. **श (sha)** – A nadi which carries prana from heart to right arm
   - बक (baka) = वायवी (vAyavI)

47. **ष (ṣa)** - A nadi which carries prana from heart to left arm
   - श्वेत (shveta) = रक्षोपधाररणी (rakShopadhArinI)

48. **स (sa)** - A nadi which carries prana from heart to right leg
   - भृगु (bhR^igu) = सहजा (sahajA)

49. ह (ha) - A nadi which carries prana from heart to left leg
- नकुली (nakulI) = लकृष्मी (lakShmI)

50. ळ (jna) - Slightly below the heart
- वशव (shiva) = हयावपनी (vyApinI)

51. कृष (kṣa) – Solar Plexus
- समवतकि (samavartaka) = माया (mAyA)

In the realm of spiritual practice and self-realization, the integration of sound, color, and bodily awareness plays a profound role. The ancient art of phoneme meditation offers a unique and transformative approach, blending these elements to deepen one's connection to the self and the divine. This practice involves chanting specific phonemes with anuswara—a nasal resonance that enriches the vibrational experience—while focusing on distinct body parts.

For centuries, such techniques were closely guarded secrets, passed down through esoteric traditions and practiced within secluded sects. Now, these sacred practices are revealed to a wider audience, providing a powerful tool for personal growth and spiritual awakening. The 51 phonemes in this practice correspond to 51 divinities, each representing a fragment of divine awareness. These divinities embody various aspects of the divine presence, and their phonemes serve as keys to accessing different dimensions of consciousness.

By aligning each phoneme with a designated body part and infusing it with the resonance of anuswara, practitioners engage in a comprehensive exploration of their inner landscape. This process

involves not only the vocalization of sacred sounds but also a deep visualization of the associated divine presence. Through chanting these 51 divine pairings, practitioners can harmonize their physical and spiritual selves, experiencing a profound sense of unity with the divine and with their own higher nature.

Each divinity, represented by its phoneme, guides the practitioner toward self-realization and spiritual integration. This practice allows for the dissolution of inner barriers and the awakening of a deeper sense of oneness with the divine essence, ultimately leading to a state of enlightened self-awareness and spiritual fulfillment

This integration helps in focusing on different body parts during the meditation practice, aligning each phoneme with its respective spiritual and physical attributes for holistic self- realization and balance.

To practice the integration of anuswara with each phoneme and its corresponding body part, chant the paired names with the anuswara sound in specific body parts. The following sequential instructions detail this process for all 51 phonemes:

1. **Om am shrikantha purnodari namaha**

- (Chant "am" with anuswara, visualizing the phoneme's color and sound enveloping the top of the head.)

2. **Om aam ananta viraja namaha**

- (Chant "aam" with anuswara, focusing on the color and resonance on the forehead.)

3. Om im sukshma shalmali namaha

- (Chant "im" with anuswara, visualizing the phoneme's color around the right eye.)

4. Om īm trimurti lolakshi namaha

- (Chant "īm" with anuswara, concentrating on the left eye.)

5. Om um amareshvara vartulakshi namaha

- (Chant "um" with anuswara, focusing on right ear.)

6. Om ūm arghisha dirgaghona namaha

- (Chant "ūm" with anuswara, visualizing the color around the left ear.)

7. Om ṛm bhavabhuti sudirghamukhi namaha

- (Chant "ṛm" with anuswara, focusing on the right nostril.)

8. Om ṝm tithi gomukhi namaha

- (Chant "ṝm" with anuswara, concentrating on the left nostril.)

9. Om ḷm sthanu dirghajihvika namaha

- (Chant "ḷm" with anuswara, right cheek.)

10. Om Īm hara kundodari namaha

- (Chant "Īm" with anuswara, visualizing in the left cheek .)

11. Om em jhintisha Urdhvakeshi namaha

- (Chant "em" with anuswara, focusing on the upper lip.)

12. Om aim bhautika vikritamukhi namaha

- (Chant "aim" with anuswara, concentrating on lower lip.)

13. Om om sadyojata jvalamukhi namaha

- (Chant "om" with anuswara, visualizing the upper teeth.)

14. Om aum anugraheshvara ulkamukhi namaha

- (Chant "aum" with anuswara, focusing on the lower teeth.)

15. Om aṁ akrura shrimukhi namaha

- (Chant "aṁ" with anuswara, concentrating on the palate.)

16. Om aḥ mahasena vidyamukhi namaha

- (Chant "aḥ", visualizing on the tongue.)

17. Om kam krodhisha mahakali namaha

- (Chant "kam" with anuswara, focusing on the right shoulder.)

18. Om kham chandesha sarasvati namaha

- (Chant "kham" with anuswara, concentrating on the right elbow.)

19. Om gam panchantaka sarvasiddhi namaha

- (Chant "gam" with anuswara, visualizing on the right wrist.)

20. Om gham shivottama gauri namaha

- (Chant "gham" with anuswara, focusing on the right palm.)

21. Om ṅam ekarudra trailokyavidya namaha

- (Chant "ṅam" with anuswara, concentrating on the fingers of right hand.)

22. Om cham kurma mantratmashakti namaha

- (Chant "cham" with anuswara, visualizing on the left shoulder.)

23. Om chham ekanetra bhutamata namaha

- (Chant "chham" with anuswara, focusing on the left elbow.)

24. Om jam chaturmukha lambodari namaha

- (Chant "jam" with anuswara, concentrating on the left wrist.)

25. Om jham ajesha dravini namaha

- (Chant "jham" with anuswara, visualizing on the left palm.)

26. Om ñam sharva nagari namaha

- (Chant "ñam" with anuswara, focusing on the fingers of the left hand.)

27. Om ṭam someshvara vaikhari namaha

- (Chant "ṭam" with anuswara, concentrating on the right hip.)

28. Om tham langali manjari namaha

- (Chant "tham" with anuswara, visualizing on the right knee.)

29. Om dam daruka rupini namaha

- (Chant "dam" with anuswara, focusing on the right ankle.)

30. Om dham ardhanarishvara virini namaha

- (Chant "dham" with anuswara, concentrating on the sole of right foot.)

31. Om nam umakanta kotari namaha

- (Chant "nam" with anuswara, visualizing on the right toes.)

32. Om tam ashadhi putana namaha

- (Chant "tam" with anuswara, focusing on the left hip joint.)

33. Om tham dandin bhadrakali namaha

- (Chant "tham" with anuswara, concentrating on the left knee.)

34. Om dam adri yogini namaha

- (Chant "dam" with anuswara, visualizing on the left ankle.)

35. Om dham mina shankhini namaha

- (Chant "dham" with anuswara, focusing on the sole of left foot.)

36. Om nam mesha garjini namaha

- (Chant "nam" with anuswara, concentrating on the left toes.)

37. Om pam lohita kalaratri namaha

- (Chant "pam" with anuswara, visualizing the right flank.)

38. Om pham shikhin kubjini namaha

- (Chant "pham" with anuswara, focusing on the left flank.)

39. Om bam chagalanda kapardini namaha

- (Chant "bam" with anuswara, concentrating on the sacrum.)

40. Om bham divranda mahavajra namaha

- (Chant "bham" with anuswara, visualizing on the umbilicus.)

41. Om mam mahakala jaya namaha

- (Chant "mam" with anuswara, focusing on the pelvis.)

42. Om yam kapali sumukheshvari namaha

- (Chant "yam" with anuswara, concentrating on the heart.)

43. Om ram bhuja~Ngesha revati namaha

- (Chant "ram" with anuswara, visualizing on the right lung.)

44. Om lam pinaki madhavi namaha

- (Chant "lam" with anuswara, focusing on the throat.)

45. Om vam khadgisha varuni namaha

- (Chant "vam" with anuswara, concentrating on the left lung.)

46. Om sham baka vayavi namaha

- (Chant "sham" with anuswara, A nadi which carries prana from Heart to right arm.)

47. Om ṣam shveta rakshopadharini namaha

- (Chant "ṣam" with anuswara, focusing on the A nadi which carries prana from Heart to left arm.)

48. Om sam bhrigu sahaja namaha

- (Chant "sam" with anuswara, concentrating on the A nadi which carries prana from Heart to right leg.)

49. Om ham nakuli lakuli namaha

- (Chant "ham" with anuswara, visualizing the A nadi which carries prana from Heart to left leg.)

50. Om jnam shiva vyapini namaha

- (Chant "jnam" with anuswara, focusing on the bottom of heart.)

51. Om kṣam samavartaka maya namaha

- (Chant "kṣam" with anuswara, concentrating on the solar plexus.)

The practice of integrating anuswara with the 51 sacred phonemes, each representing a divine fragment of cosmic awareness, offers a profound journey towards self-realization and spiritual integration. By focusing on specific body parts while chanting these phonemes, practitioners harmonize their physical, emotional, and spiritual dimensions, experiencing a deepened connection to the divine presence embodied in each sound. In much more advanced practices each pair is invoked separately and meditated upon, which is beyond

the scope of this book.For now let the yogi meditate on the pair as given above till the exercises are mastered well.

As you engage in this practice, remember that each phoneme and its associated divinity serves as a unique gateway to higher consciousness. This meditative approach not only aligns your body with the vibrational energies of the divine but also nurtures a deeper understanding of your inherent oneness with the universe. The colors and resonances infused into your practice enhance your ability to perceive and integrate these sacred sounds, fostering a harmonious relationship between your inner and outer worlds.

Through regular and mindful practice, you will likely find yourself moving closer to a state of enlightened self-awareness, where the boundaries between the self and the divine dissolve into a unified experience of spiritual awakening. Embrace this sacred journey with dedication and openness, allowing the divine phonemes to guide you towards a profound realization of your true nature.

Ultimately, this practice invites you to explore the vast inner realms of your being, uncovering the divine essence that resides within. By connecting with these 51 divine phonemes and their corresponding body parts, you cultivate a deeper resonance with your spiritual self, paving the way for transformative growth and an enduring sense of oneness with the divine.

Note: An extra consonant Jna is added in this practice, JNA is considered to be the Jnana Tatwa or the knowledge of undifferentiated state. This should be practiced in a region below the heart in a golden hue.

Conclusion: Unveiling the Veiled

As we draw the curtain on our exploration of the clandestine practices within an Indian spiritual school of monistic Shaivism, we stand at the precipice of profound revelations and enduring mysteries. This journey through the veiled corridors of spiritual esotericism has revealed a tapestry woven with the threads of ancient wisdom, clandestine rituals, and the profound quest for transcendence.

Monistic Shaivism, with its roots deeply embedded in the soil of India's spiritual heritage, offers a vision of reality that transcends the ordinary. At its core, it teaches the unity of the self (atman) with the ultimate reality (Shiva), a state of consciousness where the individual self merges with the divine cosmic essence. Yet, behind its philosophical grandeur lies a realm of practices and doctrines often shrouded in secrecy, passed down through generations of devoted practitioners.

Our exploration has uncovered several layers of these secretive practices, each revealing different facets of the school's profound spiritual architecture. We have delved into the practical intricacies that bind the practitioner to the divine, the esoteric symbols that encode deeper meanings, and the hidden teachings that challenge the boundaries of conventional understanding. These practices, while clandestine, are not mere relics of a bygone era; they are living traditions that continue to inform and inspire a select circle of adepts.

In examining the clandestine nature of these practices, we must recognize the delicate balance between secrecy and revelation. The discretion surrounding these rites is not born out of a desire for

exclusion, but rather a reflection of their profound potency and the necessity of readiness on the part of the practitioner. Such practices are often unveiled only to those who are deemed prepared and worthy, ensuring that the transformative power of the teachings is not diluted or misunderstood.

Moreover, this exploration has highlighted the dynamic tension between tradition and modernity. In a world increasingly driven by transparency and accessibility, the shadowy aspects of monistic Shaivism offer a counterpoint, reminding us of the sanctity of certain sacred experiences that transcend the limitations of verbal and visual expression. The persistence of these hidden practices underscores a timeless truth: that some aspects of the spiritual journey are deeply personal, requiring an inner resonance that cannot be fully captured by external discourse.

As we conclude, we are left with a sense of awe and respect for the sacred mystery that envelops the monistic Shaiva tradition. The clandestine practices we have examined are not mere curiosities; they are integral to the profound spiritual journey of those who walk the path of Shaivism. They serve as a testament to the rich, multifaceted nature of human spirituality and the ongoing quest to bridge the finite with the infinite.

In embracing the mystery, we honor the tradition's deep reverence for the sacred and the ineffable. The practices we have uncovered stand as a reminder that, in the world of the spiritual, some truths are meant to be felt and experienced rather than fully articulated. The journey into these clandestine realms ultimately enriches our understanding of the profound ways in which the divine can manifest in our lives.

Thus, as we close this chapter, we do so with a renewed sense of wonder and gratitude. The hidden practices of monistic Shaivism, while secretive and enigmatic, offer a profound glimpse into the depth and breadth of human spiritual potential. They invite us to explore not only the outer mysteries of the universe but also the inner mysteries of our own being, urging us to seek, to question, and to ultimately find our place within the grand, unfolding tapestry of existence

About the Author

Dr. Shreeram P.A. Iyer

Dr. Iyer is a medical doctor and a practicing surgeon. He is a priest of the Shrauta smartha lineage, representing the philosophical school of non dual vedanta (advaita vedanta).

When Dr. Iyer was 17, he started with a modality of tantra where Bhairava and Kali are worshipped. At this time, he also began working within the South Indian version of sri chakra practices to realize his true divine nature.

In 2011, he found his mentor in a tradition that was passed from mentor to disciple, the mentor only teaching one or two students in a lifetime. Shreeram's mentor requested he write a series starting with tantra from scratch, expanding the concepts of the different modalities and what they represent.

Importantly, Dr. Iyer is learned in Sanskrit, has firsthand access to rare spiritual works in museums and is familiar with the theories and practices of Western Occultism. His skillfully clear and well-ordered writing style provides the reader with access to deep spiritual knowledge and practices that have never before been made available in the West in unaltered or unadulterated form.

www.ingramcontent.com/pod-product-compliance
Lightning Source LLC
Chambersburg PA
CBHW051252130726
47987CB00004B/1501